Other Books by Arthur Kurzweil

From Generation To Generation: How To Trace Your Jewish Genealogy and Family History

My Generations: A Course in Jewish Family History

Behold a Great Image: The Contemporary Jewish Experience in Photography, edited with Sharon Strassfeld

The Strife of the Spirit by Adin Steinsaltz, edited and with an introduction by Arthur Kurzweil

On Being Free by Adin Steinsaltz, edited and with an introduction by Arthur Kurzweil

BEST
JEWISH
WRITING
2003

BEST JEWISH WRITING 2003

ARTHUR KURZWEIL

EDITOR

JOSSEY-BASS
A Wiley Imprint
www.josseybass.com

Published by Jossey-Bass
A Wiley Imprint
989 Market Street, San Francisco, CA 94103-1741   www.josseybass.com

Jossey-Bass books and products are available through most bookstores. To contact Jossey-Bass directly call our Customer Care Department within the U.S. at 800-956-7739, outside the U.S. at 317-572-3986 or fax 317-572-4002.

Jossey-Bass also publishes its books in a variety of electronic formats. Some content that appears in print may not be available in electronic books.

Library of Congress Cataloging-in-Publication Data

ISBN 0-7879-6771-8

ISSN 1542-0817

Printed in the United States of America
FIRST EDITION
PB Printing   10 9 8 7 6 5 4 3 2 1

CONTENTS

JEWISH SPIRITUAL THOUGHT

KABBALAH

POETRY

FICTION

JEWISH HUMOR

I dedicate this book to my parents,
Saul and Evelyn Kurzweil, with love,
and with gratitude for so frequently interrupting
our stimulating childhood dinner conversations,
when my brother Ken and I were young, by saying,
"Let's look it up," thereby prompting one of us
to go down the hall to find the answer to our question
in The World Book Encyclopedia.

INTRODUCTION

Arthur Kurzweil

IN THE FALL OF 1968, Dr. Robert Sobel, highly regarded economic historian, prolific author, and professor, walked into his university lecture hall, where he was teaching a course on the historical method, and announced to the students that he was no longer going to read the *New York Times* but advocated instead the daily reading of the *Wall Street Journal*.

"I have here in my hands this morning's *New York Times* and this morning's *Wall Street Journal*," remarked Dr. Sobel as he held up and displayed the front pages of each newspaper to his class. "Now, as every student of journalism knows, the most important story of the day, according to the editorial staff of the paper, appears at the upper right column of the front page. Let's look and see what the editors of each paper selected for today's lead stories."

Dr. Sobel looked at the *New York Times* and announced, "This morning's *Times* has a story about Vice President Spiro Agnew." He then picked up the *Wall Street Journal* and declared, "The *Journal* has a story about hemorrhoids."

As the students in the class snickered and giggled, Dr. Robert Sobel, author of histories of both the New York Stock Exchange and the American Stock Exchange, the author of the official history of IBM and ITT and a few dozen additional volumes, looked at his students and said, "As everyone knows, Spiro Agnew will come and go . . . but hemorrhoids are here to stay."

———— o ————

So . . . how does one make decisions about what is important and what is not important, about what is urgent and what is not urgent? Who makes these decisions, how often are these decisions made for us, and what impact do they have on who we are and how we see the world?

I vividly recall my own reaction when I read a tiny, one-inch item appearing on some back page of a daily newspaper. The headline of the little article said, "New Galaxy Discovered." New *galaxy* discovered!? Isn't this an occasion for a front-page banner headline?

A journalist once suggested that newspapers were, in fact, not really worth reading at all, and challenged his readers (in a newspaper!) by saying that the next day we should buy the paper but not read it. Instead we should put it away and take it out one year later when we would discover that there was really nothing in the paper that we needed to know.

What is big and what is small? What is foreground and what is background? These were the kinds of questions that emerged in my mind as I searched through the many Jewish and secular magazines, journals, newsletters, Websites, books, and newspapers that might contain potential material for this present volume. But it was not only my own decision-making process that preoccupied me. Rather, I had to wonder, with every issue of each publication I examined and read, how the editor of that publication made his or her choices. Which story made the cover of the magazine? Was the cover story the most important one in the issue or was it the one that would sell the most copies? Or was there perhaps some other motive that was somehow idiosyncratic to the editor of any particular publication?

Eventually I concluded that all of the above was highly subjective, as would be my own selections of these "best writings" for the past year.

○

Of the three words that make up the title of this book, two of them, "Best" and "Jewish," are problematic. We can, of course, try to establish some criteria for "best" and attempt to find examples of writing to fit those criteria. When I look at my own process, one goal I tried to achieve was balance. One need only glance through the table of contents and look quickly at the section in this book on Israel to see that I have selected a variety of points of view. It is, in a way, easier to describe what this book is *not* than to describe what it is. This book is not a platform for my own political perspectives. When it came to Middle East politics in particular, I tried to select pieces that were fine, articulate expressions of the position or positions being expressed but not necessarily my own views.

In 1979 I coedited a book published by The Jewish Publication Society called *Behold a Great Image*. It was a collection of contemporary photography that was the result of a national Jewish photography contest. As one of the coordinators of the contest (we sent posters to every synagogue and Jewish organization in the United States to have posted on their bul-

letin boards), I helped to arrange for an illustrious panel of judges to select the best Jewish photographs (first, second, and third prizes and ten
runners-up). The day of the judging arrived. The thousands(!) of entries
were piled high on the table before us, and the judges were ready to begin
the process. One of the judges quietly remarked, "What makes a photograph a Jewish photograph?"

Suddenly we were all involved in a tense and opinionated discussion.
There was little agreement in the room. Miraculously, the contest was
judged, the prize money was given to the winners, the book was published, and everyone, I think, was happy. But I still can recall one of the
judges holding up a beautiful and moving picture of a little old lady crossing a street on New York's Lower East Side. The judge said, "I know this
woman. She's Italian!"

———————o———————

It occurred to me many times during the editing process of this volume
that perhaps one day, decades or centuries from now, someone might look
at this book and try to imagine the times we live in by this book's contents. I certainly would not want anyone to conclude that this was the
only excellent Jewish writing from 2002. (With each book in this series,
writing from the previous year is selected. *Best Jewish Writing 2003* draws
from writing that was created or published or revised in 2002.) But I do
think that the general contents of this book do a good job of reflecting the
Jewish world in which we currently live.

I want to say that we live in troubled times; I believe that we do. And
I want to say that many of the selections in this book speak to those troubled times, offering us insight and wisdom. I believe that this, too, is true.
But are our times any more troubled than other times have been? While
reports of anti-Semitism are up, while the State of Israel continues to be
one of the centers of political strife in the world, while terrible acts of terrorism and suicide bombings continue to plague the Jewish State, one can
easily make the case that Jews in the United States at the beginning of the
twenty-first century have never, in the long span of the history of the Jewish people, had it as good as we do now. We can express ourselves freely,
we can run for office, we can pursue our economic interests as equal citizens, we can raise our children in safety.

In any event, I've tried to present a broad spectrum of Jewish writing
on a variety of topics. I placed the section of *Best Jewish Writing 2003*
called "Israel" at the beginning of this volume because during this past
year the situation in the Middle East in general and Israel in particular
continues to dominate the press and the minds of Jews around the world.

Diverse points of view are deliberately included in this section. I want to state clearly a second time that the points of view are not mine. They are my selections with full disclosure that I wanted, in principle, to offer a volume with a tendency toward balance.

The selections to be found in "Current Issues" reflect the fact that Judaism and the Jewish people have always been interested in every aspect of life, not just in some narrow religious realm. Feminism, stem cell research, capital punishment, drugs, and sports are just some of the countless topics that were written about by Jews from a Jewish perspective or vantage point during this past year.

"Religious Education and Practice" and "Jewish Spiritual Thought," the next two sections of this book, are also perennial topics within the Jewish universe. It is, of course, no surprise to notice that a number of pieces in this collection that appear in this section deal with a primary value for the Jewish people: education. It is in this section of the book that some of our finest spiritual thinkers and teachers, including Rabbis Adin Steinsaltz, Mordechai Gafni, and Arthur Hertzberg, are represented.

In addition to quality writing, I also looked for topics that are particularly timely. One fine example of this is the piece by Yoel Jakobovits on stem cell research. There were a number of pieces on this subject appearing in various publications. I selected the one that I thought was both well written and served the lay reader best. Similarly, while much has been written in English for the novice about Kabbalah during the last few years, the pieces by Rodger Kamenetz and Reb Zalman Schachter-Shalomi are, in my estimation, essays that serve their readers well.

Nearly sixty years have passed since the Holocaust, but it is not surprising that much continues to be written about this unprecedented event in Jewish history. I recall having a conversation with my late friend, Dr. Lucjan Dobroszycki, one of the great Jewish historians of the twentieth century. When I suggested to him that there were too many books about the Holocaust being published, Dr. Dobroszycki, whose arm retained tattooed numbers, looked at me with eyes that saw horrors and said, "It is not that there are too many books. There are not enough." In this book, the three selections in the Holocaust section certainly remind us that we continue to need gifted writers such as these to help us to even begin to grasp what it means for one third of all the Jewish people in the world to have been murdered just six decades ago.

The terrorist actions that occurred when hijacked jetliners deliberately crashed into the World Trade Towers in New York City and the Pentagon have come to be referred to as "Nine eleven" (9/11), the date (September 11, 2001) when these horrendous acts took place. How will history describe and evaluate these attacks and the chain of events that have followed? Today it seems that the very term "9/11" has become a permanent part of our vocabulary. It is the title of a section in this volume, and it is a section that seems essential. The absence of such a section at this time seems almost unthinkable.

Reports consistently indicate that anti-Semitism is on the rise in this world of ours or is simply coming out of the closet once again. It seems foolish now to think that some of us truly believed for a while that if there could possibly be some good that comes out of the Holocaust it would be a decrease in anti-Semitism. As the selections in this section indicate, anti-Semitism remains alive and well. In fact, as Phyllis Chesler writes, there is a "new anti-Semitism" that is "politically correct."

The poetry and fiction included in this volume are perhaps the most subjective and personal of all the selections I have made. The same poem can be a prayer for one reader and an unsolvable riddle for another. I hope you enjoy these selections, as I certainly did.

I close the book, quite deliberately, with a section on Jewish humor. As a person who spends time each day studying the Talmud, I know that the Jewish people have a long history of often responding to life with humor. There is much humor in Jewish life, even in our sacred texts, as "The Wit and Practicality of the Talmud" shows us. (One of the most well-known passages in the over sixty volumes of the Talmud includes an event where even God laughs!) In our time, in the United States, it seems clear that a disproportionate number of comedians are Jewish. This is no accident. It is part of a long, honored tradition of optimism and hope, introspection and self-criticism, which has always been essential to the fabric of Jewish life. Sometimes we laugh to sooth our suffering; sometimes we laugh to recognize the ironies and paradoxes of life; sometimes our laughter is actually our spiritual resistance to the evils of our world; sometimes our laughter is really a prayer.

Acknowledgments

In addition to the many authors and editors whose cooperation helped to make this volume possible, I gratefully acknowledge and thank Ariela Krevat, for your enthusiasm, skills, talents, and computer expertise; Seth Schwartz, for your editorial help as well as for your warmth and support; Alan Rinzler, for your inspiration, stimulating ideas, infectious energy, and friendship; David Horne, for your wise copyediting; Andrea Flint, for your talents, skills, patience, and care; Shira Segal, for your editorial talents, organizing skills, and loyalty; Malya Kurzweil, for your library research and for helping whenever help was needed; and my children, Miriam, Moshe, and Malya, for the joy you bring me each and every day.

Upon completion of this book, I pause to express my gratitude with the traditional ancient formula:

Blessed are You, O Lord, Our God, Ruler of the Universe, who keeps us alive, sustains us, and has permitted us to reach this season.

Passaic, New Jersey   Arthur Kurzweil
June 2003

ISRAEL

LETTER TO PRESIDENT
GEORGE W. BUSH, MAY 7, 2002

Elie Wiesel

President George W. Bush
The White House

Dear Mr. President,

Today, Prime Minister Ariel Sharon is coming to see you. He comes as the elected head of a nation that is the United States' only dependable ally in that region. He comes to you, the leader of the free world, knowing that you continue to understand the great dangers confronting Israel's very existence.

When you see Mr. Sharon,

Please remember that a majority of Israelis favor a Palestinian state alongside Israel if the terror is stopped, whereas a majority of Palestinians including Yasser Arafat support suicide killing operations against Israel.

Please remember that while Palestinian terrorists were hiding explosives in ambulances, Israeli reservists in Jenin were taking up collections out of their own funds to repay Palestinian families for the damage done to their homes.

Please remember that the maps on Arafat's uniform and in Palestinian children's textbooks show a Palestine encompassing not only all of the West Bank but **all of Israel,** while Palestinian leaders loudly proclaim that "Palestine [extends] from the Jordan River to the Mediterranean Sea, from Rosh Hanikra [in the North] to Rafah [in Gaza]."

Please remember Danielle Shefi, a little girl in Israel. Danielle was five. When the murderers came, she hid under her bed. Palestinian gunmen found and killed her anyway. Think of all the other victims of terror in the Holy Land. With rare exceptions, the targets were young people, children, and families.

Please remember that Israel—having lost too many sons and daughters, mothers and fathers—desperately wants peace. It has learned to trust its enemies' threats more than the empty promises of "neutral" governments. Today, more than ever, Israel must be trusted to decide what concessions are or are not possible within the framework of its own security.

Please remember that Ariel Sharon, a military man who knows the ugly face of war better than anyone, is ready to make "painful sacrifices" to end the conflict. In fact it was he who carried out the handing over of Yamit, displacing thousands of Israelis, in exchange for peace with Egypt.

Please remember that while Israelis mourned alongside us for our nation's tragedy on September 11th, Yasser Arafat was busy suppressing footage of his constituents dancing in the streets.

And finally,

Please remember that American Jews share your moral outrage at international terrorism as well as your determination to defend democratic ideals and religious freedom in the world. As diversified as we are in our political views, we are united in our hope that you, the leader in the campaign against worldwide terror, will recognize that terror in Israel is but another of its facets, another result of the hatred being systematically taught to Arab children by the Palestinian Authority and state-funded schools elsewhere in the Muslim world.

Years ago, we had hopes that we were entering a new era, an era of peace that would see Palestinians living alongside Israelis, in an alliance that would make the entire area flourish. If the Palestinian leadership can be persuaded to stop the abomination of terrorist attacks on innocent civilians, it may still not be too late.

For, when all is said and done, peace remains the only solution.

Respectfully yours,

Elie Wiesel
May 7, 2002

THE ELIE WIESEL FOUNDATION FOR HUMANITY,
529 FIFTH AVENUE, NEW YORK, NY 10017

WHAT EVERYONE SHOULD KNOW ABOUT THE CONFLICT

Joseph Alpher

Myth #1

Jews were absent from Palestine since biblical times, whereas Arabs have inhabited Palestine continuously for centuries. Therefore the Palestinians have a more legitimate claim to Israel.

The Facts

Arabs have inhabited Palestine for nearly fourteen hundred years, since the arrival of Islam from the Arabian Peninsula. The Jewish claim to this land goes back two thousand years earlier, to biblical times.

Jews have lived continually in the land of Israel since the destruction of the Jewish state by Rome in 70 C.E. In 1500, for example, an estimated ten thousand Jews lived in the Safed region, and in the mid-1800s, Jews constituted the largest ethnic group in Jerusalem. Many Palestinians, on the other hand, cannot trace their local lineage back very far. Two examples: the large and influential al-Masri clan in Nablus arrived from Egypt in recent centuries, and the ten thousand members of the Arab al-Turkman clan, in the Jenin area, migrated from Turkey in the nineteenth century. And during the period of the British Mandate (1920–1948), large numbers of Arabs from Lebanon and Syria settled in Palestine to take advantage of the relative prosperity that resulted from Jewish immigration.

The Palestinian historical-political narrative asserts that the Jews who settled in the land of Israel since the advent of Zionism in the late 1800s are not a people or a nation with ancient roots in the land; according to this view, Jews are either foreigners, European colonialists of the Jewish faith who stole Arab land, or "Arab Jews," no different in essence than Arab Muslims or Arab Christians. Yasser Arafat told this author in 1995 that 70 percent of Israelis—the 20 percent who are Arabs and the 50 percent who immigrated to Israel from Muslim countries—are really Arabs! And at the climax of the abortive Oslo process he asserted that "there is no historic link between today's Jews and the Haram a-Sharif (Temple Mount)."

While rejecting the legitimacy of any ancient Jewish claim to Palestine, Palestinian scholars and politicians have argued that Palestinians are descendants of the Jebusites and other biblical peoples who predated the Israelite conquest of Canaan in the thirteenth century B.C.E. This line of argument contradicts the insistence of Palestinian Muslims that they are descendants of the Arabs who swept across the Middle East and North Africa at the time of Mohammed, conquering Palestine from the Christian Byzantines in 637 C.E.

Another challenge to the Palestinian narrative of historical seniority in the land is the recent finding of several research projects carried out by American and Israeli scholars in the 1990s indicating that Jews are closer genetically to Palestinians than to any other people. This finding reinforces the theory put forth by early Zionist scholars like Yitzhak Ben Zvi (the second president of Israel), who in the early twentieth century observed unique Palestinian Arab customs in the Samaria region, such as the lighting of candles on Friday night, and postulated that at least some Palestinian Arabs are the descendants of the Jewish remnant that remained in the land of Israel after the Roman conquest and exile, and later converted to Christianity or Islam.

Myth #2

In 1947, the United Nations awarded Palestine to the Jews, who prevented the creation of a Palestinian state.

The Facts

On November 29, 1947, the United Nations General Assembly (UNGA) approved Resolution 181, calling for the creation of two independent states in Palestine, one Arab and one Jewish. The territory would be divided on a demographic basis more or less equally between the two states, allotting three barely contiguous enclaves to each. The Arabs rejected the partition plan, and Palestinian irregular forces launched attacks on Jewish civilians, killing seventy-nine Jews in just twelve days. After six months of unrest, the British completed their withdrawal from Palestine on May 14, 1948. The next day, Jewish Agency leader David Ben-Gurion declared the creation of the State of Israel in the territory allotted to the Jews by the UN partition plan. The Palestinian leadership, together with the Arab League (then numbering seven states, including all of Israel's neighbors), responded by declaring war on Israel. When the Israeli War of Independence (known by the Palestinians as the 1948 War, or the *Naqba*, disaster) ended in late 1948, Israel controlled 78 percent of Mandatory Palestine; the remaining 22 percent was controlled by Jordan (the West Bank) and Egypt (the Gaza Strip). A few feeble efforts by local Palestinian leaders in Gaza and the West Bank to proclaim a Palestinian state were squashed by these Arab states. Jordan proceeded to annex the territories it controlled— a move recognized over the ensuing years only by Britain and Pakistan— while Egypt instituted a military government in Gaza.

It was not until well after 1967, when Israel conquered the West Bank and Gaza Strip in a defensive war, that the Palestine Liberation Organization (PLO), led by Yasser Arafat, called for the creation of a Palestinian state. Thus, it was not "the Jews" or Israel that prevented the formation of a Palestinian state in 1947, or even in the years preceding 1967. It was the Arabs.

Myth #3

The Jews, not the Arabs, introduced terrorism into the conflict by deliberately expelling Arabs from Palestine to make room for European Jews.

The Facts

It is important to note that Israelis and Arabs differ radically in their definition of terrorism. Israel defines terrorism as the deliberate use of force against civilians to advance political goals. Arabs define terrorism as any act of force, whether deliberate or not, visited upon civilians, including nonviolent acts of state. Thus, to the Arabs, the building of Israeli settlements in the West Bank and Gaza is an act of terrorism that justifies a violent reaction against Israeli civilian settlers. Indeed, some Palestinians argue that Jewish settlement anywhere in Palestine (including all of Israel) is, by definition, an act of terrorism, and that every Israeli is a terrorist.

The most deeply held specific Arab grievance against Israel—the Palestinian refugee problem—was a direct outcome of the Arab invasion of the newly declared State of Israel in 1948. Approximately half of the seven hundred thousand (not a million) Arabs who fled war zones did so of their own volition or in response to evacuation instructions issued by their own leaders. The other half were, in one form or another, expelled by Israeli forces, which viewed them as enemies and, in some cases, a direct threat to Israeli supply lines or population concentrations. The flight of the Palestinian Arabs is typical of the fate that has befallen hostile civilian populations in wartime from time immemorial. Small numbers of Jews similarly fled settlements located inside the West Bank and Gaza Strip. In view of the circumstances under which the 1948 war began, it is the Arab leadership, not the Jews, that created the Palestinian refugee problem.

By the early 1950s, Israel had absorbed and resettled the Jewish refugees from the West Bank and Gaza as well as some six hundred thousand Jews who had fled Arab countries to Israel. In contrast, the Arab world and the Palestinian national movement have to a large extent (Jordan is the exception) refused to rehabilitate or grant citizenship to Palestinian refugees. Instead, by allowing refugee status to be inherited from generation to generation in a never-ending geometric expansion, the Arab world has kept the Palestinian refugee issue alive as a major focus of enmity toward Israel.

Myth #4

Israel is a racist state because it allows automatic citizenship upon request to Jewish immigrants, but denies the same right to Palestinian refugees.

The Facts

Those who make this accusation deny the Jewish people the right to statehood in the land of their ancestors. Those who spread this myth deny for Jews what they readily affirm for other people—that it is legitimate for France, Germany, Great Britain, and by all accounts the future state of Palestine to award citizenship automatically on the basis of a candidate's family association with the country or its culture. Arab states declare themselves constitutionally to be "Arab" and in some cases "Muslim," but they accuse Israel of racism for defining itself as "Jewish."

Like most countries, Israel has an orderly naturalization procedure, applicable to non-Jews, including Arabs, who apply for citizenship, usually as a result of marriage to an Israeli citizen, Arab or Jewish. Tens of thousands of Palestinian Arabs have gained Israeli citizenship in this way since 1967. Prior to then, some sixty to seventy thousand Palestinian refugees were repatriated between 1949 and 1967 under a family reunification program.

The United Nations has passed numerous resolutions since 1948 on the question of Palestinian refugees, of which the key document—UNGA 194 of December 11, 1948—does *not* prescribe an inalienable "right of return," but rather suggests possibilities of repatriation and compensation. Yet, at Camp David II, the Palestinian leadership insisted that Israel acknowledge, at least in principle, the "right of return" of refugees, in order to validate the Palestinian narrative of "the crime" perpetrated by Israel on the Palestinian people by virtue of Israel's very existence. Faithful to its own narrative, according to which its creation was just and legitimate and the refugee problem derived from the Arab attempt in 1948 to annihilate it, Israel rejected this demand, which it sees as tantamount to acknowledging that the creation of Israel was an act of "original sin."

Notably, on March 28, 2002, the Arab League ratified the Saudi proposals for Arab-Israel peace, according to which there would be a "just solution" to the refugee problem based on UNGA 194. This omission of the "right of return" represents broad Arab recognition that an Israeli-Palestinian peace agreement need not include the return of refugees, thereby in a sense vindicating Israel's position.

Myth #5

The fundamental obstacle to peace is Israel's 1967 occupation and subsequent settlement by Jews of the West Bank and Gaza Strip.

The Facts

Israeli occupation of the West Bank, East Jerusalem, and the Gaza Strip is not the cause of the conflict, but a consequence. Israel fought a legitimate war of self-defense in 1967, and successive Israeli governments have since then agreed to withdraw from occupied territories (Sinai, the Golan, Jordan) and dismantle settlements in return for peace. Israeli settlements and neighborhoods in the West Bank, Gaza, and East Jerusalem are undoubtedly an irritant, but the fundamental obstacle to peace has been, and continues to be, the refusal of the Palestinians to accept the legitimacy of the State of Israel, even within its pre-1967 borders.

At Camp David II, Israel agreed to the creation of a Palestinian state on approximately 90 percent of the West Bank and all of Gaza. It agreed to dismantle settlements on land turned over to the future state of Palestine, and it offered to continue negotiating additional compromises. By January 2001, it had offered the PLO 95 percent of the territories. But the Palestinian leadership preferred to turn to "armed struggle"—the current *intifada*.

Myth #6

It was Israel's opposition to the creation of a Palestinian state that caused Camp David II to fail and the intifada *to resume in the fall of 2000.*

The Facts

The Israeli government fully supported the creation of a Palestinian state on the West Bank and in Gaza. The talks failed primarily because of inadequate planning (the issues of Jerusalem and the refugees' right of return were not adequately addressed prior to the summit), "bad chemistry" between Arafat and Barak, and faulty negotiating techniques. For example, Israel's presentation of clearly unacceptable offers on territory (beginning with an offer of only 50 percent of the West Bank), coupled with a constant readiness to make additional compromises, weakened its position; whereas Palestinian presentation of a single ultimate position without any readiness whatsoever to compromise generated strong Israeli antagonism. Neither party based its negotiating technique on a much-needed prior shared examination of both parties' vital requirements in an agreement.

Despite these and other difficulties, the parties came close to succeeding. They radically narrowed their differences on territory, Jerusalem, security, and even refugees, to a point where President Clinton was able to offer a historic bridging proposal in December 2000 (which remains to this day the defining formula for a compromise agreement). In the end, the talks failed largely because of Arafat's insistence that Israel acknowledge the right of return for the refugees and grant the Palestinians full sovereignty over the Temple Mount.

Myth #7

The targeted killing of a Jewish child by a Palestinian terrorist is no different from the killing of an Arab child accidentally killed in a clash between Palestinian fighters and Israeli soldiers.

The Facts

For most of the Arab and Islamic worlds, there is indeed complete moral equivalency between a suicide bombing in a Tel Aviv café and the inadvertent and unintended deaths of Palestinian civilians in the conflict, or between the deliberate targeting of a Jewish child and the inadvertent and accidental death of a Palestinian child.

It might be possible to argue, on the basis of broad, internationally accepted definitions of legitimate acts of war, that Palestinian attacks on Israeli security forces, particularly inside the West Bank and Gaza, qualify as guerilla warfare or a legitimate "war of liberation" rather than as terrorism. Were Palestinians themselves to make this distinction, it might be acceptable. But most do not. They argue that their attacks on civilians are not terrorism, but part and parcel of a legitimate liberation struggle. Moreover, they insist on their right to use violence against Israeli civilians, even after an Israeli government offered them through negotiation virtually all the declared objectives of their war.

One particular weakness of the Palestinian argument emerges when some Palestinian leaders claim that, in fact, all Israelis—men, women and children, the crippled and the aged—are in fact present or future soldiers, and hence are "fair game" for attacks. This attempt to argue in terms of international standards reflects a recognition on the part of the Palestinians that the Islamic version of moral equivalency (see myth #3) is difficult to defend.

In a sense, this blurring of moral distinctions places the Israeli-Palestinian conflict on the fault line of a clash of civilizations. Hence, it is all the more appalling when, as has happened recently, some Western commentators permit themselves to justify the Palestinian rationale for killing Israeli children.

Myth #8

Israel's thirty-year occupation of the West Bank proves that it has always had expansionist intentions.

The Facts

The very act of Israel's establishment in 1948 is seen as an "expansionist" or imperialist/colonialist act by most Arabs, because they have never accepted the right of the Jewish people to live a sovereign life in their historic homeland.

It is true that, since 1967, both left- and right-wing Israeli political parties have sponsored settlement activities in the Gaza Strip and the West Bank, and right-wing parties representing settler interests and a religious-messianic ideology have sought to annex these territories. At the heart of their claim is the assertion that the West Bank, which they call Judea and Samaria, includes biblical sites, such as Bet El, Shiloh, and Hebron, that constitute the cradle of Hebrew civilization. The fact that Israel has not annexed the West

Bank (although it did annex East Jerusalem) reflects a recognition on the part of the Israeli mainstream that such a move would be unacceptable internationally; could ignite a new Middle East war; and would present Israel with the specter of an Arab demographic majority within a few decades, thereby decimating Israel's Jewish, democratic character.

Immediately after the 1967 war, Israel offered to negotiate with Jordan the return of nearly all the West Bank. Those negotiations broke down when Jordan insisted on the return of all the territory, including East Jerusalem. By 1988, Jordan, yielding to the dominance of the PLO in the territories, renounced its claim to sovereignty in favor of the Palestinians. In 2000–2001, the Barak government was close to an agreement with the PLO regarding East Jerusalem as well as the territory and settlements on the West Bank and in the Gaza Strip. This is hardly a record of expansionist aims, even if the current Israeli government seeks to retain parts of the West Bank for what it argues are legitimate security purposes.

Myth #9

The Palestinians and Israelis are equally culpable for the cycle of violence threatening the region. Sharon and Arafat are engaged in a blood feud that renders them both incapable of peace.

The Facts

During the past thirty years, a trail of blood has followed Yasser Arafat wherever he has made his headquarters. He and the PLO were expelled from Jordan in 1971 by the late King Hussein, from Lebanon in 1982 by Israel and the Lebanese Christians, and again from Lebanon in 1983 by Syria. He was accused by these Arab governments of breaking literally hundreds of ceasefire agreements. In Israel's case, since 1994 he has violated signed undertakings to avoid incitement, incarcerate terrorists, and restrict armaments. Following its military operation in the West Bank in April 2002, Israel was able to produce testimony based on documents and interrogations that Arafat himself actively supported terrorism and diverted aid funds for this purpose.

The talk of a Sharon-Arafat blood feud is basically media hype. It is rare to find attacks of a personal nature in the pronouncements of either leader, whatever their gut reactions may be. It is reasonable to say, however, that neither is capable of signing a peace agreement: Arafat because of his ongoing inability to accept Israel as a legitimate Jewish state, and Sharon because he insists on maintaining Israeli control over large portions of the West Bank and Gaza in accordance with his concept of Israel's defense. Hence, neither leader appears ready to make the minimal concessions required for an acceptable final status agreement.

Myth #10

America was attacked by Muslim terrorists on September 11 because of U.S. support for Israel. The Israeli-Palestinian conflict is the fundamental cause of political instability in the Middle East and the root of international Muslim terrorism.

The Facts

America was attacked on September 11 by Egyptian and Saudi Muslim extremists of al-Qaeda. Until that time, al-Qaeda leader Osama bin Laden consistently argued that his complaint with the U.S. concerned its military presence in Saudi Arabia, where it allegedly was violating sanctified Muslim land. Al-Qaeda had little interest in the Palestinian issue, included few Palestinians among its activists, and generally ignored the participation of other Muslim fundamentalist movements such as Hamas and Islamic Jihad in the Israeli-Palestinian conflict. It was only after the September 11 attacks that bin Laden, undoubtedly aware of the public relations advantages of linking his struggle with that of the Palestinians, introduced rhetoric concerning Israel's treatment of Palestinians into his attempts to justify al-Qaeda policies.

The Israeli-Palestinian conflict and, in a larger sense, the Arab-Israel conflict have over the past fifty-five years contributed to regional instability. But during this same period, internal Arab and inter-Muslim conflicts, such as the Sudan civil war and the Iran-Iraq War, neither of which is related to Israel, have caused far greater casualties and disruption. One can even argue that the Palestinian-Israeli conflict has been used by Arab governments to divert attention from domestic problems and avert internecine Arab conflicts.

Indeed, prior to the advent of an Israeli-Arab peace process in 1977, the conflict with Israel was the only unifying factor preventing further warfare and unrest within the Arab world. But today it seems clear to pro-Western Arab leaders, such as Egypt's President Mubarrak, Jordan's King Abdullah, and Saudi Arabia's Crown Prince Abdullah, that peace with Israel is a fundamental prerequisite to successful domestic, economic, and social stability in the region.

IF A VISITOR FROM
A FAR-AWAY GALAXY

Alan M. Dershowitz

IF A VISITOR FROM A FARAWAY GALAXY were to land at an American or Canadian university and peruse some of the petitions that were circulating around the campus, he would probably come away with the conclusion that the earth is a peaceful and fair planet with only one villainous nation determined to destroy the peace and to violate human rights. That nation would not be Iraq, Libya, Serbia, Russia, or Iran. It would be Israel. There are currently petitions circulating on most North American university campuses that would seek to have universities terminate all investments in companies that do business in or with Israel. There are also petitions asking individual faculty members to boycott scientists and scholars who happen to be Israeli Jews, regardless of their personal views on the Arab-Israeli conflict. There have been efforts, some successful, to prevent Israeli speakers from appearing on college campuses, as recently occurred at Concordia University in Canada. There are no comparable petitions seeking any action against other countries that enslave minorities, imprison dissidents, murder political opponents, and torture suspected terrorists. Nor are there any comparable efforts to silence speakers from other countries.

The intergalactic visitor would wonder what this pariah nation, Israel, must have done to deserve this unique form of economic capital punishment. If he then went to the library and began to read books and articles about this planet, he would discover that Israel was a vibrant democracy, with freedom of speech, press, and religion, that was surrounded by a group of tyrannical and undemocratic regimes, many of which are actively seeking its destruction. He would learn that in Egypt, homosexuals are routinely imprisoned and threatened with execution; that in Jordan, suspected terrorists and other opponents of the government are tortured, and that if individualized torture does not work, their relatives are called in and threatened with torture as well; that in Saudi Arabia, women who engage in sex outside of marriage are beheaded; that in Iraq, political opponents are routinely murdered en masse and no dissent is permitted; that in Iran, members of religious minorities, such as Baha'is and Jews, are imprisoned and sometimes executed; that in all of these surrounding nations, anti-Semitic material is frequently broadcast on state-sponsored television and radio programs; that in Saudi Arabia, apartheid is practiced against non-Muslims, with signs indicating that Muslims must go to certain areas and non-Muslims to others; that China has occupied Tibet for half a century; that in several African countries women are stoned to death for violating sexual mores; that slavery still exists in some parts of the world; and that genocide has been committed by a number of countries in recent memory.

Our curious visitor would wonder why there are no petitions circulating with regard to these human rights violators. Is Israel's occupation of the West Bank and Gaza—an occupation it has offered to end in exchange for peace—worse than the Chinese occupation of Tibet? Are the tactics used to combat terrorism by Israel worse than those used by the Russians against Chechnyan terrorists? Are Arab and Muslim states more democratic than Israel? Is there any institution in any Arab or Muslim state comparable to the Israeli Supreme Court, which frequently rules in favor of Palestinian claims against the Israeli government and military? Does the absence of the death penalty in Israel alone, among Middle East nations, make it more barbaric than the countries which behead, hang, and shoot political dissidents? Is Israel's settlement policy, which 78 percent of Israelis want to end in exchange for peace, worse than the Chinese attempt at cultural genocide in Tibet? Is Israel's policy of full equality for openly gay soldiers and members of the Knesset somehow worse than the policy of Muslim states to persecute those who have a different sexual orientation than the majority? Is Israel's commitment to equality for women worse than the gender apartheid practiced in Saudi Arabia?

Our visitor would be perplexed to hear the excuses made by university professors and students for why they are prepared to delegitimate Israel while remaining silent about the far worse abuses committed by other countries. If he were to ask a student about the abuses committed by other countries, he would be told (as I have been), "You're changing the subject. We're talking about Israel now." This reminds me of an incident from the 1920s involving then-Harvard-president A. Lawrence Lowell. Lowell decided that the number of Jews admitted to Harvard should be reduced because "Jews cheat." When a distinguished alumnus, Judge Learned Hand, pointed out that Protestants also cheat, Lowell responded, "You're changing the subject, we're talking about Jews."

It is not surprising, therefore, that as responsible and cautious a writer as Andrew Sullivan, formerly editor of *The New Republic* and now a writer for the *New York Times Magazine,* has concluded that "fanatical anti-Semitism, as bad or even worse than Hitler's, is now a cultural norm across much of the Middle East and beyond. It's the acrid glue that unites Saddam, Arafat, al-Qaeda, Hizbullah, Iran, and the Saudis. They all hate the Jews and want to see them destroyed."

Our intergalactic traveler, after learning all of these facts, would wonder what kind of a planet he had landed on. Do we have everything backwards? Do we know the difference between right and wrong? Do our universities teach the truth?

These are questions that need asking, lest we become the kind of world the visitor would have experienced had he arrived in Europe during the late 1930s and early 1940s.

ISRAELIS AND PALESTINIANS: WHAT WENT WRONG?

Amos Elon

1.

IN A LETTER HE WROTE shortly before his death in 1904, at the early age of forty-four, Theodor Herzl, the founder of modern Zionism, admonished his successor: "Macht keine Dummheiten während ich tot bin" (Don't make any stupid mistakes while I'm dead). It was a tongue-in-cheek remark, and I am citing it only because, of all other nineteenth-century attempts to found new nation-states, Herzl's was undoubtedly the most unusual and certainly one of the most difficult. If there was ever a national project which because of its complexity and uncertainty of success could ill-afford Dummheiten, it was Herzl's.

Zionism was a national project unlike any other in Europe or overseas. It involved colonizing without a mother country and without the support of state power. A difficult task, to say the least, in an arid country without natural resources, without financial attractions. One of Herzl's friends asked Cecil Rhodes, the great British imperialist, for his advice. Rhodes answered: "Tell Dr. Herzl to put money in his pocket." Herzl scarcely had any money. "The secret I keep from everybody," he wrote, "is the fact that I am at the head only of a movement of beggars and fools" (Schnorrer und Narren). The rich, with very few exceptions, opposed his scheme. The early settlers were mostly penniless idealists, social anarchists, Narodniks, practicing a bizarre "religion of hard labor." Ninety percent of those who arrived in Palestine between 1904 and 1914 returned to Europe or wandered on to America.

Other nationalisms aimed at liberating subjugated peoples who spoke the same language and lived in the same territory. The Zionists, by contrast, called on Jews living in dozens of countries, speaking dozens of different languages, to settle far away in a remote, neglected province of the Ottoman Empire, where their ancestors had lived thousands of years before but which was now inhabited by another people with their own language and religion, a people—moreover—in the first throes of their own national revival and, for this reason, opposed to the Jewish project as a dangerous intrusion.

One of Herzl's closest associates is said to have come running to him one day, exclaiming: "But there are Arabs in Palestine! I didn't know that!" The story may well be apocryphal, but it sums up, as such stories often do, the central facts of the case. In his answer, if there was any, Herzl would not have made an appeal to "historical rights," as many others did and still do to this day. He didn't believe in "historical rights," and he was too well informed not to know the damage that had been done by the quest for such rights during the nineteenth century by Germans, French, and Austrians, as well as in the Balkans, to name only a few examples. But he had an almost uncanny premonition of the dark period ahead. He was sure there were powerful historical currents that would justify the Zionist cause, a confidence that was fully vindicated by later events.

With so many seemingly insurmountable difficulties, it is remarkable how few stupid errors the Zionist leaders made. Fifty years after Herzl's death in 1904 they were still rare, and the damage they caused was not fatal or irreparable. The Zionist project was led by sober men, experienced in the ways of Europe and the world, unwilling to take undue risks; with the exception of a handful, whom Chaim Weizmann, the eminently rational Zionist leader in the interwar years, called disparagingly "our own D'Annunzios," they were reluctant to overplay their hand. They realized that they were conducting an unusual enterprise which in some ways ran counter to the basic trend of world events. Confronted with a mainly hostile Arab population, they wracked their brains to come up with compromises, binational solutions, and partition plans, even when these were damaging to the Zionists, as with several proposals for partition mooted over the years, which they accepted but the Arabs declined.

When you look at the maps outlining these partition plans in the 1930s and 1940s, with their contorted borderlines, narrow corridors, and British or international enclaves—the last was the UN partition resolution of 1947—you get the impression of two antagonists locked in a deadly embrace. By 1948, the British threw up their hands and quit the scene. But when, on the day they finally sailed away, the Jews declared an independent state in their part of the country, it was readily recognized by most nations, after a while even by Britain. Israel was admired for successfully defeating a combined attack by the regular armies of three neighboring Arab states.

The new state was still led by the same cautious leaders, though they were getting older. Their practical frame of mind made these men recognize their limits. They were not easily intoxicated by the recent victory of their ragged army. They usually knew the difference between force and power. Then-Prime-Minister David Ben-Gurion has since been accused of further exacerbating the Palestinian tragedy during the war—with fateful consequences later on—by authorizing his generals to expel perhaps one hundred thousand innocent villagers and townspeople, in addition to the approximately five hundred thousand who had fled the battle zones earlier during the war to seek refuge in the West Bank and the neighboring Arab countries.

And yet Ben-Gurion can hardly be faulted for his caution after the war. He firmly resisted the urgings of brash young generals to seize the rest of the country, later known as the West Bank, which made up about 22 percent of the former Palestine, including the Old City of Jerusalem with its holy places. What is now the West Bank had been annexed by the Hashemite kingdom of Jordan according to a tacit agreement with the Jewish state. The prime minister had reason to hope at that time that a formal peace treaty would now become possible with Abdullah, the Jordanian king, with whom he had remained in discreet contact throughout the war.

Ben-Gurion preferred legitimacy to real estate, even if that real estate included the Wailing Wall and other historical and sacred sites. It was a memorable decision, in the tradition of some of the wisest nineteenth-century European statesmen.

His caution did not lead to peace. The Jordanian king was assassinated by a religious fanatic. But nevertheless it paid off. Postwar Europe was guilt-ridden and contrite over the anti-Semitism of its past. For two decades, support for Israel became virtually a matter of piety in Europe. Except in Britain, the 1948 armistice lines were widely regarded in Europe and America as sacrosanct, much like the postwar partition of Europe between the Western powers and the Soviet Union. The Arabs, of course, rejected them. But it is instructive to compare attitudes in the West toward Israel's

post-1948 borders with attitudes thirty years later to Israel's de facto borders following the 1967 war. Not even Stalin, during his last years of anti-
Semitic paranoia, suggested that Israel withdraw from the 1949 armistice
lines to the much narrower confines of the original UN partition plan.
Nor did Stalin's successors in the Kremlin.

The 1950s and 1960s were the age of decolonization. Stalin and his
successors endorsed nearly all anticolonial movements (except, of course,
within their own far-flung Asian and European empire). They denounced
Israel as a lackey of American capitalism but not as a colonialist power.
Many of the newly independent, former colonial peoples favored close relations with Israel even as they condemned other settler states such as
Kenya, South Africa, or Algeria. The far left in Italy and France was by
and large free of the anti-Israel rhetoric that became familiar after 1967.
Enrico Berlinguer, the Italian Communist leader, said that Israel was a special case. In a just and rational world, he said, it might have made more
"sense" and would have even been more "just" if Israel had been established, say, in Bavaria or in East Prussia, as Lord Moyne, the British war
cabinet minister had suggested, mainly for the sake of argument. Alas,
Berlinguer added, we are not living in a wholly rational world.

The establishment of Israel was widely recognized at the time as perhaps the inevitable, even legitimate, result of a war that the Jews had neither started nor provoked; above all it was seen as a legitimate haven for
Holocaust survivors and displaced persons who, in most cases, refused to
go back to Poland or Germany. Having been rejected in their former home-
lands, many of them wanted to go to Israel and only to Israel. The reset-
tlement of more than six hundred thousand Palestinian refugees was seen
as a primarily humanitarian task, not as a political strategy. (Some had
been expelled by Israel; most had fled their villages, as villagers in battle
zones often do, and had sought temporary refuge in the Arab countries.)
Israel was expected to assume much of the responsibility for their future,
physically and financially, in the event of peace, and rightly so; after all,
the Palestinians were not responsible for the crimes of Europe, but in the
end they were punished for these crimes.

The neighboring Arab countries were expected to help and to absorb
Palestinian refugees. Many in the West held them at least partly responsible for the consequences of a war they had launched in 1948 to undo a
UN resolution. Americans, Europeans—and even the Soviet Union—urged
the Arab countries to make peace with Israel on the basis of the postwar
territorial status quo. In the UN Security Council, the American delegate,
Warren Austin, pounded the table, saying the American government be-

lieved that it was high time for the Jews and the Arabs to get together and finally resolve their problems in a truly Christian spirit.

2.

The 1967 war was the great watershed. It interrupted a decade of gradual détente between Israel and Egypt, which had raised hopes that the conflict between Israel and the Arabs might be resolved, at least partially. Though the Suez Canal remained closed to Israeli ships, they could, after 1956, move freely through the Straits of Tiran. Trade with the Far East and oil from the Iranian oil fields flowed freely to the southernmost Israeli port of Elath. Israel was at first praised in the West for scoring a spectacular victory in a war largely provoked by the bizarre miscalculations of the Egyptian and Syrian rulers, partly also by a clumsy Soviet diplomat who encouraged Egypt and Syria to threaten Israel and who soon afterward disappeared, perhaps into the gulag. (I remember chatting with a German military attaché at a party who pressed my hand and barely let go of it, saying, "This was just as Field Marshal Rommel would have done if he had had his way. . . .") We now know that it was a Pyrrhic victory. The war changed not only Israel's position in the region but even more so its self-image. Israel, which, in Isaiah Berlin's words, had always had "more history than geography," now suddenly had both. For the first time, at least in theory, it had enough territory to exchange for peace.

David Ben-Gurion was the only leading figure in the political elite who broke the general euphoria by suggesting that Israel withdraw immediately, if need be unilaterally, from all occupied territories. As he had in 1948, Ben-Gurion flatly opposed any attempts to permanently occupy the West Bank. But Ben-Gurion was old and retired and politically isolated. He had bitterly quarreled with the ruling Labor Party. Yigal Allon, the same young general who in 1948 had urged him to complete, as he put it, the "liberation" of the rest of the country, was now a prominent cabinet minister competing for the premiership with Moshe Dayan, another former general. Allon, though he spoke vaguely of the need to allow the Palestinians a state of their own, drew up a plan of settlements and annexations on the West Bank that would have left the Palestinians little more than two enclaves in the Samarian and Judean mountains, surrounded by Israeli military bases and proposed settlements. They would have had no political foothold in Jerusalem. The so-called Allon Plan grew incrementally over the years as the political deadlock continued; it embraced more and more territory to be settled and annexed by Israel.

Dayan's plans were more ambiguous but, in effect, far more ambitious. He was the first top-level secular politician whose rhetoric was loaded with suggestive biblical imagery: "We've returned to Shilo [a house of worship in the Bronze Age]; we've returned to Anathot [the prophet Isaiah's birthplace] never to part from them again," etc., etc. Dayan was the adored victor in a glorious war and, for some years, perhaps the most famous Jew since Jesus Christ. It was, I think, at his urging that the war was retrospectively named after the Six Days of Creation. Right-wing and religious fundamentalists made the most of the victory and endowed the Six-Day War with a metaphysical, pseudo-messianic aura. They pushed for the formal annexation immediately of all "liberated areas." At that time, they were still a relatively small minority.

The race between the two secular ex-generals for the premiership was more ominous, with fatal consequences to this day. Both Allon and Dayan were curiously self-centered, as politicians often are, and blind to the Palestinian presence in the region. They dismissed the aspirations of over a million Palestinians in the West Bank and Gaza Strip as of limited political importance. They had no intention to offer them Israeli citizenship. Some three hundred thousand Palestinians already lived in Israel proper, increasingly embittered by their status as second-class citizens. The Jewish population in 1967 was 2.7 million; the combined Arab population west of the river Jordan was 1.3 million. It was as though France had decided in 1938 to absorb as many as 20 million restive, potentially subversive Germans within borders that were surrounded, as Israel was, by more than a hundred million of their hostile, heavily armed co-nationals. Today, thirty-five years later, 4.1 million Palestinians live between the river Jordan and the sea (3.1 million in the West Bank and the Gaza Strip and 1 million Palestinians in Israel proper.) Despite heavy Jewish immigration since 1967 there are still only some 5 million Jews, a ratio of only 1.2 to 1. Higher Palestinian birthrates are certain to ensure an absolute Palestinian majority within ten or fifteen years.

Cabinet sessions in Israel are always long and verbose affairs but never as long and frequent as they were in the summer of 1967. The ministers deliberated on what to do after the great victory. The crucial session, on the status of the occupied West Bank, began on a Sunday in mid-June and lasted, with brief interruptions for food and sleep, until the following Wednesday. The decision finally made was—not to decide. In the absence of a decision, Dayan, by now a national demigod, Allon, and assorted right-wing and religious fundamentalist militants and squatters were able to successfully establish very dubious facts on the ground—settlements and so-called *heachsujot* (outpost positions) that multiplied over the years through formal and semi-informal arrangements. Squatters were gradually legalized, lavishly subsidized, and eventually hailed as national heroes. It was said of the British Empire that it was born in a fit of absentmind-edness. The Israeli colonial intrusion into the West Bank came into being under similar shadowy circumstances. Few people took it seriously at first. Some deluded themselves that it was bound to be temporary. Those re-sponsible for it pursued it consistently. They included a few ministers who believed that it might even induce the Arabs to sue for peace sooner rather than later, before too many "irrevocable" facts were established on the ground.

An ostensibly dovish Labor minister of housing—a declared opponent of the settlement project who nevertheless very generously subsidized it—cynically remarked that after the settlements were evacuated, as he was certain they would be, the United States would compensate Israel at a rate of one dollar for every lira spent on it in vain. The few who protested the settlements on political or demographic grounds were ignored. They were no match for the emerging coalition of religious and political fundamen-talists. The Knesset never voted on the settlement project. The settlements were at first financed mostly through nongovernmental agencies, the United Jewish Appeal, the Jewish Agency, and the Jewish National Fund. The U.S. government went through the motions of mildly protesting the settlement project. It took none of the legal and other steps it might have taken to stop the flow of tax-exempt contributions to the UJA or JNF that financed the settlements on land confiscated for "security" reasons from its Palestinian owners. For all practical purposes, the United States served as a ready partner in the settlement project. The National Coalition cab-inet, which was slapped together hastily on the eve of the 1967 war, re-mained in power long after. It was presided over at first by Levi Eshkol, a weak prime minister who died soon after the war and was succeeded by the hard-line Golda Meir, famous for her smug maternalism and for say-ing, "Who are the Palestinians? I am a Palestinian."

The government informed the United States that Israel was ready to withdraw from occupied Egyptian and Syrian territory in return for peace, but it explicitly excluded withdrawal from the West Bank or Gaza Strip. No evidence has turned up so far that American diplomats actually sounded out Cairo and Damascus about a deal based on Israeli with-drawal. An attempt, a few years ago, by *The New York Review of Books* to induce the U.S. National Archives to release diplomatic documents per-tinent to these exchanges under the Freedom of Information Act produced no results. Not a single U.S. cable, report, or verbal communication turned up to indicate that in the summer of 1967 an attempt was made by the

United States to begin a peace process. We can only speculate on the reasons for U.S. failure to do so.

Apart from being happy, apparently, that Israel had humiliated the Soviet Union's main clients in the region, the United States was in no hurry to end the Arab–Israeli conflict. The Arab–Israeli War was becoming a proxy conflict between the superpowers, a testing ground for their hardware. The Suez Canal remained conveniently blocked.

At the height of the Vietnam War, the United States, under Lyndon Johnson, might have had good reasons to keep it closed as long as possible and force Soviet supply ships to North Vietnam to take the long route around Africa. Soon afterward, at a summit meeting in Khartoum, the Arab countries announced the "Three No's"—no to recognizing, negotiating with, or making peace with Israel. The ensuing stalemate lasted several years. An Arab-Israeli writer, with something like Schadenfreude, borrowed an Oriental image to describe the Israeli dilemma: "Instead of stepping on the snake that threatened them, they merely swallowed it," he wrote. "Now they have to live with it, or die with it." A dilemma, by definition, is a conflict between equally undesirable alternatives. But was this really the conflict facing Israel? We now know that it wasn't. Peace was a distinct possibility—with the Palestinians as early as the summer of 1967, with Jordan and Egypt in 1971 and 1972. Soon after the 1967 war, two senior Israeli intelligence officers—one was David Kimche, who later served as deputy director of Mossad and director general of the Israeli Foreign Ministry—interviewed prominent Palestinian civic and political leaders throughout the West Bank, including intellectuals, notables, mayors, and religious leaders. He reported that most of them said they were ready to establish a demilitarized Palestinian state on the West Bank that would sign a separate peace with Israel. The Palestine Liberation Organization (PLO) at the time was still a fairly marginal group.

Kimche's report, as far as we know, was shelved by Dayan. It was never submitted to the cabinet. In the hubris of the first few months following the war, even a tentative effort to explore this possibility would likely have been rejected by the cabinet. Dayan believed that as long as the natives were treated kindly and decently—at first they were—it would be possible to maintain the status quo on the West Bank and in Gaza for generations. The Palestinians were still remarkably docile; they had allowed the West Bank to be conquered in a few hours without firing a single shot. Dayan—and nearly the entire political and military establishment—were convinced that not only the Palestinians but also Egypt and Syria would be unable to present a military threat for decades. Dayan's opinion of the Arab armies was reflected during a visit to Vietnam. Asked by General

Westmoreland how to win in war, Dayan is said to have responded: "First of all, you pick the Arabs as your enemy." He told me a few weeks after the war: "What is it really, this entire West Bank? It's only a couple of small townships."

We may forget that top political leaders live very different lives from the rest of us. Their escorts whisk them through red lights and they often travel about by helicopter. From the cockpit of a helicopter, the West Bank might indeed look like little more than a handful of wretchedly small townships. Dayan's mood was reflected in an interview he gave at the time to the editor of *Der Spiegel*. Asked how Israel hoped to achieve peace, his answer was: "by standing firm as iron, wherever we are now standing, until the Arabs are ready to give in."

Q: Then it's only King Hussein who is likely to qualify as a partner in negotiations. But he isn't strong enough to agree to [your] conditions.

DAYAN: In this case let them find themselves another king.

Q: But Jordan as a country may not be strong enough to agree to peace on Dayan's conditions.

DAYAN: In this case let them find themselves another country.

Q: Under these circumstances, it is hard to hope for peace soon.

DAYAN: That's probably right.

Before the Yom Kippur War of 1973, Dayan's position toward Egypt was that it was preferable to retain Sharm el Sheik and half the Sinai peninsula without peace than to have peace with Egypt without retaining Sharm el Sheik. After the Yom Kippur War, Dayan's position toward Egypt changed, and he was willing to leave the occupied Sinai. As for the occupied West Bank, in complete disregard of demographic realities, he remained an annexationist. Henry Kissinger complained that whenever he asked the Israelis about their political intentions there, he failed to receive an answer.

The truth was that despite the "Three No's" of Khartoum, direct negotiations with Jordan began soon after the Six-Day War, by 1970 with King Hussein himself. Even while Golda Meir was publicly lamenting, "If the Arabs would only sit down with us at a table like decent human beings and talk!" her representatives were secretly meeting the King. Hussein flew his own helicopter to Tel Aviv and was taken by Dayan on a tour of the city by night. The king was ready to make peace with Israel if Israel withdrew from much of the West Bank as well as from East Jerusalem and if the Muslim and Christian holy places in the Old City were restored to Jordan. The king was ready to make concessions to Israel along the narrow coastal plain and at the Western Wall in the Old City of Jerusalem.

Israel would not hear of it. The expanded municipal area of Jerusalem— by now it included not only Arab East Jerusalem but a part of the former West Bank—was declared Israel's capital for "all eternity." In addition to this Greater Jerusalem area, which was being intensively settled by Israelis on land confiscated from its Palestinian owners, Israel insisted on the latest (expanded) version of the Allon Plan. It called for the annexation of the entire Jordan Valley from the Lake of Tiberias down to the Dead Sea, the heavily populated area between Jerusalem and Hebron in the south, and the slopes of the western and northern mountain range of Samaria in the north. The king indicated that for such far-reaching concessions the Israelis would have to negotiate with the PLO. In retrospect, it is tragic that no agreement could be reached with Palestinian leaders in the West Bank or with Jordan in the late 1960s and early 1970s.

We are speaking of a time, thirty years ago, before the Palestinians were radicalized by an increasingly humiliating occupation regime and by large-scale expropriation of Palestinian land for the exclusive use of Israeli settlers. Neither Hamas nor Hezbollah existed, and the PLO was not recognized internationally. Hamas was, in fact, encouraged by the Israelis as a counterweight to the PLO, much as the CIA supported the Islamic extremists in Afghanistan. An autonomous Palestinian entity, at peace with Israel, would not have removed the PLO from the scene, but it might have considerably weakened its impact. Alternatively, in a peace settlement with Jordan the Palestinian issue might have reverted to what it had been before 1967: mainly a Jordanian problem.

The failure to reach an agreement seems all the more tragic, since at that time there were still relatively few settlers—fewer than three thousand— and they would not have been able to veto all concessions, as they do today. Today there are two hundred thousand settlers in the West Bank and Gaza Strip—their number has been allowed to almost double since the Oslo agreement of 1993. With two hundred thousand more settlers on former Jordanian territory in East Jerusalem, the total number has now reached four hundred thousand.

The settlement project continues to grow even now. Imagine the effect on the peace process in Northern Ireland if the British government continued moving thousands of Protestants from Scotland into Ulster and settling them, at government expense, on land confiscated from Irish Catholics.

The occupation was, by and large, a paying proposition. Until the first *intifada* twenty years later its costs were more than covered by taxes on the Palestinian population as well as by turning the West Bank and Gaza into a captive market for Israeli-produced goods and services. Michael Ben-Yair, Israel's attorney general in the Rabin government, recently wrote in *Ha'aretz:*

> The Six-Day War was forced on us; but the war's Seventh day, which began on June 12, 1967—continues to this day and is the product of our choice.
>
> We enthusiastically chose to become a colonialist society, ignoring international treaties, expropriating lands, transferring settlers from Israel to the occupied territories, engaging in theft and finding justifications for all this.

These are harsh words, but it is a characteristic of the tragic folly I am describing that Ben-Yair did not put forward such views in a legal brief when he was still attorney general, as he could have done nine years earlier.

The settlers now are the strongest political lobby in Israel. In recent years they have been supported by lavish subsidies, grants of land, low-rent housing, government jobs, tax benefits, and social services more generous than any in Israel proper. The settlements are now a kind of suburbia of Israel proper: most settlers commute daily to their jobs in Jerusalem and the greater Tel Aviv area. With few exceptions, the settlements have not made Israel more "secure" as was sometimes claimed; they have made Israel less secure. They have greatly extended the country's lines of defense. They impose a crushing burden of protecting widely dispersed settlements deep inside densely populated Palestinian territories, where ever-larger numbers of Palestinians are increasingly infuriated by the inevitable controls, curfews, and violence, as well as by humiliation imposed on them by insensitive or undisciplined recruits and army reservists.

Two examples: an entire armored regiment has been tied down for years protecting a small colony of nationalist, religious fanatics in downtown Hebron, a deeply fundamentalist Muslim city. The colony believes that the Kingdom of God is near and—at first against government orders—squatted illegally in a couple of abandoned, half-ruined houses.

In the Gaza Strip some of the well-established, prospering settlements are only a few hundred meters away from the vast refugee camps, populated by third- and fourth-generation Palestinian refugees. In five minutes a visitor might feel as if he were passing from Southern California to Bangladesh—through barbed-wire entanglements, past watchtowers, searchlights, machine-gun positions, and fortified roadblocks: a bizarre and chilling sight.

The Palestinians are infuriated as well by seeing their olive groves uprooted or burned down by settlers while their water faucets go dry and their ancestral land reserves and scarce water resources are taken over for the use of settlers who luxuriate nearby in their swimming pools and consume five times as much water as the average Palestinian. The settlements themselves occupy less than 20 percent of the West Bank, but through a network of so-called regional councils they control planning and environmental policy for approximately 40 percent of the West Bank, according to figures recently published by B'tzelem, the Israeli human rights organization.

It is not difficult to imagine what the settlers' lobby means in a country with notoriously narrow parliamentary majorities. Though 70 percent of Israeli voters say in the polls that they support abandoning some of the settlements, four hundred thousand settlers and their right-wing and Orthodox supporters within Israel proper now control at least half the national vote. They pose a constant threat of civil war if their interests are not fully respected. At their core is a group of fanatical nationalists and religious fundamentalists who believe they know exactly what God and Abraham said to each other in the Bronze Age.

The settlers are no longer outsiders or squatters as they once were. A great many became settlers for purely pragmatic reasons—cheaper housing in what they hoped would be more pleasant surroundings within easy commuting distance to Israel. For almost twenty-five years the settlers have been praised by every Israeli government as patriots, good citizens, good Zionists. At least in the West Bank, the settlement project long ago became a cornerstone of Zionist and Israeli national identity. By now there is a second generation of settlers who see no difference between themselves and other Israelis who live in Tel Aviv or Tiberias. Since the outbreak of the most recent *intifada* and the emergence of reckless suicide bombers, moreover, they are not merely defending an idea; as they see it, they are defending "home."

As a result, on both sides now, the extremists are dominant: in Israel and Palestine they veto all progress toward peace. Disasters follow one after another daily and the end is not in sight. Hamas seems to have usurped the Palestinian national movement while hard-line religious groups seem to be usurping the Jewish national cause. The situation seems all the more tragic, since thirty years after Hussein's first peace proposals in 1970 a similar peace scheme was tentatively endorsed by the Barak government. At Camp David, one of the worst-prepared peace conferences in history, Clinton, not Barak himself, conveyed to the Palestinians

several "bases for negotiation" calling for a Palestinian state in which Israelis would continue to occupy roughly 9 percent of the West Bank; as
Robert Malley and Hussein Agha wrote in these pages, Arafat was "unable to say yes to the American ideas or present a cogent or specific coun-
terproposal of [his] own."[1]

After more secret meetings between Israeli and Palestinian diplomats
during the autumn, Clinton, on December 23, 2000, conveyed to Arafat
what he called the "parameters" of an improved scheme, which the Israeli
cabinet accepted;[2] Arafat's reply to Clinton was delayed ten days, and
when it finally arrived it expressed both interest in the new proposals and
reservations about them. The negotiators (but not the principals) met
again at Taba in Egypt between January 21 and 27 in 2001 and issued a
statement saying, "The two sides have never been closer to reaching an
agreement and it is thus our shared belief that the remaining gaps could
be bridged . . ." It was too late: Clinton had left office, and the Israeli elections were impending. Like every other observer, Arafat was aware that
Barak would lose.

We can only speculate on his reasons for not clearly accepting at least
the basic outlines of an agreement. He may have thought he might obtain
better terms under the incoming Bush administration. Or he may have de-
spaired of ever restoring the West Bank and Gaza to Palestinian rule by
diplomatic means. According to Robert Malley, who was present at the
Camp David negotiations, the Palestinian negotiators were divided and
competed with one another. Arafat apparently lost control over some of
his own internal factions. He may have hoped at this moment that just as
Hezbollah terror had succeeded in driving Israel out of southern Lebanon,
so Israel could be forced by continuing violence to abandon Gaza and the
West Bank. Arafat's strategy at this stage, or perhaps even before, could
even have been to hold out for a kind of Greater Palestine—just as powerful Israelis had long been planning a Greater Israel from the sea to the
river Jordan. Sharon has long said he has been in favor of a Palestinian
state east of the river, i.e., in what is now Jordan.

I don't pretend to know what makes Arafat tick. He and his henchmen
certainly underestimated, grossly so, Israel's power, resilience, resolve, and
international support. Arafat may, or may not, have decided already in
1993 to exploit the Oslo agreement in order first to consolidate a power
base on the West Bank and then try to enlarge it later on to include a
Greater Palestine, taking over all or parts of Israel proper. This is what
the hard-liners in Israel claim and they may be right. Or they may be
wrong: the Palestinians invested $3 billion in new tourist facilities on the
West Bank during the past seven years; they may not have done so if the
plan had always been to wage an all-out struggle. Such an investment

would make sense for the Palestinian state that Arafat has often said he wants and Sharon is determined to prevent.

I interviewed Arafat in his Tunis headquarters in 1993 while the secret Oslo talks were still going on. He never hinted even vaguely that he knew of the talks, though one of his aides did. Arafat complained at great length about Rabin. At one point I asked him: "What do you want Rabin to do?" He said: "He is not a De Gaulle. Let him be at least a De Klerk." To Israeli ears, this sounded ominous. Under De Gaulle, the entire French population quit Algeria. Under De Klerk, the whites were allowed to remain in a Greater South Africa controlled by the black majority. Arafat refused to clarify this remark. It may have been mere rhetoric. Out of Arafat's hearing, one of his assistants later said sarcastically: "Well, the old man is no De Gaulle either."

The right wing in Israel may be correct in claiming, as they now do, that no workable compromise is possible with the Palestinians, but if they are right, there is all the more reason to regret the strategically senseless extension of Israel's defense lines to embrace a multitude of vulnerable, widely dispersed, often isolated Israeli settlements deep in heavily populated Palestinian territory. Instead of minimizing friction, they increased it. Almost two hundred settlements on the West Bank and in the Gaza Strip and more than two hundred thousand settlers in East Jerusalem are potentially explosive irritants that can undo any possible historic compromise. How much easier would it now have been, if Israel were poised more or less along the 1967 line (from which, after all, it defeated three Arab countries in six days).

Instead Sharon's government is now trying, mostly for domestic political reasons, to build high walls along this line and innumerable other high walls around each settlement and each Palestinian town. Every other day it dispatches tanks and combat helicopters to patrol the roads leading to each settlement. It nevertheless suffers heavy casualties, calls up the reserves, and deploys huge forces in Jerusalem to prevent suicide bombers from making their way into Jewish neighborhoods. In too many cases, these extensive security measures fail—inevitably perhaps, since in Jerusalem Palestinian and Israeli residential and business quarters are intermixed, suicide bombers seem to get through the tightest controls, and retaliating strikes don't discourage them.

In Israel and in Palestine, the center has collapsed. The much talked about "two-state solution" may no longer be practicable since on both sides all confidence is gone. The extremists of Greater Israel and the extremists of Greater Palestine mutually veto all progress. I use the terms "Greater Israel" and "Greater Palestine" with deliberate bitterness. We know the evil wrought by similar "Great" projects elsewhere: "Greater Serbia," "Greater Bulgaria," "Greater Ustashi Croatia," and "Greater Greece."

Israel is now likely to remain in physical control of millions of restive Palestinians. We don't know for how long. It is possible that the long-sought "solution" will be delayed by another generation, perhaps more than one. For what does Ariel Sharon mean when he says he aims at dismantling what he calls the "infrastructure" of terror? The true "infrastructure" is not in some odd garage or workshop where belts loaded with explosives and steel nails are prepared and homemade mortar missiles are built. The true infrastructure is more dangerous: it consists of both the growing willingness of enraged young men and women to blow themselves up and the religious and political culture in twenty-one Arab countries that praises the suicide bombers as martyrs. This "infrastructure" is diffuse. It may not have a center. The most powerful air force can't defeat it. In Afghanistan the Americans defeated the Taliban but not al-Qaeda, which continues to exist.

The race between Netanyahu and Sharon for the leadership of Likud is pushing both men further to the right. Sharon says he will not dismantle a single settlement. For both men, this may or may not be a bargaining position. But for their political survival, both men depend on right-wing and religious extremists. By effectively consuming the one thing Israel had to offer the Palestinians in return for peace—Palestinian land—the extended settlement project, I fear, may yet prove Israel's undoing. It may lead to two equally awful alternatives: wholesale ethnic cleansing or permanent violence, terror, suicide bombers, and possibly all-out war.

3.

Perhaps Israel's greatest tragedy has been the deterioration over the years of the quality of Israeli leadership. A flawed electoral system had a lot to do with this, since it discourages clear majorities. Recent attempts to tinker with the constitution have increased political instability. In less than a decade, one prime minister was assassinated by a right-wing fanatic and three prime ministers have been unable to serve out their terms. Government continues to depend on forming unwieldy coalitions that give undue leverage to religious and other splinter and pressure groups. The perennial instability has encouraged waste, xenophobia, and demagoguery. The moral bankruptcy of the Labor Party made inevitable the ascendancy of Likud and its religious, nationalist, and semifascist allies.

It remains to be seen if in the few weeks left until the Israeli election Amram Mitzna, the new Labor leader, will succeed in reversing this trend. It seems unlikely. By promising to renew peace talks unconditionally with the Palestinians and to withdraw from Gaza and from some of the more remote West Bank settlements, Mitzna has at least offered voters a clearer alternative to Sharon than has been the case so far. He faces the enormous task of reeducating a terrorized electorate driven by recent events to support harsh measures against Palestinians. He must also try to rebuild a discredited party shattered by shameless opportunism and infighting among special interest groups.

It could be argued that the missed peace opportunities would have saved a lot of needless bloodshed and it could, of course, also be argued that such a "peace" might have proved to be illusory, a short-lived cease-fire with an adversary resolved to remove an intrusion, as the Crusader state was wiped out after a series of cease-fires and armistices. The jihad, according to this line of thought, would go on and on. I am not saying that it won't; but the peace treaties with Egypt and Jordan, which have survived many a tough moment, seem to suggest that the wider Arab–Israeli conflict can only end if Israelis and Palestinians arrive at a compromise.

The nature and details of such a compromise have been known for years: the partition of a country over which the two national independence movements have clashed for almost a century now. The bazaar diplomacy of the past ten years has clearly been counterproductive. The so-called "incremental" Oslo peace process was abused by both sides; by relegating the most difficult problems to the very last stage it encouraged both sides to cheat. When force did not work, there was a tendency to believe in using more force, which led, as we are seeing, only to another dead end. The search for secure borders—even when it did not involve the domination of one people by another—was carried too far. No border is ever deemed absolutely secure before it seems absolutely insecure to the other side and so makes the next war inevitable.

The vast settlement project after 1967, aside from being grossly unjust, has been self-defeating and politically ruinous. "We've fed the heart on fantasies,/the heart's grown brutal on the fare," as William B. Yeats put it almost a century ago in a similar dead-end situation in Ireland. The settlement project has not provided more security but less. It may yet, I tremble at the thought, lead to results far more terrible than those we are now witnessing.

NOTES

1. See "Camp David: The Tragedy of Errors." *The New York Review,* August 9, 2001.
2. See Malley and Agha's reply to Ehud Barak in "Camp David and After: An Exchange." *The New York Review,* June 13, 2002.

FICTIONS EMBRACED
BY AN ISRAEL AT WAR

David Grossman

A DANGEROUS AND DECEPTIVE plot line has become superimposed on the story that Israeli society tells itself about its conflict with the Palestinians. Since the outbreak of the current *intifada* two years ago, it is as if the Israeli mind has turned to a new page in the chronicle of the conflict and, at the same time, erased many of the pages that preceded it.

It's as if the thirty-three years of repression, occupation, and humiliation that Israel imposed on the West Bank and Gaza between June 1967 and September 2000 vanished with the wave of a magic wand. The majority of Israelis take comfort today in believing that the horrifying deeds committed by Palestinian terrorists in the last two years somehow "balance the books" for those long years of subjugation, and that all the guilt for the current state of affairs rests on Palestinian shoulders. Furthermore, they believe, the suicide bombings, and the broad support they have received from the Palestinian population, have revealed things about the Palestinians that ex post facto justify the injustices of the occupation. In a contorted way, many Israelis believe that the new wave of Palestinian terrorism has granted their country absolution for its problematic past.

Of course, the Israeli occupation is not the entire story. During those thirty-three years the Palestinians contributed their share to the march of blood and folly by being intractable in their positions and murderous in their actions. And we must not forget that the Six-Day War was not a war that Israel wanted. Yet, despite this, the historical story that Israel chooses to tell itself is astoundingly obtuse and superficial.

The story that now reigns nearly unchallenged in the media and political discourse obliterates more than thirty-three years of roadblocks, thousands of prisoners, deportations, and killings of innocent people. It's as if there were never long months of closures in cities and villages, as if there had been no humiliations, no incessant harassment, no searches of houses, no bulldozing of hundreds of homes, no uprooting of vineyards and olive groves, no filling up of wells and, especially, no construction of tens of thousands of housing units in settlements and large-scale confiscation of land, in violation of international law.

The new narrative leaps back through the manipulative fog created by the prime minister and his cabinet, his supporters, and his various spokesmen straight to the Six-Day War, our pinnacle of justice. And looking forward from that point in 1967, there is a kind of desert devoid of history, devoid of responsibility, devoid of blame, until we suddenly emerge from the miasma right at the Oslo accords, the proposals that Ehud Barak made to Yasser Arafat at Camp David and, after Camp David, like thunder on a bright and sunny day, the second *intifada*.

According to this story, the Palestinians suddenly exploded in September 2000 in an uncaused natural eruption, spewing out lava and ash and igniting the entire region. They had no logical reason for exploding and there was no prior Israeli provocation. Ehud Barak made them a generous offer, and they betrayed him with an outburst of violence—because they, by their nature, are motivated solely by destructive, irrational forces that make impossible any future compromise with them.

This theory is also the basis of another right-wing claim that now seems to be accepted by the majority of Israelis. It is that the Oslo accords, and their supporters, were what in fact caused the second *intifada*. In other words, it wasn't the intolerable conditions in which the Palestinians lived for more than three decades. It wasn't the tacit support that most Israelis lent to the ongoing occupation, all the while persuading themselves that it was such an enlightened occupation that it was barely an occupation at all. It wasn't the refusal of every Israeli government before the second administration of Yitzhak Rabin to try to reach a true, if painful, accommodation with the Palestinians. It wasn't the doubling of the number of Israeli settlers in the territories in the years after Oslo. Nor was it the way in which Ehud Barak conducted the Camp David talks, presenting to Yasser Arafat as ultimatums proposals that, while they were generous compared with Israeli positions in the past, were entirely insufficient in Palestinian eyes.

None of these factors are now viewed as sufficient reason for a popular uprising by a subjugated and despairing people. No, it's the Oslo accords that are to blame, as if in the absence of Oslo the Palestinians would have come to terms with the Israeli occupation, accepting it tranquilly, even lovingly, to this very day; as if the Oslo agreements were a match, not a fire extinguisher.

Obviously, one of the reasons this storyline has gained acceptance is that it seems to give a logical structure to a chaotic and threatening reality. Along the way, it also seems to justify the use of massive and unrelenting military force against the Palestinians.

But this view of reality is fraught with danger because it is simply not realistic. It's true that the Palestinians have committed serious errors and war crimes in the last two years. It also may well be true that, had they acted otherwise, they would have a state today. But if Israel is interested not just in punishing the Palestinians but also in extricating itself from the trap it's in, it must wake up and reinsert into the tragic story of the conflict those parts that have been expunged from its consciousness during the last two years. If we do not replant the recent *intifada* in its historical context, no change of any minimal mutual understanding will sprout. And without context, we will never be truly cured.

LETTER FROM
AN ANGUISHED SOUL

David A. Harris

THE BAD NEWS JUST KEEPS COMING. One terror attack after another. More and more fatalities. No place in Israel today is safe. No Israeli can feel immune from the danger.

Tragically, the response to each calamity takes on a rather eerie predictability.

Israelis are killed, and the mourners, together with an entire nation, weep, while the government vows to crush the terrorists, and the people stoically resolve to carry on their "normal" lives. Of course, this government, just like its predecessors, is unable to find a foolproof method to stop the terrorists. Who could? And what constitutes a normal life these days in a totally abnormal situation?

Israeli spokesmen are too many in number, perhaps the price to be paid for a democratic society where everyone is eager to speak, and foreign journalists, who are in Israel by the hundreds, are in need of filing a story and always looking for an angle.

Some Israeli spokesmen are on message, others not; some come across well on television, others do not; some speak fluent English, others do not; some talk the language of war, others of peace. In other words, to borrow a favorite Israeli expression, it's a bit of a *balagan,* chaos, and efforts to control the messenger and the message have been only partially successful.

In the wake of President Bush's landmark June 24 speech, glib Palestinian spokesmen—Arafat's minions—now appear before Western reporters to ritualistically denounce the terror attacks against Israelis but then never fail to add that, in the final analysis, these attacks are all Sharon's fault and certainly not the Palestinians'. Following a carefully controlled script, they then quickly slip in the Palestinian buzzwords that inevitably surface whether the interview lasts five seconds or fifty—Israeli "occupation," "humiliation," "economic strangulation."

Not only are the Palestinians better at controlling the message and the messenger—unless it's Arafat speaking—but they have another advantage. They are practiced liars.

They can look unblinkingly at the television cameras and declare that hundreds of Jenin residents were massacred by Israeli troops, or that Israeli doctors have injected HIV in Palestinian children, or that the Israeli army is using depleted uranium shells, or whatever other outrageous fabrication comes to mind. These spokesmen know all too well that such accusations will be reported dutifully—and often uncritically—by an often gullible media that's "only doing its job," and that there are a certain number of nations, human rights groups, and individuals who are only too ready to believe the latest charge against Israel and repeat it ad nauseam. History has taught us something about the "big lie" theory, hasn't it?

Meanwhile, back in Gaza or Nablus, the deaths of Israelis, whatever their age, ideology, or denomination, are cause for feverish celebration among the many who take to the streets. Compare this to the anguished discussion within Israel when Palestinian civilians, especially children, become unintended casualties of military action to combat terror.

The United States, to its everlasting credit, can be counted on to quickly and unambiguously denounce the terror, express its understanding of Israel's situation, and defend Israel's right to strike back.

The Europeans, by contrast, stumble all over themselves, trying, but never terribly convincingly, to show sympathy for the Israeli victims but unable to hide their profound antipathy for the Sharon-led government and their general dislike of military responses to what they believe to be political problems.

In fact, to this day the European Union cannot even bring itself to agree on designating Hezbullah, a group openly dedicated to Israel's destruction, as a terrorist organization, largely due to French objections that there are other, more "benign" aspects to the group, such as its "social welfare" agenda and participation in the Lebanese "political" process. (By contrast, Hezbullah, together with Hamas and Islamic Jihad, have been on the U.S. terrorism list for many years.)

The media, with few exceptions, feed us the "moral equivalence," "cycle of violence," and "an eye for an eye" lines, essentially two sides in an atavistic struggle to the end, with no clear distinction between democrats and dictators. The *New York Times* is still not prepared to label Hamas, which is hell-bent on Israel's complete destruction, according to its own charter, a terrorist group, instead antiseptically referring to its members as "militants." And, as we know, the *Times* is far from the worst offender. That title would clearly go to one of several European candidates.

Countries like Egypt and Jordan, which, in private, express undisguised contempt for Arafat, are fearful of saying anything remotely similar in public.

The United Nations, needless to say, is a hostage of the numbers game, and the numbers are heavily stacked against Israel. That helps explain why the Geneva-based Commission on Human Rights, for example, was able to devote 30 to 40 percent of its time at this year's six-week session to bashing Israel. It passed no fewer than eight anti-Israel resolutions, when no other problematic regional situation was the object of more than one resolution, if that.

When was the last time anyone remembers the UN meeting in special session because of a Palestinian terror attack against Israel? Don't count on it anytime soon, either.

American Jews react in various ways. There are those—the clear majority, according to a national survey just released by the American Jewish Committee—who identify ever more closely with Israel and recoil in horror at these repeated terrorist attacks.

Then there is a significant minority that remains essentially indifferent to the attacks, devoting, at best, passing attention but then moving on, since Israel is far from their lives.

And, finally, there is a much smaller minority, but a vocal one at that, people who have essentially determined that Israel has only itself to blame for its current situation and who are ready to sign on to any ad or join any protest to heap scorn on Sharon et al., while self-righteously wrapping themselves in the mantle of the Jewish ethical tradition.

Thus, on the day after the horrific tragedy at Hebrew University, one Jewish letter writer to the *Times* could contemptuously blame it all on Sharon, while others publicly call on the American government to pressure Israel by withholding foreign aid.

I confess that sometimes I just don't get it.

A spokesman for Hamas publicly declares that the group's objective is to rid Israel of its Jewish population. He couldn't be more clear, nor could the Hamas charter. The same goes for Islamic Jihad, Hezbullah, and other terror groups. Israel is in a war for its survival against an enemy that celebrates death, especially Jewish death. What exactly is Israel supposed to do in response? If there's a playbook for this crisis, I'm not aware of it.

Israel has just about tried it all.

The dovish Shimon Peres replaced the slain Yitzhak Rabin as prime minister, eager to continue the work of building peace, and was almost immediately faced with one deadly terrorist bombing after another in the spring of 1996. As a result, he lost the election to his rival, Benjamin Netanyahu, who promised the nation security.

Under Prime Minister Barak of the Labor Party, and with the full support of President Clinton, Israel made a breathtakingly tantalizing offer to the Palestinians for peace and statehood on 97 percent of the disputed land less than two years ago, only to see it turned down flat. Now the Palestinians, once again seeking to rewrite history, flail about, asserting variously that the offer was never actually made in writing, or was less than meets the eye, or would have created Bantustans, but the people actually in the know—President Clinton, Prime Minister Barak, Ambassador Dennis Ross, and Foreign Minister Shlomo Ben-Ami—all reject these contentions out of hand.

Israel has tried unilateral ceasefires, restraint in the face of severe provocation, offers to ease economic conditions, and even expressions of regret when Israel Defense Forces mistakes occur, but that hasn't done much good either.

Let's acknowledge certain inescapable truths.

The Palestinian leadership has not prepared its people for peace with Israel or even acceptance of Israel's right to exist as a Jewish state, whatever its final boundaries. To the contrary, the years since the 1993 Oslo Accords have been devoted to quite the opposite—the teaching of hatred and incitement, and the creation of a military/terrorist infrastructure.

Remember that this is the very same Palestinian leadership that introduced the world to a whole new era of international terrorism in the 1970s, that was expelled from Jordan, that caused a domestic civil war in Lebanon, that violated more ceasefires in Jordan and Lebanon alone than Barry Bonds hit home runs last season, that has been utterly corrupt in the use of aid money, that supported Saddam Hussein in the Gulf War, that colluded with Iran to purchase sophisticated weapons, and that, during the Cold War, embraced just about every communist dictator from the Soviet Union's Brezhnev to Cuba's Castro.

Despite all the attempts at spin and recasting, Arafat has not changed his spots. It's tough to admit, perhaps, but he managed to pull the wool over the eyes of just about everyone, including the Nobel Peace Prize Committee.

To state the painfully obvious, there are no easy or off-the-shelf answers for Israel in the face of this situation. As I've written on previous occasions, both the left and the right have flawed approaches.

The left has a blind spot. It refuses to see things as they are. Instead, it substitutes wishful thinking for reality. Since it cannot bring itself to admit that its analysis was so off base, it chooses, instead, to persist in its dangerous thinking.

The right lives under its own illusion. The Palestinians cannot be crushed militarily. Or, let me put it differently: they can be, but Israel is not prepared to do what would be required, because there are built-in restraints on Israeli behavior, both as a democracy and as a Jewish state. And don't think the Palestinians, for all their accusations against Israel, don't know it. They know it very well.

To be sure, the Palestinians can be made to pay a heavy price for their support of terror, but, as we've seen, it didn't take long after the Israeli-launched Operation Defensive Shield for the Palestinian terror infrastructure to regroup and launch more attacks.

I don't pretend to have the answers. Indeed, for years I have contended, whatever the government of the day in Jerusalem, that it is for Israel to decide how to respond most appropriately to the challenges both of war and peace.

Those of us on the outside—however close to the situation, however well-intentioned—need to exercise restraint and intellectual modesty. It would be sheer chutzpah to believe that we want peace for Israel more than Israel wants peace for itself, or that we have solutions to Israel's military challenges that Israel, which has managed to defend itself against all the odds since 1948, has not yet come up with. And do we still need reminders that, at the end of the day, it is Israel and its citizens—and not we in the Diaspora—who will bear the most direct consequences of decisions made?

Our job, I believe, is to help Israel achieve the time and space it needs to make its own decisions on these existential questions. That does not necessarily mean that Israel is incapable of making mistakes, or that its highly pressurized society doesn't come up with some pretty bad policy from time to time. Of course it does.

Israel is an imperfect society, but then so is every other democracy. But those other nations are not faced with the same immediate threats as Israel is today. Yes, the United States and India, in particular, currently understand the menace of terrorism, but surely few citizens in either country ever stop to wonder whether their national existence is imperiled.

Israel is fighting tooth and nail to defend its citizens, who have been declared fair game by a whole host of terrorist groups fueled by hatred and a sense that they have found the Israeli Achilles' heel through suicide bombings and remote-controlled explosions.

Israel desperately needs our support, now more than ever. We have our work cut out for us here in the United States, but we've also been given an extraordinary opportunity.

How will history judge us at this defining moment?

Do we have any excuse for passivity or indifference?

Are there those who will be able to claim, down the road, that they were unaware of what was actually going on?

Are some so focused on the trees—grievances about this or that Israeli policy or tactic—that they fail to see the forest, namely, the attempt to destroy all of Israel, to kill as many Jews as possible, and to propagate a vicious anti-Semitism unknown since the days of Hitler and Stalin?

Do some hold Israel to such an unrealistically high standard of behavior that Israel will never be able to meet it, if it is to survive and win this ugly war?

It's long overdue for everyone in the American Jewish community to wake up and, as they say, smell the coffee.

We need to stand up and be counted. Now. Not at some distant time down the road, but now. Events aren't going to wait for us. There is much to be done by us, and if we're not going to do it, who will?

What do we need to do?

More than anything, we need to find ongoing ways to express our collective solidarity with Israel and its people.

We need to engage fellow Jews who don't yet grasp the importance of the moment or may not have a full appreciation for the history that led to this point.

We need to make certain that all of our political leaders know exactly where we stand, and that we support candidates for elected office of both major political parties who share our views and are prepared to act on them.

We need to reach out to our non-Jewish friends, colleagues, and neighbors more than ever and help them understand what Israel is up against and why America must continue to stand foursquare with our democratic ally.

We need to make the point to the world that if Israel succumbs to the scourge of suicide bombing then every democratic nation becomes vulnerable to the very same threat.

We need to go out of our way to buy Israeli products and otherwise support the battered Israeli economy.

We need to continue traveling to Israel, in spite of the dangers or, yes, maybe because of the dangers. We cannot allow Israelis to feel alone and abandoned. Their struggle is our struggle. They must not be asked to shoulder it by themselves.

We need to be vigilant with the media, on university campuses, and in civic groups, where anti-Israel activists are seeking to make inroads.

We need to stress that Israel's yearning for peace is unquenchable and has been demonstrated again and again, but that peace with the Palestinians requires a willing and credible partner.

We need to ask our rabbis, who are soon to preside over High Holy Day services, when vast numbers of American Jews will be attending services, to use the occasion to mobilize the community.

And we need to support those Jewish organizations that are on the front lines in this battle. As individuals, our influence is usually quite limited, but as members of influential groups we leverage our power.

The Israeli people time and again have shown the world what they are made of. It's now time for us American Jews, asked to play a supporting role, to do the same. Given our track record of support for Israel over the past fifty-four years, I have no doubt that we can and will rise to the challenge.

TORAH, WAR, AND
THE "GENTLE HEART" TODAY

ISRAELI SOLDIERS' REFUSAL TO SERVE
IN THE OCCUPATION ARMY

Arthur Waskow

THE TORAH TEACHES: "The officials shall go on addressing the troops and say, 'Is there anyone afraid or gentle-hearted? Let him go back to his home, lest he melt the heart of his brothers, like his heart!'" (Deuteronomy 20:8).

More than 250 Israeli reserve soldiers and officers have publicly announced that they will serve in defense of Israel's boundaries but refuse to serve in the army of occupation in the West Bank and Gaza.[1] They have named themselves "Omets Lesarev/Courage to Refuse."

Adding also the previous group "Yesh Gvul" ("There is a border/ There is a limit") and the shiministim (students on the verge of conscription) who have also said they will defend Israel but refuse to serve in the occupation army, there are more than a thousand such Israelis.

Is there any connection between their decision and the passage of Torah in Deuteronomy?

First, it is noteworthy that the biblical tradition has a place for individual exemption from national military service (Deuteronomy 20:5–8):

> Then the officials shall address the troops: "Is there anyone who has built a new home but not yet dedicated it? Let him go back to his home, lest he die in battle and another dedicate it.

"Is there anyone who has planted a vineyard but has never harvested it? Let him go back to his home, lest he die in battle and another initiate it.

"Is there anyone who has paid the bride-price for a wife, but who has not yet married her? Let him return to his home, lest he die in battle and another marry her."

The officials shall go on addressing the troops and say, "Is there anyone afraid or gentle-hearted [*rakh halevav*; also 'disheartened,' or 'softhearted']? Let him go back to his home, lest he melt the heart of his brothers, like his heart!"

I Maccabees 3:56 reports that even in the moment of resistance to the Syrio-Hellenistic empire ruled by Antiochus, Judah Maccabee applied this passage of Torah and ordered back to their homes the newly married, the new homebuilders, etc., and those who were gentle-hearted.

Notice that this war was being fought against an imperial occupation of the Land of Israel, against an enemy that had desecrated the Temple and commanded idolatry.

About three centuries after the Maccabean wars, when the Rabbis took up the question of interpreting this Torah passage, some of them asked why the last verse specified both "afraid" and "gentle-hearted" as reasons to exempt a man from military service.

According to one interpretation, those who must be exempted from army service are not only those who are afraid to be killed but also those who are gentle of heart lest they become killers.

The Tosefta Sotah 7:22 quotes Rabbi Akiva as saying, "Why does the verse then say 'and the disheartened'? To teach that even to the mightiest and strongest of men if he is compassionate (*Rachaman*) he should turn back."[2]

Notice that the gentle-hearted MUST be exempted; if that is how they feel, there is no discretion, not the Army's and not theirs, to conscript them.

And notice that the Torah's concern is both for conscience and for practicality: if they stay in the Army, their example may bring other soldiers to become unwilling to kill or to die.

This provision operates also as a rough public check-and-balance to measure whether the people really believe a specific war is worth dying for and worth killing for.

If many soldiers begin to take the position that a specific war is not worth their dying or killing, the war may become impossible for the nation to fight.

If, on the other hand, most eligible fighters rally vigorously to the cause, the war can probably be fought.

In the Talmud,[3] the Rabbis limited the exemptions by distinguishing different types of wars—an "obligatory war" from a "voluntary war" (*milchemet chovah* versus *milchemet reshut*)—and said that the exemptions named by the Torah applied in the second case but not in the first.

But what is an obligatory war? Not so easy:

Raba said (Sotah 44b): "The wars waged by Joshua to conquer Canaan were obligatory in the opinion of all; the wars waged by the House of David for territorial expansion were voluntary in the opinion of all; where they differ is with regard to wars against heathens so that these should not march against them."

Note that there was a real difference of opinion about whether a preventive/defensive war was voluntary or obligatory.

So one could argue that only a war to establish a Jewish place in the Land of Israel, like Joshua's wars and the war of 1948, was obligatory; once that place for sustainable self-government was carved out, all other wars were (thought by some to be) voluntary. So in our own day, the occupation of the West Bank and Gaza could be argued to be an expansion of territory beyond what is necessary for a sustainably self-governing Jewish community, and therefore a voluntary war in which the exemptions would apply.

It is certainly not an open-and-shut case that the occupation is a *milchemet reshut*; but it seems a reasonable extrapolation.

The fact that the electorate and the Knesset may have authorized the present level of war to control the West Bank and Gaza does not settle the matter.

To declare a VOLUNTARY war, according to the Talmud, required the approval of a Sanhedrin of seventy-one. So even if the Sanhedrin (or an elected analogue today) voted for such an expansionist war, the exemptions would still apply.

In assessing the situation we face today, there is a second dimension to apply:

There are many aspects of our lives, and this is one, that are profoundly different from the context in which the Talmud evolved.

Indeed, the Maccabees, far more nearly than most later rabbinic communities, lived in the situation of a state or state-in-the-making in the Land of Israel that would have to decide whether and how to make war.

One would think that if ever there was a war the Rabbis might have defined as "obligatory," in which the Deuteronomic exemptions would have been suspended, it would have been the kind of war the Maccabees were fighting against Antiochus. Yet the Maccabees understood the Deuteronomy text to apply even in their extreme situation. They applied the Torah, and evidently because many of the people did support that war, they fought and won.

Of course the "Book of Maccabees" does not control the halakha, and was not even canonized by the Rabbis as sacred text. But it does make clear what Jews who lived in this situation thought and did. So today we might take their responses into account.

Another of the most important differences between our lives and those of the Rabbis is that today we are intertwined with an effort by the human race to develop an international law of war which includes the UN Charter, the Geneva Conventions, etc., and includes not only an Israeli state but a law of that state itself REQUIRING a soldier to disobey an unlawful order, including one unlawful under international law.

This does not end our questioning, but does enrich and complicate it a great deal. We might even, borrowing from but not necessarily standing inside the rabbinic mindset, think of this whole weave of international law as the effort of the Children of Noah to develop the *sheva mitzvot*—the seven commandments—by which, according to the rabbinic mind, the whole human race is bound.

So the Talmudic law of *milchemet chovah* and *reshut* may not for us exhaust the question.

Finally, what weight and value do we give the life-experience of our own generation(s)? Some of us would say that our lives continue to distill Torah, if we open our experience to God.

In that case for sure, and probably even if we would not go so far, it behooves us to listen to the direct reports of those involved.

The reservist refusers who have signed the recent statement do not think that the State of Israel is under occupation or in any danger of being occupied. Just the reverse. They do not believe that the occupation army is acting in a way that protects Israel. Just the reverse. Two reports:

Shuki Sadeh, a paratrooper reservist who was among the signers, told a newspaper how he had seen an Israeli soldier kill a young Palestinian boy at a distance of 150 meters. "What angered me at the time," Sadeh explained, "was that our soldiers said, 'Well, that's another Arab who has disappeared.'"

Ariel Shatil, an artillery master sergeant recently on duty in the Gaza Strip, recalled that while it's claimed that the Palestinians shoot first and Israelis just respond, in reality, "We would start shooting and they would fire back."

As an appendix to this essay, I am including the original statement of the Refusers and their first public leaflet for other soldiers.

So today some Israeli soldiers are, in a new situation, applying much the same basic sense of values that are marked out in Torah, attempting to distinguish defense from a war of conquest and occupation—and appealing to the individual "heart" as one of the crucial elements in making that decision.

At the level of reexamining, revitalizing, and renewing Torah, we might imagine bringing together some members of Omets Lesarev with rabbis of various streams of Jewish life and with ethicists who have addressed the questions of just war, nonviolence, and civil disobedience.

Courage to Refuse: Reserve Combatants Letter

• We, reserve combat officers and soldiers of the Israel Defense Forces, who were raised upon the principles of Zionism, sacrifice and giving to the people of Israel and to the State of Israel, who have always served in the front lines, and who were the first to carry out any mission, light or heavy, in order to protect the State of Israel and strengthen it.

• We, combat officers and soldiers who have served the State of Israel for long weeks every year, in spite of the dear cost to our personal lives, have been on reserve duty all over the Occupied Territories, and were issued commands and directives that had nothing to do with the security of our country, and that had the sole purpose of perpetuating our control over the Palestinian people.

• We, whose eyes have seen the bloody toll this Occupation exacts from both sides.

• We, who sensed how the commands issued to us in the Territories, destroy all the values we had absorbed while growing up in this country.

• We, who understand now that the price of Occupation is the loss of IDF's human character and the corruption of the entire Israeli society.

• We, who know that the Territories are not Israel, and that all settlements are bound to be evacuated in the end.

• We hereby declare that we shall not continue to fight this War of the Settlements.

• We shall not continue to fight beyond the 1967 borders in order to dominate, expel, starve and humiliate an entire people.

• We hereby declare that we shall continue serving in the Israel Defense Forces in any mission that serves Israel's defense.

The missions of occupation and oppression do not serve this purpose—and we shall take no part in them.

Excerpts from the Leaflet

SOLDIER:

We all want to defend our country. We're all sick and tired of terrorism. We all want peace. But do our actions permit of an end to the cycle of bloodshed?

Since 1967, Israel has ruled over 3.5 million Palestinians, running their lives by means of a forcible occupation, with continual violations of human rights.

Ask yourself whether your actions in the course of your military service enhance national security? Or do those actions merely fuel the enmity and the acts of violence between us and our Palestinian neighbors?

SOLDIER: THE OCCUPATION BREEDS TERRORISM!

When you take part in extrajudicial killings ("liquidation," in the army's terms), when you take part in demolishing residential homes, when you open fire at unarmed civilian population or residential homes, when you uproot orchards, when you interdict food supplies or medical treatment, you are taking part in actions defined in international conventions (such as the 4th Geneva Convention) and in Israeli law as war crimes.

Soldier, is there a people anywhere in the world that will not resist an occupation regime? If you were in the Palestinians' shoes, would you be willing to bow your head to a foreign ruler?

SOLDIER: THE OCCUPATION UNDERMINES OUR COUNTRY

The occupation and the violence that it prompts drag the economy down into recession. Investors are in flight, tourists stay away, entire sections of the economy are in collapse.

SOLDIER: IT'S IN YOUR HANDS!

NOTES

1. See [seruv.nethost.co.il/defaulteng.asp].
2. See Jacob Milgrom, ed., *The JPS Torah Commentary: Deuteronomy*, note 22 on p. 379, citing Tosefta 7:22. See also Midrash B'reshit Rabbah 76:2 and Rashi on Genesis 32:8, which use similar logic to understand Jacob's feeling both "fear" and "distress" at Esau's approach: fear lest he be killed, distress lest he kill. Thanks to Rabbi Everett Gendler, Rabbi Marc Gopin, and Devorah Shubowitz for helping guide me along this midrashic path.
3. See especially Sanhedrin 2a [the Mishna], 16a, and 20b, and Sotah 44a-b).

EUROPE'S UNIFIED VOICE AND PASSION

Andrei S. Markovits

RECENT EVENTS ACROSS EUROPE indicate a vigorous passion targeted against Israelis and what they represent. This passion hails from a confluence of many things, all immensely complex that, when merged together, form a very potent brew. Certainly that passion is driven by a massive reemergence of old-fashioned European anti-Semitism which— some silly optimists thought—had miraculously vanished from its thousand-year European existence after the Holocaust. Of course it never did. It merely lay dormant in the post-1945 world of the Cold War. But once this world had come to its definite end in 1989/1990/1991, the discourse on many things changed drastically, among them that on the Jews. The threshold of shame gradually subsided in the course of the 1990s, thus increasing attacks on Jewish institutions (such as cemeteries) and the ever more open way in which anti-Semitic insults became socially completely acceptable.

For example, Daniel Bernard, France's current ambassador to St. James's Court, publicly referred to Israel as "that shitty little country" that the world ought to abandon (to what, exactly, he left to his listeners' imaginations). As well, it has become part of accepted discourse in good society to deride Israel as an entity, not merely (and completely legitimately) its policies. A new tone has also entered all strata of German and European society, where criticizing Jews—not merely Israel and Israelis—has attained a certain urgency that reveals a particularly liberating dimension. "Free at

49

last, free at last, we are finally free of this damn Holocaust at last!" In this context Europeans—and not only Germans—posit that Jews, who created a culture of shame and kept Europeans from speaking their minds, behave just like they did. The lid is off; Jews are a target yet again.

By constantly bringing up the truly shameful and disgusting analogy of the Israelis with the Nazis, Europeans absolve themselves from any kind of remorse and shame and thus experience a sense of liberation. As well, one hurts the intended target by equating it with the very perpetrators that almost wiped it off the earth in the most brutal genocide imaginable. Lastly, Israel—partnered with the United States—also represents a certain modernity that European intellectuals of the left and right have always feared. For the right, Jews (thus Israel) and America have always stood for a soulless and disruptive modernity that was antithetical to any kind of an imagined tradition, so dear to the right's heart. And for the left, America and the Jews were the epitome of an unbridled capitalism that was bad everywhere but that exhibited its most stark characteristics in these two related entities.

Suffice it to say that America and the Jews have always been negatively and fearfully intertwined as particularly despised protagonists of modernity for both the European right and left throughout the twentieth century, if not before. Only thus can one explain the antiglobalization movement's massive support for the Palestinians. Why did Jose Bove show up in Ramallah and not in Gujarat, where many more Muslims were slain in multiple pogroms perpetrated by Hindus? Rather than explaining this as simple hostility toward Israel, it is a hostility aimed at globalization, which has become synonymous with the United States, and by extension Israel and Jews.

And this brings us to Europe's irritation with the United States that has less to do with policy differences than with values. When Europeans in the 1990s embarked on the arduous process of building the European Union, they began to raise the issue of having different, perhaps incompatible, values from those of the Americans. While it will long remain a question what values and identities Europeans themselves share, it is becoming clear that they have begun to embrace one negative value with considerable fervor: that of not being American.

This helps explain why many Europeans fast abandoned their post–September 11th sympathies for the United States and reverted to their default of seeing America as an uncouth bully. By viewing Israel as an extension of the United States, this mechanism of a negative identity reaches to the Middle East as well. It is not so much sympathy for the Palestinians but antipathy for the Israelis and the Jews that drives European opinion in this crisis—an antipathy that also draws much of its vigor from hostile feelings toward the United States.

CURRENT ISSUES

ORTHODOX, FEMINIST, AND PROUD OF IT

Blu Greenberg

AFTER THIRTY YEARS OF steadily pulsing its messages into the culture, feminism has reached deeply even into the most traditional religious communities. The radical transformation of divorce law in Egypt—making it easier for women to end a marriage—is but one example. Discussion among American Catholics about the ordination of women is another.

Orthodox Judaism, too, has been touched by this new social movement. Orthodox feminism, once considered an oxymoron, is a fact of life. Questions about women's roles and rights are raised daily on issues that were uncontested for centuries.

The consciousness of the entire modern Orthodox community has been raised, with rabbis readily acknowledging women's issues to be a primary concern in their congregations. Conferences on feminism and Orthodoxy in 1998 and 2000 turned out record numbers of participants, two thousand strong; many showed up unregistered, boarding planes the night before as if impelled by some mysterious force. The explosion in Jewish women's higher learning is unprecedented, with women studying Talmud as if by natural right. One would not guess that these texts were virtually closed to women for two thousand years.

New Orthodox synagogue architecture reflects the desire to create space in which women will not feel at the periphery, creating a women's section on par with the men's section. Orthodox women's prayer groups, though not universally welcomed, have grown in number and in size. Models of women's leadership—congregational interns (the female equivalent to assistant rabbis), presidents of synagogues, principals of Jewish day schools, advocates in the Jewish divorce courts, advisers in halakic (Jewish legal) matters—all are new to the Orthodox scene.

Yet, just as all these gains are being made, *feminism*—the very word itself—has increasingly become a red-flag word inside Orthodoxy. When feminism mattered not at all, it was not a subject for discussion. But suddenly, feminism is at the door—or halfway through the door—of modern Orthodoxy. And many inside have squared off.

Some examples: A mainstream Orthodox women's organization was invited to join as cosponsor of the 1998 Orthodox feminism conference, a role that same group had played the previous year. The organization's leadership said yes, but only on the condition that conference organizers drop *feminism* from the title. (They refused.) And this year, women from eleven countries met to form an international Orthodox feminist organization, but the issue of whether *feminism* should be part of the title went unresolved. Probably half the Orthodox women who would be described by any objective standard as feminist shy away from the word in defining themselves.

At some level, I understand this. During the first ten years of the women's movement, I often used the word *feminism* to criticize excesses; during the next ten, I'd begin statements with "I'm not a feminist but . . ."—though clearly I was speaking the movement's values.

Perhaps the expedient thing to do would be to drop this internally fractious word. Yet each time I consider the idea, I reject it, for many reasons.

To excise *feminism* from the lexicon of Orthodox Jews would constitute a colossal act of ingratitude. Like all women of these times, I have reaped the fruits of the labors of the founding mothers. They took a dedicated and lonely stand for many years, electing to make themselves vulnerable while others lashed out or clucked their tongues.

A second reason not to run scared is that the movement has undergone a great deal of fine-tuning. Men are no longer perceived as the enemy, nor is the family considered the locus of abuse for women. Indeed, feminism serves as a model of how all social movements need time to mature and rebalance.

But there is yet another reason to retain the word: precisely because it continues to rankle and irritate. Even in the midst of fundamental societal change, the temptation to pull back to the old ways is always there. *Feminism,* with its steady beat of cognitive dissonance, prevents that slide.

Carrying the term also offers an Orthodox feminist the opportunity to define what she is, namely, a woman who believes in the equal dignity of women within Orthodoxy; expanding the spiritual, intellectual, ritual, and communal opportunities for women to the fullest extent possible within halakah; the elimination of all injustice and suffering for Orthodox women arising out of hierarchical laws, such as Jewish divorce law (which puts power to end a marriage totally in the hands of the husband).

What is she not? A nullifier of women in family roles, as the stereotypical charge goes. Nor does she reject the chain of authority; rather, she stays within community, observes *halakah,* and attempts to resolve complaints by engaging those who hold the interpretive keys in their hands, the rabbis.

But as Orthodox feminism is also a movement in its infancy, so it must remain open-minded. As we seek to redefine the role of women in Orthodoxy, we do not yet know what will be preserved as distinctive-but-equal gender roles and what will be judged as hierarchical and unjust, and therefore discarded. Thus, the more dialogue, the more input, the more well-intentioned criticism, the sooner will we be able to sort out matters. All voices should be heard in this process of discovery, even oppositional ones, and they should be heard in the presence of each other, rather than in whispered campaigns and innuendo.

Despite the fact that some believe feminism will destroy or water down Judaism, Orthodox feminism should be understood as a service to the community, a building up of faithfulness and commitment. Women are asking to enter the tradition more fully, not to walk away from it. Thus, feminists should see themselves not as supplicants at the door, but as bearers of a great tradition, refreshing that tradition with women's new spiritual energy and revitalizing it with the ethical challenge of equality for women, thus bringing us one step closer to perfection of the world.

STEM CELL RESEARCH

WHAT DOES HALACHAH SAY?

Yoel Jakobovits

WITH ONE SPECTACULAR DEVELOPMENT tumbling over the next in ever more rapid succession, our generation is witnessing the compression of history in the scientific and medical realm just as much as in the geopolitical realm. Indeed, it may well be that in the long term, the direction of humanity and its history ultimately will be affected more profoundly by these scientific and medical developments than even by the current unprecedented global political upheavals.

New Technology—New Issues

Medical ethics concentrates largely on the opposite ends of life. For example, at the beginning of life, questions relate principally to abortion, contraception, and conception issues even before birth. At the other end of life, inquiries relate to the management of dying, the moment of death, autopsies, and organ harvesting even after death. The intervening years prompt relatively few medical ethics problems.

Over the past several decades, "end of life" issues have been the focus of much attention, largely due to the new life-prolonging technologies. Some of the issues raised relate to advanced life supports, defining the moment of death and the allocation of expensive, scarce resources to prolong life. In contrast with the great advances in life-prolonging technologies, perhaps the most exciting recent medical developments have been related to life-creating techniques at the other end of life. These developments include the mapping of the Human Genome Project, ever more sophisticated in vitro fertilization techniques, stem cell development, and cloning technology.

In addition to the "old" technical questions concerning abortion and contraception, the new technology has spawned a whole new range of ethical issues concerning the beginning of life. The stage for these developments was set already half a century ago by the pioneering work of Watson, Crick, and others who discovered and described the fundamental elements governing the structure and function of DNA. Over the ensuing decades, there has been an ever-accelerating application of these basic scientific advances, culminating in successful mammalian cloning and effective stem cell therapy.

In writing this article, limited to an analysis of stem cell issues, I have set myself two chief objectives: to outline the essential medical facts pertaining to stem cell research and therapy and to summarize the principal halachic approaches which have been proposed thus far. Clearly, given the novelty of these innovations, both the medical and scientific questions as well as halachic answers are in flux and must be tentative at this point in time.

What Are Stem Cells?

Every discussion of medical ethics must be governed by the axiom: good ethics—and good halachah—require good facts.

All the various parts of a plant or tree—the trunk, branches, leaves, and fruits—develop from the stem. Similarly, all the cells of a living organism develop from "precursor" cells known as stem cells.

Mammalian development begins with the union of a male's sperm cell with a female's egg. The resultant cell has the inherent potential to develop into the entire gamut of cells forming the organism. This prime cell divides, within several hours of fertilization, into two identical duplicate cells, each of which retains this broad potential. After several more divisions, by about the fourth day, these cells begin to specialize, forming a hollow sphere called a blastocyte, which is composed of an outer and inner layer of cells. Cells of the outer layer are destined to form the placenta and other supporting tissues of pregnancy. The inner layer cells go on to develop into all of the organs and tissues of the developing fetus. These cells are now somewhat more limited in their potential—they can give rise to many but not all the types of cells necessary for fetal development. As stem cells "mature," their potential to develop into any kind of human tissue decreases. Soon after, these stem cells undergo further specialization (called differentiation), becoming cells committed to developing into a given line of cells.

Ultimately, stem cells develop into "master cells," designed to multiply into specific tissue types. For example, blood cell stem cells will develop into the various types of blood cells; skin stem cells into the various types of skin cells. Once they reach this level of specialization, they are committed to developing specific tissues.

The cells related to developing the blood are the best-understood stem cells. They reside in the bone marrow of all children and adults, and are, in fact, usually present in very small numbers in the circulating blood stream as well. Because red and white cells in the peripheral blood have limited life spans, these stem cells are crucial to maintaining an adequate blood supply in the healthy person.

Parenthetically, a few words about the techniques involved in bone marrow transplantation are in order. Bone marrow is not a solid organ; it is transplanted by transfusion from the donor to the recipient. Bone marrow cells are almost all stem cells, committed to producing mature blood cells. The donor is treated to prompt his marrow to become overactive, spilling large numbers of cells into the circulating blood stream. From here, these cells can be readily harvested by phlebotomy (opening a vein). The collected bone marrow stem cells can then be transfused through a vein into the recipient. Patients with leukemia, for example, are treated with powerful medications which completely eradicate their diseased bone marrow. Healthy stem cells, which have been previously harvested from a matching healthy person's circulation, can be administered by transfusion to replenish the now barren bone marrow of these patients. This procedure is the essence of bone marrow transplantation.

A fairly widely used variation of this process can also be applied to patients with a variety of cancers. Treatment with sufficiently high doses of chemotherapy, designed to destroy all traces of their cancer, often leads to the incidental eradication of their bone marrow. In these circumstances, bone marrow stem cell transplants can be offered to rescue the patient by replenishing the destroyed bone marrow.

Cells early in the chain of developmental events are less clearly committed to any specific tissue line. Therefore in trying to induce cells to develop new and controlled tissue lines, these early "omnipotent" cells are the most desirable. Once cells differentiate into specific cell lines, they can generally be expected to develop only into cells of that family. Getting cells to climb back up the chain of development, and thereby regain the ability to develop into other cell types forms the basis of cloning technology.

The technological and ethical issues involved in cloning, however, are beyond the scope of our current discussion.

Where Are Stem Cells?

At present there are several sources of stem cells:

- Early human embryos. In general these embryos are developed as a result of couples using in vitro fertilization to conceive a child. The union of sperm and eggs in a petri dish produces many embryos. Implanting them all into the mother's uterus would present a grave danger to her because of the multiple fetuses she would have to carry. Therefore only a few are implanted; the remaining are leftover or spare. These pre-implanted embryos are a widely used source of stem cells.
- Tissue obtained from aborted fetuses.
- Cells obtained from the umbilical cord.
- Using "somatic cell nuclear transfer" (SCNT), an adult cell's gene-containing nucleus can be combined with an egg from which the nucleus has been removed. Using special techniques, the resultant cell can be induced to divide and develop as an early stem cell to form a blastocyte from which very potent cells can be obtained. This is the basis of cloning.

Stem Cell Research and Implications for the Future

Why isolate and develop pluripotent stem cells, that is, stem cells that have the ability to become any human tissue? At the most fundamental level, stem cell research will help enormously in understanding the complex events of early mammalian development. Secondly, such research could dramatically change the way in which drugs are developed and tested. Specific healthy and diseased cell lines could be exposed to specific drugs, largely obviating the need for much more dangerous and expensive human testing.

The most far-reaching applications would come in the area of "cell therapies." Thousands of people are on waiting lists for organ transplants. Because the supply of donors is much smaller than the number of waiting patients, many patients will die of their illnesses before suitable donors can be found. Incidentally, a major cause of limited donor supply is the strict application of seat belt laws! Ultimately it is hoped that stem cells could be stimulated to develop into a source of replacement cells to create banks of transplantable human tissue. There is already reason to believe that this will be possible in replenishing the diseased or absent brain cells caused by Parkinson's and Alzheimer's diseases, strokes, spinal cord injuries, various heart diseases, diabetes, and arthritis.

Halachic Considerations

We begin the outline of the halachic approach to stem cell research by stressing some general overarching principles. In contrast with other religions, Judaism has no problem with "playing God," provided we do so according to His rules as expressed by authentic halachic mandate. Far from being shunned, "playing God" in the Jewish tradition is, in fact, a religious imperative: "*Mah Hu af atah,*" the concept of *imitatio Dei* is implicit in the mandate to heal and provide effective medical relief wherever possible. Of note, the only two "professions" ascribed to God Himself are those of teaching (". . . *hamelamed Torah l'amo Yisrael*") and healing (". . . *ki ani Hashem rofecha*"). By teaching and/or healing, we fulfill the obligation to "play God."

There is no reason that microscopic manipulation of a faulty genetic blueprint should be any different than surgical manipulation of a defective macroscopic—that is, visible to the unaided eye—tissue or organ. Normative halachah sanctions—nay, encourages—medical intervention to correct both congenital and acquired defects and makes no distinction between stem and somatic (body) cell tissues. The crucial distinction here is between the permissible act of correcting a defect (sanctioned by "*verapo yerapeh*") and the forbidden act of attempting to improve on God's creations (generally proscribed by the laws of *kilayim,* cross-breeding). For example, it would be permitted, were it possible, to correct the genetic defect which leads to Down's syndrome, but manipulating genes to produce a "perfect-bodied" six-footer with blue eyes would be prohibited.

There would, therefore, be no halachic problem with using stem cells derived from adult tissue. Similarly, it would appear that using cells from umbilical cord tissue would be permissible. A rather minor concern here might be the following: may one have umbilical tissue collected and frozen so that the cells will be available in case one requires stem cell therapy some time in the future? Is this degree of *hishtadlut,* effort, in trying to insure one's health appropriate or excessive?

While there are few halachic objections to deriving stem cells from adult or umbilical cord tissue, the problems arise, however, with deriving stem cells from embryonic tissue. Post-implantation embryonic tissue (that is, an embryo already implanted into the uterine wall) is after all, an early fetus; clearly no sanction would be given to aborting a fetus in order to obtain stem cell tissue. Even were fetal tissue necessary to provide life-sustaining therapy for a patient, no sanction would be given to sacrifice an innocent fetus even in the interest of *pikuach nefesh* (saving a life). The only exception to this rule is the obligation to forfeit the life of the "non-innocent" fetus when its continued existence constitutes a danger to its mother by virtue of the fetus's *rodef* "pursuer" status.

Even fetal life before the fortieth day of gestation—which is considered *"maya b'alma"* ("mere water")—could not be aborted in order to obtain stem cell tissue. Prior to forty days, a miscarried fetus does not cause *tumat leidah* (Niddah 30a) and therefore is of lesser status than a more mature fetus (Rabbi Y. Y. Weinberg in Seridei Aish, III: 350, 7; however cf. Seridei Aish: III: 127). Though Chavot Yair argues that even pre-fortieth-day feticide is prohibited because of the restriction of seminal seed, Rav Yaakov Emden (in She'eilot Ya'avetz 43) counters that *zera levatalah* cannot apply once implantation occurs. Rabbi I. Unterman (Shevet Miyehudah I:9) also holds that destruction of even the earliest embryo is feticide because the Shabbat may be violated for its welfare (based on Ramban's *Torat Ha-Adam* citing Yoma 85b). On the other hand, Rabbi Chaim Ozer Grodzinski (Achiezer III, 65:14), and others, argue for a less stringent status in embryos before forty days of gestation.

The prime source of embryonic stem cell tissue is embryos that have not been implanted into the uterine wall. As discussed above, they are usually the "by-products," spare embryos left aside during in vitro fertilization in order not to dangerously overload the mother's uterus. The halachic status of these "spare," non-implanted embryos is somewhat unclear.

Some rabbinical options suggest that in addition to the forty-day milestone, an embryo doesn't reach fetal status until it is implanted into the uterus. Prior to that, while still in a petri dish, or other artificial medium, it cannot develop into a viable fetus. Therefore, such early embryos have no real life potential at all and are not considered alive. Consequently, there would be no halachic opposition to disposing of them, researching on them or deriving stem cell tissue from them.

The status of pre-implantation embryos has another potentially important halachic consequence. Pre-implantation genetic diagnosis (PGD) offers a promising approach to prevent the birth of genetically defective children. By studying embryos before implantation into the uterus, it is possible to identify those defective genes. By selecting only genetically intact embryos for implantation, the development of genetically defective fetuses would be avoided. Assuming the pre-implanted embryo has not reached the level of a fetus, halachic sanction may be possible.

The ethical issues raised by stem cell research and therapy are, of course, not only of interest to Jews. In an unprecedented national broadcast, shortly before and largely overshadowed by the events of September 11, President Bush defined some fairly restrictive regulations. Just recently the Administration argued strongly in favor of banning all research into human cloning. Evidently the crossroads of medical science and the generation of life itself raises fears and genuine concern in the minds of many thinking people.

It appears that halachah may be more permissive than is generally understood. Clearly, it behooves us, as Jews, to avail ourselves of whatever Torah and scientific knowledge we can—not only as we try to find halachic guidance for ourselves, but, perhaps equally importantly—as we strive to fulfill our national mandate to be an *"ohr lagoyim"*—to help shed light on these vexing issues for society at large.

JESUS WHO?

Amy-Jill Levine

THAT MANY CHRISTIANS have misperceptions about Judaism, views ranging from the slightly humorous (all Jews are smart, all Jews can read Hebrew) to the blatantly obscene (Jews are children of the devil; Jews seek world domination) is common knowledge to us Jews. We would like our Christian neighbors to appreciate Judaism as a tradition of spiritual depth, profound practice, rich culture, and moral emphasis, and we would also like them to know that we Jews do not have horns, do not worship a God of wrath and law as opposed to a God of love and compassion, and do not spend much time worrying about the state of our immortal soul.

But ignorance cuts both ways. It's time for us to learn more about Christianity: not just its history of anti-Semitism, but also its theological depth and system of morality.

Most Jews know little about Christianity, and what we know— impressions often gleaned from benign mall decorations of elves and bunnies to the spoutings of narrow-minded ministers convinced that they have a lock on heaven's doors—is likewise often mistaken. Our errors range also from the harmless (thinking that "Christ" is a last name) to the horrifying (thinking that all Christians are anti-Semites).

Even today, many of us would never set foot in a church, refuse to read the New Testament, even ban copies of *Bible Review* from our homes because an article in it deals with Christian Scriptures as well as the Hebrew Bible.

Yet, in fact, since the birth of the Christian church, we have been asking questions about this moment. Today, with the rise in Christian missionary efforts to convert Jews, on the one hand, and with the current congeniality of interfaith dialogue on the other, it's time to revisit these questions.

Learning more about Christianity helps us in at least two ways. Not only does this type of inquiry tell us how anti-Jewish attitudes developed within the church,[1] but also, informed historical discussion enables us both to appreciate the traditions of our Christian neighbors and to enhance our appreciation for the choices Judaism made.

As a professor of the New Testament at a predominantly Christian divinity school, I do get a lot of questions from Jews interested in what their Christian neighbors are thinking. Here are some of the issues I am most frequently confronted with:

- Jesus was a Jewish man who after his death was proclaimed to be divine. The whole megillah—virgin birth, walking on water, resurrection from the dead, ascending to heaven—is nonsense that no intelligent person could possibly believe.

- Christianity is primarily a pagan religion: although they have the "Old Testament," they dumped all the laws; instead of recognizing that God is "One" (as expressed, for example, in the statement "Hear O Israel, the Lord is our God, the Lord is One"), they worship three gods, a Father, a Son, and a Holy Spirit (who used to be called the "Holy Ghost"), and some worship the Virgin Mary. They are also idolators because they worship statues and paintings.

- Christians believe they eat the real body and the real blood of Jesus when they "take communion" and are thus engaged in some sort of cannibalism.

- Christians are necessarily anti-Jewish, think all Jews are going to hell, and therefore the proclamations of the church lead directly to the ovens of Auschwitz.

Each of these positions, however, is based on partial evidence only, and that evidence has been sifted through centuries of Christian persecution of Jews.

What do Christians really believe?

The response begins with a word of warning. We can no more claim that "all Christians believe" something than we can claim that all Jews hold to a particular view. There are numerous groups within what is broadly called the "church": Roman Catholic, Anglican, Eastern Orthodox, and Protestant; some churches are organized according to a particular system of leadership (popes or patriarchs, bishops, deacons, elders, etc.); some are independent. Some ordain women, and some do not; some approve of birth control and abortion, and some do not; some think that all Jews are going to hell, and some do not.

And not all church members agree with the official teachings of their church: some Roman Catholics favor birth control, but the church's official line condemns it; some Presbyterians and United Methodists favor the ordination of gays and lesbians, but the official teaching of their denominations still forbids this. A few years ago, the head of the Southern Baptist Convention proclaimed that "God does not hear the prayers of the Jews"; numerous Baptists disagreed. In other words, Christianity in terms of its diversity looks very much like Judaism. Thus, any comments that might be made about "what Christians think" are true only in a general sense.

Is the whole system nonsense? No, it actually makes a great deal of sense when seen in its historical context. The Christian proclamation was both developed and accepted by a number of Jews, so it must have made sense to them, and it clearly made sense to the greater number of pagans who joined the church. The reason many of the claims of the church appear so alien to Jews today is the passing of time; to understand how the church could begin within Judaism, we need to go back several generations before Jesus.

The Judaism that developed in the late fourth century B.C.E. in the wake of Alexander the Great incorporated Greek cultural views, just as Jews have always been influenced by the countries in which we live. Thus, we find in the centuries leading up to the Maccabean revolt in the second century B.C.E. an increasing penetration of Greek thought within Jewish communities. This synthesis of earlier Jewish tradition and new ideas is called "Hellenism," and it is in the crucible of Hellenism, supported by the Roman Empire that gained control over Israel in 63 B.C.E., that Christianity was conceived.

We can see the influence of Hellenism in the Septuagint, the Greek translation of the Hebrew Bible. For example, the Greek translation of Isaiah 7:14 mentions that a "virgin" would conceive a child who would be called "Immanuel" (the Hebrew means "God with us"). This verse is cited in the New Testament's Gospel according to Matthew as being fulfilled by the birth of Jesus. Otherwise put, some of the attributes accorded Jesus by his earliest followers make sense when seen in a Jewish, Greek-speaking context. Actually, the underlying Hebrew is not "virgin," but "young woman."

By the early first century C.E., more than just Greek language had fully impacted Jewish life and thought in Israel and the Western Diaspora. Retelling their traditional stories in Hellenistic and Roman terms, many Jews began to think of their ancient heroes such as Moses and Abraham, as well as less-well-known figures such as Enoch and Melchizedek, as divine men. Moses and Melchizedek were attributed miraculous births; Abraham became known, along with prophets Elisha and Elijah, as a miracle worker; Enoch, transported into heaven, took on the role of future judge of the world. The Jewish philosopher Philo of Alexandria spoke of the manifestation of God on earth; he called this the "Logos" (Greek for "word"), which is the same term some early Christians applied to Jesus (as in the opening words of the Gospel of John, "In the beginning was the word").

At the same time, Jewish wonder workers began to appear: Honi the Circle-drawer, who could make it rain; Haninah ben Dosa, whose prayers could cure the sick. Accompanying this intensification of the miraculous and marvelous was an increasing attention to the afterlife. The Pharisees promulgated the idea that during the Messianic Age the dead would be raised; hundreds of Jews went into the Judean desert by the caves of Qumran to await the final battle between the "sons of light" and the "sons of darkness" (as we know from the Dead Sea Scrolls); a Jewish prophet named John (the Baptist) began to immerse fellow Jews in the Jordan River as testimony to their having repented of their sins and in preparation for the coming Messianic Age (from the Greek term for immerse comes the term "baptize").

This period in Judaism not only witnessed speculation about the Messianic Age or the "world to come"—the time when the prophetic vision of universal peace would arrive—it also saw the rise of several claimants to be the inaugurator of that age. One first-century C.E. candidate, named Theudas, announced that a new era had arrived (Rome executed him); another, called "the Egyptian," proclaimed that the walls of Jerusalem would fall (although he escaped, Rome killed many of his followers). In the early second century C.E., Rabbi Akiba proclaimed the Jewish military leader, Bar Kochba, the Messiah (Rome killed them both). That Jews in Israel might follow a visionary and a healer who spoke of the Kingdom of God should not be unexpected; nor should that visionary's execution by the Roman Empire.

It is also not surprising—it is in fact quite "Jewish"—that those who followed Jesus saw him as a wonder worker, recognized that his birth signaled something special, and even believed that after his death he was raised from the dead. If he was the Messiah, surely he would be raised. Jewish messianic belief at the time, and even now, incorporated the idea that the Messianic Age is marked by the resurrection of the dead. Although it has been argued that the disciples stole Jesus' body and invented the resurrection (the Gospel of Matthew states that "this story has been spread among the Jews to this day"), the followers of Jesus were neither hypocrites nor charlatans. That someone would experience such a vision in these times is hardly surprising, especially in cases of extreme stress.

These visionaries lived then with a missionary zeal and commitment to their tradition, a tradition that happened to be Judaism. This is why many of Jesus' first followers believed that shortly after the crucifixion and his resurrection, there would be a general resurrection of the dead. When this did not happen, a number of these Jews probably returned to wait for the Messiah. For the most part, among Jews, the mission in the name of the crucified and resurrected man from Nazareth was a flop. The majority of Jews at that time and subsequently did not find a need for Jesus in their lives: he filled no gap in their souls; he was not needed to take away their sons; he did not bring about the Messianic Age; they believed in resurrection already. Yet among gentiles the movement took hold: It offered the antiquity (in antiquity, "old" was "good"), morality, and community of Judaism, and it also offered what Jews already had: a covenantal relationship with heaven that would lead to eternal life.

Was that direction toward the gentile world one of pagan polytheism and idolatry? Christians, of course, would say "no," as would most historians of the early church. Granted, it is not incorrect to think of Christianity as having adopted numerous pagan practices, from setting the date for the birth of Jesus—December 25, the day dedicated to the ancient sun god—to the adoption of yule logs, Christmas trees, and Easter bunnies. But adaptation of cultural practices is an important way that religions develop; we might think of Jewish non-scriptural traditions, from jelly donuts and latkes at Hanukkah, to Hamantashen at Purim, to whatever the latest bar mitzvah fad is. Showing a shared good taste, Jews and Christians both have eggs for our spring festivals (respectively, Passover and Easter).

In terms of its relationship to Jewish practice, the earliest Christian movement had at first only one sacred Scripture, the Bible of the synagogue (*Torah, Nevi'im, Ketuvim,* or Torah, Prophets, and Writings). However, rather than insisting that all gentiles who joined the new movement convert to Judaism, the church after some debate concluded that this was unnecessary. Gentiles were not to be obligated to perform any distinctly Jewish practice. Thus, gentile Christians were not bound by circumçision, kashrut, etc. That decision itself, however, was quite kosher: resident aliens in Israel were not bound by these laws; the few scriptural statements about the "world to come" do not indicate that gentiles must convert to

Judaism. Further, during the Hellenistic period, Judaism developed the idea of the Noahide Laws—seven laws given to Noah and hence binding all humanity, not just Jews. Gentiles who followed these laws (prohibitions of murder, sexual sins, theft, idolatry, blasphemy, eating the limb from a living animal; the establishment of courts of justice) were considered "righteous" (as today we have the category of the "righteous gentile") and accordingly were worthy of eternal life. Thus, gentiles in the church were required to conform to basic moral precepts only.

As for polytheism, the earliest Christian texts, which were written by Jews (such as Saul of Tarsus, a Pharisee who came to be known as St. Paul), do not encourage one to pray "to" Jesus. Rather, one prayed "through" him to God (the Father). This is also the role of the Saints and the Virgin Mary in some church teachings (most notably, the Roman Catholic Church). These figures are not "divine," but are viewed as having special intercessory powers. The idea that the righteous have a special pipeline to God is not unknown in Judaism. Not only is it anticipated in Second Maccabees, a similar system can be seen in Israel today, where the pious pray at the tombs of Jewish "saints." Jesus himself, in the so-called "Lord's Prayer," speaks only of prayer to "our father, who is in heaven" (throughout my grade school years in the Massachusetts public school system, children recited the "Lord's Prayer" every morning. I had no idea this was a "Christian" prayer; there's nothing in it a Jew could not say).

As for the "Holy Spirit," this is the Jewish *ruach,* spirit—or "wind" or "breath" to give a literal translation to this Hebrew word—used in Genesis when God hovered over the face of the deep, according to Bereshit (Genesis 1). The idea of the Spirit coupled with the concept of Wisdom, as found in books such as Proverbs, coalesced into the Christian Holy Spirit (the Greek term for "spirit," *pneuma,* can also mean "wind" or "breath"; hence, pneumonia). Later on, when this Jewish movement intersected with Greek philosophical thought and as its adherents attempted to explain how God the Father, Jesus the Son, and the Holy Spirit were related, the doctrine of the "Trinity" developed.

Finally, Christians are not idolators. Statues and icons are like prayer tools: They are the means to the end, which is the worship of God. We may compare this to the kissing of a Torah scroll during a Jewish worship service; the scroll is not divine, but it is honored, and even "dressed" in such a way that an outsider might see it as an idol.

Speaking of errors outsiders sometimes make, consider the matter of what Christians call either the "Eucharist" (Greek for "thanksgiving") or "communion" or "the Lord's Supper." Ask Christians if they believe they are eating the body and blood of Jesus when they take communion. Ironically, just as Christians from the Middle Ages until the early twentieth century accused Jews of using the blood of Christian children to bake matzah (a charge made by the notorious Nazi anti-Semite Julius Streicher and recently promulgated by some within the Islamic world), so in the early years of the church, Christians were accused by pagans of using blood in their worship services. Christians did not use blood, but they did use the language of blood.

While the idea of consuming blood is considered anathema in Judaism—it is forbidden throughout Jewish tradition—that Jesus might have spoken about bread and wine served at his last supper as being his body and blood is not completely odd, when seen in historical context. In the first century, animal sacrifice was a major part of religious culture. Both Jews and gentiles believed in the power of blood to cleanse sin, to honor or appease heaven. Thus, in what is clearly a hyperbolic, extreme statement, Jesus, knowing he was to die, may well have spoken of his body in sacrificial terms.

During the Middle Ages, Christian Europeans told stories of Jews stealing the sacred bread (called the "host") and sticking pins into it—at which point the bread would bleed real blood. Concurrently, when government-sponsored disputations between Christians and Jews were popular (disputations in which the Jew was inevitably going to lose; when Jews appeared to have gained the audience's sympathy, cartloads of Talmuds were burned), the notion that the "real presence" of Jesus was in the bread and wine eaten during the Christian worship service was a target of Jewish polemic. As one rabbi put it: if Jesus descended to earth to inhabit the bread each time it was consecrated and served, heaven would be full of holes, like cheese.

Since the so-called Protestant Reformation, started by Martin Luther in the sixteenth century, churches have disagreed on the question of the real presence in the Eucharist. This is where the concepts of "transubstantiation" and "consubstantiation" come in. The former, which is associated primarily with the Roman Catholic Church, is the belief that indeed the bread and wine used in the Eucharist are actually converted into the body and blood of Christ. The latter belief, developed by Luther in opposition to Roman Catholic teaching, states that the wine and bread are not actually transformed, but exist together in union with the body and blood.

Although the theology underlying this practice is alien to Judaism, the origin of this meal is not. The meal in memory of Jesus' death originally was a full meal, not just a piece of bread and a sip of wine (or in some of the newer traditions, grape juice). It finds its origins both in the seder meal celebrated at Passover and in fellowship meals celebrated by first-century Jews.

Finally, is Christianity necessarily anti-Jewish and, if so, does it lead inexorably to Auschwitz? No, and no. That the New Testament has anti-Jewish material I do not doubt, but it is equally true that not all Christians read the material as anti-Jewish. Similarly, I do not read the Exodus story as casting a negative shadow on Egyptians today. To limit "Christianity" to the New Testament is no more appropriate than to limit Judaism to our earliest texts.

What about the relationship of Christianity to Germany's Nazi beliefs? In September of 2000, about 170 rabbis and Jewish academics signed a statement called "Dabru Emet" ("Speak Truth"), subtitled, "A Jewish Statement on Christians and Christianity." Among the eight assertions the signatories supported was that Nazism was not a Christian phenomenon. This plank continues to be the subject of often-heated discussion. It is certainly true that the various Christian movements and *machers* have more than had their anti-Jewish moments, as a flip through the recent best-seller *Constantine's Sword* powerfully demonstrates. And newspaper stories on the recently disclosed Nixon tapes have revealed that even Billy Graham believed Jews controlled the U.S. media and were a danger to U.S. society. But for much of history these anti-Jewish voices simply sought to convert Jews.

Not so for the Nazis. The baptized nun was just as "Jewish" and therefore just as expendable, as the Hasidic rebbe. The Nazi focus was not Judaism as a belief or practice, it was Jews as a race. Did the various anti-Jewish attitudes inculcated through centuries of Christian preaching, art, and teaching facilitate National Socialism's program? Of course. But was the church a cause of National Socialism? That is a much more difficult claim to make. Indeed, if one were to make this claim, then the numerous righteous gentiles—Protestant, Catholic, and Orthodox—who because of their religious beliefs sheltered Jews at the risk of their own lives, become inexplicable.

It is this brave and benevolent response that anticipates the vast improvements the past half-century has witnessed in Jewish-Christian relations. On the academic front, Christian scholarship for the most part no longer sees the synagogue as a foil for the church or regards Judaism as a depressing and repressing religion marked by numerous unbearable restrictions. Christian scholars and teachers now emphasize that Jesus cannot be understood apart from Judaism. If you want to understand Jesus, you must understand the Jewish world in which he lived. Christians in numerous churches—Roman Catholic, United Methodist, Presbyterian,

Episcopalian, Lutheran, and others—have made formal statements praising the depth of Jewish traditions, theology, and commitment to social justice. In Sunday schools and adult education programs, people in these groups and others are continuing to learn about and therefore appreciate Judaism. It is time for the synagogue to reciprocate.

In church and synagogue, our forms of worship, sacred Scripture, understanding of the divine, and views of salvation differ, but we do have shared moral principles. When asked by a potential follower, "Teach me the Torah while standing on one foot," Hillel responded: "What is hateful to you, do not do to your fellow. All the rest is commentary, go and learn." When instructing his disciples, Jesus announces: "Whatever you wish that people would do to you, do so to them, for this is the Law and the Prophets." The point is not to debate which is the "better" formula: the "don't" of Hillel or the "do" of Jesus; both teachings import the same guideline, that we treat our neighbors as ourselves.

Both traditions similarly promote both orthodoxy (literally, "right belief") and orthopraxy ("right action"), even as both debate internally what those positions should be. Although Christianity will typically emphasize that action comes from belief (as Martin Luther put it, "Good works don't make a good man, but a good man bears good fruit"), the Epistle of James—a text, by the way, that Luther did not like—insists that "faith without works is dead." And although Judaism will typically emphasize action, halachah, that action is premised on the covenant between God and Israel. A first-century Jew was asked, "Which commandment in the Law is the greatest?" He responded "You shall love the Lord your God with all your heart, and with all your soul, and with all your strength . . . And you shall love your neighbor as yourself." The citations are from Deuteronomy 6:5 and Leviticus 19:18; they are quoted here from the Gospel of Matthew.

NOTE

1. See Ben Birnbaum's "A Legacy of Blood—Can Christianity Be Purged of Anti-Semitism Without Changing the Gospels?" in the October 2001 issue of *Moment*.

JUDAISM AND THE ULTIMATE PUNISHMENT

Daniel Polish

DOES JUDAISM CONDONE capital punishment?

Supporters of the death penalty often cite the Bible to bolster their position. "Ye shall take no ransom for the life of a murderer . . . he shall surely be put to death" (Numbers 35:31). Indeed, the Torah specifies a full litany of offenses for which a person may be put to death, including murder, idolatry, blasphemy, adultery, violating the Sabbath, wizardry, and rebelling against one's parents. The punishments for each transgression are noted as well—stoning, burning, and slaying by the sword.

But the recording of these laws in Scripture may give a false impression about the actual practice of capital punishment in ancient Israel. While the Torah supports the death penalty in principle, it places formidable obstacles to its implementation. HUC-JIR Bible Professor Dr. David Sperling has observed that the well-known *lex talionus* (law of retaliation) "Thou shalt give life for life, eye for eye, tooth for tooth, hand for hand, foot for foot, burning for burning, wound for wound, stripe for stripe" (Exodus 21:23–25) may appear to endorse capital punishment, but it is actually a formula for *restricting* the punishment to be meted out. "In contrast to the Code of Hammurabi [an earlier legal code well known in the ancient Near East]," Professor Sperling writes, "biblical law limits the death penalty to the murderer—a family member cannot be executed in his/her place" (Exodus 21). Moreover, the defendant may not be put to death unless two (or in some cases three) eyewitnesses testify against him or her. Each witness must be so certain of his testimony that he personally would be willing to carry out the execution. Deuteronomy 19:31–21 asserts that a false witness is subject to the same punishment as the defendant—including, presumably, death.

The Torah also distinguishes between a premeditated murder and unintentional killing. In the case of an unintentional slaying, the killer is permitted to take refuge in one of six cities on the other side of the Jordan River (Numbers 35:9–15, Deuteronomy 4:41–43, Joshua 20). The pattern of not inflicting the ultimate punishment is established early in the Bible. After Cain kills his brother Abel in a fit of rage, God does not demand Cain's life in retribution; instead, Cain is set free to wander the earth. The mark God places on Cain's forehead is not a sign of punishment, as is commonly assumed, but one of protection; it served as a kind of mobile "city of refuge," warding off anyone seeking to avenge the wrong Cain had committed.

Interpretations in the Rabbinic Age

The rabbis who compiled the Talmud in the first centuries of the Common Era interpreted and expanded upon the biblical laws governing capital punishment. They too stipulated transgressions deserving of death, among them idolatry, bestiality, blasphemy, illicit sex, violating the Sabbath, witchcraft, and adultery in certain circumstances. Then, in meticulous detail, they linked each crime with its corresponding method of execution (stoning, burning, strangulation, or slaying by the sword).

Grisly punishments all—but it is highly doubtful that the rabbis ever actually imposed the death penalty. After a long, elaborate discussion of the class of capital crime befitting the stubborn and rebellious son and a description of how the execution was to be carried out, the Talmud states: "It never happened and it never will happen." The passage then explains that the entire matter is presented purely for study: "That you may study [the Torah for its own sake] and receive reward" (Sanhedrin 71a). In other words, the discussion of capital punishment in the Talmud seems to exist only in the realm of theoretical speculation, just as—after the destruction of the Temple in Jerusalem—all the laws of sacrifice were retained and studied long after the sacrifices ceased to be offered.

The Trial

Capital cases were heard by a court of twenty-three judges (Sanhedrin 2a) and, in some cases, seventy-one judges (Sanhedrin 2a, 15a, and 16a), all of the highest character. "Anyone fit to try capital cases could also try monetary cases," the rabbis stated, "but a person fit to try a monetary case may still be unfit to try a capital case" (Nida 49b). According to Rabbi Judah, a person whose disposition is cruel should be excluded from sitting in judgment in such cases (Sanhedrin 36b). Not only should a person's own record be pure and righteous, but his ancestry had to be free of blemish before he could sit on this court (Sanhedrin 36b). The judges sat on three rising semicircular tiers, as in an amphitheater, in order to see one another, and all murder cases were tried in the light of day; in these ways, everything could be open and aboveboard. Two judge's clerks stood before them, one to the right and the other to the left, and wrote down the arguments of those who would acquit and those who would condemn; both clerks were necessary as a precaution against any mistake. Rabbi Judah said that there were three such clerks: one to record arguments for acquittal, a second to record arguments for conviction, and a third to record arguments for both acquittal and conviction. Witnesses stood in front of these tiers of judges.

The stringent demands on witnesses in capital cases rendered almost impossible the likelihood that a defendant would be convicted. To ensure that a witness's testimony was not based on conjecture (e.g. circumstantial evidence), hearsay, simple rumor, or the observations of another witness, the court would "fill the witness with fear." Witnesses were asked to establish the day and hour of the crime and explain the circumstances surrounding it (Sanhedrin 2b). They were then warned that they would be subject to rigorous questioning and relentless cross-examination and held personally responsible should the accused be falsely condemned. Bearing false witness in a capital case was in itself a crime punishable by death (Sanhedrin 9b, 32b, 86a, and 89a).

A witness in a capital case had to have seen the entire crime as it was being committed; circumstantial evidence was inadmissible. For example, Rabbi Simeon ben Shatach witnessed the following incident: "I saw a man chasing another man into a ruin; I ran after him and saw a sword in his hand dripping with the other's blood, and the murdered man in his death agony. . . ." Even though he was convinced of the man's guilt, the rabbi could not testify against him, because he did not see the actual crime (Sanhedrin 37b).

Not only did witnesses have to see the crime take place, they had to have warned the perpetrator prior to the act that he was about to commit a capital offense. According to Rabbi Judah, a warner even had to inform the perpetrator of the type of execution prescribed for his crime (Sanhedrin 8b). The perpetrator was then obliged to have verbally acknowledged this warning by saying something like, "I know I am warned not to do this"; to have admitted his liability to death by adding something like, "even though I shall be punished by such-and-such manner, yet I want to go ahead and commit this crime"; and to have committed the murder within the time needed to make such an utterance (Makkot 6a). The great eleventh-century commentator Rashi explains this last restriction by suggesting that if a murder was delayed longer than the time necessary to make an utterance, the plea might be accepted that the perpetrator had forgotten the warning altogether. Furthermore, two or three witnesses had to have similarly interacted with the accused. And on the unlikely chance that such witnesses could be found, the court could convict the accused only if guilt could be proven beyond a reasonable doubt. According to the Talmud, "A doubt in capital charges should always be for the benefit of the accused" (Baba Batra 50b, Sanhedrin 79a). In reaching a verdict, a judge was free to argue in favor of the accused, but not against him. A judge who had argued initially for condemnation could subsequently argue for acquittal, but one who had argued for acquittal could not argue later for condemnation. Acquittal in capital cases required a majority of one vote, condemnation a majority of two. A verdict could be reversed for acquittal if errors were revealed, but no new evidence was allowed which would reverse a decision from acquittal to condemnation.

Staying the Execution

Following a guilty verdict, provisions were made to stay the execution. A herald was dispatched to announce something like: "So-and-so, son of so-and-so, is going to be stoned because he committed such-and-such offense, and so-and-so are his witnesses. If anyone has anything to say in his favor, let him come forward and state it." If someone offered to make a statement in favor of the condemned man, a retrial followed. A person was stationed at the door of the court holding a signaling flag, while a horseman stood at the ready within sight of the signalman. If one of the judges said he had something further to state in favor of the condemned, the signaler waved his flag, sending the horseman to postpone the execution. Indeed, even if the condemned said he had something further to plead in his own favor, the court was obliged to reconvene (Sanhedrin 42b).

Rabbinic attitudes concerning the death penalty are also reflected in statements such as "a Sanhedrin that effects an execution once in seven years is branded a destructive tribunal." Rabbi Elizer Ben Azariah said "once in seventy years." Rabbis Tarfon and Akiba said, "If we were members of a Sanhedrin, nobody would ever be put to death." In that same Gemarra, however, Rabbi Simeon Ben Gamaliel dissented: "If we never condemned anyone to death, we might be considered guilty of promoting violence and bloodshed. . . . [We] could also multiply shedders of blood in Israel" (Makkot 7a).

Forty years before the fall of Jerusalem in 70 C.E., the rabbis abolished capital punishment altogether (Soncino Talmud, Sanhedrin page 161, footnote 10). Rather than applying the four methods of execution themselves, they ruled that punishment should be carried out by divine agencies (Sanhedrin 37b, Ketubot 30a and 30b). In other words, a punishment so awesome as the taking of a person's life should not be entrusted to fallible human beings, but only to God.

This ruling does not mean the rabbis dispensed with punishment altogether. On the contrary, they expressed no compunction about decreeing corporal punishment—harsh physical suffering. If the rabbis/judges were convinced of a defendant's guilt in a capital case, but the high standard of evidence did not permit execution, he would be sentenced to prison on a ration of bread and water.

The thrust of Jewish tradition and the historical positions of the Reform Movement impel us to oppose capital punishment in principle and in practice. A person wrongfully flogged for robbery can heal. A person improperly imprisoned for murder can be exonerated and set free. But someone put to death for a crime he/she did not commit can never be redeemed. If we are true to our faith and our tradition, we must respond to the imperative of its teachings and do everything we can to keep our society from committing the ultimate of injustices: the wrongful execution of an innocent person.

ISRAEL AND THE DEATH PENALTY

So great is the Jewish revulsion against capital punishment that when the Jewish state was established in 1948, even though the death penalty was initially permitted and death sentences for murder handed down, these sentences were never carried out; instead the convicted were sentenced to life in prison.

At Israel's first murder trial, both the Ashkenazi and Sephardi chief rabbis sent a cable to the Minister of Justice, urging him to abolish capital punishment at once and warning the court that punishment of death was incompatible with the teachings of Judaism and a sin against Jewish law. Partly as a result of their statement, when the penal laws were revised six years later, in 1954, the death penalty was abolished, with one exception: if the accused was found guilty of participation in genocide and treason during a time of war. Only one person has been executed in Israel since 1948: Adolf Eichmann, administrator of the Nazi destruction of the Jews of Europe.

WHY ONLY THE ORTHODOX CAN AVOID INTERMARRIAGE

David Saks

ONE OF THE DOMINANT TOPICS of discussion in American Jewish circles in recent years was the 1990 National Jewish Population Survey, its findings and implications. Indeed, few surveys of this nature can have been as analyzed, quoted, and argued over as this ground-breaking study. One figure was quoted so often in connection with the survey that it practically became synonymous with it. That figure, of course, was "52 percent."

There is hardly any need to elaborate; "52 percent," according to the survey, was the rate at which Jews in the United States were marrying non-Jews by the second half of the 1980s. Of the children of these marriages, barely a quarter were being raised as Jews, and the rate of conversion was little more than 5 percent. The effect of these findings cannot be exaggerated. For the first time, American Jews were confronted with the prospect of their ultimately disappearing altogether as a distinct religious group, and because of the size and importance of the American Jewish community, the sense of consternation was shared in other parts of the Diaspora. Nor was the attrition solely an American phenomenon; nearly every Jewish community of note (Mexico and South Africa were rare exceptions) had similar problems. Outside of Israel, in fact, Jews were increasingly looking like an endangered species.

A new national population survey is currently being conducted, but few people expect the news to be any better. Indeed, many communal workers are bracing themselves for even more sobering results. It is clear that the number of Jews in the United States who disapprove of intermarriage is shrinking; well over half now see nothing wrong in marrying someone of another faith, with or without a conversion. Nor should we be surprised at this. The various denominational groups within Christianity also show high rates of outmarriage; far higher, in fact, than the Jewish one. It is now generally accepted that in an open society, such intermingling is inevitable, and may even be a good thing.

Add to this the fact that American Jews are no more than 2 percent of the total population. This means that a Jewish person should in theory come into contact with fifty times more gentiles than fellow Jews. In other Diaspora centers, of course, the ratio will be much larger, somewhere in the region of 250:1 in the case of the United Kingdom; at least 100:1 in France; and as much as 1000:1 in Argentina. Given these statistics, a Jew who mixes freely with gentiles is overwhelmingly more likely to strike up a lasting relationship with one of them, often even before coming into contact with a Jewish potential partner.

Take away the Jewish religion and there is no way whatever of justifying opposition to intermarriage. One will occasionally hear people say Jews should not intermarry lest they "give Hitler a posthumous victory" (Emil Fackenheim's famous quote), but this assertion is considered by some to be deeply offensive because it effectively equates intermarriage with mass murder.

One group within Diaspora Jewry that did not feel particularly threatened by the burgeoning intermarriage statistics were the religiously observant Orthodox. A distinction needs to be made from the outset between these and the non- or partially observant Orthodox. The latter make up the majority in countries like England and Australia and are also very much affected by intermarriage, albeit not to the same extent as Reform and secular Jews. Observant Orthodox live their lives strictly according to halacha, the code of Jewish law, and do not question its Divine origins or its relevance and absolute authority in every age, regardless of the prevailing norms and values of contemporary society. For this grouping, intermarriage is a marginal phenomenon.

For the Orthodox, this risk of marrying out is minimized by their deliberately keeping themselves and their children apart from the general society, certainly at the social and school level and as much as possible in the workplace. One of the crucial reasons why children from Orthodox families intermarry at a dramatically lower rate—less than 5 percent—is because they are so seldom allowed to come into contact with non-Jews. True, with their more intensive religious background, such children would in any case be far less likely to be tempted into relationships with non-

Jews, but there is no guarantee. People are people at the end of the day, and mutual attraction and compatibility can often overcome even the most formidable religious and ethnic barriers. Jews, in other words, do not keep themselves apart from "the *goyim*" because they "don't like" them. In fact, they do like them, enough to want to intermarry with them, and for this practical reason they set up social barriers.

However, the Orthodox ability to withstand intermarriage goes beyond mere physical separation. Staying physically apart is only the "how" of avoiding intermarriage. More important, the ideology of Orthodox Judaism also provides the all-important "why"—why Jews should strive to be a people apart and not become lost among the nations. The Orthodox stance on the Torah and prophetic writings is that these constitute no less than a communication from the Creator Himself, not the philosophical musings of charismatic oriental mystics and not a body of ethnic folklore. Central to this Divine communication is that the Jewish people have been set apart to keep the laws of the Torah and thereby to become a holy nation and bearers of G-d's wisdom to all humanity. If this understanding of the Jewish Scriptures is true, then it provides a pretty good reason for marrying within the fold, thereby ensuring Jewish continuity.

The Jewish will to survive in exile was predicated on the absolute conviction that Jews were a people with a G-d-ordained mission and that the Creator had directly intervened throughout history on their behalf and given them an immutable Guidebook through which to accomplish their destiny. It was this absolute conviction that enabled Jews to withstand the despair and defeatism that nineteen centuries of exile must have engendered, an exile replete with humiliation and suffering.

Then, late in the day, new interpretations emerged, new schools of modern Judaism that essentially said, "Well, actually, no. The Jewish Bible was really put together by some of our ancestors as a way of making sense of the universe as they saw it then, and much of it has no relevance to us today. Nevertheless, it remains a valuable source of Jewish morals and ethics."

I realize that I am caricaturing the non-Orthodox approach, yet at bottom I think that is precisely what its theologians were saying. Torah is not Divine; at best, "Divinely inspired" is the message that comes through. Those parts of it that jar modern sensibilities are to be regarded as being of antiquarian interest only and set aside.

Rabbi Eric Yoffie, president of the Union of American Hebrew Congregations, once summed up the new Reform commitment to tradition with the words "Torah! Torah! Torah!" One would expect even Orthodox Jews to approve of this ringing undertaking until one takes a closer look and asks the question, "Just what 'Torah' does Rabbi Yoffie mean?"

Not the sacrificial laws, surely, nor the detailed laws concerning *kashrut,* mixtures of wool and linen, and levirate marriage. The first half of the book of *Exodus* is fine, with its theme of freedom from oppression, but what about the second half, devoted almost in its entirety to the building of the Sanctuary in the desert? Then there are the "sexist" divorce laws and, of course, that dreadfully homophobic passage in *Leviticus.* One could go on. The truth is that in the version of Judaism Rabbi Yoffie espouses, more than half of the Torah would end up being rejected as being of no spiritual relevance, at best, and as hopelessly reactionary and intolerant, at worst. The obvious question an intelligent young Jew will ask is, if the author of the Torah managed to get so much wrong, why trust him on everything else, particularly if it means making important lifestyle changes?

Let us also suppose, for argument's sake, that the non-Orthodox view is the correct one, and that, after all, G-d the Creator never really communicated with our ancestors, or made a covenant with them, or gave them the Torah. In my view, quite frankly, this would mean that thirty-five hundred years of Jewish history, with all the suffering and striving it entailed, will then have been based on a pitiful delusion, and under the circumstances, intermarriage should be welcomed, not opposed. Indeed, we should even be grateful to our non-Jewish neighbors for their willingness to intermarry with so wretched a bunch of dupes.

The bottom line with regard to intermarriage is that if you are going to ask a Jewish person to give up his or her Catholic girlfriend or Episcopalian boyfriend, then you have to provide a very good reason. The non-Orthodox movements, for all the undoubted sincerity of their leadership, do not seem to be capable of doing it, of stemming the tide of intermarriage. This is not "Ultra-Orthodox Triumphalism." It is simply a fact.

Y MARKS THE SPOT

William C. Speed

AS A CHILD, I used to flip through the white pages to find my grandmother's telephone number. To my surprise, right above "Speed, Katherine," and right beneath the listing for "Speed, Mr. and Mrs. C. William," was someone else: "Speed, Gregory." I ran to my mother with the good news: I had just found a long-lost brother, right there in the phone book. I remember getting irritated with her nonchalance: "Honey, it's just someone else with that last name." Visions of unknown cousins and great-aunts had filled my head. I wanted proof. We had none.

What we did have was a family photo album. Many families have them—each photo labeled: Aunt Meredith, Cousin Joseph, Grandpa Seth. We know how we are related to each of these faces, by blood or marriage. We might even see physical characteristics, such as a widow's peak or curly hair or tall stature, evident in many family members. We all have childhood memories of that embarrassing aunt hugging us too closely and proclaiming that we have our grandfather's eyes, or that we are the spitting image of our great-grandmother.

Instead of using anthropological data from photo albums and marriage records, however, geneticists are coming up with genetic tools to look backward along a family tree. They are using a person's own genetic material to find out about his or her family's history. For example, geneticists were able to show that it is highly likely that Thomas Jefferson had a child with his slave Sally Hemings, confirming a family tradition preserved by descendants of that union. In other studies geneticists have identified genetic markers that support independent anthropological and archaeological data that the human species originated in Africa and migrated from Africa eventually to populate the entire world.

In the past several years, a number of scientific papers have been published bearing on issues of special interest to the Jewish community, most notably purporting to trace the genetic markers of Aaron, the brother of Moses, to the present Jewish population.

In Jewish tradition, priests, or *kohanim* in Hebrew, are descendants of Aaron. According to Exodus 28:1, God tells Moses to bring forth his brother Aaron and his sons as priests. They shall be consecrated "to minister to me as priests." The priesthood in Israel is ordained only once; henceforth, priests are defined as the male descendants of this line (in contrast to females through whom the status of "Jew" has descended since Rabbinic times).

Kohanim are given no certificate testifying to their status as priests. The status is a presumptive one. There is no certain way to be sure in each case. The status is simply passed on, often preserved in names, from father to son. There are a myriad of names signifying this status. Cohen is only one. Others are Cohn, Kohn, Kahn, Kahan, Kahana, Kagan, Cowan, and Katz (an acronym for *Kohen Tzadek*, literally "righteous priest"). But many kohanim do not bear "kohanic" names.

Even today kohanim know who they are. And they are still accorded special ritual privileges. They are given the first *aliyah* (literally "call up") when the Torah is read in synagogues. (The second aliyah is typically reserved for a *Levi*, traditionally a member of the priestly tribe of Levi. While every member of that tribe was a priest, the kohanim in the tribe were at a higher level and it is to them primarily that ceremonial Temple service was reserved.) In some synagogues, the congregation's kohanim are still called up to bless the congregation with the priestly blessing attributed to Aaron and his sons in Numbers 6:22–27. Prior to this, the congregation's Levites ritually wash the hands of the kohanim. The status also has some restrictions—regarding whom they may marry and a prohibition against contact with the dead.

Studies that purport to trace a "kohanic" genetic link back to Aaron identify shared genetic markers. Genetic markers are unique spots in the human genome, or, more technically, specific places on specific chromosomes. Imagine taking your car and parking it next to ten other cars of the same make, model, color, and year. That's the human genome. Could you find your car? They all look almost exactly the same. But suddenly you remember a small nick in the windshield where a truck kicked up a stone. Or a dent on the bumper from a parking lot incident. You could tell which car was yours by looking at these small identifying marks, the variation between your car and all the others. However, unlike dents and dings, most genetic markers are chosen by scientists because they have no physical manifestation; they are, in this sense, anonymous. For these studies, geneticists choose as their markers areas in the DNA that are not part of any gene or protein, that is, any key functional component of the cells. So far as we know, these entities have no function. They are simply genetic markers. These are the same kinds of genetic markers that are used in forensic analyses of crime scenes or in the paternity analyses seen on mid-morning tabloid TV shows.

All humans are genetically unique (except identical twins). Nevertheless, all humans are very similar genetically. For this reason, when geneticists study a human population, they don't just look at one or two genetic markers. They look at several genetic markers in the same genetic region. Combinations of these markers are known as haplotypes, and they are powerful analytical tools for geneticists.

To take a simple example of how a genetic haplotype can be used, consider the case of an English geneticist named Bryan Sykes.[1] From English voter registration lists, he took a random sample of people whose last name was the same as his, Sykes. These people had no known relationship to each other, other than sharing their last name. Sykes looked at the genetic material passed from fathers to sons—the Y chromosome—since the Sykes name was passed from father to son. He looked at four genetic markers on the Y chromosome, a haplotype of markers, on forty-eight people with that last name. Of those forty-eight people, 44 percent shared this haplotype. In contrast, DNA taken from twenty-one next-door neighbors of these Sykeses, as part of the scientific control group, had none of this haplotype, and were much more genetically diverse. None of the neighbors' chromosomes looked like the Sykes chromosome (15-23-11-14, in scientific geek-speak). Clearly, the Sykes men had much more of this DNA haplotype than the rest of the population. This suggests that hundreds of years ago one man named Sykes was the single forebear of the Sykes lineage.

Does this mean that anyone with this 15-23-11-14 haplotype is also a Sykes? No. And despite the fact that none of the twenty-one neighbors had this haplotype, there are undoubtedly some other men out there with different names who share these genetic markers.

What if a person doesn't have the 15-23-11-14 haplotype? Does that mean he isn't a "true" Sykes? Again, no. This family name has been handed down from generation to generation. To suggest that the 56 percent of

Sykeses who do not fit the majority's profile are not "real" Sykeses would be ludicrous.

Does the data support the idea that people with the same family name generally share a larger genetic identity? Yes. Indeed, that was the question asked of the DNA.

The studies pertinent to our inquiry deal not with a family history based on family name, but with religious history based on a cultic designation. Do kohanim share genetic markers passed down from Aaron to his sons and their sons, from father to son, for three thousand years? Although small genetic variations in the DNA will have accumulated over time due to rare, random changes, the Y chromosomes should have remained very similar even over thousands of years.

One study identified a haplotype of twelve genetic markers on the Y chromosome and studied 306 Jewish men who were categorized first as Ashkenazi or Sephardic and then subcategorized into kohanim, Levites, or Israelites (all the rest). The result: the kohanim showed much less Y chromosome variation than the rest of the Jewish population. The kohanim shared the set of genetic markers (the "Cohen modal haplotype") 96 percent of the time among the Ashkenazi kohanim and 88 percent of the time among the Sephardic kohanim. The Levites and Israelites had much more genetic diversity on their Y chromosomes than the kohanim.[2]

This does not, however, mean that 96 percent of the Ashkenazi Cohens are "real" priests and the rest are not. Nor does it mean that Levis or Israelites who share these genetic markers (this haplotype) are "lost" priests who are really kohanim. In television dramas we may see a doctor walking into a room with a large manila folder holding the DNA test results that show the patient has sickle-cell anemia or Down's Syndrome. He is dealing with genetic questions that have yes or no answers. In population genetics, however, scientists deal in frequencies and probabilities, seldom with yes or no answers. We ask: Are kohanim genetically similar? The answer is yes, astonishingly so. But this does not mean that we have identified any particular person as being a descendant of Aaron. The fact is we have no genetic proof that Aaron existed. Science has shown only that our oral and written history are consistent with the genetic data. "Consistent with" and "proof of" are very different.

Furthermore, there is no such a thing as "Jewish DNA." Judaism is a religion and/or ethnic group, not a race of people.

Geneticists have recently been accused of fueling racism by relying on studies like the one I mention above.[3] But race is a social construct. No population geneticist argues that the data establishes "races." Most genetic variation we find is a subset of the original variation found in the

African populations. As various groups of Homo sapiens migrated out of Africa, some genetic variation was lost; as other groups migrated over the Siberian land bridge to North America, more genetic variation was lost. For the most part, genetic variations found in Welsh and Cheyenne and Russian and Ashkenazi are all found in peoples in Africa, the most genetically diverse Homo sapiens in the world. What we find through genetic study is that we all share the same genetic stuff: there is no Chinese DNA or African DNA; there is no genetic test to see if someone is Finnish.

In most genetic studies, people are self-identified. A researcher doesn't simply arrive on the scene and say, "Hey, you look like you're an Ashkenazi. Can I have some DNA?" The individuals who consent to participate in the study choose whether or not to identify themselves in a particular way. People designated kohanim designate themselves. They are not put in this category because of their genetic (or other objectively identifiable "racial") characteristics. The questions population geneticists ask are based on how self-identified groups of people behave DNA-wise. From these larger sample sizes, we can find only *statistically* significant similarities and differences.

The scientific method—hypothesis, experiment, conclusion—doesn't work in both directions. We cannot look at genetic markers on the Y chromosome and say, "Aha! A kohen!" We can look at the genetic markers of people who self-identify as kohanim and say only, "Genetically similar! Much more so than other peoples in their population!"

Similarly, peoples of various national origins may show statistically significant genetic variation. It should therefore come as no surprise that the Jewish and non-Jewish populations of the Middle East are closely related genetically and that these populations share most genetic haplotypes. These genetic haplotypes form a genetic pool that is statistically distinct from, for example, the European pool. A recent paper shows just how closely Kurdish Jews are related to Ashkenazi and Sephardic Jews, as well as to the Muslim Kurds and Palestinians.[4]

Rather than giving support to racist claims, population geneticists have shown just how similar, almost to the point of being indistinguishable, we all are. Yet, as a group, kohanim bear strikingly different genetic characteristics from the rest of the Jewish population.

NOTES

1. See Bryan Sykes and Catherine Irven, "Surnames and the Y Chromosome," *American Journal of Human Genetics*, vol. 66, pp. 1417–1419 (2000).

2. M. Thomas, K. Skorecki, H. Ben-Ami, T. Parfitt, N. Bradman, and D. Goldstein, "Origins of Old Testament Priests," *Nature,* vol. 394, pp. 138–140 (1998).

3. See, for example, Joseph L. Graves Jr., *The Emperor's New Clothes— Biological Theories of Race at the Millennium* (New Brunswick, N.J.: Rutgers University Press, 2001).

4. See, for example, Almut Nebel, et al., "The Y Chromosome Pool of Jews as Part of the Genetic Landscape of the Middle East," *American Journal of Human Genetics,* vol. 69, pp. 1095–1112 (2001).

DRUGS AND JEWISH SPIRITUALITY

THAT WAS THEN, THIS IS NOW

Lawrence Bush

1.

Rabbi Kahana explained an inconsistency: the word for "wine"
is spelled tirash but pronounced tirosh. If a man merits it, wine
makes him rosh, "chief"; if not, it makes him rash, "a poor man."

Rava explained another inconsistency: as spelled, the text reads,
"Wine that desolates [yeshammah]" (Ps. 104:15), but we
pronounce the last word, "yesammah [that maketh glad]."
If a man merits it, wine makes him glad; if not, it desolates
him. That is what Rava meant when he said:
Wine and spices stimulate my mind.

—Babylonian Talmud, Yoma 76b, in H. N. Bialik
and Y. H. Ravnitzky, *Sefer Ha-Aggadah/The Book of Legends*

The first time I ever stayed up all night and saw daylight return, I was seventeen years old and "tripping" on LSD. The solidity of the New York cityscape as dawn spread through the streets was profoundly comforting to me: after the radical shifts in perception that I had weathered through the night, here I could affirm that the world does not dissolve during the hours of sleep, but "remains the same forever" (Ecclesiastes 1:4).

Uncertainty about such existential fundamentals eventually drove me to abandon LSD and all other drugs. By dint of personal wiring and family history, I was lacking in *emunah,* the faith to know that I could have such experiences and land in a grounded reality. Looking back, today, on the twenty-plus "acid trips" that I took as a much-too-young adult, I sort them into two varieties. At their most gentle, psychedelic drugs evoked some superb sensory experiences: the half-hour examination of the exquisite symmetry of a dew-hung spider web, the glimpsing of a smile on a trotting dog's face, the sudden apprehension of cubism as a form of realism. "Hallucination" belittles these experiences: dogs, after all, *do* smile.

More problematic were the "mystical" moments, tinged with madness, that involved a greatly intensified sense of metaphor and meaning, the dissolution of ego borders, the powerful "perception" of what was real and illusory, natural and bizarre, holy and profane—and the manic longing to organize these insights into a redemptive system. Such episodes, deeply challenging to the rationalism that my family held dear, would leave me incapacitated by ambivalence. *Bouncing ego can't be free, boundless ego won't be me,* I wrote in a poem at age eighteen. And so, like the Hebrew people at the foot of Sinai, I "fell back and stood at a distance" ("Let not God speak to us, lest we die," Exodus 20:15–16). I left psychedelic drugs behind, far less with a sense of relief than with a sense of failure, incompleteness, and envy for those free spirits who *could* safely ascend the mountain.

Such Jewish imagery probably would not have occurred to me during my drug-using days, when I identified more with the Woodstock Nation than with the Jewish People. Today, however, I do know more than one rabbi and Jewish professional who either postponed or extended the baby-boomer rite of drug experimentation to a time when Jewish metaphors came naturally to them. Their psychedelic experiences thus became tightly interwoven with their Judaism and deeply influenced their professional practice.

Rabbi C., for example, never took LSD during the sixties heyday, but waited until he was in his late forties. With his own rabbi serving as his (drug-free) "guide," C. spent some six hours rapturously experiencing the Revelation at Sinai. He had an overpowering sense of *devekut,* oceanic union with God; he could "see" the entire cosmos, micro and macro, and experienced what he calls "an unbearable feeling" of having his own boundaries stretched to encompass it all. This piercing perception of the infinitesimal yet infinite nature of his individual identity was accompanied

by an overpowering infusion of faith, a certainty about there being meaning in the universe and interconnection among all life. This mystical encounter served as the bedrock of Rabbi C.'s creative theology for the next
eighteen years. "What I experienced and felt," he reports, "was not un-
real or less real but *more* real than my daily perception of reality. I've never
felt any other way about it."

Another rabbi, N., an executive within Jewish organizational life, was
a weekly user of marijuana and hashish and "tripped" several times annually for a twelve-year period before entering rabbinic school. Rabbi N.
believes that "drug experiences opened me up for prayer experiences and
a relationship to God—there are even similar feelings of community in
getting high with people and praying with them." He especially deplores
the criminalization of drugs in America, which has made drug use into
"the leading source of crime and waste of government money." Instead,
N. believes, "a way should be found to allow marijuana and psychedelics
to expand people's spiritual consciousness in a safe environment."

A Jewish educator and day school principal, B. took psychedelic drugs
about a dozen times, "always with a sense of spiritual mission." She remembers a Shavuot some twenty years ago when she and three other wom-
en (all prominent in Jewish life today) "borrowed" a Torah scroll from a
day school ("It was locked away on Shavuot!"), took it to a state park,
ate hallucinogenic mushrooms, and spent the day reading Torah, along
with "woodland creatures, frogs, and deer," who "came out and participated!" B. admits that "the fact of connectedness or 'oneness' that the
Sh'ma expresses first became clear to me on LSD."

A successful editor of Jewish books, F. had numerous psychedelic experiences in the 1970s. "I look back on nearly all of them with great awe
and respect," F. says. "Each time was a 'big occasion' with a consistent
teaching: that there are all kinds of things going on in the spectrum that
my normal waking consciousness doesn't pick up. It's like a dog whistle—
your ear doesn't hear all frequencies. But with each 'awakening' there is
some residue left in the senses, as with the lightning bolt described by
Rambam [Maimonides], which briefly illuminates the sky."

A third rabbi, J., who heads a vibrant congregation in the Northeast,
undertook two LSD experiences during and shortly after college and feels
that they strongly influenced his later rabbinic practice. "I remember sitting outside our apartment in the snow," reports J., "drawing a circle in
the snow to make a pie, putting jelly on it, cutting up slices and eating
them. Looking through the patio doors of the next apartment, I saw a
very fancy cocktail party. I realized at that moment that every social interaction is a construct, a kind of pretense. The perception didn't require

me to 'drop out,' but it did help make me radically unregimented as a rabbi. I saw that there is no particular activity or time that has a meaning beyond that which we humans have attached to it. Nothing is sacred, in other words, except when we choose to make it sacred—which is something I really value and love doing."

2.

Were the great ritual moments of Judaism used as reminders (or recreators) of states of elevated consciousness, as they once were used to some extent by the Kabbalists, those of us who have gained religious insight through the use of drugs might indeed find great excitement in the ritual life.

—Rabbi Arthur Green, writing pseudonymously
as Itzik Lodzer, in *Response,* Winter 1968

The Jews I have quoted are certainly among the more radical in contemporary Jewish life. They are hardly alone among baby-boomer Jews, however, in their experiments with psychedelic drugs and their positive associations between those experiments and their Jewish spirituality. Nor are such Jews limited to the liberal denominations: "I know many *ha'alei teshuvah,*" reports F., speaking of Orthodox and Hasidic friends and neighbors, "who cannot deny that their spiritual journey included 'getting high with a little help from their friends.'"

"Awakenings" via drugs have often led to a desire to awaken Judaism itself. In particular, many psychedelic voyagers have spent subsequent years pushing against what Rabbi Arthur Green called, in his thirty-year-old *Response* article, the "cult of God-as-father" that "has been allowed to run rampant for hundreds of years" in Jewish life. "As presented today," wrote Green,

> Judaism . . . has lost the creative mystic drive which led beyond its own images into a confrontation with the Nothing *[Ein Sof].* The Judaism which contemporary Jews have inherited is one of a father figure who looms so large that one dare not *try* to look beyond Him. We have indeed become trapped by our image.

This trap, according to Rabbi Green, guaranteed that "most psychedelic voyagers" in the 1960s, including Jews, "sought their religious guidance in the traditions of the East," which encourage altered states of consciousness and are tolerant of fluid images of divinity. Against such a backdrop, the creative metaphysics of tripping (what Green called "the construction of elaborate and often beautiful systems of imagery which momentarily seem to contain all the meaning of life") seemed less heretical and more resonant.

Green's article proceeded to offer an alternative to the stodgy ol' Judaism of the 1960s by drawing four analogies between psychedelic drugs and kabbalistic mysticism. First, he wrote, the "everything-has-been-changing-but-nothing-has-changed" experience of tripping is analogous to "the Kabbalists' descriptions of God as *Sefirot*," in which "there is no limit to the ever-flowing and ever-changing face of the divine personality." Second, LSD's "terribly exhilarating liberation . . . from the bondage of all those daily ego problems" has analogy in Judaism's "'stripping off of the physical' (*Hitpashtut ha-Gashmiyut*)," an "interpretation that some of the Kabbalists give to the act of fasting on Yom Kippur." Third, the acid-induced sense of time as a "union of moment and eternity" is parallel to the kabbalistic view that "all future moments were contained within creation, and creation is renewed in every moment."

Finally, Green wrote of "the deepest, simplest, and most radical insight of psychedelic/mystic consciousness . . . the realization that all reality is one with the Divine." Despite Judaism's built-in "fears and reservations" about this insight, he declared, "the feeling of the true oneness of God and man is encountered with surprising frequency in the literature of the Kabbalah."

This theology of immanence (God is everywhere) is a typical hallmark of many Jews whose résumés have "LSD" invisibly written in the white space between the lines. So is a deep interest in Jewish mysticism and a desire to broaden the Jewish agenda from survivalism/group solidarity to "God-consciousness" and spiritually meaningful observance. To the extent that these interests have become pervasive among a wide variety of Jews, so do we glimpse their influence.

Yet the impact of psychedelic drugs on these innovators goes unacknowledged, even three decades after Rabbi Green's ground-breaking article. Perhaps his analogy between drugs and Jewish mysticism holds here, too, as the Talmud (Hagiga 13a) warns that "The things that are as sweet as honey," i.e., arcane knowledge, "should remain under your tongue." Most tongues have been tied less by reverence, however, than by the "Just Say No" propaganda of the past two decades, which has made saying "yes" or even "maybe" into a major career risk. It seems you cannot become president—not even in the Conference of Presidents of Major American Jewish Organizations—if you admit to having inhaled.

3.

Our masters taught: Four men entered the Garden, namely, Ben
Azzai, Ben Zoma, Aher, and Rabbi Akiva. . . . Ben Azzai cast
a look and died. . . . Ben Zoma looked and became demented. . . .
Aher mutilated the shoots. Rabbi Akiva departed unhurt.

—Babylonian Talmud, Hagaig, 14b in H. N. Bialik
and Y. H. Ravnitzky, *Sefer Ha-Aggadah/The Book of Legends*

There is no stronger antidote to the intoxication of youth than the fears accompanying parenthood, and when I contemplate the prospect of my children (twelve-year-old boy/girl twins) "entering the Garden," I become very sober.

The hazards are many. An LSD trip is not an amusement park ride, delivering safe thrills within set parameters; it is an intense, day-long experience of altered brain chemistry, and its outcomes are strongly influenced by many factors, both subjective and environmental. Psychosis and exaltation walk side by side; the dissolving of ego borders and the uprooting from mental certainties can be terrifying, even lethal. The thirteenth-century Jewish kabbalist Abraham Abulafia could easily have been discussing LSD when he wrote of "spirits of jealousy" that gathered around him during his own mystical "trip," even as "God touched my mouth" and "a spirit of holiness fluttered through me." Over the course of the next fifteen years, "I was confronted with fantasy and error," Abulafia admitted. "My mind was totally confused, since I could not find anyone else like me, who would teach me the correct path. I was therefore like a blind man, groping around at noon" and "Satan was at my right hand to mislead me."[1]

Beyond psychosis, I dread having my kids physically injured or even killed while intoxicated by misjudging their own physical limits, disregarding the laws of physics, or simply driving a car. Although LSD is known for its peculiar virtue of provoking fantastic visions while maintaining an objective, "watcher" frame of mind, I would not want my children's lives to depend on the steadfastness of that "watcher." Instead, *I* want to serve as their watcher: the principle of *s'yag l'Torah*, making a fence around the Torah, has no greater application for me than in protecting the lives of my children through prudent parenting.

It is, however, the criminalization of drugs, rather than their inherent dangers, that most prevents me from serving as "watcher" over my children's safety and mental health. Certainly, the hostile policies of America have kept me from discussing drug use in as honest and nuanced a way as I would like with my kids, for fear that their naïve interpretations and adolescent gossip might lead to serious stigmatization, despite our being a drug-free household. As a result, their main source of drug education has been their school's DARE (Drug Abuse Resistance Education) program— a program awash with a repressive mystique that violates my values, while its deterrence power is very questionable. My own father, a pharmacist with detailed knowledge about the dangers of drugs, gave up a two-pack-a-day cigarette habit in the 1960s to deter my drug use by example. If such intimate heroism failed to halt my experimentation, why should a local sheriff's corny propaganda be effective?

Criminalization further ensures that if my kids ever do mess with drugs, I will be helpless to ensure "quality control" and maximize their safety. They will be left to procure their substances from whatever unsavory sources, in whatever dosages, for use in whatever environments, because they will lack my cooperation and guidance—guidance that could lead me to prison and loss of custody. American law thus throws up a huge wall between me and my children and all but ensures that the spiritual possibilities of their drug use, if it transpires, will be seriously compromised.

What about Jewish law? "I brought the issue of substance use to a teacher of mine in the traditional world," reports F., the editor. "He told me there are two problems. The small problem is that the halachah teaches us to be law abiding: *dina malkhuta dina,* 'the law of the land is the law.' The larger problem is embodied in the question: Who is the master and who is the servant?"

F.'s rebbe was talking about addiction—a scourge that directly challenges my open-mindedness about drug use. Drug and alcohol addiction, after all, are powerful catalysts of crime and social blight. Statistics on child abuse, domestic violence, rape, robbery, and murder reveal the central role addiction plays in facilitating human misery.

Advocates for the legalization of "soft" drugs, moreover, strike me as naïve when they deny that there is any link between use of marijuana and psychedelics and use of the harder stuff. "Sin begins as a spider's web and becomes a ship's rope," teaches Rabbi Akiva in *Genesis Rabbah* (22.6). Even as a reasonably sensible, self-aware, and middle-class pothead in the sixties, I tried almost every available drug at least once, including cocaine, amphetamines, tranquilizers, opium, and angel dust (nasty!). Only heroin, with its reputation for addictiveness, fatal overdose, and nausea for novices, provoked me to "Just Say No."

Addiction is not limited, moreover, to "hard" drugs. Several of my friends, for example, became psychologically "addicted" to marijuana well into their mature years. The narcissistic qualities of getting high—the sense of achievement, loosened inhibition, personal brilliance, and hilarity— provided a buffer against the frustrations of thwarted ambition, relational *ennui,* and existential boredom that most human beings face. Only when these individuals realized that a plunge into the depths of humility was pre- requisite to their growth were they able to stop medicating themselves.

Is their drug use fundamentally different or somehow less reprehensible than those of inner-city folk who smoke crack to rise above their blighted landscapes? The truth is that any drug, whether used to "awaken" the soul or to "deaden" it (a very subjective and culturally determined distinction), can be overused and misused. And all such abuse, to my mind, deserves a compassionate, psychospiritual response. Criminalization simply max- imizes the degradation of the human beings involved—and turns my parental fears into nightmares.

4.

> When I can undergo the deepest cosmic experience via some minuscule quantity of organic alkaloids or LSD, then the whole validity of my ontological assertions is in doubt. [Yet the] psyche- delic experience can be not only a challenge but a support of my faith. After seeing what really happens at the point where all is One . . . I can also see Judaism in a new and amazing light. The questions to which the Torah is the answer are recovered in me.

> —Rabbi Zalman M. Schachter, writing in a *Commentary* symposium on "The State of Jewish Belief," August 1966

Apart from legal impediments, why shouldn't psychedelic drugs be used in Jewish life as they have been in other faith traditions—as a tool for wrench- ing open the mind and heart to "God's presence"? Why not embrace the spiritual power of the psychedelic experience and try to elevate it, as we do with sexuality, above the recreational and into the sacramental zone? Why shouldn't the roster to Jewish life-passages include the opportunity to have a psychedelic experience (perhaps after the age of forty, Judaism's traditional age of enlightenment and mystical initiation, or perhaps at an earlier stage of development)—with rabbinic guidance and community ap- proval? If Abraham's Voice and Moses' Burning Bush and the Revelation at Sinai are the archetypal encounters that inform our faith, why not strive to recreate such experiences throughout our "nation of priests"?

One "why not" is rooted in a spiritual work ethic. Arthur Green put it as follows in a second article in *Response,* published three years after his pseudonymous one: "That which you don't work out on your own, in a struggle that has to begin way down here in the world of ordinary week-day consciousness, somehow just isn't going to last."

True, LSD is promiscuous in its power: you needn't read Hebrew, study Torah, or make any Jewish commitments before you stand on "holy ground." The logic of banning such a powerful tool of religious awakening, however, would also have us banning English translations of holy texts, cross-referenced CD-ROM versions of the Talmud, and all such tools of "easy" access—as well as outreach strategies that seek to provide Jewish contexts for people's "real life" passions and hobbies (Jewish elderhostels, Jewish environmentalism, Jewish ski weekends, etc.). Jewish life has simply moved too far in the direction of democratization and cross-cultural pollination to retreat now.

Another "why not" targets mysticism itself. Writing in *Contemporary Jewish Religious Thought* (ed. by Arthur A. Cohen and Paul Mendes-Flohr, 1987), the late Israeli philosopher Yeshayahu Leibowitz devoted his entire essay on "Idolatry" to a denunciation of mysticism, which "is another name for idolatry." In particular, he wrote, the kabbalistic *sephirot,* which are "thoroughly imbued with . . . aspects of the divine . . . directly contradict the scriptural view of God," which ascribes holiness to God and to nothing else. "How difficult it is," Leibowitz continued,

> for man [sic] to accept the distinction between the holy and the pro-
> fane, between the creator, who alone is "truly real" . . . and utterly
> holy, and his own status in God's world, which is contingent and
> profane.

Such a critique, though rare in contemporary Judaism, has dogged Jewish mysticism for centuries. In particular, the Hasidic flowering of the mid-1700s was violently opposed by traditionalists (the *Mitnaggedim*) who viewed the Hasidic emphasis on ecstatic worship over study and *mitzvot* as heretical and idolatrous. Similarly, Rabbi C.'s LSD-induced experience of *devekut,* B.'s conviction that "connectedness and oneness" is the meaning of the *Sh'ma,* and Rabbi J.'s humanistic perception that "nothing is sacred except when we choose to make it sacred," would all likely have been denounced by the Gaon of Vilna, leader of the *Mitnaggedim*—or by Yeshayahu Leibowitz—as egotism writ large.

Mysticism nevertheless seems integral to the spiritual upsurge of the 1990s. For better or worse, "getting high on God" far outweighs "submitting to the yoke of the *mitzvot*" in most Jewish circles, while courses in

Kabbalah, meditation, and other Jewish techniques of consciousness expansion have full enrollments. Unless our community turns away, en masse, from this quest to "get high" through Jewish ritual, there is little ground here for excluding psychedelic explorations from our sacramental roster.

The fact is that psychedelic drugs have already been part of the "sacramental roster" for many baby-boomer Jews, who sensed while under the influence that "Surely the Lord is present in this place, and I did not know it!" (Genesis 28:16). Rather than emulating Jacob and erecting a pillar at the site of their discovery, they have been forced by two decades of repressive social policy to bury and hide it. Like the Marranos of old, they have bought respectability and influence with silence—a choice that has facilitated many innovations in American Jewish life. But that silence has also left our children to fend for themselves. It has left psychedelic voyagers without a Jewish port-of-call—and tens of thousands of human beings to wallow in prison without Jewish protest. It has left the heritage of the sixties vulnerable to slander, while the "War on Drugs" rages out of control, with inquisitors and cowards calling the shots.

"Truth is the center of the circle," wrote Abraham Ibn Ezra, the world-wandering Hebrew poet, commentator, and holy man of the twelfth century. Perhaps the time has come to step into Ibn Ezra's circle, face outwards to America, and admit to having inhaled.

NOTE

1. Tr. by Aryeh Kaplan; see Diane M. Sharon's essay in *The Fifty-Eighth Century,* ed. by Shohama Wiener, 1996.

KING OF THE JEWS

Jane Leavy

YOM KIPPUR IS THE HOLIEST DAY of the Jewish calendar, the Day of Atonement. Those who repent their sins are inscribed in the Book of Life. On October 6, 1965, Koufax was inscribed forever in the Book of Life as the Jew who refused to pitch on Yom Kippur. Bruce Lustig, who would grow up to be the senior rabbi at the Washington Hebrew Congregation in Washington, D.C., was seven years old and attending services in Tennessee with his parents that day. He took a transistor radio with him, the wire running up the inside of his starched white shirt. When the rabbi called upon the congregants to stand and pray, the earpiece came loose and the voice of Vin Scully crackled through the sanctuary. His mother walloped him with her purse and banished him to the synagogue library, where the television was tuned to NBC's coverage of the game. Live and in color when live and in color was something to brag about.

The Dodgers lost but Koufax won. In that moment, he became known as much for what he refused to do as for what he did on the mound. By refusing to pitch, Koufax defined himself as a man of principle who placed faith above craft. He became inextricably linked with the American Jewish experience. As John Goodman put it in the movie *The Big Lebowski:* "Three thousand years of beautiful tradition: from Moses to Sandy Koufax."

Koufax was a purist. "Too nice to be so great," Wills always said. Unlike Drysdale, who glowered for effect and exploited his reputation for all it was worth, Koufax burned inwardly. Jeff Torborg thought his eyes might just burn right through his head.

More than one of his African-American peers attributed Koufax's rectitude and reticence to his being a minority. "Stayin' right in his own house," as Lou Johnson put it, knowing he would be held to a higher standard. Perhaps Johnson was projecting. But if Koufax had been a White Anglo-Saxon Protestant who played clean and kept his nose clean, he'd have been proclaimed the second coming of Jack Armstrong. But he was a Jew. So he was moody, aloof, curt, intellectual, different.

His portrait hangs in the L.A. County Museum. The painting, by the esteemed Jewish artist R. B. Kitaj, is striking for several reasons; among them, it does not attempt to make him beautiful. The artist chose to illuminate duress, that portion of his delivery when his chest preceded his lower body and his elbow, cocked to a breaking point, trailed behind him like the tail of a kite. The squinched eyes, pursed lips, skin drawn taut by effort, even the distorted maw of his glove make palpable his exertion. The artist's palette is equally thought-provoking. Hues of muted peach inform the fabric of his uniform; his cap and arm a fiery orange. They leap from the pastel blue background of the sky. The choice of color is eclectic and disconcerting. It is not the color of baseball, decidedly not Dodger blue. It is, in fact, a perfect rendering of his Otherness. What baseball executive Dick Cecil calls "the mysterious Hebrew."

At the heart of any bias lie inchoate assumptions, the stereotypes to which we unconsciously yield. Thus: Jewish men are nebbishes or wise men, shylocks or scholars, concave-chested specimens with two left feet who walked to Hitler's ovens rather than resist their fate. The stereotype is expressed in seventeenth-century European monographs and twenty-first-century online Haiku: "Seven-foot Jews/in the NBA slamdunking!/ My alarm clock rings." Early twentieth-century Zionist leaders advocated a new "muscular Judaism" to counter such bias. This did not deter Henry Ford, America's best-known anti-Semite, who declared in 1921: "Jews are not sportsmen. Whether this is due to their physical lethargy, their dislike of unnecessary physical action, or their serious cast of mind, others may decide. . . . It may be a defect in their character, or it may not; it is nevertheless a fact which discriminating Jews unhesitatingly acknowledge."

In this regard, two incidents from the 1965 season are particularly revealing. On May 26, Koufax faced the Cardinals and his nemesis, Lou Brock, in Los Angeles. In the first inning, Brock led off with a bunt single, stole second, stole third, and scored on a sacrifice fly. In the dugout, Drysdale told rookie Jim Lefebvre: "Frenchie, I feel sorry for that man."

When Brock came up again in the third, Koufax hit him hard and with intent. "So darned hard that the ball went in and spun around in the meat for a while and then dropped," catcher Jeff Torborg said.

It was the first time, the only time, Koufax threw at a batter purposefully. He didn't brag about it. He didn't tell anyone he was going to do it. He didn't acknowledge it until long after his career had ended. "I don't regret it," he told fans more than a quarter century later. "I do regret that I allowed myself to get so mad."

You could hear it all over the stadium. In the Cardinals' dugout, it sounded like "a thud that had a crack in it," outfielder Mike Shannon said. Other Cardinal players insist Brock was hurt doing the limbo prior to the game. Drysdale would remember, wrongly, Brock collapsing in the base-path and being carried off the field, a story he loved to tell because for once Koufax wasn't perfect. In fact, Brock stayed in the game and promptly stole second. The morning papers reported the incident in passing, noting that Brock left in the fifth inning and that X rays were negative. He appeared only once in the next five days, as a pinch runner.

Three months later, the simmering violence of a savage summer erupted in Candlestick Park. Koufax was pitching for the Dodgers; Marichal for the Giants. It had been a season of enmity between the two teams, a series fraught with knockdown pitches and threats. On August 22, bad blood turned to spilled blood. Marichal, practiced in the art of intimidation, had already decked Fairly and Wills. Roseboro was equally adept in the subtleties of retribution. When Marichal came to the plate, Roseboro purposefully allowed Koufax's 1-and-2 pitch to drop at his feet, whizzing the return throw just east of Marichal's ear.

Marichal raised the stakes when he lifted his bat and cracked it over Roseboro's head, leaving a two-inch gash in his skull and an enduring dent in baseball's beatific reputation. Koufax and Mays rushed to intervene. Koufax tried to grab the bat. The anguish was visible on his face as he raised his hand to prevent another blow. Mays dragged Roseboro away, stanching the blood and the violence, assuring him the wound wasn't as bad as it seemed. Shag Crawford, the home plate umpire, still refuses to talk about it. (Roseboro sued Marichal for $110,000, yet another unwelcome harbinger of the modern age. Nine years later, the suit was settled out of court and later still they became friends. Roseboro was one of the first people Marichal called when he was elected to the Hall of Fame.)

In the telling and retelling of the tale, Koufax, the pacifist, allows Roseboro, the tough black enforcer, to take care of business. "We had talked about it on the bench," Roseboro said. "I told him, 'I'll take care of it, knock him down behind the plate.'" Which is true as far as it goes. What

Roseboro's account leaves out, others who heard the dugout conversation say, is that Koufax prefaced his remarks with the pertinent question: "Who do you want me to get?" Also, the dugouts had been warned by Crawford. A knockdown would have resulted in Koufax's suspension in the middle of the pennant race.

The legend, as handed down, reinforced the already established notion that Koufax wouldn't knock anyone on his ass, wouldn't protect his players. In the machismo-driven world of professional athletics, this was not a compliment. It also wasn't true. Koufax believed in protecting his players; he just didn't believe in throwing at someone he couldn't get out. In 1962, when Bill Skowron was still a Yankee, he made Marichal look bad in the world series. Next season, Moose was a Dodger. "First time up, he low-bridged me," Skowron said. "I'm hitting like two-twenty. I go back to first base. Willie Mays comes up. Sandy threw one up tight and Willie's cap flew off. They said Sandy didn't throw at anyone, but he protected his players. I blew him a kiss."

Nor did he disdain throwing inside. "The art of pitching is instilling fear," he always said. Wise batsmen avoided crowding his plate. Shannon still regrets a game-winning two-run home run he hit off Koufax in 1966—and the inside fastball he saw next time up. "I think you pissed the big Jew off," Roseboro told him.

When, on September 9, 1965, Major League Baseball announced that the World Series would open on October 6 in the American League city, it wasn't at all clear that the Dodgers would be in it. But as they won eighteen of their last twenty-two games, headlines began to appear: "Koufax Problem: Jewish Holiday." Koufax told reporters, lightly, "I'm praying for rain." He also said he would consult the rabbis (as Greenberg had done) to discuss a dispensation. He was joking. He never intended to pitch on Yom Kippur. He never had.

Twice, in the fall of 1960 and 1961, manager Walter Alston scheduled him to pitch on Jewish holidays. An hour after sundown marks the end of holiday observances in the Jewish faith. On September 20, 1961, after sundown, Koufax went to the mound and beat the Cubs 3-2 in thirteen innings, striking out fifteen. Soon after, a fan sent Alston a 1962 calendar marked with all the Jewish holidays. From then on, the manager made sure to consult Danny Goodman, director of advertising and novelties, before making out his starting rotation.

Far from being distraught over Koufax's willingness to pitch that evening—even if it meant missing afternoon services—Jewish authors of present-day online encomiums salute his toughness. Imagine pitching thirteen innings without eating or drinking! His observance of the fast is assumed without a shred of documentary evidence.

Koufax was presumptively devout. Teammates still testify to the strength of his faith. "Like Muhammad Ali's," Lou Johnson said. "His Jewish belief was bigger than the game." How else could they understand his decision not to pitch on Yom Kippur except as a reflection of compelling belief? Why else would anyone voluntarily skip the World Series? Others needled him about getting religion only after he got famous. "I used to jokingly say that Sandy didn't become Jewish until he had his first great years," Stan Williams said.

Their assumptions were rooted in ignorance. In fact, like Greenberg, Koufax was neither a devout nor a practicing Jew. "His Jewishness has nothing to do with whether he wears a yarmulke every day," Fred Wilpon said. "And I will tell you this—he is very Jewish. He is a Jewish being. And unlike most of us who aren't very religious, he is very Jewish in his thinking because he's very New York in his thinking and his background."

It's a sensibility. To wit: one night in Philadelphia, Koufax and the Sherry brothers went out for Chinese food. They got in a cab and told the driver to take them to a good place. Norm Sherry remembers: "The cab pulls up at a restaurant and Koufax says, 'This is not where I want to eat.' So, the cabbie takes them to another and another and another. Finally, Koufax says, 'This is okay.' Larry says, 'What the hell is the difference?' Koufax says, 'You don't go to a Chinese restaurant unless it has an awning like they have in New York. It's gotta have an awning.'"

The Jewish boys from Southern California didn't get the humor.

Choosing not to work on Yom Kippur was not a difficult decision. It's what Jews do. His roommate, Tracewski, doesn't remember him agonizing over it. "It was a given with him. So, you pitch a day late. Big schmeer." And, as Osteen said, "It wasn't a real bad choice having Drysdale."

Drysdale started in his place and got hammered. The score was 7–1 when Alston came to the mound to relieve him. "Hey, skip, bet you wish I was Jewish today, too," Drysdale said. For Jews, the loss was a win. If Big D could joke about being one of the Chosen People, that was already something, a tacit acknowledgment of their acceptance into the mainstream. *Shtetl*, farewell.

Koufax started and lost game two. The flight back to Los Angeles was difficult, especially for Osteen, who was scheduled to start game three. He sat on the aisle, and every coach and player walking by made sure to touch his left shoulder. With each reassuring pat and each pat rejoinder— "You'll get 'em!'"—his shoulder got tighter. Koufax and Drysdale loosened everyone up with humor. "Don looks at Sandy and goes, 'Well, we sure got ourselves in a hell of a mess, didn't we?'" Jim Lefebvre said. "And they started laughing."

The Dodgers won three straight in Los Angeles—Osteen, Drysdale, and

Koufax outdid themselves and each other. In the final home game of the series, Koufax shut out the Twins, 7–0. After the game, Koufax cheerfully told Scully, "I feel like I'm a hundred years old."

The Dodgers needed only one more win but they needed to go back to Minnesota to get it. They were confident. Lou Johnson packed enough clothes for a one-day business trip. The Dodgers checked out of the team hotel the morning before game six was played. Osteen lost, forcing management to scramble for rooms and Alston to make a difficult decision. Parker, the first baseman, went into the bathroom and cried. Alston summoned his coaches—Preston Gomez, Danny Ozark, Lefty Phillips—to a gloomy tribunal. Drysdale was the logical choice to pitch game seven. It was his turn in the rotation. He would be pitching on a full three days' rest; Koufax on two.

The players were showering; no one had popped a beer. All three coaches put their heads between their knees when Alston broached the question. Ozark recalled the scene. "'Jeez,' Lefty Phillips says, 'Koufax does real well against them, maybe he can go.' Alston says, 'Who's gonna ask him?' Everyone got laryngitis. Me, the big dumb Polack says, 'I'll do it.' I find out later on that there were differences between him and Alston. They may have been going back to '57. I don't think he could overlook what happened. It was his career. They held him back."

His teammates knew how he felt. "He felt he always had something to prove with Walter Alston," Ron Perranoski said. "He wasn't used when he was young and when he was used he wasn't trusted. He always had this thing in the back of his mind about the way he was treated, that he didn't get a chance. He knew what he was made of, what he was capable of."

When Ozark approached him at his locker at Metropolitan Stadium on the eve of the seventh game of the 1965 World Series, Koufax told him, "I'm okay for tomorrow." It would be his third start in eight days. "He didn't want to be known as a person who couldn't have the strength and the ability to take the ball on two days' rest," Wilpon said. He did so eight times in his career, winning six; three were complete-game wins with a combined total of thirty-five strikeouts. He never lasted less than seven innings. How much, if at all, this represented for him a refutation of stereotype is unknowable. How much it represented a retort to early doubters is easier to guess. But it spoke volumes to the Jewish community.

Alston told Mel Durslag, the Los Angeles writer, it was the hardest decision he ever made as a manager. Drysdale subsequently made it easier by volunteering to go to the bullpen. "He was worried about Drysdale's feelings and afraid of saying something anti-Semitic," Durslag recalled. "He was an upright guy, not a loose guy. People intimated—he was a farmer from the middle of Ohio—that he might have been anti-Semitic. Maybe he felt if he didn't give it to Koufax, he'd look anti-Semitic."

The heart of bias is as intangible as it is corrosive. When he was interviewed by Charley Steiner for ESPN's *Sports Century* series, Koufax was asked, off camera, whether he believed anti-Semitism played a part in the way he was used early in his career. "I don't even want to think about that," Koufax replied. It violates his code of honor to argue with the dead or the past. He has never addressed the issue publicly and he won't. But as Steiner, now the voice of the Yankees, says, "When he says he hasn't thought about something, you know he's thought about it a lot."

Among his black teammates a degree of bias was presumed. Like Ozark, they noticed who pitched on Opening Day, whose face appeared on year-books and press guides and newspapers. "Don was blond and blue-eyed and more marketable as far as being the Dodger image," Wills said. "Sandy was second fiddle. All the black players felt that. Don was the poster boy; it was always Don and Sandy. We knew it was Sandy and Don."

Rumors started flying on the bus on the way back to the hotel. Coaches, rookies, other members of the pitching staff all weighed in. Opinion was unanimous. "You don't have to ask our ball club, 'Who do you want to see pitch?'" said Gomez. "The whole world is going to say, 'Give the ball to the Jew.'"

Wills: "We might not have gone on the field if he hadn't."

Koufax and Drysdale arrived at the ballpark the next morning unshaved—a signal that neither knew the skipper's decision. In fact, it was a ruse. Koufax knew but wasn't supposed to tell anyone, not even his roommate, Trixie. Alston announced his decision at a team meeting before the game, explaining with soothing if impersonal logic why he had chosen Koufax. "He says, 'We're going to start the left-hander,'" Tracewski remembered. "'After that we have Drysdale in the bullpen, and if we need it we'll finish off with Perranoski. And if that's not good enough, we are in trouble.'

"It was a very quiet meeting and it was a very quick meeting and Sandy said, 'He called me the left-hander,'" Tracewski said. "He felt he should have called him by his name."

Watching the videotape of the seventh game of the 1965 World Series is like looking at a piece of American folk art. There is an innocence about the broadcast as primitive as the production values. There were marching bands and decorous cheerleaders, skinny ties and vendors selling straw boaters to polite Minnesota fans. "Not a smokestack crowd," as infielder Frank Quilici described them. "Nice." The Twins' front office sat Dodger wives behind home plate. In Los Angeles, the Twins' wives were given seats way out in right field. Between innings, go-go dancers did a decorous frug, and Gillette hawked a new super stainless-steel blade with "miracle edges" to a clean-shaven nation. Harry Coyle, the director, had only a couple of cameras to work with, and a batboy who kept wandering into the frame. The narration is uncluttered and understated, so quiet you can hear the sound of an airplane buzzing the outfield. On the pregame show, Vin Scully and Ray Scott talked about the pitching matchup: Sandy Koufax and Jim Kaat for the third time. No one mentioned Yom Kippur. Today, ESPN would be doing man-on-the-street interviews at the Wailing Wall.

The broadcast is a staple of *Classic Sports* television. Sam Mele, the Twins' manager, has seen it nine, maybe ten times. "Lost every goddamn game," he says. He, too, remembers the quiet. "They normally weren't that quiet," Mele said. "I think everybody could sense—even my bench and me—that it's Koufax out there. You know what I mean? You can't get too excited because this guy's going to knock the jubilance out of you, you know?"

That morning a thunderstorm of biblical proportions inundated the Twin Cities. Helicopters were brought in to dry the field. By game time, the skies had cleared. Temperatures were in the fifties. Osteen, who had lost game six, went down to the bullpen to see if he could help out, standing in an imaginary batter's box so that Koufax would have someone to throw to. Osteen had never seen his curve from that vantage point before. He remembers thinking, so that's why they can't hit it.

Koufax was pitching on fumes. When he walked two batters in the first inning, Drysdale got up in the bullpen. He was a two-pitch pitcher without a second pitch. Roseboro kept calling for the curve; Koufax kept shaking him off. Finally, Roseboro went to the mound for a conversation. For the first time, Koufax acknowledged how bad his elbow was. "He said, 'Rosie, my arm's not right. My arm's sore.' I said, 'What'll we do, kid?' He said, 'Fuck it, we'll blow 'em away.'"

The game was scoreless when Johnson came to bat in the fourth inning. He had called his mother before the game, vowing, "I'm going to do something today, Ma. I told Sandy I was gonna get him a run."

He kept his promise, hitting Kaat's fastball long and deep to left field. It was curving foul when the foul pole got in its way. Home run! Johnson applauded as he rounded the bases. The rest of the stadium was so quiet Tracewski could hear Johnson's footsteps as he came around third. "So quiet," Johnson said, "you could hear a cat pissing on cotton."

The crowd remained nicely catatonic until the bottom of the fifth. Quilici, the Twins' second baseman, doubled, and the next batter walked. With one out, Zoilo Versailles hit a ball hard down the third-base line. It was past Junior Gilliam when he realized it was in his glove. Somehow he beat Quilici to the bag. In the press box, the game was officially declared over.

The afternoon sun waned. Koufax pitched from the shadows. His royal blue sweatshirt appeared navy; his beard darkened inning by the inning. His mouth hung open after every pitch. Drysdale got up in the bullpen again. Scully wondered aloud how far a man could go with only one pitch. "Everybody sat there with their mouths open," Ozark said. "He pitched like it was going to be his last breath."

In the ninth inning, the 360th of his season, Koufax faced the heart of the Minnesota order: Tony Oliva, Harmon Killebrew, Earl Battey, and Bob Allison, a two-time batting champion, a six-time home-run leader, a four-time All-Star, and a onetime Rookie of the Year. With one out, Killebrew singled sharply to left, the Twins' third hit of the game. Battey came to the plate. One swing, he thought, and I could be the world series MVP! By the time the words formed a sentence in his brain, the umpire had signaled, "Strike three."

Up to the plate strode Allison, a formidable slugger whose two-run home run off Osteen had forced the seventh game. He fouled off the first pitch and looked at two others for balls and then swung at the next. "It's two and two," announcer Ray Scott informed the television audience. "Koufax is reaching back. Every time he's had to reach back, he's found what he needed."

Killebrew watched from first base as Allison swung through strike three for the final out of the series. "I told Bob, 'If you'd have swung at the ball as hard as you swung at the ground after you struck out, you might have hit it.'"

It was his second shutout in four days, his twenty-ninth complete game of the season. The locker room was joyously subdued, partly because a phalanx of sportswriters had gotten stuck between floors in the press elevator and partly because everyone was so drained. Scully wrapped an arm protectively around Koufax, the bright light of live television highlighting his fatigue. "Here's the fella who gave the Dodgers the championship. Sandy, in Los Angeles, when you pitched a seven-nothing shutout, you were quoted as saying, 'I feel like I'm a hundred years old! So today, Sandy, how do you feel?'"

Koufax was too tired to do anything but smile and tell the truth. Viewers at home saw a grin so wide his dimples threatened to implode. "Well, Vinnie, I feel like I'm a hundred and one. I'm just glad it's over and I don't have to do this again for four whole months."

Time devoted a page in its next issue to baseball, a cut-and-paste story cobbled together from Series coverage, recycled quotes, and McWhirter's unused file. The tone was decidedly "cool"—grudgingly appreciative at best. It got right to the point: "Just because a man does his job better than anybody else doesn't mean that he has to take it seriously—or even like it."

And it continued: "Alone among ballplayers, Koufax is an anti-athlete who suffers so little from pride that he does not even possess a photograph of himself. TV and radio interviewers have learned to be careful with personal questions—or risk a string of billingsgate designed to ruin their tapes."

To his teammates, even to his few close friends, Koufax's aloofness is often downright annoying. "Imagine," says Dodger catcher John Roseboro, "being good-looking, well off, single—and still be so cool. I know guys who would be raising all kinds of hell on those stakes." Dodger vice president Fresco Thompson considers him a heretic. "I don't think he likes baseball," mutters Thompson. "What kind of a line is he drawing anyway—between himself and the world, between himself and the team?"

In his autobiography Koufax wrote an impassioned fourteen-page protest against the myth of his alleged anti-athleticism.

"I have nothing against myths. But there is one myth that has been building through the years that I would just as soon bury without any particular honors: the myth of Sandy Koufax, the anti-athlete. The way this fantasy goes, I am really a sort of dreamy intellectual who was lured out of college by a bonus in the flush of my youth and have forever after regretted—and even resented—the life of fame and fortune that has been forced upon me."

Mordecai Richler reviewed the book in the November 1966 issue of *Commentary* magazine. The fact of the review by the distinguished Jewish author in the distinguished journal of Jewish thought was testimony to Koufax's standing among his people, especially the literary intelligentsia. The review was scathing, damning the effort as a "very bush-league performance, thin, cliché-ridden." In short, a typical ghostwritten sports autobiography. (Had Richler read more closely he might have heard an authentic voice in the opening cri de coeur.)

Getting to the heart of the matter, Richler wrote: "Anti-Semitism takes many subtle shapes and the deprecating story one reads again and again, most memorably recorded in *Time,* is that Sandy Koufax is actually something of an intellectual. He doesn't mix. Though he is the highest-paid player in the history of the game, improving enormously on Lipman E. Pike's $20 a week, he considers himself above it."

Then he goes further: "In fact, looked at one way, Koufax's autobiography can be seen as a sad effort at self-vindication, a forced attempt to prove once and for all that he is the same as anybody else. Possibly, Koufax protests too much." In denying his putative intellectualism, Richler seemed to be saying, Koufax was denying an essential part of his Jewish-ness. Which no doubt accounted for the deluge of letters to *Commentary's* editors accusing Richler of being anti-Semitic.

The significance of Koufax's decision has been debated ever since in synagogues and at dinner tables, by Talmudic scholars and baseball play-ers. How much did he change the way Jews are perceived? How much did he change the way Jews perceive themselves? "He gave little Jewish boys some hope," said pitcher Steve Stone, who was one of them. "The series went seven games instead of four," said general manager Buzzie Bavasi. "I always told him, 'You made Walter O'Malley a million dollars.'"

Rabbi Lustig, who as a boy wired a transistor radio to his seven-year-old person and took the World Series into the synagogue, understands why Koufax is hardwired into the psyche of the American Jewish com-munity and his congregation—why grown men are transformed by putting on Koufax's jersey. The decision not to pitch was a transforming event, providing the catalyst for an unknown number of lawyers and Little Lea-guers to acknowledge and honor their religion in like kind. Koufax made them brave. By refusing to pitch, he both reinforced Jewish pride and en-hanced the sense of belonging—a feat as prodigious as any he accom-plished on the field.

"The Six-Day War was important to Zionism," Lustig said. "It changed the image of the Jew in the world. He could be a true soldier. The World Series was important to the whole community. What could be so Ameri-can? We had finally made it. We had earned the right to be as interested in baseball as in our Jewish identity."

Koufax refused to be a Jew's Jew or a gentile's Jew. He may have been different but he refused to be anything other than himself. In the Talmud, it is written that some attain eternal life with a single act. On Yom Kip-pur, 5726, a baseball immortal became a Jewish icon.

RELIGIOUS
EDUCATION
AND PRACTICE

WHO IS AN EDUCATED JEW?

Paula E. Hyman

THERE HAS BEEN no consensus on the issue of "Who is an educated Jew?" for more than two hundred years. If one were to have posed the question in 1750, say in Poland, the answer would have been obvious. The educated Jew was a mature male who had devoted his life to talmudic study, debating fine points of *halakha* in *yeshiva* and *beit midrash*. He was familiar with all of the classic rabbinic texts and their commentaries, the *rishonim* and the *aharonim*, and the languages in which they were written, Hebrew and Aramaic, in addition to the Jewish vernacular that he spoke—in Poland, Yiddish, of course. No women were given such an education because the teaching of classical religious texts in Hebrew to women was neither halakhically nor socially legitimated; it was also irrelevant to their roles within the family and society. While regional variations in learning styles and in the details of the curriculum existed, the substance of what educated Jews should know was widely shared in the Jewish world.

That shared commitment to a curriculum, and therefore to a vision of Jewish knowledge, was irretrievably disrupted with the social and political changes that occurred at the end of the eighteenth century. The Western states' desire to reshape the socioeconomic and cultural configuration of their Jewish populations, and the emergence of a cohort of Jewish intellectuals and businessmen who were eager to respond to the opportunities that integration into the larger society (the *maskilim*) seemed to promise, led to a sharp dissent from the consensus about Jewish learning that had prevailed, at least within Ashkenazi communities in Europe. For a growing number of Jews, the *talmid hokhm* was no longer the model of the educated Jew.

Instead, modernizing educated Jews, following the model set by the *maskilim,* saw Western culture as an essential component of their consciousness and created a canon that placed secular education at the fore. They expected educated Jews to be at home culturally in both traditional Jewish and secular learning. A good example is the scarcely known Puah Rakovsky, who was an educator and director of a girls' school in Warsaw that taught Hebrew and secular studies, a translator, and a Zionist and feminist activist. Born in Poland in 1865 to a traditional family, she lost her faith as an adolescent and was assertively secular. Still, her Yiddish memoirs are replete with allusions in Hebrew to biblical and midrashic sources, and she was convinced that her Jewish learning was the source of her values. Because she witnessed growing indifference to Jewish culture among youth in the years before World War I, Rakovsky was able to discern that the goal of modern Jewish education had to be transformed from the "regeneration" of Jews under the influence of secular knowledge to the "rejudaization" of Jews bereft of Jewish knowledge.

Modernity fractured Jewish experience, destroying the hegemony of rabbinic Judaism and the authority of traditional Jewish elites. Contemporary currents of thought like postmodernism and multiculturalism have challenged virtually all certainties and shaken all canons. No canon is fixed, and all guardians of cultural transmission are required to make hard choices. We are fortunate that the Jewish canon has always been a relatively open one, for the traditional Jewish system of interpretation of classical texts has provided a mechanism for ongoing revision. The development of interpretive strategies, in midrash, for example, as literary scholars have argued, demonstrates a way to recover oppositional strands within traditional texts. Insofar as we focus on the spaces for debate and contestation within the traditional Jewish canon, we acknowledge the need for, and sustain the possibility of, multiple cultural expressions for the diverse people that we are. Although the term "open canon" sounds like an oxymoron, it simply reflects the recognition that every canon is constructed and merits a healthy combination of respect and skepticism and regular revision if it is to speak to its intended audience. A truly "open canon" affords opportunities for choice and for the inclusion of ongoing cultural creativity.

Once we acknowledge that unity is neither possible nor desirable, though, we must ask what models of educated Jews we seek to promote.

What, if anything, will educated Jews of different *paideias* (educational visions and curricula in the broadest sense) share?

I can think of three prerequisites—necessary but not sufficient—for all educated Jews: the Hebrew language (in all its variants, from the Bible to the present—not just street Hebrew); an acceptance of biblical and rabbinic texts as one's own; and a general knowledge of Jewish history. Hebrew is an essential tool for reading much of what Jewish culture has produced. But it is more than a tool. Without Hebrew there is no visceral, as distinct from intellectual, connection to Jewish creativity across time and space. Accepting Tanakh and rabbinic texts as one's own does not necessitate ascribing to them sacredness or religious authority. But it does necessitate grappling with their meaning and their role in world culture as w~~ll~~ as Jewish culture and in the choices that contemporary Jews make. ~~...~~dge of the broad outlines of Jewish history enables us to un-~~...~~l and intellectual contexts in which Jewish culture has

~~...~~riculum is only the first step in becoming Jew-~~...~~wish canon in the twenty-first century draws ~~...~~genres. It must embrace all the Jewish cultural ~~...~~turies—that is, the different forms that Jews ~~...~~of their existence as Jews. Secular forms in ~~...~~terature, memoirs, folklore, film, and the ~~...~~ssed as lacking in cultural significance.

~~...~~ that educated Jews would share a core ~~...~~foundational texts, and knowledge of ~~...~~ld then follow a multiple-track model ~~...~~ng, according to their own interests, ~~...~~l expression than is commonly con-~~...~~ge." Although biblical and rabbinic texts would ~~...~~ Jewish knowledge, further learning would not privilege ~~...~~ngle genre of cultural production or any single text.

Changes within the past generation necessitate a rethinking of Jewish learning as thorough as the *Haskalah* critique of two centuries ago. While the majority of Jews have acquired secular education, as *maskilim* advocated, they have not always applied their knowledge to Judaism or Jewish culture. I am not referring here to the willful ignorance of what modern scholarly inquiry has to say about classical Jewish texts. Rather, I am speaking about the failure of most Jews who consider themselves Jewishly educated to contend with recent trends in studies of culture.

Thanks to the work of theorists in anthropology, history, and gender studies, it is widely acknowledged today that culture cannot be subsumed in the writings of an elite. However varied those writings, and however weighty, they reflect the values and considered opinions of one segment of society alone. "Says who?" is an essential question when studying any text. As we have learned from multiculturalism, the ways in which silent or silenced, generally subordinate, groups within society conferred meaning on their own lives and accepted or resisted the values promulgated by elites are part of cultural history. That is as true of Jews as of other groups.

Popular Jewish culture has always existed, and we must be willing to look for it and to reflect on its relation to the elite culture that we have considered the sum total of Judaism and of Jewish cultural creativity. Familiarity with the varieties of Jewish culture instills in Jews a recognition that Jewish culture is not fixed or reified, nor limited to one social segment of the Jewish people. Rather, it is malleable and ever changing, shaped by the interaction of internal forces and external circumstances, and created by Jews through a combination of consciousness and behavior.

The multicultural model, which disputes the very idea of canon (but may also accept the concept of an open canon) and pays heed to the voices that resist and subvert authority, appears quite suitable to the diversity of Jewish patterns of behavior and thought in a post-emancipation world. It mandates willingness to acknowledge the multiplicity of Jewish voices and accept their authenticity. The multicultural model is particularly appropriate to the ambiguous position of Jews in Diaspora, who create Jewish culture in the space between being a part of the larger society and apart from it (or, in the words of a recent book, insider/outsiders). The adoption of a multicultural stance, however, requires a recognition of the diversity of Jewish life as a value rather than an unfortunate fact; that is, it requires a conversion of diversity into pluralism.

Living in a multicultural society, we have the opportunity and the obligation to shape a fluid Jewish canon for our own time and for the future. Engaged with the richness of the culture we have inherited, which links us with Jews of other times and places, we must be sensitive as well to the incompleteness of our legacy, to the voices that have been suppressed (women's and others) and to the interpretations that have lacked authority. The legacy of our generation may well be a postmodern hermeneutics of suspicion and a recognition that a diverse people requires cultural diversity.

RABBINICAL EDUCATION FOR THE TWENTY-FIRST CENTURY

Lewis D. Solomon

TODAY, AMERICAN JEWS ARE disappearing from Judaism in massive numbers—through intermarriage, broken or blended families, and indifference. Although increasingly alienated from Judaism, they still ache in their souls for spiritual guidance and healing.

At the same time, there is a growing shortage of congregational rabbis across the United States, due to greater demand. More congregations feel the need for a second (or perhaps a third) rabbi to serve different groups within their walls. Privacy and family time constraints increasingly make full-time pulpits unattractive. New positions have also opened for rabbis in community centers and organizations, college campuses, and a variety of chaplaincies. Some leaders, such as Rabbi Eric H. Yoffie, president of the Union of American Hebrew Congregations, describe the current shortage problem—one that will continue for most of this decade—as "exceedingly serious."

The four major Jewish denominations have established seminaries (or graduate academies) that not only serve as gatekeepers for admission and ordination but also provide a centralized placement system. Not unexpectedly, the denominations express a concern, as evidenced by one responsum issued by the Central Conference of American Rabbis, that "the ordination of students by individual rabbis whose programs of study are not supervised by any responsible authority endangers the maintenance of any and all standards of educational excellence." Similar to other professional associations intent on credentialing, the established denominations want to restrict membership in the rabbinate to those meeting proper educational standards, at least as they see them.

Before discussing the course of study a modern rabbinical seminary should offer and the requisite standards for rabbinic ordination, three questions must be considered: (1) Who are the customers of Judaism in the United States, and what do they value? (2) What functions do (and should) rabbis perform? (3) Who are the prospective rabbinical students?

Who Are the Customers, and What Do They Value?

Religion has become far less of a guiding force in the life of most American Jews. Many consider Judaism and Jewish observances peripheral to their lives except for the High Holidays, Passover seders, bar/bat mitzvahs, and funerals. Judaism competes with other institutions and organizations for their time, attention, and financial support. They have other leisure-time options. They have discovered other ways of finding meaning, fulfillment, and happiness in life from twelve-step programs to Eastern religions.

Today's Jews live outside the halachic mindset of traditional Judaism, with its multitude of rules, regulations, and directives, to be followed along with, not unexpectedly, exceptions and compromises. They have moved away from a commitment to Jewish law and its centrality to life. Textual interpretation and the halacha do not interest them. Despite the arduous efforts of rabbis, synagogues, and adult education organizations, most American Jews do not read the Torah, the Talmud, or legal codes to arrive at rules and ethical standards for daily living or to help them meet life's challenges. They do not view the Hebrew Bible as the word of God. Thus, they do not look to the Torah (and to its lifelong study) as the foundation of life. They do not feel "commanded" by God to perform various ritual acts. They do not take seriously the heart of the Jewish tradition, notably, observance of the dietary laws and Shabbat. They do not attach much importance to studying Hebrew. Exploration and experience, not doctrine and ritual, characterize most contemporary American Jews.

Moving beyond a past-oriented, rather pedantic interpretation and dissection of Jewish texts—intellectual puzzles for those who like these sorts of things—how can rabbis bring Judaism to those alienated by current approaches and to the unaffiliated, who evidence a negative attitude to synagogue participation and affiliation? If not ritual and law, how can we make Judaism become meaningful to more lives?

Today's Jews hunger for spirituality. Instead of looking back to more traditional forms of rituals and observances—to the dietary laws and the

Sabbath, to more and more Hebrew in group worship services and at life cycle events, and to ever greater reliance on the Torah as an authoritative document for the Jewish people—they want Judaism to provide a framework to give meaning and purpose to their lives. They ask why is each of us here, they seek help in facing life's challenges for which they are otherwise unable to cope, and, ultimately, they must face the contemplation of their own mortality. Realizing that something is missing in their lives, they search for guidance in their own spiritual quest and for assistance in developing their relationship with God, including an image of the Eternal as a loving, creative Presence.

The Role of the Modern Rabbi

In the twenty-first century, rabbis will continue to perform a variety of functions. They will preach and lead public worship services and ritual ceremonies as well as officiate at life cycle events—interfaith weddings, naming ceremonies, and funerals. They will provide pastoral counseling, visiting the sick, and comforting the bereaved. They will also teach, facilitate meetings, and administer organizations. However, most will not be expected to function as textual scholars or religious authorities for obedient throngs who will follow their halachic prescriptions. They will not serve as legal decision makers relying on Jewish law—the Talmud, legal codes, commentaries, and responsa.

To meet their spiritual hunger and desire for spiritual insight, contemporary Jews want a rabbi, in whatever capacity he or she serves them, to function as their spiritual guide and counselor, struggling with them as a co-seeker, creatively and constructively using the Jewish tradition and its wisdom to provide a direction for life's journey. They want rabbis who will help them on their way to faith and to God; to provide guidance to facilitate a more meaningful and purposeful life, thereby enabling them to achieve their fullest potential and act out of a sense of concern for and responsibility to their neighbors and fellow citizens; to partner with God in repairing our shattered planet and bringing us nearer to the messianic era; and to begin to fathom the existence of evil, pain, and suffering in the world.

They want help with what I call Spiritual Judaism, namely, how to understand and apply the enduring virtues of the Jewish tradition—both personal (self-esteem, humility, joy, optimism, inner peace, serenity, and equanimity) and interpersonal (love, compassion, forgiveness, and truthfulness)—to the ups and downs of daily living, and to meet life's vicissitudes, including the despair arising from death and dying, bereavement and grief, serious and chronic illness, the tragedies of divorce as well as business and career reversals. Those searching for a Jewish anchor in a secular world also need assistance with spiritual tools, such as personal prayer, meditation, relaxation techniques, and imagery, for self-discovery, spiritual development, and transformation, to facilitate healing, which will thereby enable them to attain a wholeness of mind-body-spirit.

The modern rabbi must confront contemporary Jewish institutional arrangements. Many seekers need the support of inclusive communities to relate the insights of Spiritual Judaism to the challenges of everyday life. In the future, Jewish spiritual centers may replace the urban synagogue-cathedral, the suburban temple complex, or the community center as the central institution for Jewish communal life. These spiritual centers may become the primary entry point to Jewish education, involvement, and commitment. Along with spirituality, Jews search for community—human connectedness in a world marked by loneliness and isolation. They want small groups, perhaps demarcated by age, marital status, or special interests, in which they can become family for each other.

Beyond offering group worship; child, teen, and adult education; and holiday and life cycle celebrations rooted in a spiritual approach to Judaism, this new institutional model will creatively act to build nurturing communities of people and meet their spiritual needs. It will serve as the vehicle to teach people about Spiritual Judaism, offering the tools to deal with the stresses and complexities of life.

Modern rabbis serving at such centers will address the full range of seekers' personal and interpersonal needs through one-on-one and group counseling and instruction in virtues and the spiritual techniques for transformation. As spiritual guides and facilitators, modern rabbis will assist in the search for meaning and personal renewal through life development and marriage enrichment seminars; they will deal with addiction, abuse, grief, and divorce recovery, recognizing that many currently do not find worship services inspiring or edifying; for those interested in group worship, these centers will pioneer in creative liturgy and music—contemporary, authentic, and accessible—for the High Holidays (as well as monthly services throughout the year, healing services designed to unite and promote the wholeness of body-mind-spirit) and meaningful haggadahs for home Passover seders. They will also reevaluate current bar/bat mitzvah practices. In short, these Jewish spiritual centers will provide new communities of healing, of openness, and of trust.

Whether or not a modern rabbi operates out of a spiritual center (or a more traditional congregation), he or she will extend the insights of Judaism to all open-minded spiritual seekers. As spiritual guide and counselor, the modern rabbi will help give meaning and purpose to lives, addressing spiritual dilemmas—identity struggles, personal problems, and questions of faith—and aiding seekers in finding the moments that reshape one's earthly existence. As a co-seeker, the modern rabbi will empower and inspire others in their quest for meaning and understanding with life's "big questions."

Who Wants to Serve as a Modern Rabbi? Today's Rabbinic Students

Increasingly, rabbinic students are midlife individuals, not twenty-somethings. They have struggled with life and its challenges; they have faced life's losses. They yearn for a second, more meaningful career—as a full-time or part-time rabbi. They bring to the seminary valuable professional and business skills as well as significant life experiences and perspectives (and their accumulated Jewish knowledge). They are sensitive to others' struggles and their spiritual journeys. They often are not searching for a denominational credential as a basis for future employment, that is, to gain a congregational pulpit, or to serve in a "movement" or an organization.

The Modern Rabbinical Seminary and Its Course of Study

The modern seminary as a professional school for the training of rabbis needs to deal with these individuals entering the rabbinate as a second (or perhaps even a third) career. They will study on a part-time basis, generally through distance learning programs facilitating study many miles removed from the seminary's physical location and using traditional print materials and electronic technologies. Many will readily gravitate to self-study. Two questions then come to the fore: (1) Who are candidates for admission and ordination? (2) What should a modern rabbi's course of study look like; more specifically, what is the discrete body of knowledge to be mastered, what is the particular set of skills to be learned, and how should the seminary integrate the academic, the conceptual, and the intellectual with the practical, the emotional, and the spiritual?

Besides maturity (often evidenced by one's age and life experiences, but not always), emotional stability, and spiritual depth, a seminary in admitting a student (and as a prerequisite to ordination) must assess his or her character, a rather intangible and subjective inquiry. Character assessment includes level of self-esteem, humility, love, compassion, patience for and sensitivity to others, inner strength, leadership ability, and potential. Also: Does the student relate well to people (seeing the good in others) and have the ability to get along well with others? Is he or she the kind of person one would look to as a spiritual guide and counselor? What is his or her readiness to serve the needs of the Jewish people and other spiritual seekers? In short, is he or she a *mentsch?*

Considerable curricular flexibility ought to exist in a seminary training modern rabbis. The midlife students come from different backgrounds (Jewish and secular). They have diverse interests and career aspirations. Some want the congregational life of a "general practice" rabbi, a Jack or Jill of all trades. Others will opt to serve as specialists, for instance, as spiritual counselors, chaplains, or educators. They come with various personal hurts inflicted upon them and losses they have experienced, as well as challenges they have faced and overcome. They have different intellectual, personal, and professional abilities. To facilitate the development of an individual's unique personal rabbinical style, one size, one type of education, does not fit in. There is a need for more flexible, individualized programs. What, then, are the educational requisites for a modern rabbi in order to meet the needs of twenty-first-century Jews and other spiritual seekers?

Looking to develop rabbis expert in Spiritual Judaism, a nonlegalistic path, expertise in Jewish law as a basis for religious leadership and authority is not needed. The modern rabbi will not have judicial authority to render decisions based on Jewish law. Hair-splitting and logic-chopping halachic study is not necessary. An introduction to rabbinic texts—the Talmud, legal codes, commentaries, responsa, and the analytical method— is helpful, but nothing more. There is no need for the minute analysis of the array of texts of rabbinic Judaism.

If most American Jews no longer look to the modern rabbi for halachic rulings but rather for spiritual guidance, pastoral counseling, and a Jewish theological and historical perspective—what I call Spiritual Judaism anchored in enduring virtues—then the development of the Jewish tradition and its application to contemporary life rests first on the Hebrew Bible, not as a document revealed by God to ancient Jews but rather as the source for the legendary stories of the Jewish people, the teachings of the Hebrew prophets, and the Wisdom Literature (the Psalms and Proverbs); and second, on the mystical Jewish tradition (the Cabbalah). Familiarity with these two nonlegal Jewish sources need not approach the scholarly level. Rather, the Hebrew Bible and the Cabbalah serve as the primary sources for the formulation of an image of God, considerations of theodicy, the development of personal and interpersonal virtues, and spiritual tools for transformation (including prayer, meditation, imagery, use of Psalms, and the crying out to God). They provide the foundation for the spiritual guidance offered by a modern rabbi. A seminary could facilitate the educational process by using secondary sources to help guide students by means of a topical approach, for instance, to an image of God and the various virtues, not a chapter-by-chapter, section-by-section analysis of primary sources.

The education of the modern rabbi rests on five additional building blocks: first, on introductions to philosophy, ethics, and theology (Jewish and non-Jewish), focusing on modern dilemmas, including serious illness, euthanasia, reproductive technology, and sexual orientation; second, on a grounding in Jewish history for its contemporary relevance; third, on a basic knowledge of Jewish holidays and life cycle events, but not legalistic aspects of rituals and observances; fourth, on practical rabbinics, including pastoral and counseling skills, sermon preparation and delivery, and officiating at life cycle events; and finally, on a degree of Hebrew literacy. For those who aim at officiating at life cycle events that match the steps along life's path, as well as spiritual healing and pastoral work, only a limited knowledge of Hebrew is requisite; those striving to be pulpit rabbis and group worship facilitators, especially with traditional congregations, require more extensive Hebrew language skills.

Rather than using an examination format, students should demonstrate their knowledge and skills through a series of short papers. Skills could also be enhanced through a mentoring program, matching each student with one or more experienced rabbis in a student's immediate geographical area. Thus, a student would gain practical, supervised experience in his or her chosen rabbinic area(s), for instance, pulpit, officiant, counselor, or teacher. Again, flexibility is the keynote with respect to a mentoring program. Because of their professional or business careers, many students already possess numerous skills easily transferable to the rabbinate.

Beyond striving to unite theory and practice, a rabbinical seminary must facilitate each student's own spiritual and moral life and quest—his or her growth and development. It needs to challenge each student to develop his or her own inner resources to become an independent, critical, lifelong inquirer and spiritual seeker.

To promote a life of spiritual growth and development, two avenues could be pursued. In addition to one (or more) practical mentors, a student could also be paired with a spiritual mentor to discuss and cultivate his or her inner life and to nurture his or her soul.

Furthermore, requiring some sort of comprehensive preordination paper or project, certainly not a research thesis, would serve several ends. It would enable each student to tie together the various threads of his or her education and evidence the formulation of his or her own comprehensive and coherent Jewish spiritual approach to God, life, and the world that will serve as the springboard for his or her future spiritual and moral growth and development and the pursuit of lifelong learning.

A word or two is in order regarding the time frame requisite. Given the curricular goals for training the modern rabbi, the current five-year, full-time program (including one year in Israel) is simply too long. Rather, the course for study outlined here requires a flexible, but more limited, time frame dependent on each student's intelligence, understanding, and diligence. When a student feels he or she has prepared sufficiently and is fit to be a rabbi, let him or her come forward, subject, of course, to the approval of the seminary's administrators. For most, it may be two years; for others, ten years; for a few, never.

The modern rabbi requires an educational process transcending the traditional patterns of thought—the historic paradigms—of more than a century of American rabbinical seminaries. I cannot say whether the existing denominational rabbinical schools will be up to the challenge of training the modern rabbis required to meet the needs of contemporary American Jews. Probably not. The forces of tradition hold them back.

Denominational synagogues will continue to employ credentialed rabbis, steeped in the textual content of traditional rabbinic education—classic Jewish book learning. To fill the void, independent, post-denominational seminaries will flourish as professional schools, not graduate academic programs, training modern rabbis for the twenty-first century and responding to the tragic dilemma of the disappearing Jew.

OOPS! I SHOULDN'T SAY THIS . . .
OR SHOULD I?

Margaret Moers Wenig

"I've heard first-, second-, and third-hand gossip circulating at my synagogue—mostly untrue or, at best, only partially true," says a past president of a Reform congregation. "The most damaging gossip was about our rabbi. People assumed the worst about his conduct or motives, discredited him in ways that ranged from petty to slanderous. As a result, we lost members, teachers, staff . . . and the gossip hurt important temple relationships, both with local Jewish organizations and the non-Jewish community." Another past president concurs. "While sometimes congregants raised legitimate concerns with me in sensitive ways, at other times people were cruel. The net effect was, the synagogue felt less like a sanctuary, less holy, than it might have."

In Judaism, damaging a person's reputation through gossip is akin to taking his life. The Talmud teaches: "A person's tongue is more powerful than his sword. A sword can only kill someone who is nearby; a tongue can cause the death of someone who is far away" (Babylonian Talmud Shabbat 15b).

Rabbinic laws governing gossip, or *lashon hara*, are as extensive as they are strict. We are forbidden to relate *anything* derogatory about others. Even if a negative statement is true, it is still considered *lashon hara*. If it is false, even partially so, the offense is the more severe *motzi shem ra* (defamation of character). Also prohibited is *rechilut* (talebearing, or reporting to someone what others have said about him). *Lashon hara* violates no fewer than thirty-one biblical commandments, among them: "do not utter (or accept) a false report" (Exodus 23:1), "do not go about as a talebearer among your people" (Leviticus 19:16), and "cursed be one who smites his neighbor secretly" (Deuteronomy 27:24).

In 1873, Rabbi Israel Meir Kagan, a commentator on the *Shulchan Aruch* and a teacher of *musar* (ethics), collected the laws of *lashon hara* and *rechilut* into one volume titled *Sefer Chofetz Chayim*. So widely studied is this work that its author became known as the Chofetz Chayim, a reference to Psalm 34:13–14: "Who is the person who desires life (*chofetz chayim*). . . . Guard your tongue from evil and your lips from speaking deceit." According to the Chofetz Chayim, we are forbidden

- To discuss a person's negative character traits or to mention his or her misdeeds, even to a person who witnessed them
- To make derogatory remarks about someone, even when the information is common knowledge, and even if it causes no harm
- To convey a negative response about a person through hints, hand motions, facial expressions, coughs, winks, or tone of voice
- To make any statement, even if not explicitly derogatory, which might cause financial loss, physical pain, mental anguish, or any damage to reputation
- To reveal any personal or professional information about someone which he or she admitted to us, even if he or she did not request confidentiality
- To speak ill of a *talmid chacham* (scholar) or to ridicule his teaching—a particularly egregious sin if he is the practicing rabbi of a community

We are even forbidden

- To listen to or sit next to someone who speaks *lashon hara*
- To praise another person excessively, for doing so might provoke a listener to disagree
- To make a seemingly neutral comment (such as, "Have you seen Sam lately?"), for it may prompt others to speak ill of him

The Chofetz Chayim adds that the greater the number of people who hear one's *lashon hara,* the greater the sin. One who gossips habitually commits sins greater than idolatry, adultery, and murder.

Dangers of *Lashon Hara*

If some of the rabbinic injunctions against *lashon hara* appear exceptionally strict, consider what is at stake:

- Lashon hara *can destroy a human being's livelihood.* The "blacklisting" that was characteristic of the McCarthy era left many people jobless, and worse.

- Lashon hara *can inflict psychic pain and damage self-esteem.* "For all the misery that's crossed my path, no pain is more searingly etched in my memory than the relatively slight deprecations I've endured or inflicted," writes UAHC board member and social activist Evely Laser Shlensky. "Relatively minor personal humiliations can elicit a powerful enduring sense of degradation. I think of these intimate acts which crush the human soul as 'little murder.'"

- Lashon hara *can compromise truth.* Since standards of proof are rarely invoked in gossip, *lashon hara* violates the legal principle: innocent until proven guilty.

- Lashon hara *can violate our privacy.* "When other people intervene by telling someone information about us," Rabbi Margaret Holub observes, "they are violating our control of our personal information. This can feel like theft or even rape."

- Lashon hara *about an entire group of people can lead to racial/ ethnic/religious hatred and violence.* Jews as a people have often been victimized by slanders emanating from pulpits, the media, and now the Internet.

- Lashon hara *can undermine a sacred community.* Congregants may flee from or avoid assuming leadership roles in synagogues in which backbiting is rampant, privacy is violated, and people are constantly being judged.

What makes *lashon hara* even more insidious is the near impossibility of undoing its damage. The Chofetz Chayim tells the story of a penitent who asks him for a way to repair the harm done by his gossip. The Chofetz Chayim hands the man a feather pillow and instructs him to take it outside, slit it open, and shake its contents into the wind. When the penitent returns with the empty pillow, the Chofetz Chayim says, "Now, go collect the feathers."

Benefits of *Lashon Hara*

Gossip can cause irreparable damage to a person's reputation and well-being, but it can also play a *constructive* social role. "Gossip provides an individual with a map of his social environment, including details which are inaccessible to him in his own everyday life," writes anthropologist John Beard Haviland in *Gossip, Reputation and Knowledge in Zinacantan.* Quoting F. G. Bailey, he explains, "An event or an action is public not only to those who see it, but also to those who hear about it. . . . The map which a man has of the community around him, of what is going on and of how he should respond to others, is a map created by the spoken word, by the information circulating around his community." In *Scorpion Tongues: Gossip, Celebrity, and American Politics,* columnist Gail Collins says, "By revealing behavior that's normally hidden, [gossip] helps people understand how things really work in the mysterious world behind closed doors." Philosopher Sisela Bok adds: "If we knew about people only what they wished to reveal, we would be subjected to ceaseless manipulation; and we would be deprived of the pleasure and suspense that comes from trying to understand them. . . . In order to live in both the inner and the shared worlds, the exchange of views about each other—in spite of all the difficulties of perception and communication—gossip is indispensable."

Gossip also helps to create and define the boundaries of a community of shared values. It may even be instrumental in forming what F. G. Bailey calls "a moral community"—that is, "a group of people prepared to make moral judgments about one another." In fact, the first definition of a gossip in the *Oxford English Dictionary* is: "One who has contracted spiritual affinity with another by acting as a sponsor at a baptism (from god sib)." Consider the positive value of former classmates or camp buddies sharing information about members of their group: who is ill, who is getting divorced, whose child is having trouble, who is changing careers, who could use a friendly call. In other words, there is an appropriate connection between the intimacy of family or the closest of friends and the intimate information they share with one another.

In the realm of politics, *lashon hara* may be necessary in order to exercise our responsible roles as citizens in a democratic society. To vote, to speak out for justice, to respond intelligently to the dilemmas of our era, we need access to information about the actions of our public officials, good and bad. "Consider the implications of Daniel Ellsberg's leaking the Pentagon Papers to *The New York Times,*" writes Rabbi Margaret Holub. "One could make the case that gossip ended the Vietnam War."

For the oppressed, *lashon hara* may serve as a means of resistance. "For much of human history," Gail Collins writes, "[gossip] was one of the few weapons available to the powerless: servants who spread stories about their masters, peasants who irreverently speculated about the most private aspects of life in the manor. . . ." Today, if an employee suspects she has been discriminated against, speaking *lashon hara* may lead to confirmation of her belief and may become the first step in mobilizing resources, her own and others', to fight the discrimination.

Lashon hara can lead to self-understanding and connection with those closest to us. For example, discussing with a spouse, partner, or trusted friend a negative encounter with one's boss, though considered *lashon hara,* may help our loved one better understand why we are angry, uncommunicative, or depressed. Unburdening in this way may also result in our gaining a more balanced perspective on our situation and brainstorming strategies for resolving the conflict.

Lashon hara also plays a role in fostering creativity and self-expression. In commenting on society and the human condition, literature and the performing arts often describe people with satire, irony, and humor. "If we are honest," adds Rabbi Margaret Holub, "there is probably some percentage of that awful gossip we all do which is just fun. It really doesn't fan the flames of our negativity. It doesn't keep us from more serious and intimate conversation. It doesn't harm the person at whose expense we laugh. I think we each need a little free zone—a few minutes a week, a single trusted companion, something like that—to keep ourselves from being insufferably self-conscious or, worse, sanctimonious. The very same energy which allows us to laugh and mock also keeps us curious and alive."

In Jewish law, *lashon hara* is permitted when it is the only means available to alert someone of possible danger, and it is *required* when the intent is to warn others not to follow in the footsteps of one who has transgressed *mitzvot*. For example, *lashon hara* may be necessary if in private premarital counseling a rabbi learns that the groom-to-be has engaged in unsafe sex and refuses to be tested for HIV. In this case, telling the bride-to-be that her fiancé's behavior and attitude might pose some risk to her and to their future is a *mitzvah*.

In business dealings as well, under certain limited circumstances, the rabbi is permitted the exchange of negative assessments of a person's character and behavior. When asked for an employee reference, Rabbi Zelig Pliskin explains that you are "obliged to give a truthful answer, even if [your] reply . . . contain[s] derogatory facts . . . in order to prevent an unqualified person from being mistakenly hired." In such cases, a person is permitted to listen to *lashon hara* for cautionary purposes, but the listener is forbidden to take any negative information as the absolute truth.

A consumer is also "permitted to speak of the poor quality of a [vendor's] merchandise in order to prevent [a potential customer] from being cheated." And "it is permitted to speak *lashon hara* if you believe your words will help an injured person receive compensation."

Finding the Right Balance

How, then, do we determine when engaging in *lashon hara* is destructive and when it is desirable? The first step is to become more aware of the ramifications of our own speech. Try these guidelines for a week:

- Take note of everything you say about another person or about a group of people.
- Refrain from repeating anything you do not know firsthand to be true.
- Each time you are tempted to speak about another person, ask yourself: "Is there a better way to accomplish my goal [e.g., to become closer to the listener, to help a friend, to correct a problem]?"

Preventative Strategies

We can learn to avoid committing *lashon hara* in the first place by implementing "preventative" strategies, such as giving another benefit of the doubt, rebuking with compassion, and nurturing appreciation for the good in others.

Giving others the benefit of the doubt. When we witness the infuriating behavior, instead of automatically ascribing to the offender the worst of motives and then sharing our judgment with others, we might instead assume the best of intentions—or that the offender was simply misguided. "As we judge others favorably, so will God judge us favorably" (The Babylonian Talmud, Shabbat 127b).

Rebuking wisely. If a situation arises which cannot be simply "explained away," our tradition enjoins us to rebuke the presumed offender directly and privately (publicly embarrassing someone is prohibited). Leviticus 19 states: "You shall surely rebuke your neighbor (*hocheyach tochiach et amitecha*), but incur no guilt [because of him]." Notably, this *mitzvah* appears immediately after the prohibition, "Do not go about as a talebearer" and immediately before, "You shall not take vengeance or bear a grudge against your kinsfolk. Love your neighbor as yourself. I am the Eternal God."

Although we may hesitate to offer rebuke (*tochecha*) for fear of "hurting another human being, ruining a relationship, engaging in an unhealthy power struggle, or opening up our own sense of vulnerability and insecurity," says Rabbi Matthew Gewirtz of Rodeph Sholom Congregation in New York City, "we are nevertheless commanded to rebuke." To minimize the risk of causing hurt feelings, Rabbi Gewirtz offers these guidelines from Jewish tradition: Be aware of your motives before proceeding. Do not rebuke someone out of anger or jealousy arising out of your own sense of failure. Maimonides advises us to "speak to the offender gently and tenderly, so that he can hear the critique" (Mishneh Torah Hilchot Deot 6:7).

Nurturing appreciation. While rebuke, or direct criticism, can be a *mitzvah,* we must be mindful not to nurture negativity in human relations. As Rabbi Gewirtz says, "Let us not allow our responsibility to offer *tochecha* to prevent us from also seeing the good in each other. We all need to be appreciated. We all need to be loved. We all want to live with each other in peace. . . . [But] love unaccompanied by criticism is not love. . . . Peace unaccompanied by reproof is not peace" (Genesis Rabbah 54:3).

Sacred Speech, Sacred Communities

Just as *lashon hara* can diminish the sanctity of synagogue life, rebuke can enhance it. Even in a sacred community, a community in which each person is regarded and treated as a creature of God, members still err. Sacred communities cannot grow stronger by ignoring the genuine weaknesses or faults of their members, leaders, or collective culture. A truly sacred

---

HOW TO AVOID LISTENING TO *LASHON HARA*

If someone begins speaking *lashon hara* which you do not wish to hear:

- Change the subject

- Encourage the speaker to address his concerns directly to the person about whom he is speaking, and offer to help him do so

- Walk away (if in a group)

- If you have no choice but to listen to the *lashon hara,* do not believe it, act on it, or repeat it

community acknowledges that people transgress and that *tochecha* (rebuke), *teshuvah* (repentance), reconciliation, and forgiveness are, in most situations, not only possible but advisable. As Zelig Pliskin writes in *Guard Your Tongue: A Practical Guide to the Laws of Lashon Hora Based on Chofetz Chaim:* "If a person diligently applies himself to studying the laws of *lashon hora,* God will remove his *yetzer hora* (his urge) for forbidden speech. But if an entire group will resolve together to guard their speech, the merit is [much] greater."

Should the Reform Movement establish standards of acceptable and undesirable *lashon hara?* Just as libel laws vary from state to state and have changed over time, guidelines for *lashon hara* should be developed at the local level to address each community's unique circumstance. Congregations notorious for stoking the destructive fire of *lashon hara* may have to emphasize prohibitions and sanctions; on the other hand, congregations in which all negative comments are suppressed may need to concentrate on opening channels for permissible *lashon hara.*

Every synagogue can benefit from implementing steps to address the underlying causes of *lashon hara.* Congregants whose insightful questions or concerns are ignored may gossip out of frustration. Those who persist in raising thorny questions may be pegged as "chronic complainers" and dismissed. Others who may have legitimate complaints may simply leave the congregation without a sound. "A leader who is uncomfortable with dissension, who is unable to encourage others to express their differences, [and] who negatively judges those who do surface disagreements is going to cause even more organizational difficulty," says Stephen B. Leas, director of consulting for the Alban Institute, in *Leadership & Conflict.* The key to stemming the tide of *lashon hara* is to open avenues for direct criticism and honest feedback—practices which require good leadership.

When I arrived at Beth Am, The People's Temple, in New York City in 1984, a bitter conflict between two warring factions had not yet been resolved. Though the focus of that conflict was no longer an issue, the war continued. To "create an atmosphere where gossip would not breed—in other words, to drain the swamp"—the temple president, Judah Rosenfeld, mandated a monthly "Liaison Committee" meeting, with representation from both sides as well as those with their ears closest to the grapevine and those in positions of power. Every month, committee members brought complaints from the congregation to my attention. One Liaison Committee member who had opposed my hiring carried a little notebook and, after each service, solicited criticism from those he knew might be dissatisfied; at each Liaison Committee meeting he drew the notebook from his pocket and went down that month's list.

For the first few years, the constant criticism was painful for me to hear. But I preferred knowing the substance of congregants' complaints to the anxiety of not knowing what people were saying about me behind my back. In time, when it became clear that the criticism would not scare me away, the Liaison Committee meetings became the place where the synagogue leaders (who eventually came to see themselves not as adversaries but as allies) helped me figure out how to respond to the criticism and how to avoid provoking it in the first place. The committee also allowed me to air my own concerns and enlist help in addressing them.

Rosenfeld's strategy had succeeded. The creation of an appropriate avenue to discuss issues curtailed gossip which arose from congregants' legitimate concerns and grievances.

While the Chofetz Chayim prohibits "disgracing, belittling, or ridicule" of a rabbi as *lashon hara,* legitimate disagreement with a rabbi's teaching is permitted. And so, at Beth Am, following a tradition established decades earlier by Rabbi Israel Raphael Margolies, *z'l,* after each Shabbat evening service the congregation sat down for cake and coffee and an hour-long discussion of that night's sermon. I was granted absolute freedom of the pulpit; the congregation was granted equal freedom to disagree. I never worried that congregants might whisper about my sermons behind my back; they shared their reactions to my face—blunt, trenchant, no holds barred. On occasions when there was no sit-down discussion, congregants who objected to a sermon would tell me so on the receiving line, in a letter, or by phone. In recent years, online discussion of my High Holiday sermons sometimes lasted months and involved an ever-widening group of congregants. As a result of the objections voiced directly to me, valuable dialogue replaced *lashon hara,* turning the temple into a community energized by the exchange of viewpoints.

Excommunicating "Clergy Killers"

Sometimes, even in congregations with open channels of communication, a few members will intentionally introduce dissension by spreading nasty rumors. In *Pastoral Stress: Sources of Tension, Resources for Transformation,* Anthony G. Pappas of the Alban Institute refers to such members as "clergy killers"—people "with power needs and other pathologies" . . . who find congregations—composed mostly of "warm, loving, and tolerant" people—"a viable environment to act out their internal illness. Ideally, the congregation will react in responsible ways to transform or at least contain the harmful behavior. . . ." If all other strategies have failed, Pappas advises that "key congregational leaders [educate themselves] about the reasons and procedures for censure, removal, and/or excommunication of members."

Jewish law considers *lashon hara* against rabbis and other Jewish communal leaders a particularly egregious offense. If we witness a communal leader's transgression, we are instructed to assume that our eyes deceived us, or that the behavior was in error, or an aberration. And if we tell someone else what we saw, our punishment is the more severe because we committed *lashon hara* against a sage. In *Gossip: The Power of the Word,* Rabbi Stephen M. Wylen of Temple Beth Tikvah in Wayne, New Jersey, rejects the Chafetz Chayim's hierarchy giving sages the greatest benefit of the doubt. Rabbi Wylen's wisdom has been borne out by revelations of sexual abuse of congregants and children by clergy who had been given the benefit of the doubt by their superiors.

With the exception of complaints from "clergy killers," grievances about synagogue leaders merit serious attention. In most cases, it is preferable that a synagogue president not censor a member's *lashon hara* by saying, "*Lashon hara* is a sin; I cannot listen to you," or cut off the objection midstream by refuting its contents. In many complaints there lies valuable information about the subject of the *lashon hara,* its speaker, and/or the circumstances which gave rise to its utterance. Rabbi Wylen advises: "Even a tongue-lashing from a spiteful person may contain some surprising insight into our character that we can use to our own advantage if we will only listen . . . 'Rebuke a wise man and he will love you' (Proverbs 9:8)."

As synagogue leaders will inevitably receive direct or indirect criticism, they are well advised to ask themselves: "What support do I need to listen to *lashon hara* (or rebuke) without feeling so vulnerable that I am compelled to respond defensively?" How well a leader meets this challenge will affect the synagogue's well-being. "The quality of interpersonal transactions between members of a congregation," writes Rabbi Lawrence Kushner, "is the single most important factor in determining its health. Do they bear witness to the piety the congregation claims to perpetuate? Where the human relationships are self-righteous, deceitful, and toxic, congregational life is wretched. Where they are tolerant, honest, and nurturing, congregational life can be a transforming joy."

In Mendocino, California, Rabbi Margaret Holub and members of her community have been discussing passages from the Chofetz Chayim and experimenting with standards of "right speech." "More than once of late, I've heard someone stop a sentence and say, 'Oops! I shouldn't say this,'" Rabbi Holub writes. "The very process of being aware of how we speak about others and how we hear others will itself guide us in the direction we want to go. This process . . . is exactly the opposite of the kind of frozen silence that I fear when speech is thoughtlessly curtailed. I have every confidence that we will find our answers as we keep talking."

As we keep talking, may we remember the wisdom of Proverbs 18:21: "Death and life are in the power of the tongue."

CREATING A MORAL LEGACY
FOR OUR CHILDREN

Susan Berrin

AFTER BEING A PARENT for seventeen years, I know enough about children and about myself as a mother to acknowledge that any smugness when reading newspaper headlines would be unwarranted. "That couldn't happen to my family" is no longer part of my vocabulary. Seventeen years of exploring the landscape of babies, toddlers, children, adolescents and teens has led me through wadis and rivers, mountain peaks and valleys. Most trails have been marked, and sometimes I've been guided along them. Other times I feel like a pioneer, traversing a terrain inhospitable to family life. But along the trails I've noticed that families—even Jewish families—form and sustain themselves in many different ways. And what I might have held unimaginable years ago no longer surprises me. What I assumed could never happen to a Jewish family happens. As folk-singer and 1960s cultural icon Phil Ochs sang, "there but for fortune go you and I."

How do we create families that do not make horror headlines? How do we nurture children so that they live within a moral framework? What mother's milk does not contain love, what pablum is not stirred with sweet kisses? But, at what point—and how—do we begin to instill—along with love and sweet kisses—a moral dimension to our parenting?

When our son was four years old, and we were spending the year in Jerusalem, his preschool teacher taught him and us a wonderful song. The words, *Sh'ma beni musar avicha v'al tichtosh torah emecha,* are from the Book of Proverbs, and mean, "Listen my child to the *musar,* the morals, of your father and to the *torah,* the teachings, of your mother." So what is that *musar?* What are the morals with which we live? What ethics guide our journey as families, what teachings help to make us good people? After the horrific killings last spring in Colorado, we all wanted to ask, "Are there any guarantees that we can raise our children to love life and honor it?"

While we have no guarantees about life, least of all about our children, we can take an active role in *creating* the families we live in. And along with planning for schools, lessons, and babysitters, part of our educational master-plan should be the instilling of the vital moral lessons that make us *menschen,* good, kind, generous, moral human beings. Instilling our lives with Jewish values enriches my family's experience. Our children know that although we may be week-weary, each shabbes we try to invite friends or family to our table. Together we reflect on the week, its ups and downs, the incidental experiences we each had, the ways our lives made others happy or sad. Before beginning the meal, we bless our children, helping them to understand their unique holiness. We ask that they grow to reflect the best qualities of our ancestors, that they use their hearts like Sarah, their eyes like Leah. When we bless the wine we recall our liberation from Egypt, our journey towards freedom, our obligation to ensure that all people live free lives. *HaMotzi,* the blessing over the challah, is an opportunity to acknowledge our partnership with God. As we bless the Source that brings bread from the ground we are aware that farmers grow wheat, which is then made with hands into braided loaves. We end our meal with *birkat hamazon,* the blessing after eating. We always remove knives from the table because as symbols of destruction, they do not belong on our symbolic altar—a powerful, weekly reminder to our children of the evils of killing.

As a Jewish mother, some of what I teach my children necessarily separates them from others and creates boundaries. For example, keeping kosher draws a line around what we eat, and observing shabbat limits some of my children's weekend activities. Adhering to these boundaries, especially in a society that often judges them artificial and unnecessary, is challenging. But it is part of how I invest the daily lives of my family with Jewish values.

How do we create a family that instills moral virtues? Primarily, by living these values daily—some simple like honoring our elders and others more complex. What our children learn from us is what they observe us doing. Rather than listening to our words, children watch our actions. With keen eyes, they observe the informal, daily minutiae: how we speak to a waitress, how we handle injustices, how we affirm our humanity, whether we ever lie (even that little white lie). If they observe compassion, they will have compassion as a behavior to model. I am forever amazed at what, and how much, my children (and even my young children) re-play from my conversations and behaviors. Like flies on the wall, they are absorbing the nuances of our lives.

At home we strive to create a nurturing environment, where children know we are available to listen, to sit and to be completely present with them. As a full-time working mother, I often find the hardest piece of my life is balancing my professional commitments with the time I need to be physically and emotionally present with my children. We all know that the most insightful, poignant parent-child conversations occur spontaneous-ly. Sometimes they happen at night, at "tuck-in, kiss-me-goodnight time." Sometimes they happen driving in the car, on the *shlep* circuit. But they can only happen when we're together, and for many families today, stretching that together-time is like pulling at a very worn-out elastic. Those times of profound communication cannot be scheduled, and if we don't happen to be home when a child needs us, or decides to shed her outer layer and ex-pose herself, we won't be witness or partner to the experience.

As more women struggle with this balancing act, and more families lose a stay-at-home parent, we are challenged on many fronts. Not only are we pressed for time, and not only do our lives take on a more frenetic veneer, but we can also be tempted to embrace more fully the normative culture—a culture that does not reflect the moral values we are aspiring to establish in our homes. We are tempted to sit a child in front of a TV program while we make dinner, we become more lenient about what video games the child purchases, what movies he watches, where he "hangs" after school.

As parents we hold unique and powerful positions as teachers of moral virtues. But we are not their only teachers. We can also surround ourselves with other families who serve as role models, and we can join communi-ties that mirror and encourage the values we affirm. As our children grow, we know their horizons expand, and that our control over their lives di-minishes. But children who are connected to a community can move out of the parental orbit while staying within our stratosphere. Not only do our children learn by observing a larger pool of interactions, they feel con-nected to people outside the nuclear family, outside the inner sanctum. That feeling of belonging is one of the most essential aspects of develop-ing a positive sense of self, a self-image that reflects being responsible, being loved, being part of a nucleus that moves, grows, creates, and sustains life.

Some of my greatest fears in life revolve around my children. Because I love my children more than anything, the fear of losing them, losing their trust, their love, their embrace, their future is ever present in my heart and mind. A simple but powerful Rebbe Nachman song helps calm my anxiety: "The world is a narrow bridge. And the essence is to not be afraid." To live unafraid with my children and guide them, to foster in them a positive Jewish self-image, is my greatest, and also my most rewarding, challenge.

The daily news shakes every family in America. The headlines provoke a call to reexamine certain assumptions American society—and many Jewish families living in the United States—hold. The first is that violence on TV, in movies, and on the computer screen, will not adversely affect our children. In fact, the violence children experience through the media has a strong impact on the way they view themselves and their relationships to others.

I have spent seventeen years nurturing my children: teaching them to feel the pain of an uncaring society, the sadness of a homeless woman. But also, to feel empowered to act courageously and with principle to change their world. We look at the world not only through our own individual eyes, but also through Jewish eyes. Our feet not only walk on American soil, but also carry a history of footsteps traversing deserts and rivers around the globe.

My children are sometimes resentful that I curb their "entertainment," set limits on what they view and on the instruments of their play. But I am confident that the prism I am helping them to create, the ways they engage the world, will be more satisfying, more in tune with Jewish tradition and yet, perhaps, unconventional by some middle-class American standards. If only I teach them to think and analyze autonomously and creatively, I will feel a measure of success. If only I teach them to stand tall and yet walk humbly with all others, *dayenu!* The path I walk along is very Jewish: sometimes it is in harmony with the broader society, sometimes it is not. It is a gentle path, one that crosses many narrow bridges, but one that opens to expansive fields, to fields sprouting with wildflowers in an array of colors.

As parents, we need to develop the strength to say "no" to violence in all of its forms, to resist the violent, dehumanizing toys and games and media that American culture has promoted. Creating a nonviolent home, a sanctuary from the frenzied lives we encounter through TV, the Internet, and news, is not only about controlling the flow of weapons into our living rooms. It is also about creating a family environment based on values of cooperation, love, trust, and creativity. It is about teaching our children to resolve conflict with words and insight, about choosing friends who reflect similar values, about trusting oneself with the pervasiveness of the media. It is about learning responsibility and accepting it. It is about building self-esteem so that a child doesn't feel a need to prove his or her toughness to others. Creating a nonviolent home means modeling that behavior every day: treating children, at all ages, with respect and gentleness, with kindness and through offering a measure of autonomy and indulgence.

The balance between autonomy and parental guidance, however, is critical. My children know I have no tolerance for mean-spirited behavior or unkindness, and no tolerance for actions that harm or *simulate harm* to others. I am firm on issues of children and violence: they should never meet. We learn what we do and practice. So when I say to my children, "no weapons," there is no relenting, even when it is difficult to adhere to that principle (in the face of our children's friends and their parents, and the current consumer marketplace). My children definitely know where I stand on this issue. They have years of experience resolving conflict without force, years of playing without guns or video games, years of developing a sense of self that nurtures rather than harms.

We have ample opportunities as a Jewish family to learn about our tradition's responses to violence and our prophets' visions of peace. We have opportunities to celebrate life, which is antithetical to violence. We have opportunities to nurture family experiences that value life, that support healthy families, that build trust and loving memories, that cement sibling bonds. As a parent, one of my most important responsibilities is to raise a child who recognizes the ultimate value of life and who sees him- or herself and is seen by others as a *mensch*.

Being a parent is an affirmation of one of Judaism's most important values—hope. Being hopeful as a parent means that even when we face difficult times with our children, we know that the possibility for change exists. That even when our children do not appear to hear us, they are absorbing our lessons, or fragments of those lessons, that will long encase their hearts. Being hopeful also gives us—and our children—courage and strength to make the world a healthier and safer habitat for all of its people.

Tshuvah, the act of return, of changing from an unacceptable way, is an important component of Jewish life. While it is a central theme of the Rosh HaShanah and Yom Kippur liturgies, it should not be relegated only to these Fall months. *Tshuvah* recognizes that *we all make mistakes,* that we all have the potential to change, to become better people. It should be a part of our personal repertoire as parents.

Grounding our attitudes to life and death, to kindness and violence, in Jewish terms is one more facet in creating a values-based, Jewish family life. It teaches our children to resist cruelty, to think deeply, to think autonomously. Making these issues Jewish issues grounds the universal dream of a peaceful world in particular symbols and metaphors. It pushes us to bring the most compelling issues of our lives home, to a place where we can daily cast our vote for life. It helps our children choose richer, safer, happier lives.

HEBREW VS. YIDDISH—
THE WORLDWIDE RIVALRY

Norman Berdichevsky

ISRAEL HAS SUCCEEDED in "reviving" an ancient language, thus linking it to its historic past. In the State of Israel, independence was recreated along with a cultural revival in the face of great odds and massive doubts concerning the viability of both state and language. Even Theodor Herzl, the founder of the Zionist vision that launched the political efforts to create a Jewish state, skeptically asked in 1897 at the time of the First Zionist Congress: "Who among us can as much as ask for a train ticket in Hebrew?" His skepticism was shared by many European Jews, who felt that reviving the ancient language was an impossible task (or a profane, even sacrilegious one). In Herzl's romantic, utopian novel of a future idealized Jewish state, *Altneuland,* Jews are pictured as cosmopolitan multilingual speakers of German and other major European languages. Neither Yiddish or Hebrew is mentioned.

One hundred and twenty years ago, there were ten million Yiddish-speaking Jews. None was a habitual, primary, or native Hebrew speaker who had learned the language at home from his parents. For centuries, Hebrew had been used as a liturgical language of prayer and, on occasion, as the means of communication between educated Jews traveling abroad whose native languages were unintelligible. It was in wide use both for religious commentary and also as an eminent, "high" language for philosophical, legal, and even scientific texts by learned Jews who addressed themselves largely to a Jewish but not necessarily Orthodox readership.

The pioneer work of Eliezer Ben-Yehuda[1] to make it a spoken language had its initial impact in Palestine in the late nineteenth century.

Ben-Yehuda's efforts were looked upon as eccentric by most educated Jews living in the country and as a profane sacrilege by the ultra-Orthodox for whom the language was reserved for God's word. Today, Hebrew is the everyday spoken language of more than five million people, including non-Jews, in the State of Israel and understood or read by at least another million people in the Diaspora.

The Jewish "Hybrid Languages"

Although Hebrew ceased to be the spoken language of the majority of Jews in their Judean homeland between the second century B.C.E and the second century C.E., it remained as the most important language of religious commentary and heavily influenced the various "hybrid" languages that arose in the Diaspora such as Yiddish (Judeo-German), Ladino (also called Judezmo, or Judeo-Español), and several other varieties, all of which used the Hebrew alphabet. It is estimated that Hebrew words constitute close to 15 percent of the Yiddish vocabulary and a lesser proportion of the other hybrids. Many Hebrew words absorbed by Yiddish indicate religious beliefs and abstractions. The Yiddish word usually has the stress on the first syllable and characteristic diphthongs *aw*, *ow*, and *oy*.

ORIGINAL HEBREW	YIDDISH	ENGLISH
shabbát	shábes	Sabbath
yom tóv	yuntev	"a good day"—a holiday
brit	bris	ritual circumcision
mazzál	mázl	luck
tallít	tális	prayer shawl
zikarón	zikórn	memory
rachmanút	rakhmónes	mercy
melaméd	milámed	teacher
chatán	khósn	bridegroom
milchamáh	milkhúme	war
mishpacháh	mishpúkhe	family
kó'ach	kóyekh	power

These Yiddish words are just a few of the most important of several hundred words of Hebrew origin and used in Yiddish with a slightly different stress and different pronunciation of several sounds.

The Hebrew-Yiddish Rivalry

For a time, a lively rivalry existed between Hebrew and Yiddish, vying for the loyalty of several generations of literary figures—writers, playwrights, and philosophers. In 1908, supporters boldly proclaimed Yiddish "a Jewish National Language" at a famous conference held in Czernowitz, Austria-Hungary. They could always point to the fact that Yiddish was spoken by millions of Jews, whereas Hebrew was not a spoken vernacular but rather more of an experiment to breathe life into a moribund language incapable of meeting the demands of twentieth-century life. Hebraists, on the other hand, laid claim to Hebrew as *the* Jewish National Language at their congress in 1913 in Vienna. They pointed out the superiority of Hebrew's historical continuity—the immense prestige of the Bible and its influence upon much of European literature, as well as its venerable age. By contrast, Yiddish was essentially regarded as a "jargon" or "dialect." Early in the twentieth century, Yiddish speakers in Europe, and among recent East European immigrants to the "New World," constituted a vast majority of the world's Jewish population. The largest Jewish socialist party in Poland, The Bund, cultivated an independent Yiddish culture, and most Jewish immigrants to Palestine until the 1930s were native Yiddish speakers.

Visitors to Israel today can scarcely believe or appreciate the enormous difficulties that were involved in the restoration of Hebrew as a living language. The Hebrew conflict with Yiddish in Palestine took three generations to resolve. Hebrew's triumph, which seems such a foregone conclusion today, was a tenacious struggle. It was greatly aided by the natural process of territorial concentration, plus immigration to Palestine by Jews who already were sympathetic to the revival of Hebrew as part of their Zionist beliefs. But it faced intense skepticism from critics who labeled it "artificial," until the first group of children played unselfconsciously in Hebrew and expressed a full range of emotions without the assistance of another language.

Many individuals who possessed a love for both languages experienced a soul-wrenching dilemma over the necessity of "choosing sides" in the increasingly polarized atmosphere of the new society being built in Eretz-Yisrael. For many committed Zionists, even those who grew up with Yiddish as their first language, there was a conscious identification of the language with the ghetto Diaspora existence that Zionism sought to eradicate.

Ze'ev Jabotinsky was not atypical in his categorical rejection bordering on hatred of Yiddish when he attacked the very intonation of Yiddish with its "sing-song melody." He proclaimed:

Do not sing while you speak. This ugliness is infinitely worse than every other defect, and regrettably, it is taking root in our life. Both the school and the stage are guilty; the first, out of sloppiness, the latter out of an intention to "revive" for us the ghetto and its whining. The tune of the ghetto is ugly not only because of its weeping tone which stirs unpleasant memories in us."[2]

The Yiddish Counterattack

Detractors of Hebrew who ridiculed "Modern Hebrew" mocked the halting Hebrew speech of native Yiddish speakers unable to converse freely and the obviously stilted character of Hebrew novels attempting to portray real conversations in a language that was not yet the vernacular of a community outside the struggling Zionist colonies in remote and backward Palestine. Several Yiddish "spokesmen" critical of Hebrew compared it to the artificial character of Esperanto[3] when both languages were still in their infancy.

Yiddish as the Authentic *Mame Loshn* (Mother Tongue)

Supporters of Yiddish seized on the inevitable shortcomings in the early days of Hebrew's rebirth to argue that only Yiddish reflected a distinctly Jewish social environment that could be recreated in Palestine. Non- or anti-Zionists and the ultra-Orthodox throughout the world were hostile to the notion that Hebrew could be successfully transformed into a vehicle of modern communication and cultural creativity. The argument repeated by fervent Yiddishists was that Yiddish was the natural vehicle of expression for millions of Jews who had learned it at home, were fluent in it, and had already elevated it into a literary language capable of fully expressing all the needs and desires of an entire people. Moreover, several generations of Yiddish authors had raised the status of the language in the eyes of the world. In the opening address of the First Yiddish Language Conference, Nathan Birnbaum[4] spoke of the great progress made by Yiddish. His speech was also an attack on assimilation and a dismissal of Hebrew supporters as "lost wanderers" turning themselves into "ramblers," "torn from home and nationality" and going off to the desert-wilderness.

"Turning the Clock Backwards"

Critics of Zionism pointed to the apparent absurdity of "trying to turn back the clock" to an eccentric recreation of an extinct culture thousands of years old. It was "nonsense" to struggle learning an "ancient language" and trying to make up for the loss of two thousand years of development. These arguments were partially correct but ignored the reality of finding a common language in the multilingual Palestinian society with its substantial "Sephardic" or Middle Eastern Jewish population. Not only were Turkish and Arabic of prime importance in the revived Jewish homeland, but competing Zionist agencies encouraged the use of French, Russian, and German. Moreover, the enormous and continually growing American Jewish population was in the process of rapidly giving up Yiddish and fully embracing English.

Yiddish progressively lost strength through assimilation in Europe and America with continued Jewish emigration from Poland and Russia, while Hebrew grew in power and prestige due to territorial concentration through migration (aliyah) to Mandatory Palestine and then Israel. Yiddish did reflect the folkways and religious life of the mass of European Jews. But Zionists correctly foresaw that Yiddish could never achieve the status of a "National Language" linked to a specific territory or independent state anywhere and that it would suffer an inevitable decline, even though it had brilliantly met the requirements of sophisticated urban life and modern literature. As late as 1978, Yiddish could boast a Nobel Prize winner in the field of literature (Isaac Bashevis Singer, whose works have been translated into dozens of languages), but the Holocaust and assimilation have dealt it a mortal blow.

In Palestine, the rivalry of the languages reached a fever pitch in the late twenties and early thirties. The arrival of tens of thousands of German-speaking Jews from Germany and Austria following the Nazi assumption of power radically changed the balance of the language controversy. The new immigrants, who had been proud of their fluency in German and had always looked down upon Yiddish as the "jargon" of East European Jews, were enthusiastic converts in identifying with the Zionist cause and the Hebrew language. It also became increasingly clear that most Jewish immigrants from all backgrounds had at least a basic reading knowledge of Hebrew as the result of their early religious training. For speakers of Arabic, the transition was even easier, as the two languages have many structural similarities and many almost identical words.

Hebrew and Yiddish in the Interwar (1920–1940) Lithuanian Schools

The reborn Lithuanian government, in need of Jewish support during the negotiations leading to the Versailles Treaty, provided a measure of national autonomy for the Jewish minority that even guaranteed its own educational system in Hebrew and/or Yiddish. The Jewish community was recognized as a legal institution with the right to legislate binding ordinances, and all Jews were subject to the decisions of the Jewish National Council (*Va'ad Ha'aretz*). The Zionist Minister of Jewish Affairs in the Lithuanian government, Soloveichik, often delivered speeches praising Jewish autonomy and the right of the Jews to shape their own development in the "two national languages" (Yiddish and Hebrew), declaring that "we are rehearsing here towards a Jewish state." This measure of recognition of the Jews as a "national minority" (rather than a religious one) was a major step on the road to achieving eventual recognition of a Jewish state. The Ministry of Jewish Affairs was abolished in 1924. The ostensible reason given was internal bickering between the supporters of Hebrew and Yiddish, but a more fundamental underlying cause was the dissatisfaction of Lithuanian nationalists, who regarded such minority rights as divisive. Although Jews were initially viewed in a more favorable light than the Russian, Polish, and German minorities, Jewish economic preeminence, especially in commerce and retail trade, aggravated tensions.

The Creation of a "Base Society" of Hebrew Speakers

Hebrew's amazing success has been paralleled on a smaller scale only by the relative success of Esperanto, the only devised language to emerge within a generation of its appearance as the idiom of a dispersed, non-ethnic, non-territorial but functioning community able to use the language in many walks of life and with its own literature. When Eliezer Ben-Yehuda began his work, Hebrew lacked much of the simplest vocabulary necessary to deal with many domains and needs of modern society and technology. The problems were not simply those of a lack of new words but modes of speech to express spontaneous emotions or reflective thoughts and moods.

There is one essential requirement that Hebrew needed to grow and survive and without which its fate would have been similar to thousands of other intellectual designs of invented languages that never got beyond the laboratory stage. This requirement is what Benjamin Harshav[5] has called "a base society" or "the social existence of the language"—i.e., a community of a sufficient number of speakers for whom the language is the essential tool of communication and information in all areas of human experience, throughout every social and institutional situation: "the bureaucracy, the universities, the slums and the hospitals, the highways and the cinemas, the tanks and the airplanes."[6] Only when children who were educated in Hebrew schools began to hear Hebrew spoken by adults in such roles as policemen, shopkeepers, lifeguards, government clerks, and postal workers, rather than by their own parents or their formal "teachers" in school, could they begin to imitate and even invent Hebrew words and expressions that seemed "natural" to them. The founding of The Hebrew University immediately made the world aware that Hebrew indeed had reached a level of maturity as a modern tongue and could function as a language of research and scientific investigation.

The Importance of the Hebrew Schools, the Radio, and the Press

Perhaps the most critical early achievement that enabled Hebrew speakers to surmount a major obstacle was the ability of Hebrew high school graduates in Palestine, for whom Hebrew had become their "second language" (the language predominantly used outside the home), to marry and then raise their children in an all-Hebrew-speaking environment. This began to happen sometime between 1905 and 1915. This served to establish a new Hebrew-reading and speaking "base society."[7] Even before Eliezer Ben-Yehuda arrived in Palestine, a Hebrew language press had begun as a weekly journal of information in Jerusalem. *Halevanon* and *Hahavatzelet* began publication just a few months apart in 1863 in Jerusalem. Both employed a very stilted form of Hebrew with countless new words "invented" by the editors, who imitated French, German, or Russian words for modern concepts. Both competed for a limited readership and were not reluctant in maligning each other before the Turkish authorities, who eventually closed both of them down.

Immediately after World War I, official recognition of Hebrew as the language of the Jewish community and Zionist institutions, renewed immigration, a stability and prosperity fostered by more secure British rule, and the growth of Tel Aviv all fostered a more secular Hebrew reading public and encouraged a Hebrew daily press. By 1948, the Hebrew press was already one of the most journalistically competitive in the world. Some new immigrants made the transition to full literacy by first reading *HaMat'hil* (The Beginner), a fully vowelled newspaper (*nikud*) encouraged by teachers during the period of government- and kibbutz-sponsored intensive Hebrew courses in live-in facilities (*ulpanim*). Israelis have always been fond of saying that Hebrew is the only language that "the children teach their parents," and this theme became a popular motif in many propaganda posters. Radio programs in the new spoken standard modeling proper pronunciation became a feature of the Hebrew language broadcasts avidly listened to during the Mandatory period.

The Twin Sources—Native and *Lo'azi*

Israel's national language is in danger. Internationally based words, immediately recognizable to a foreign audience, are edging out long-established Hebrew equivalents that were in common use before independence and generally contain the recognizable three-letter consonantal roots. The following list is by no means exhaustive. It appears that this trend is increasing—an example of "sociolects" (words characteristically employed by a distinct socioeconomic level of society) with "reverse snob appeal"—exactly the opposite of the situation that prevailed during the Hebrew renaissance when new words of Hebrew (or Arabic or Persian as indigenous to the Middle East) origin were coined and the public encouraged to use them instead of the internationally recognized words—largely with German or Russian suffixes. An English speaker without any knowledge of Hebrew can easily make out the *lo'azi* words in the left hand column.[8]

MODERN WORDS OF *LO'AZI* ORIGIN (FOREIGN ORIGIN)	WORDS BASED ON INDIGENOUS HEBREW ROOTS
aggresivi	tokpani
addict	mimukar
adminsitratzia	minhal
situatzia	matzav
adeptazia	histaglut
breksim	blamim
illuzia	ashlayah
illustratzia	iyur
immunizatzia	hisun

Better Hebrew Usage, a standard text by Dr. Reuben Silvan, published in 1969, lists well over seven hundred such pairs of words. Today, the number has grown substantially to more than twice that. A generation ago, the Hebrew press catered to a veteran Hebrew-speaking, literate population familiar with the root structure of the language and its mechanisms for word derivation. This made it easy for someone with a firm grasp of the language to recognize the new words based on the Hebrew letters forming the basic root concept and who could often venture a correct guess as to the exact meaning of the new word. Today, many readers with a minimal grasp of the language and not familiar with the written language can much more easily relate to the words of foreign origin, the majority of which bear a close resemblance to Yiddish! Probably any English reader without any previous knowledge of Hebrew can guess the meaning of the words in the left-hand column of the table above.

"The Soviet Zion" in Birobidzhan and Yiddish as a Jewish National Language

Because Israel served as the focal point of Zionist efforts to "ingather the exiles" to create a Jewish homeland, it is necessary to examine the competition between Hebrew and Yiddish, Hebrew's major competitor on a global scale. According to Marxist theory on the "national question," small peripheral and marginal ethnic groups were simply anachronistic remnants of the previous precapitalist economic system. They were thus "destined" to be completely assimilated within the integration of a worldwide proletariat linked by class solidarity and absorbed within the larger nations. The "backward" or "quaint" peoples in remote areas would, according to the Marxist theory, soon lose their distinctiveness. Each mile of railroad track and telegraph wire was destined to integrate these groups into larger frameworks and to encourage the rapid adoption of the national languages, standards of speech, literacy, dress, and folkways. The Jews, because of their "fossil-like" existence—a non-territorial historical remnant of the ancient world that had lost the identifying characteristics of a common territory and language—particularly vexed both Marx and Lenin.

The Jews, lacking a territory, more literate, urban-dwelling, and more ready, willing, and able to participate in the new capitalist economy than the other minorities, should "wither away" first. The new regime, however, was uncertain what policy to adopt with regard to the Jewish minority remaining in the country, after so many had emigrated from tsarist Russia to escape persecution, discrimination, and religious intolerance. Although many Jews initially welcomed the fall of the tsarist regime, their place in the new society was subject to contradictions. Many Jews in the rural areas of the Ukraine and White Russia were overwhelmingly still speakers of Yiddish[9]; they included many skilled craftsmen, simple unskilled workers, farmers, petty merchants, and shopkeepers. As late as 1937, the U.S.S.R. issued postage stamps representing the flags, nationalities, and the respective languages of all the Soviet Republics. The stamp representing Byelorussia (White Russia) bears the slogan "Workers of the World Unite" in Byelorussian, Russian, Polish, and Yiddish (reissued in 1948 but with the Yiddish and Polish inscriptions omitted).

The appeal of Zionism in its secular, and even Socialist form, exercised an immense appeal on the popular consciousness of the Jewish masses.

By 1928, the regime decided to confront this challenge to the loyalty and integration of the Jewish minority by fully recognizing a Jewish national identity based on Yiddish. It was located in a strategic area of Soviet interest in the Far East. At that time, over 70 percent of Soviet Jews indicated Yiddish as their mother tongue. The chosen area of Birobidzhan in the Amur River Valley near Manchuria would also act to prevent Japanese expansion. The "Jewish Autonomous Oblast (District)" was officially inaugurated in 1934, and Soviet President Kalinin stated that it would achieve recognition as a Soviet Republic when it reached a population of one hundred thousand.

From the Soviet point of view, the remote location of the intended Jewish Autonomous Republic would provide a new society for Jews, moving them far away from their earlier environment with its traditional religious influences. It would garner sympathy from secular Yiddish-speaking Jews throughout the Diaspora and aid in the movement to make the Jewish economic profile more productive in areas such as agriculture and industry. It is noteworthy that even a small group of disillusioned Zionist pioneers who left Palestine in 1932, following several years of economic depression in Palestine, chose to settle in the much more productive Crimea rather than go to the "New Zion" in Birobidzhan, which had been their original choice. In 1935, the Jewish population in Birobidzhan reached fourteen thousand, which constituted 23 percent of the total population, its high point. Yiddish schools begun with great initial hopes were closed down in 1948, even though the Jewish population had increased to almost thirty thousand. Since then, there has been a continuous decline, and the Jewish population today accounts for less than 5 percent of the total. Although now both Yiddish and Hebrew are taught, there is little hope that the "Jewish identity" of the region will survive.

The Brief Soviet-Israeli "Honeymoon"

Soviet policy towards the District was always contradictory. During World War II, the Jewish Anti-Fascist Committee was formed to win sympathy for the U.S.S.R. Nevertheless, a long-term ban on the teaching of Hebrew remained in force, and even Yiddish was suppressed. A relaxation during the Khrushchev era allowed the Jewish Autonomous District capital to publish the Yiddish language newspaper *Birobidzhaner Shtern* (Birobidzhan Star) and the monthly literary review *Sovietish Heymland* (Soviet Homeland). Both were heavily subsidized by the Soviet regime and primarily designed for consumption abroad, as a way of still influencing Yiddish-speaking and sympathetic leftwing Jews in the Diaspora. The region has, however, produced no major literary, musical, or other Jewish artistic work of any note. Further emigration from the region to Israel has reduced the Jewish population to a tiny proportion of the total, very few of whom have continued to speak Yiddish.

The ironic outcome of continual Soviet opposition to Zionism "as a reactionary tool of British imperialism" was the complete turnabout of the entire Eastern Block in 1947–1949 as a result of the Zionist underground's successful opposition to British rule. In spite of the myth that America was primarily responsible for Israel's birth, the United States imposed an embargo on all weapons shipments and purchases to both sides. It was Czech-equipped Zionist forces that defeated the British-trained-and-equipped Egyptian, Iraqi, and Jordanian armies. On January 7, 1949, Israeli aircraft shot down five British-piloted Spitfires on patrol over the Sinai Desert. The Israeli fighters were former German Luftwaffe Messerschmidts provided by Czechoslovakia to the nascent Israeli Airforce. The British aircraft had been ordered to patrol Egyptian- and Jordanian-controlled territory to make sure that Israeli forces had not made incursions and caused a diplomatic crisis.

The Soviet press, which had always maligned Zionism and praised the "Soviet patriotism" of Russian Jews, portraying Jewish heroism in terms of Yiddish speaking proletarians, now lauded the new Hebrew-speaking fighters for independence and socialism against the reactionary invading Arab armies backed by British imperialism! The turnabout was breathtaking. In 1948–1949, two other events stimulated Russian-Jewish identification with the new state—the arrival in Moscow of Israel's new ambassador, Golda Meir, and a performance in Moscow by Paul Robeson, the great American black singer, who unexpectedly electrified a sell-out crowd with his rendition in Yiddish of the "Song of The Jewish Partisans." The Communist party quickly recognized it had made a colossal error in stimulating emotions of Jewish patriotic identification with the new heroic state of Israel and quickly made another about-face—intensifying its ban on the teaching of Hebrew and even closing down Yiddish schools; the leaders of the Jewish Anti-Fascist Committee were executed.

The Hebrew-Yiddish Reconciliation in Israel Today

For two generations, the language debate in Israel was marked by a polarized controversy that reached the level of street brawls, social ostracism, picket lines against Yiddish theater, a polemical literature, and self-proclaimed boycotts by rival groups of the "other language." Although Hebrew emerged the "winner" and has increased its legitimate authority as the official language and bearer of the majority culture in the State of Israel, elements in the Jewish population, especially among the ultra-Orthodox of East European origin, maintain a hostile attitude toward its modern role as a secular language and insist that its use be prescribed only as the *loshn kodesh*—holy language of the Scriptures. Extremist wings of the ultra-Orthodox, notably in Jerusalem and Bnei-Brak, can study the Talmud and Bible using Yiddish. For them, the Hebrew language in its modern form represents a sacrilegious and blasphemous transgression. On numerous occasions, demonstrators have defaced the house of Eliezer Ben-Yehuda and monuments in his memory. One can well understand the reaction of those for whom the tabloid press, cheap detective and cowboy novels, pornographic magazines, books on sexual matters, the football lottery, and a thousand and one other secular concerns are printed in a language made holy by God's written word.

Nevertheless, the authorities, and a large segment of the Hebrew-speaking public, have regained a sympathetic attitude toward honoring the language of many of their parents and grandparents.[10] Israel's broadcasting system "Kol Yisrael" (The Voice of Israel) maintains a full range of Yiddish programs. The Yiddish theater and Yiddish singers have a devoted audience, and there is a host of degree-granting programs offered by Israeli universities in Yiddish linguistics, language, and literature. Today Yiddish is an optional subject in Israeli secondary schools and honored by all segments of the Israeli cultural establishment. The famous Habimah Hebrew theater now offers plays in Yiddish. Subsidies for cultural and scholastic endeavors in the language have been made available by the government, local municipalities, and institutions abroad—notably from Germany. Countless Yiddish expressions have entered popular Israeli Hebrew speech, and the language may be said to have risen from the bottom of the social ladder of languages spoken in Israel.

Language Decline and Retention—Yiddish and Hebrew in the United States

From a prewar population of more than ten million Yiddish speakers throughout the world, the number of speakers worldwide had been reduced by more than half by the end of the war in 1945. The Yiddish press in New York City reached a high point in the early 1930s when daily circulation reached almost half a million. The estimate of the number of speakers currently varies widely.[11] Today there are no more than one million American Jews with knowledge of the language, 200,000 in Israel, and only 154,000 "native language speakers" in the U.S.S.R. (1989 census). Almost all of these are elderly, bilingual, or multilingual in Russian and several other languages, and about half of them have since immigrated to Israel. The U.S. census shows a steep decline among Yiddish speakers, in spite of recent popular attempts to maintain the language. In data on "mother tongue claimants" collected by the U.S. Census in 1970, Yiddish still stood as the sixth most common mother-tongue foreign language in the United States, with just over a million and a half claimants, behind Spanish, German, Italian, French, and Polish.[12]

Twenty years later, Yiddish speakers in the United States had fallen to sixteenth rank with 213,000 speakers, barely ahead of Hebrew, in twenty-third place with 144,000 speakers. Most young people study Hebrew either because of religious obligations or else as an identification with the still young, vibrant Israeli society in contrast to the image of Yiddish as a somber reminder of the Holocaust.

Hebrew's Success

Hebrew's success was the result of a combination of unique circumstances that other nations were unable to repeat. Jews migrating to Palestine had no common language, and no other argument could so successfully establish Jewish attachment to Israel. Countless everyday documents, scrolls, tombstones, and monuments from past millennia written on wood, stone, clay, and papyrus have been uncovered, all of which "speak Hebrew," confirming the Jewish connection to the land. As Hillel Halkin so succinctly put it: "Any alternative to Hebrew would have meant the loss of Zionism's historical content, the political consequences of which would have been to degrade the movement into the mere colonizing enterprises its enemies always viewed it as being and so doom it in advance."[13]

NOTES

1. See "Ben-Yehuda and the Revival of Hebrew Speech" in *Ariel, Quarterly Review of the Arts and Sciences in Israel,* no. 25, 1969, pp. 35–39; and Jack Fellman, "Eliezer Ben-Yehuda," *Ariel,* no. 104, pp. 26–31, Jerusalem.

2. Ze'ev Jabotinsky, *Hebrew Pronunciation.* Tel Aviv: HaSefer, 1940, pp. 37–38.

3. For a comparison of the similarities between the introduction of Esperanto and modern Hebrew, see Norman Berdichevsky, "Esperanto and Zamenhof," *Ariel,* 1986, no. 64, pp. 58–71.

4. For complete text, see the Website: http//www.bibiblio.org/yiddish/Tshernovits/birnbaum-op.html

5. Benjamin Harshav, *Language in a Time of Revolution.* Berkeley, Calif.: University of California Press, 1993.

6. Ibid., p. 40.

7. B. Spolsky and R. L. Cooper, *The Languages of Jerusalem*. Oxford: Clarendon Press, 1991, p. 63.

8. See also the humorous article "Hebrew As She Is Spoke" by Hillel Halkin, *Commentary*, December 1969, pp. 55–60.

9. Estimates from the 1897 census indicate that mother-tongue Yiddish speakers numbered well over 95 percent of all Jews in the rural area of White Russia and the Ukraine.

10. Eliezer Ben-Rafael, *Language, Identity and Social Division—The Case of Israel*. Oxford: Clarendon Press, 1994, p. 231.

11. John Geiple, in "*Mame Loshn; The Making of Yiddish* (1982), takes the optimistic view that there are still upwards of four or five million speakers (or readers) of Yiddish worldwide. This seems exceedingly optimistic. The 1997 *World Almanac and Book of Facts* lists the principal languages of the world with over one million speakers: it includes Yiddish but without an exact figure—the only language in the table without one. Undoubtedly this is due to the difficulties of taking an accurate census when speakers are so geographically dispersed.

12. Table 2. "Mother Tongue of the Population by Nativity and Parentage," 1970 U.S. Census.

13. Hillel Halkin, op. cit., p. 60.

THE PARENT IS THE CHILD'S FIRST TEACHER

Carol Diament

I DID NOT GROW UP on Cinderella or Little Red Riding Hood. In some of my earliest childhood memories, I am sitting on a high chair in my mother's kitchen while she recounts the exploits of King David. Between spoonfuls of farina, she would tell me about David's triumphs over Goliath and Saul, of his bloody battles with the Philistines, of his lust for Bathsheba, and of his punishment by God. David was so real to me, I could touch him. The sense of wonderment and suspense I felt when listening to those tales has remained with me forever. I'm still proud of David, as I am of Moses, Ruth, Joseph, and Esther. They are my brave and true childhood heroes.

My mother didn't stop with the Bible. She told me of Bruria, Rashi, Ben-Gurion, Theodor Herzl, and the Ba'al Shem Tov. Never did she have trouble feeding me.

Often I reflect on those mystical moments when I felt so intimately connected to her and to the whole Jewish people. The sense of trust and belonging that was communicated to me through the language of stories never left me. I became an avid student of Jewish history. My mother also sang to me from her repertoire of Yiddish songs and lullabies. To this day, I sing for my children and for others. Stories and songs were beautiful vessels for transmitting Jewishness to me, and they continue to be—even in an age of television and hard rock—of inestimable efficacy in passing on Jewish feelings, values, and a sense of identification to the new generation.

Another early memory is of my father's morning *davening,* the black *tefillin* straps wound tightly around his left arm, the little black box sitting just above the graying hairline of his forehead. Once the *siddur* fell, and he stooped to pick it up and kiss it. To this day, I always kiss a *siddur* or Bible when it falls. I can't even bring myself to treat a Hebrew newspaper cavalierly. Reverence for the Jewish word, instilled early, lasts forever.

My maternal grandparents lived around the corner. They, too, were among my early Jewish educators. My parents, my older brother, and I spent most Friday nights and Sabbath afternoons with them. The universal questions about God I saved for my grandfather. I knew that only he could answer complex questions of this nature: Is God a man or a woman? If He's a man, does He have a wife? When will He die?

When my own children ask these questions, I try to respond from my current intellectual perspective and with integrity. Often, it doesn't wash—but I know I must not dismiss their questions without attempting some answers: We can't see God. God is a kind of spirit. He is the intelligent force in the universe. For my grandfather, God was God. You simply accepted this on faith. You could argue with God, you could protest and rail against Him. There certainly was plenty of cause for railing in the 1940s, when I was growing up, but you never ceased to believe in Him.

My grandfather was a *maskil,* a disciple of the Hebrew Enlightenment in Eastern Europe. His love for the Hebrew language was real. He read *Hadoar* and Hebrew journals and books. I learned to read the Hebrew alphabet before entering first grade. If my grandpa couldn't practice with me, my mother did, or my father. I have tried to pass on this love of the Hebrew language to my children by giving them a modern-day school education, in which Hebrew is taught as a living language. To them as to me, Hebrew is the key to the treasured sources of the Jewish people.

Friday nights at my grandparents' house were otherworldly. The fragrance of Sabbath still lingers, as do the tastes of gefilte fish and chicken soup with the little round golden eggs you can no longer buy at the kosher butcher. My grandmother always enlisted my help with the preparations, shining the candlesticks, baking the *halla,* chopping the meat. My mother taught school, so these Friday night and Sabbath afternoon dinners, which she did not have to prepare or worry about, were, for her, the epitome of women's liberation. Involving children in concrete tasks related to Jewish holidays is still the best way to get them to feel a part of the observance.

When my brother went to *shul* with my father and grandpa, the quiet time between the lighting of candles and their homecoming was surely a foretaste of heaven. The language of stories was not spoken here. Instead, there was a kind of silent teaching that transmitted to me a sense of the

Shekhina. These magical moments alone with my mother and grandmother were the closest I ever came to a spiritual transcendence. The experience of the Sabbath and the transition from workday to Sabbath can instill Jewish values, even if only in their being different from the rest of the week.

Gender roles were sharply delineated in those calm days before the women's movement. I was deeply jealous of my brother's being able to read the Torah, of his bar mitzva, and of his box seat in the men's section. Later, I made sure that my daughter would participate fully in the rites of passage. But I would not have traded that quiet time with my mother and grandmother for anything in the world.

There is a midrash that tells that angels accompany Friday night worshipers on their way home from the synagogue. Surely, I felt, when my grandpa blessed me to grow up to be like Sarah, Rebecca, Rachel, and Leah and my brother to be like Ephraim and Manasseh, the angels were hovering over us. When our children would later ask about heaven and hell and the devil, I was sure there were no devils, but I could never be certain about the angels.

Today I try to parent Jewishly the way I was parented. It's not quite the same; it is not so easy as it was in my own childhood. My parents do not live around the corner; my children cannot come home to their grandparents for lunch and listen to the Yiddish radio. My busy schedule doesn't always allow me time to tell them long, magical tales, but my husband and I do other things that my parents could not do for us.

We have three children, a daughter of twenty-three and two sons, one twenty-two and the other thirteen. When our big kids were four and five, we took them to Israel for a year. My grandfather, who was a Zionist and a Hebraist, was not blessed to see the Land of Israel. Neither was my father-in-law, who was a Yiddish writer. My parents did not go until they were close to fifty; there was never enough money or time.

But Israel was already alive and bustling for my children when they were very young. They went to school there, played house, rode the bus, and got lost among its streets. They still sing Shabbat *zemirot* and popular Hebrew tunes with an Israeli accent. Even our young bar mitzva read the Torah with an Israeli accent on his special day. He never got to spend a year in Israel as did his brother and sister, but he was there for a long summer. Any exposure children get to the Land of Israel is invaluable.

All our children dream of making *aliya* and one day, perhaps they will. Their connection to the land is deep and intense. In December 1987, when the *intifada* began, they were consumed with anxiety. They could hardly think of anything other than Israel embattled; they, too, felt embattled.

There were endless expressions of remorse about not living there. The spate of forest fires in Israel during that time was particularly painful. Who can spend one's childhood pasting stamps on JNF (Jewish National Fund) branches and dropping coins into little blue boxes and remain indifferent to trees?

In other ways, however, it is more difficult now to carry forth the traditions. Our family is more nuclear than when I was young. My husband and I are mostly on our own in raising our kids Jewishly. We have affixed *mezuzot* to every room in the house, built our *sukka* annually, hung our Israeli paintings, eaten our Friday night and holiday meals, kindled our *menora,* dispensed our *mishloah manot* (Purim gifts), most often with friends rather than with family. We have searched for *hametz* and have soaked our glass dishes in the bathtub in preparation for Passover by ourselves. Our parents were only sometime, weekend guests; when my mother, mother-in-law, and father were younger, however, we spent many holidays together. Still, it was not the same as when I was growing up.

Our older children knew my father well, but our youngest son was only six when he died. None of our children ever knew my father-in-law. Perhaps because of this, we are more open about death than were my parents. When my niece named her first child for my father, Hayyim Noah, the *brit* became for us a symbol of Jewish continuity. It helped to heal some of the wounds we experienced at my father's funeral.

My mother has since remarried and lives in Israel. In her twilight years, she is living out her lifelong Zionist dream of homecoming. My children are very proud of her. It makes their connection with the land even more intense and personal. Parents and grandparents who demonstrate sincerity in what they advocate are powerful role models for young people. Zionist attachment to Israel and Jewish communal and political involvement are two possibilities that can serve this purpose.

Our middle child, who spent his junior year at Cambridge University in England, came on winter vacation to Israel after traveling through Europe. He called from Tel Aviv to tell us how at home he felt with his *savta* (grandmother). All her old Brooklyn furnishings were there, her lamps and china cabinet, her books and umbrella stand, even the dusty yellow tennis balls she neglected to leave behind. *Savta* was home, and home was Israel. He had just been to Spain and to Auschwitz, exploring his Jewish background at the sites of some of the historic epochs we had talked about over the years.

Often when I have time, I sit with my youngest son and read the Torah portion or some Hebrew story or ethical tract. Sometimes we say the nightly *Sh'ma* together, although mostly we forget. I remember that when he was only two, he would say amen after every blessing. Now he asks me if God really takes back his soul at night and returns it to him in the morning. I can't always answer that question. I know only that the Jewish soul exists: King David and my grandfather certainly had one, and so do my children.

Our daughter, who is married and in medical school, is expecting a baby soon. My husband and I look forward to grandparenting and to the miracle of a new and precious Jewish soul.

ETHICAL KASHRUT

Yitzhak Husbands-Hankin

AS EACH YEAR WE ENTER the season of Passover, we find an enduring spark of hopefulness that derives from our awareness of the transformative message of Pesach. We again experience the vision of liberation as we eat the humble matzah and we sing our song of gratitude:

DAYEINU—IT WOULD HAVE BEEN ENOUGH.

Today humanity is tormented by the rage, hatred, and fear that are concomitant with war, milchama. The root of the word "milchama" is L-CH-M, the word "bread." It is impossible not to wonder about the relationship of these two words "war" and "bread." Is it our fear of not having enough bread, enough sustenance to go around, that brings people to fight wars? Is it a lack of faith in the One Who Sustains All that leads people to become enemies fighting over a real or imagined inadequate supply of sustenance?

When the moon circles to show us its fullness, we exchange our eating of leavened for unleavened bread. I see within this exchange a powerful message that can serve as a framework of understanding toward our own liberation. We set aside the fullness and feeling of abundance associated with leavened bread and we meditate on the qualities of the simple unleavened matzah.

When we consider the nature of enslavements in our own time and place on this planet, we see a societal illness recently identified and named "affluenza." Affluenza is the sickness of "wanting and consuming too much." It is the sickness of not knowing how to feel satisfied and to endlessly and in futility pursue fulfillment through acts of acquisition and consumption. This illness not only affects those who personally suffer from the symptomatic lifestyle, it also affects others who find that their fair share of essential consumables is not available to them.

We live in a society that has cultivated in many of us a sense of entitlement to endless material abundance. It is only in recent years that the impact of our overconsumption is becoming recognized. We are just beginning to understand the harm that this behavior brings to our own health and well-being in addition to the harm and deprivation that it causes others.

Our halachic tradition provides us with some useful models that can serve us well in our efforts to liberate ourselves from this contemporary enslavement. The halachic framework provides shaping disciplines for all of our natural appetites. It guides us to gain mastery over them rather than remaining enslaved to them. There are constraints placed upon our appetites for food, sex, and money. We learn from these disciplines that we are capable of saying and experiencing what it means to have "enough." Creating communal covenants that shape our consumption practices into sustainable patterns can allow us to support one another in redefining success and well-being in new ways that counteract the models and values that led us to our current overindulgences.

The development of a Halacha of Ethical Kashrut can provide us with a road map out of the debilitating and unsustainable condition of affluenza. Americans have too long lived with the illusion that we are driving a global economy that will eventually bring the world to a level of material abundance equal to our own. The reality is that with current technologies, for the world population to live at the same level of resource consumption as the population of the United States, four planet Earths and nine atmospheres would be required.

A system of Ethical Kashrut must envision and have as its goal a sustainable global reality in which consumption patterns of food and a wide range of other resources allow for enough Lechem, sustenance, to go around—to turn us from the anxiety that leads to milchama-conflict. As we develop a system of Ethical Kashrut that certifies that a product is made through a process that does not cause environmental degradation, exploitation of workers, or the cruel treatment of animals, we will also be aligning with practices that create a global sustainability.

Ethical Kashrut would lead us to diets that utilize foods lower on the food chain so that there would be a diminishment in the land usage for raising beef and other livestock and the earth's abundance would become available for growing foods that could sustain our global population.

Ethical Kashrut can lead us from utilizing vehicles that consume fossil fuels that are altering the global climate, endangering lives, and causing immense harm to the health of countless people as well as other life forms.

A certification of Ethical Kashrut could serve as a positive market incentive to producers. Our already well-organized faith communities would be relatively easy to educate through newsletters, Websites, etc., about the availability of ethically certified products. Other faith communities could utilize their particular linguistic equivalent to "kosher" but could be similarly well organized in their ability to have an impact on production processes and goods. Together we can unify in developing a global ethic that truly brings us through grassroots organizing, a sustainable global system. Our tradition teaches—V'achalta—you shall eat (consume), V'savata—and you shall be satisfied, U'verachta—and you shall Bless. May we soon know the beauty of feeling satisfied and the sense of gratitude that comes from having simply enough.

HALACHA

DIVINE OR HUMAN?

Gilbert S. Rosenthal

IS HALACHA, JEWISH LAW, Divine or human? Or is it an amalgam of both elements? This is a fundamental question for understanding Judaism, which is, after all, a religion of law, not merely of theology; of action, not just of faith. Law plays a crucially important role in Judaism that cannot be ignored without distorting the Jewish faith. To ignore halacha is to misconstrue Judaism.

But what is the nature of halacha? Interestingly, the sages seemed to believe that halacha is a process, an unfolding of laws. Moreover, there is a parallel process of expounding the law that proceeds in heaven and on earth. God and His celestial Beit Din study, debate, interpret, and vote on legal rulings simultaneously with the terrestrial courts and academies. An unusual midrash in the name of Rabbi Yehudah states that "not a single day goes by in which the Holy One, blessed be He, does not pass new halacha in the celestial Beit Din, for it says in Job 37:2, 'Hearken well to His thundering voice, to the rumbling that comes from His mouth'" (Genesis Rabbah 49:2). Doubtless, this is the inspiration for the statement of the eminent Kabbalist, Rabbi Isaiah Horowitz (Selah, died 1630) that "the Holy One, blessed be He, gave the Torah and gives it at every moment; the flowing fountain never ceases."

So we know that the sages viewed Torah as an evolving process with God Himself actively involved in its renewal. What place in the process do we humans occupy?

One school of thought, championed by Rabbi Akiva, insisted that all is in heaven; that everything was given at Sinai. Some partisans of this approach insist, in what Abraham Joshua Heschel dubbed "a theological exaggeration," that the entire corpus of the oral law, including every future decision of the sages, was revealed to Moses (Berachot 5a and parallels). Furthermore, Mar Samuel asserted that three thousand halachot given at Sinai were forgotten during the mourning for Moses, and it is our task to try to discover those lost laws (Temurah 16a). Rabbi Eliezer ben Hyrcanus was the great exponent of this position. His legal rulings either were based on traditions from ancestors and previous scholars or else were conveyed to him from heaven via supernatural channels. The famous debate over the purity of a certain type of stove highlights the difference between Rabbi Eliezer and his colleagues. He ruled that an Achnai stove is ritually pure while his colleagues demurred and declared it impure (Bava Metzia 59b):

> "If the halacha is according to my view, let the carob tree prove it." And the carob tree was uprooted and moved 400 cubits. Said the sages, "We don't bring proof from a carob tree." "If the halacha is according to my view, let this stream of water flow backwards." And the stream flowed backwards. Said the sages, "We don't bring proof from a stream of water." "If the halacha is according to my view, let the walls of the academy prove it." And the walls of the academy inclined as if to fall.
>
> He persisted and said, "If the law is according to my view, let Heaven prove it." Whereupon a Bat Kol (echo of a Divine voice) issued from heaven proclaiming, "Why do you challenge Rabbi Eliezer? The law always follows his views." Said Rabbi Joshua ben Hananiah, "It is not in heaven" [Deuteronomy 30:12]. Said Rabbi Jeremiah, "The Torah has already been given at Sinai; hence, we pay no attention to a Bat Kol, for You have written in Your Torah at Sinai, 'Follow the majority'" [Exodus 23:2].

Clearly, Rabbi Eliezer was relying on his learning and prestige plus a few miracles and Divine intervention against the majority of the sages. But as the great Polish commentator Rabbi Samuel Edels (Maharsha, died 1631) notes: "This shows that the power of the majority supersedes a Bat Kol, because the Torah was not given to angels in heaven."

Another well-known tale on the issue of human versus Divine prerogatives in halacha is found in the Talmud (Eruvin 13b), again in the name of Mar Samuel:

> For three years Beit Shammai and Beit Hillel debated. Beit Shammai
> said, "The halacha is according to us." Beit Hillel said, "The halacha
> is according to us." A Bat Kol came forth from heaven and proclaimed,
> "Both these and those are the words of the living God, but the halacha
> is according to Beit Hillel."

This famous tale, which, as Professor Avi Sagi notes, conceals more
than it reveals, seems to reinforce the notion that, whereas humans may
debate halachic rulings, the final arbiter is God in heaven. This approach
denigrates the role of human beings: humans may neither create, nor
change, nor reinterpret the law. At best, they may only discover or recover
the original, concealed halachot via *pilpul* (debates, dialectic), and offer
chiddushim, novel interpretations and insights.

The second school of thought, championed by Rabbi Yishmael, denied
that all was given at Sinai. Indeed, only general principles were revealed
to Moses; the rest was filled in by succeeding generations of scholars
(Chagigah 6a and parallels). Consequently, the role of humans in the halachic process is affirmed and strengthened. After all, even in the Talmudic controversy about the stove, cited above, we are informed that "the law
is not in heaven" any longer, or, as Professor Menachem Fisch puts it, "[I]t
is beyond the reach of heaven." Several *aggadic* texts, some of which display legendary or mythic qualities, buttress this view.

> Said Rabbi Yanai: "Were the Torah given cut-and-dried, it would not
> have a leg to stand on." Said Moses: "Master of the universe, teach
> me the halacha." God said to him, "Follow the majority. If the ma-
> jority rules 'innocent,' he is innocent. If the majority rules 'guilty,' he
> is guilty. In this way, the Torah may be interpreted 49 ways to rule im-
> pure and 49 ways to rule pure" [Yer. Sanhedrin IV, 2, 22a].

○

Clearly God expects humans to debate all sides of issues in arriving at a
conclusion by majority vote. Not only that, but we are told that God affirms and confirms decisions arrived at by human courts and ratifies them
on high. So we read in the Talmud (Makkot 23b and Megillah 7a) on the
verse in Esther 9:27: "[T]he Jews undertook and irrevocably obligated
themselves" to observe Purim and that "three laws passed by Israel were
confirmed in the heavenly Beit Din." The three laws are the reading of the
Megillah of Esther, greeting persons using God's name or a divine epithet

such as "shalom," and imposing tithes on the Levites to be given to the priests. In short, "they confirmed on high what was accepted below."

The same principle applies in setting the calendar: Heaven approves of human decisions on halachic matters. The sages insisted that the Torah conferred on them the authority to proclaim which day is prohibited and which day is permitted, which labor is prohibited and which labor is permitted (Chagigah 18a). And they went even further in strengthening rabbinic prerogatives:

> If the Beit Din ruled to move Rosh Hashanah to the next day, at once the Holy One, blessed be He, says to the angels, "Remove the bimah . . . because My children have ruled to move Rosh Hashanah to the next day, as it says, 'For it is a law for Israel, a ruling of the God of Jacob.' If it is not a law for Israel, so to speak, it is not a ruling for the God of Jacob . . ." [Yer. Rosh Hashanah I, 3, 57b].

In other words, God originated the core of the law but now it is up to us humans to continue the process of explication and interpretation. God merely confirms or assents to human actions.

This view of human involvement in the legal process is found in a quaint *aggadah* in Gittin 6b:

> The sages disagreed in the interpretation of the verse in Judges 19:2, "Once his concubine played the harlot." Rabbi Aviatar said that the husband found a fly in his food. Rabbi Jonathan said he found a pubic hair in his food. Rabbi Aviatar came across Elijah and asked him, "What is the Holy One, blessed be He, doing?" He replied, "He is discussing the question of the concubine in Gibea." "And what does He say?" Elijah responded, "My son Aviatar says such-and-such and my son Jonathan says such-and-such." Said Aviatar, "Can there possibly be uncertainty in the mind of the Holy One?" Elijah replied, "Both answers are the words of the living God."

In an even bolder legend, God and His Beit Din are depicted as turning to humans for help in deciding the law. This is the tale found in Bava Metzia 86a:

> They were debating in the heavenly academy the rule of a skin lesion. If the scab precedes the white hair, it is unclean; if the white hair precedes the lesion, it is clean (Leviticus 13:1–3). But what if we are unsure which came first? The Holy One, blessed be He, ruled "pure," but

the members of the heavenly academy ruled "impure." They wondered, "Who will decide the issue? Only Rabbah bar Nachman who is a great expert in skin lesions and the laws of impurities." They sent the angel of death to summon him, but as Rabbah was engrossed in Torah study, he could not kill him. The angel then caused a wind to blow so that the leaves rustled mightily. Rabbah thought that a cavalry troop was approaching. He stopped studying and exclaimed, "Better that I should die than fall into the hands of the government." And he died proclaiming, "Pure, pure" [thereby upholding God's opinion].

This *aggadah* is clear evidence that at least some sages believed that God Himself as well as His celestial academy turn to human beings for halachic rulings, and the authority of the sages supersedes even God's.

○

That halacha is not stagnant or frozen, and that we humans have a role to play in its growth and development, is clearly the point of one famous text that comes down firmly on the side of human creativity in the halachic process. I refer to the legend in Menachot 29b, a tale that reveals more than it conceals. Its purpose was clearly to indicate the methodology of Rabbi Akiva in expounding the written Torah by which each jot and tittle on the letters is built into great structures. Instead, we learn much about how we humans create and expand God's Torah. Rabbi Yehudah quotes the tale in the name of Rav:

> When Moses went on high, he found the Holy One, blessed be He, sitting and tying crowns on the letters of the Torah. He asked God, "Who prevented You from writing whatever You wanted [Rashi: that You have to add additional crowns]? He replied to Moses: "There is a certain man named Akiva ben Joseph who, after many generations in the future, will interpret every single jot and tittle of the letters and build mounds of halachot." Moses replied: "Master of the universe, show him to me." He said, "Turn back to the future." Upon doing so, Moses found himself in the academy of Rabbi Akiva, so he sat at the end of the eighth row. He did not understand a single word of the discussion, and he felt faint. They reached a certain matter in the discussion, and one of the pupils challenged Rabbi Akiva, "Rabbi, how do you know this is the law?" Rabbi Akiva responded, "It is a halacha given to Moses at Mount Sinai." And Moses' strength returned to him [Rashi: since Rabbi Akiva quoted him by name even though he had not yet received this legal ruling of Torah].

This unusual legend teaches some very profoundly crucial lessons. First, as Rashi observed, we see from the text that contrary to Rabbi Akiva's viewpoint, Moses had not received all of the Torah at Sinai. Second, we learn that the law develops and grows; it is not static or frozen. Third, each human being is free to explore and expand the Torah. Fourth, the Torah is clearly broader than the written text; its boundaries are set by human inquiry. Finally, human beings are God's partners in fashioning halacha.

It is apparent from these sources I've marshaled that the majority of the sages seem to have endorsed Rabbi Yishmael's understanding of the halacha, by which humans are invested with the authority to flesh out the basic Sinaitic principles. Indeed, it seems to be God's will—or challenge to us—that we humans continue the task He inaugurated. Let us remember the tale of the Achnai stove, which I cited earlier and which ends with God laughingly proclaiming, "My children have defeated Me!" God wanted us to uncover and reveal, explain and elucidate, interpret and reinterpret, expand and amplify, improve and renew His essential Torah. An early medieval midrash (Seder Eliyahu Rabbah II, p. 172) offers an analogy of Torah and raw materials. It states that when God gave us the Torah, it was like wheat and flax. Just as it is up to us humans to convert them into bread and cloth, so must we refine and enhance the basic teachings of Torah.

Am I reading too much into these texts? Have I distorted their true meaning? I think not, and I have assembled some later commentaries to prove the point.

Rabbi Yom Tov ben Abraham Isbili (Ritva, Spain, thirteenth to fourteenth centuries) replied to a query about rabbinic authority from French rabbis by indicating that God had shown Moses forty-nine different possibilities to permit or prohibit a matter, but He indicated that "the prerogative will be handed over to the sages of Israel in every generation to rule according to their discretion." His younger colleague, Rabbi Nissim Gerondi (Ran, Spain, fourteenth century), considered it God's will that the wise men, not the prophets of each generation, reveal the halacha. In one of his sermons, he notes that the Talmud had indicated that after the destruction of the Temple, prophecy was taken from the prophets and given to the sages (Bava Batra 12b). Consequently, "the power of deciding such matters has been transmitted to the scholars of the generations, and their consensus is what God has commanded." Rabbi Joseph Albo (Spain, fifteenth century), the last of the great Spanish theologians, subscribed to the position of Rabbi Yishmael and argued that only "general principles were given orally to Moses at Sinai, briefly alluded to in the

Torah, by means of which the wise men of every generation may work out the details as new issues develop."

Shifting to Poland, I cite the great legalist Rabbi Solomon Luria (sixteenth century), who interpreted the phrase, "both these and those are the words of the living God," as follows:

> It is as if each sage received his ruling from God or from Moses even though no such thing was ever uttered by Moses. . . . Therefore, the Torah transmitted the authority to the sages of each generation, each according to his intellect, to enhance and add to the teachings with the approbation of Heaven.

Rabbi Samuel Edels adopted a bolder view of the human role in shaping halacha. He interpreted the verse from Isaiah 42:21, "that he may magnify and glorify [His] Torah," in a strikingly original way:

> You must not consider it wicked in God's sight for humans to add from their own intellect laws and prohibitions to those written in the Torah given by God. . . . The Holy One, Blessed be He, wants us to glorify and strengthen that which we increase so that it might be even more glorious and strong than the body of the Torah of the Holy One. . . . And lest you argue, "Who appointed puny humans to make themselves partners of God who gave us the Torah and *mitzvot* by adding a new Torah and *mitzvot?*" To this God responds by citing the verse, as if to say, "Just the opposite! The Holy One wants this to happen. . . ."

I turn to a modern giant of Jewish learning, Rabbi Baruch Epstein (Russia, died 1942), who discusses this matter in several places in his renowned commentary on the Pentateuch, *Torah Temimah*. He notes the view of Rabbi Yehoshua ben Levi in the Talmud, who agrees with Rabbi Yishmael that "every future teaching of great scholars has already been given to Moses at Sinai," but he interprets it in quite a different way. He suggests that only the principles (*ikkarim*) of the laws were given; the ultimate decisions will be arrived at by students through their analytical powers and ability to fashion rules based on those principles. But his statement is not to suggest that the actual *pilpulim* were conveyed to Moses, "as the narrow-minded have endeavored to prove in their interpretations of the Talmud, thereby undermining the effects of human striving and struggles in the Talmudic debates." Elsewhere, he proposes that the text, "by the hand of Moses" (Numbers 4:37) should be linked to the verse, "it is not in heaven" (Deuteronomy 31:2), indicating that "it is in human hands to resolve all doubts that accompany specific laws."

In short, it is the will of God that we humans abet the unfolding process of interpreting and elucidating the Torah begun at Sinai, for the Torah must be interpreted and reinterpreted in every generation, in every land, in the light of new and changing circumstances. Just as we are God's partners in completing the creation of the world (Shabbat 119b), so are we His partners in continuing the evolving understanding of Torah and halacha, of teaching and law. As Rabbi Joseph B. Soloveitchik put it, we humans are God's partners and a reflection of God the Creator as we seek novel interpretations of the law, for the "goal of the halacha is uniting the creative force in man with the Creative Force of the universe." Professor David Weiss Halivni describes our role as "active partners in the creative process."

This understanding of halacha as an ongoing process bestows on us both an honor and a challenge. It certainly is an honor to be viewed as a partner of the Divinity in shaping halacha. But it is also a challenge to remain faithful to God's mandate to cultivate, invigorate, and reinterpret the halacha.

Judaism without halacha is no longer Judaism; it is an anarchical system of several loosely held beliefs. How can there be a Jewish religion if individual autonomy is the rule so that chaos reigns? As the eminent Reform rabbi and scholar W. Gunther Plaut complained, ". . . our people lack a Jewish lifestyle. . . . To defend the emptiness of their lives they shout, 'Freedom!' but they mean *hefkerut,* license to carry on with as little as possible, or at best, with what is convenient." Yet another renowned Reform leader and thinker, Rabbi Arnold J. Wolf, formulated the problem differently when he wrote, "Accordingly, the Reform movement will suggest or even instruct its adherents what political measures to support, while hardly requiring any ritual obedience, except for converts. . . . But there is no coherent standard for changing Jewish law except the spirit of the times, an epoch that is hardly worthy of emulation."

Conversely, Judaism with a frozen halacha is an anachronism and irrelevant—a betrayal of the dynamism that has always shaped it, as the sources I have selected clearly indicate. Let us recall that the word *halacha* means going, walking; it implies movement, process, activity—not stasis. Additionally, the noun is feminine (even as the word Torah is feminine), implying fecundity and growth. The very nature of halacha is to grow and reproduce and multiply. "The law must be stable but it cannot stand still," wrote Justice Benjamin Cardozo. And Professor Louis Ginzberg urged that "immutability must not be confounded with immobility." It is intolerable that the plight of the *agunah,* the woman unable to receive a *get*

(Jewish divorce) because the husband is either missing or recalcitrant, has not been properly addressed or resolved in the Orthodox community. It is even more galling, knowing that the remedies exist within the parameters of halacha. For example, there are five cases in the Babylonian Talmud of annulment of marriages—a procedure invoked on any number of occasions by the great adjudicator of the last century, Rabbi Moshe Feinstein. Yet, when Rabbi Emanuel Rackman and a handful of courageous colleagues invoke these remedies, they are pilloried and shunned for their heroic efforts.

Our faith is a tree of life; it has flourished and foliated in the past because we were bold and audacious in accepting the Divine mandate to serve as God's partners in creating new insights into Torah. When Jews were slaughtered by Greeks because they would not take up arms on the Sabbath, the sages reinterpreted the halacha and conceived of the category of *pikuach nefesh*—saving a human life supersedes all the *mitzvot* including Shabbat. When the Torah's prohibition against any person "arising from his place" grew so onerous and strangling as to destroy the pleasure of Shabbat, they eased the halacha to allow movement as far as two thousand cubits. When economic pressures and the refusal to grant loans to the needy became unbearable, the sages circumvented the Biblical prohibition against usury and conceived of a variety of legal loan instruments. That is how they kept halacha alive; that is how they preserved Judaism as a living entity.

So the question with which I began this essay can now be answered: "Halacha: Divine or Human?" The answer is: both. God, the source of Torah and halacha, entrusted to us mortals the sacred task of partnering with Him in exalting and glorifying Torah and *mitzvot*, in bringing all beneath the wings of the *Shechinah*, the Divine Presence. Whether or not we are up to the challenge may well determine the future of Judaism.

RABBI ABRAHAM JOSHUA
HESCHEL OF APT ON LISTENING

Peninnah Schram

JEWS ARE CALLED THE People of the Book, but also the People of the Word, because God had created the world through His word, *Bereshit* (In the beginning). From the beginning, words have always been important to the Jews, namely the words of the sacred books, The Torah (First Five Books of the Old Testament, the Pentateuch) and the Talmud (the commentaries on the Torah),[1] along with the prayers, proverbs, stories, and songs, all part of the oral and written traditions.

In Judaism, listening is a central theme. The keynote of all Judaism is the creed "*Shma Yisrael: Adonai Eloheinu, Adonai Ehad*" (Deuteronomy VI:4), usually translated as "Hear O Israel: The Lord Is Our God, The Lord Is One." This is essentially a summation of the first two Commandments. The *Shma*, referred to simply by the first Hebrew word of the paragraph in Deuteronomy, has been Judaism's "watchword and confession of faith throughout the ages."[2] This creed, the most important prayer in the Jewish liturgy,[3] is repeated twice each day, at morning and evening services, *aloud*. The reason for speaking it aloud is so that our own ears hear these words. In addition, this prayer is recited before going to sleep. So perhaps it would be more accurate to say that the Jews are the People of the word *Shma*, listen!

> It is no accident that "*Shema Yisrael*—Listen, O Israel" has become imperative in Judaism. God needs an audience. Thus, the quality of any exchange depends upon the listener.[4]

At an earlier moment in the Bible, after Moses had ascended Mt. Sinai to receive the Laws of Torah, Moses "wrote all the words of the Lord" (Exodus XXIV:4). Then after a peace-offering, Moses read the Book of the Covenant to the people of Israel. Their answer is most instructive. They responded with ". . . *naase v'nishma*" which means "We will do and we will listen" (Exodus XXIV:7).

In both these places, the word *shma*, to hear/listen is used. Rabbi Shlomo Riskin discusses the etymology of this key word:

> When we examine the etymology of the word "shma," we discover its linguistic link to another word which at first glance seems to have nothing to do with hearing: me'i, (guts, innards, intestines)—compare the mem and ayin of "shma" and the mem and ayin of "me'i." This suggests that the word "to hear," in the holy tongue, is not simply the act of registering an auditory sensation and then proceeding to the next sensation, but it is to go through an experience that takes what one hears and internalizes it. "Seeing" may be believing, but hearing is more than belief: hearing is making it your own, making it so close to you that it actually enters your innards, your guts, the very essences of your being.[5]

In essence, listening is an active process of hearing, attention, under-standing, and remembering,[6] a concept central to Judaism, as it is a major component in the communication process. George Bernard Shaw once said: "It is the audience that keeps the speaker speaking." In order for a speaker to successfully deliver a message, the speaker must also be aware of feed-back, audience receptivity, and speaker adjustment. Listening then involves more than hearing. What then are the differences between hearing and lis-tening?

Hearing refers to *"the physiological sensory process by which the ear receives auditory sensations and transmits them to the brain."*[7] However, listening goes beyond the physiological sensory process by also encom-passing a psychological process. *"Listening is a complex psychological process that deals with interpreting and understanding the significance of auditory sensation."*[8]

According to Klopf and Cambra,[9] the word *listening* derives from two Anglo-Saxon words: *hlystan,* which means "hearing"; and *hlosnian,* which means "to wait in suspense." "Listening, then, is the combination of hearing what the other person says and a suspenseful waiting, an in-tense psychological involvement with the other." The authors conclude that "Listening is a 4-stage process—the first of which is hearing, the other stages are attention, understanding and remembering." In other words, the listener must first take what he hears and internalize it, understand it, make it his own, remember what he hears and, only then, be able to act on it. Thus, when the children of Israel shout out *We will do and we will listen,*" in most translations you will see instead these words: "We will do and we will *obey.*" The agreement "to obey" apparently can only happen if the people really *listen,* according to the explication of Rabbi Riskin and the entire concept of *listening.*

As a storyteller as well as a teacher of communication, I have often thought about this concept of listening and its importance in our oral tradition. I also wondered whose contributions, among the various teachers in our Jewish tradition, have helped to shape understandings of the phenomenon of communication. Five teachers sprang to mind. For each teacher, in turn, there was a good argument to be made as to why that one should be chosen. I could then imagine how these five would come together, each to present his case as to why he should be the one chosen to represent the Jewish oral tradition. (In Judaism, there is even a midrash/story about the debate between mountains, each one vying for the honor to be chosen to be the site of Revelation.) Thus if mountains debate, why not teachers coming together—breaking the chronological time barrier—and each presenting his case?

Based on the above discussion of "listening" as the key concept in Judaism, I have chosen the following five Jewish leaders to present: Moses, Aaron, Solomon, Hillel, and Abraham Joshua Heschel of Apt. The first four will get but a brief mention with a focus on why they qualify to be a leading contributor to communication. However, it will be the last of these five that I will then discuss in more depth as my nominee for the significant Jewish contributor to the field of communication.

Our Sages say that a person can learn from everyone and everything. They say we can learn industriousness from an ant and modesty from a cat.[10] The first and best reason to learn anything worth knowing is to share it and transmit it to someone else; to plant metaphorical (and actual) trees so that future generations will be nourished with their fruit. Each generation in turn plants for the next one, and the next one, and the next one.

But how are we to do that? How do we determine the ability to teach at the right level of comprehension and need? In Judaism we have a tradition of telling stories. A person is considered a great teacher if he or she has the ability to transmit knowledge in a form that people will understand.

Moses was said to be such a teacher. Listen to the way Dr. J. J. Horovitz interprets a passage about Moses:

In the Ethics of the Fathers 4:25, the transmission of knowledge to the young is compared to the marking of clean paper with symbols in ink. Our Sages tell us that when Moses, our great Master, taught the Torah to his disciples in the wilderness, he had the ability to hold back the flow of ink so that it should not pour forth to excess from his pen; in other words, Moses had the talent of discrimination and discretion, to ensure that the quantity of knowledge to be communicated to his disciples should not be overly great, lest the whole effort of education prove a failure. In this manner his teaching could penetrate the minds of all, even those of little learning. . . . And as for Moses himself, his dignity did not suffer because he transmitted his own vast knowledge in the simple language that all of his listeners could understand.[11]

Moses, the first and greatest Prophet of the Jewish People, seems to have had a speech impediment (a stutter of some kind, perhaps). Pleading with God that he is not eloquent and thus assuming the leadership of the Jewish People would be impossible to a man not skilled in rhetoric and fluency, Moses says: "Oh Lord, I am not a man of words, neither heretofore nor since Thou hast spoken unto Thy servant; for I am slow of speech and of a slow tongue" (Exodus IV:10). But it is Moses, in spite of this speech stammer, who is referred to in the Bible, and to this day, as "Moses Our Teacher" (Moshe Rabbenu), for he is the archetype for all true leaders, teachers, and righteous judges. He understood how to reach each person on his or her own level of comprehension. Truly a great communicator!

Aaron, the High Priest, was the older brother of Moses and a person known as a peacemaker. It was during the time of the Jews crossing the desert, a time for stress and infighting among the people, that Aaron acted in his role as peacemaker between people, between couples, through patience and understanding. He personally aided them in their conflicts. As a teacher, he taught people how to pray and study, according to their own level. No doubt he learned this from his brother Moses, for after all he did sometimes serve as the spokesman for his brother.

Aaron did not, however, consider his task restricted "to establishing peace between God and man," but worked to create peace between the learned and the ignorant, among the scholars themselves, and between man and wife. Hence, the people loved Aaron and when he died, men *and* women mourned his death.

According to rabbinic legend, he would go from house to house, and whenever he found one who did not know how to recite the Shema, he taught him to recite it. He did not, however, restrict his activities to "establishing peace between God and man," but strove to establish peace between man and his fellow. If he discovered that two men had fallen out, he hastened first to the one, then to the other, saying to each: "If thou didst but know how he with whom thou hast quarrelled regrets his action!" Aaron would thus speak to each separately, until both the former enemies would mutually forgive each other, and as soon as they were again face to face greet each other as friends.[12]

Aaron was truly a great mediator who used words in order to resolve conflicts and pursue peace!

The third effective teacher of communication is Solomon, King of Jerusalem (961–920 B.C.E.). His name in Hebrew is Shlomo, which means "peace," because peace and prosperity reigned in his kingdom during his forty-year rule. Famous for his solving of riddles and as a judge, his greatest accomplishment was the building of the First Temple in Jerusalem. As a communicator dealing with people, keeper of the peace, and a wise judge, Solomon gained a reputation as a wise King and one who was sought out for resolving many disputes.

When God asked Solomon to choose what he wished for himself, Solomon requested a *lev shamaya* (I Kings, III:9), "a heart that listens" or often translated as "an understanding heart." As a result, Solomon possessed a wisdom beyond all others. "When Alexander the Great conquered Jerusalem, he found there Solomon's books of wisdom which he gave to his teacher Aristotle, who drew all his knowledge from them. The wisdom of the Greeks is accordingly entirely dependent upon Solomon."[13] If so, then in a sense all the credit for communication theory derived from Aristotle belongs to Solomon. But as we see, the concept of listening, an empathic response to hearing the message, is what Solomon desires most for the purpose of being able to discharge his responsibilities as king so as "to discern between good and bad" in order to better promote the welfare of the people.

Hillel, a contemporary of King Herod the Great, was the president of the Great Sanhedrin, the Jewish higher court of law during the time of the Second Temple. The role of the Great Sanhedrin was to interpret biblical law and enact new laws. (The Lesser Sanhedrin tried civil and criminal cases). Hillel reinterpreted the law so it would keep on developing into a living tradition that could be applied to any age.

Hillel is most famous for his teachings. And of those, his best known is "Do not unto others that which is hateful to you." This is a reformulation of the commandment in the Book of Leviticus, "Love your neighbor as yourself." Another famous saying of his is "Do not judge your neighbor until you are in his place."

Hillel's rival, Shammai, often took opposing points of view. However, Hillel always listened carefully to his opponent with patience and, only then, would he give his answer which would first incorporate what Shammai had said and then continue with his own argument. Jewish tradition presents both of these schools of thought, Beth Hillel (the House of Hillel) and Beth Shammai (the House of Shammai), but most often, if not always, agrees with Hillel in practice.

> . . . For three years there was a dispute between Beth Shammai and Beth Hillel, the former asserting, "The *halachah* (law) is in agreement with our views" and the latter contending, "The *halachah* is in agreement with our views." . . . Since, however, "both are the words of the living God," what was it that entitled Beth Hillel to have the *halachah* fixed in agreement with their rulings?—Because they were kindly and modest, they studied their own rulings and those of Beth Shammai and were even so (humble) as to mention the actions of Beth Shammai before theirs . . .[14]

From Hillel, we learn to be succinct and to listen fully to the other side, acknowledging the other's argument, before presenting our own view. Indeed this is sound communication logic!

Now we come to our fifth, and final, candidate, Rabbi Abraham Joshua Heschel of Apt. How is it then that I chose him to be the most significant contributor from Judaism that has helped to shape our understanding of communication? And who is he?

Abraham Joshua Heschel (1749–1825) is one of the outstanding Hasidic leaders of his generation.[15] His name in Hebrew is Avraham Yehoshua Heschel. Called the Apter Rabbi, he was a disciple of Rabbi Elimelekh of Lizensk. Heschel served as rabbi in the communities of Kolbuszowa Apta (Opatow) from 1809 to 1813 and then two years later in Medzibozh (Podolia), remaining there until his death. As a leader working to maintain peace and unity among the various hasidic groups, Heschel was regarded as an authority and respected for his decisions and counsel. He was a peacemaker. He could be said to have an extraordinary personality because he would recount his revelations about events he himself had witnessed in former incarnations as high priest in the Temple, and as other personages in past history. A great "lover of Israel," this is what he chose to be his epitaph. His main goal was to serve God without ulterior motive. He was the author of two books: *Ohev Yisrael* (*A Lover of Israel*) and *Torat Emet* (*A Torah of Truth*).

But what is it that identifies Heschel as an outstanding teacher of communication? What qualities or characteristics did he exemplify or expound that could give him that accolade? He did seek peace and unity among the various groups, as did Aaron. He had a wild imagination and revelations, but that could better qualify him as a mystic, or even a madman. Teaching the love of Israel and complete devotion to God were not his teachings alone.

Rather it was his commitment to the concept of "listening" that exemplifies the great lesson in communication. Perhaps he learned this well from his teacher Elimelekh of Lizensk. Rabbi Elimelekh "listened so well that he eventually became almost a copy of the Maggid."[16] (The Maggid here refers to the Great Maggid Dov Baer of Mezeritch, 1704–1772.)

Third in the line of assuming leadership of the Hasidic movement after the founder, the Baal Shem Tov, and then after the "architect" of the movement, the Maggid of Mezeritch, came Elimelekh the teacher, "the practical man who translated abstract concepts into simple language for simple people."

> A story: When Elimelekh of Lizensk felt his hour approach, he made his last will known. To Mendl of Riminov he bequeathed his brain, to Yehoshua Heschel of Apt, his tongue; to Yaakov-Yitzhak of Lublin he left his sight, and to Israel of Kozhenitz, his heart.[17]

And so how did Abraham Joshua Heschel of Apt use "the tongue"? He told stories which made others listen.

> The rabbi of Apt liked to tell tall stories. You might have taken them for meaningless exaggerations, and yet not only his disciples but others too saw meaning in them and found enlightenment.
>
> Once when he was visiting Rabbi Barukh of Mezbizh, a grand-son of the Baal Shem, and was just about to begin a story, Rabbi Barukh asked him to accompany him to the well which was called "the spring of the Baal Shem." The moment they reached the well the rabbi of Apt started talking and Rabbi Barukh stood by, leaning on his cane and listening. Among other things, the rabbi of Apt told about his son's wedding: "The batter for the noodle dish was spread on leaves over the fences and even hung down from the roof-tops!"
>
> The Mezbizh hasidim who surrounded the two watched the wise lips of their rabbi and prepared to burst out laughing as soon as he

did, but they saw that he was listening attentively and his lips were not twitching. Later, when the rabbi of Apt had left, Rabbi Barukh said: "Never have I heard such a golden tongue!"[18]

At another time, the Rabbi of Apt visited another hasidic rabbi and began telling a story about the time "when he was a rav in the town of Jassy they wanted to build a big bridge in front of his house, and what huge quantities of wood they had carted to the spot. A merchant who often went to Jassy to trade was among the listeners, and nodded eagerly: 'Yes, Rabbi, that's just the way it was!' The rabbi of Apt turned to him in surprise. 'And how do you know about it?' he asked."[19]

The Rabbi of Apt also understood the concept of listening.

> Once a great throng of people collected about the rabbi of Apt to hear his teachings. "That won't help you," he cried to them. "Those who are to hear, will hear even at a distance; those who are not to hear, will not hear no matter how near they come."[20]

We can see by the word "hear," he really meant active listening; to hear, to attend, to understand, to remember, the psychological process of listening.

Finally, Abraham Joshua Heschel of Apt used his tongue which he inherited through listening to his mentor to pray for better listeners. It is for this prayer that I have chosen the Rabbi of Apt as the teacher from our Jewish tradition who has taught the most important communication lesson.

> Master of the Universe, . . . Well, you know I have discovered the knack of telling stories. So I tell stories. And believe me, Master of the Universe, I swear to You, I want You to believe me, I invent nothing. Whatever I tell is true. Whatever I tell did really occur to me—yes, to me. All the incidents and episodes in my stories—I remember perfectly when and where they took place. I take them from my own memory, my own soul. But the people—you know them. What do they say? They say that the Apter Rebbe is exaggerating again. Could I exaggerate even if I wanted to? What wonders could I invent in a world which is full of wonders?
>
> Listen, I tell them, for instance, that I have already lived here in previous centuries. Well, that is absolute truth. Have I not heard the thunder and seen the lightning at Sinai? Have I not joined my voice to those saying "*Naaseh v'nishma*," shouting their fidelity to You and Your Covenant and Your Torah? Then why should it be surprising that I also remember my years in Jerusalem? Indeed, I was high priest. I can

still see the Jew who brought his cow as an offering. The cow escaped, and the Jew ran after her. It was so funny a sight that I burst laughing. And even now, in retelling it, I cannot help but laugh. But the people who listen also laugh. I laugh with joy because I remember the Temple and its splendor. They laugh because I amuse them. I entertain them. They say, "Here he goes again, the Apter Rebbe and his stories, his miracles, his fantasies."

The fools. Some think I make miracles, others think that I simply exaggerate. But I say to them, "You are the greatest miracle of all, you who are alive, you who listen to each of my words. Everything I say is true." My only prayer, God, is that You give me good listeners—listeners like Reb Barukh of Medzebozh, the great-grandchild of the Baal Shem Tov.[21]

This prayer, which was translated and incorporated into an essay by Elie Wiesel, contains the essence of what is so important in Judaism, namely the tale and the listener. Wiesel continues

Once I asked my own master, "I understand why the *mitzvot*, the laws, were so scrupulously transmitted from generation to generation, but why the *aggadot*? Why the legends?" And my master answered, "They are important because they stress the importance of the listener."

. . . So, stressing the importance of the listener is part of the tale, what Buber called the I-and-Thou. When one tells a tale, one relives it. One does not talk to the listener. One talks with the listener. To listen is as important as to talk, sometimes more so. Some Hasidim used to boast that they went to the Pshiskher, the master of the Kotzker, "to listen to the rebbe's silence."[22]

"To listen is as important as to talk, sometimes more so." That is what the Jewish leaders I have discussed in this essay learned to do in order to achieve their goals of teaching at the proper level (Moses and Aaron), gaining and pursuing peace amongst rivals (Aaron, Solomon, and Abraham Joshua Heschel), listening to your rival's argument and incorporating his side into your case (Hillel), listening with empathy and wisdom (Solomon), and telling stories in order to make the stories one's own experience through the telling and the listening (Heschel). To listen is to remember. To remember is to retell. And so the communication cycle continues. . . . What I pray for as a teacher and as a storyteller is the same prayer that Rabbi Abraham Joshua Heschel of Apt made, to have "good listeners." Listening is the key to more effective communication, conflict resolution, and a more peaceful world filled with good stories.

NOTES

1. Talmud, the most sacred Jewish text after the Bible, comprises the Mishna and the Gemara. These are the commentaries on the Bible and the Oral Law that were transmitted through the generations. It is a storehouse of Jewish history and customs and is two-thirds *aggada* (homilectic expositions of Bible, stories, legends, folklore, maxims) and one-third *halachah* (law).

2. J. H. Hertz, Editor, *The Pentateuch and Haftorahs* (London: Soncino Press, 1981), 769.

3. Morris Silverman, Editor, *Sabbath and Festival Prayer Book* (New York: Rabbinical Assembly of America and United Synagogue of America, 1980), 378.

4. Elie Wiesel, "The Storyteller's Prayer," *Against Silence: The Voice and Vision of Elie Wiesel*, ed. Irving Abrahamson (New York: Holocaust Library, 1985), 57. This essay also appears as the Foreword to *Jewish Stories One Generation Tells Another* by Peninnah Schram (Northvale, N.J.: Jason Aronson Inc., 1987), xi–xvii.

5. Shlomo Riskin, "The Art of Listening," *The Jewish Leader* XV:3 (February 9, 1989), 9. Rabbi Riskin writes a weekly syndicated column from his home in Efrat, Israel, and which is published in a number of Jewish weekly newspapers across the United States.

6. Donald W. Klopf and Ronald E. Cambra, *Personal & Public Speaking* (Englewood, Colo.: Morton Publishing Company, 1989), 172.

7. Klopf and Cambra, 169.

8. Klopf and Cambra, 171–172.

9. Klopf and Cambra, 172.

10. Louis Ginzberg, *The Legends of the Jews I* (Philadelphia, Pa.: Jewish Publication Society, 1909), 43.

11. Benno Heineman, *The Maggid of Dubno and His Parables* (New York: Feldheim Publishers, 1978), x.

12. Hertz, 659 f.

13. Ginzberg, VI, 282–283. For more on this, see Ginzberg, "Aristotle in Jewish Literature," in *The Jewish Encyclopedia*.

14. I. Epstein, ed., *'Erubin, Seder Mo'Ed* (Hebrew-English Edition of Babylonian Talmud) (New York: Traditional Press, 1979), 13b.

15. Neil Rosenstein, *The Unbroken Chain* (New York: Shengold Publishers, Inc., 1976), 530.

16. Elie Wiesel, *Souls on Fire: Portraits and Legends of Hasidic Masters* (New York: Random House, 1972), 117.

17. Wiesel, *Souls on Fire*, 132.

18. Martin Buber, *Tales of the Hasidim: The Later Masters* (New York: Schocken Books, 1948), 112–113.

19. Buber, 113.

20. Buber, 115.
21. Wiesel, "The Storyteller's Prayer," 55–56.
22. Wiesel, "The Storyteller's Prayer," 56–57.

FACING AN UNCERTAIN FUTURE

WHAT JEWISH MEDITATION TEACHES

Sheila Weinberg

TODAY IS NOVEMBER 11. Two months have passed. That is a very short time in the world of emotional shock and grief. It is also Veteran's Day, which used to be called Armistice Day, commemorating the eighty-third anniversary of the end of the war to end all wars. Sadly, these last eighty-three years have witnessed war upon war, grief piled on top of grief.

I was asked a few weeks ago to try and address September 11 and its aftermath from the viewpoint of Jewish meditation. It is a humbling task. I was in Massachusetts on September 11, not in New York or Washington. I was born in New York but I haven't lived here since before the Towers went up, over thirty years ago. But I have friends and family in this city, and I serve as the rabbi of a congregation among whom there is barely a soul who was not personally touched by September 11. There are circles of shock and grief, loss and confusion that spread out in waves from the radius of Ground Zero.

Coming to New York is a little like making a Shiva call. One is going to a house of sorrow. The tradition enjoins the Shiva visitor to enter the house in silence. The mourner is not obligated to get up and open the door or even greet the visitor. The visitor is required not to speak but to simply offer one's silent presence and wait. To wait until the mourner begins to speak. One is supposed to simply listen—to be there—to wait—to receive.

When we cultivate a calm, alert spacious awareness, a capacity to be present and tranquil to all that arises, we are preparing to make a Shiva call. When we practice mindfulness, the quality of attending moment to moment to the arising and passing of experience, we are getting ready to be in the house of sorrow.

The visitor must combine two potentially paradoxical qualities—calmness and attention. These are the same qualities required of any leader, parent, good friend, teacher, or healer. It is much easier to remain calm if you are remote, caught in fantasy, or not available either physically or emotionally. On the other hand, it is perhaps more natural to show up and get caught in the anxiety of a situation or one's own discomfort and insecurity and be an agitated presence. It's a lot easier to be calm when you are half-asleep. The trick in paying a Shiva call or in meditation—perhaps the trick in life—is to be calm and alert.

But we are really talking about something that is more than a Shiva call. September 11 caused collective shock and grief. The comforters are also the mourners. The mourners must comfort each other. Innocent victims proliferate—from the unemployed in New York and Hawaii to the refugees and their children, running as bombs "carpet" (such a gentle term) their homes in our name.

Innocent people and things do look more suspicious. Crazy jokes upset great systems. All year my friend is consoling me that my son is in Jerusalem and I wait for the 6 A.M. news with ice in my chest. Now I am comforting my friend whose son works for a New York Congresswoman in Washington, D.C.

September 11 reminds me of other days that remain identified by their dates. In the Jewish calendar the starkest example is Tisha B'Av—the Ninth of Av. That day commemorates the calamities in Jewish history—primarily the destruction of the first Temple by the Babylonians in 586 B.C.E. and the destruction of the second Temple by the Romans in 70 C.E. Other sorrows from other periods coalesce around that day as well. The Ninth of Av never got another name. It just stayed the Ninth of Av, a date to remember, to reflect upon and contain the sorrow that otherwise might hover like a cloud around the rest of the calendar.

The Book of Lamentations, or Eicha, is chanted on the Ninth of Av. It is a collection of five poems that release the words and melody beneath the silence of a communal Shiva call. Its purpose is to comfort and strengthen the fallen city.

The first poem is a conversation between the narrator and the daughter of Zion. She is the victim, the personification of the city. She tells the story of her suffering. Most of all she asks to be seen. She wants someone—God or human—to pay attention to her suffering. In contrast, the narrator is remote. He rants and blames. He is not engaged.

In the second poem, things shift. The narrator responds. He becomes her witness. He joins the grieving woman in her pain. He takes her words into himself and in this way gives her life, identity, a path to wholeness. He addresses her with these extraordinary words: "Shifchi KaMayim Libaych—Nochach Pnay Hashem" "Pour out your heart like water in the presence of God."

God never actually appears to comfort the city. Only in the empathy, compassion, and receptivity of the narrator is the divine quality of pure, loving awareness made manifest.

Nothing is finally resolved in Eicha. The word *eicha* in fact is a question—"How Come?" Many voices offer contradictory explanations of blame and fault throughout the poems. Verses of hope appear in poem three and then disappear again when another wave of sorrow crashes against the shore.

But, as in the practice of mindfulness, there is a container and a structure, which allows the light of pure presence to shine. We sit with the daughter of Zion, the city woman, the city as woman, and allow her truth to be known, heard, seen—without trying to fix, without judgment, without ridicule. Just as it is. Just as it is—as open as a question that may not have an answer.

Many words have been uttered since September 11. Words that try to control, explain, understand, and comfort. Words that try to draw conclusions. Terror is the biggest word of all—intense fear. Terror is organized violence done to innocent people as a political tactic or as a way of getting power or as a way of relieving oneself from feeling threatened. It simultaneously grows from and seeds revenge, rage, and fear.

Rage and fear seem to circle each other in a loop of misery, merry-go-rounds fueling each other.

When I sit with the contents of my own mind this is what I understand. When something unpleasant arises and I treat it with hostility, judgment, or inner violence, my suffering increases. The more I fight, the more exhausted and defeated I feel. In meditation I can investigate fear and rage. I can explore how painful it is to shut my heart. Through the power of steadfast, gentle, and persistent awareness, returning to this moment, the rage and anger that arise can be held, explored, transformed into guidance and wisdom before they become solidified in cruel speech and violent action.

I don't really understand the nuances that some use to distinguish among the kinds of violence done to innocent people. I know violence and war only yield violence and war. If I fight in order to achieve peace, don't I justify that very violence?

I don't understand how violence is justice. I thought justice was connected to wisdom and the rule of law and courts and evidence. I thought justice was joining with others to uphold moral norms and calling those who do not uphold moral norms to account.

A lot of words yield a lot of questions. I sit with the questions. I sit with my own mind and I see that when I generate hatred, I suffer. I become a victim of my own animosity. I become smaller, more isolated, less alive.

Words can mean so many things. Take the word "emptiness," for instance.

We note the profound emptiness that has been revealed since September 11th—the empty space in lower Manhattan where those mighty towers stood, and the gaping hole in the Pentagon.

We also note the emptiness in the hearts of so many lovers and friends, parents and children waiting for their dear ones who will never come home. Instead they must notice, feel, and receive their own inner aching emptiness. Empty chairs, empty beds, and empty arms. There are empty hotels and theaters, airplanes and conferences. This very room itself is relatively empty, compared to the dreams and intentions of its planners.

There is emptiness halfway around the world as women and children leave their homes with the shutters flapping in the frosted air and rush to shelters at borders that might be safe, or simply the site of deeper despair.

And there is another kind of emptiness that flows from silence and is revealed in mindfulness, in the close attention to this moment, this breath as it rises and falls, as it is born and dies. There is the emptiness that is "the infinite pause before the next inhale of the breath that is breathing us all into being" (Oriah Mountain Dreamer).

All our rushing for explanations and blame, grabbing for substances, people, work, rage and revenge, are an effort to avoid the emptiness and the fear we have of that abyss. Our spiritual practices are structured activities that prod us into that very emptiness. They push us, against the resistance we all share, to be with the mystery, the unknown, the vulnerable, the soft edges where we merge and disappear and reappear again.

When we practice mindfulness, awakened attention, we experience reality, including our own self, as nonfixed, as process and change, as constantly arising and passing in relation to other phenomenon. Let us pause for a moment and sit in silence. Let us note the body as a flow of energy and change, and let us know the mind as an endless flow of energy and change.

What is solid? What is stable? What is lasting? If we are afraid to ask the questions or receive the answers, let us be with the fear itself and with the vastness of what we do not know. As we sit in the silence and the flow of energy and change, we relax. We see that we are not separate. We are not independent. We are the stuff of life that keeps flowing and changing. In the silence, in the stillness, in the emptiness, we touch life. We face ourselves and we face God.

Jewish practices, stories, and symbols teach us about emptiness, the emptiness that renews and sustains and leads to compassion and wisdom. Therefore, when we practice mindfulness in the context of Jewish teachings, the practice itself is sustained and enriched. Here are a few examples.

1. There is a passionate rejection of idol worship in Judaism. An idol is anything, anything at all—a person, idea, animal, mountain, work of art, flag—that is conceived of as fixed and all-powerful—worthy of devotion and ultimate obedience. Because anything at all that is separate is also changing, partial, limited. Only the invisible, nameless emptiness that is holiness and wholeness suffusing and uniting all is worthy of worship.

2. The empty place, the wilderness, is the place where true meeting and connection occur. Moses first meets the One whose name is simply given as Ehyeh Asher Ehyeh—pure being becoming—in the wilderness of Midian at the burning bush (the sneh). Then he returns to the same place—Sinai—with the newborn nation of freed slaves. An ownerless people journey to an ownerless spot to meet a God with a name that cannot be pronounced. Then Moses leaves the people alone. But emptiness is not so easy to tolerate, as the Israelites indicate by constructing a statue of gold to fill the void.

3. God asks the Israelites to construct a dwelling place for the divine presence—"Build me a dwelling place and I will dwell among you." This is the emptiness that is ready to perceive and receive the sacred. The holy place is akin to the open heart, no longer grasping or seeking, no longer fearing or resisting, just present to the indwelling love that abides in each moment.

4. The center of Jewish worship in space and time is the Torah, the scroll that tells the story and contains the laws for living a life of peace and justice. As long as we keep entering the story with our own voices and keep practicing the principles of love and fairness embodied in the ways of Torah, we are not worshipping idols.

The discipline of law holds up the possibility of an alternative to war. The Torah offers an ethic of care, protection for those in need, mutual respect, and cooperation. It acknowledges the interrelationship of all creation and the dynamic consciousness that liberates, sustains, renews, and holds all suffering in mercy and love. The way of Torah is the way of law.

It partakes of the divine emptiness in its fluidity, inclusivity, and attentiveness to process.

The path of war, on the other hand, is based on absolute dichotomies between good and evil, victory and defeat. Its illusory certainty encourages reckless violence. In war the end justifies the means. In law and in Torah, the end remains embodied in the means.

5. Each week of the Jewish year revolves around an empty day, the Sabbath, day of rest. All the energy and creativity of the other days of the week derive from the Sabbath. It is the center candle on the seven-branched menorah of the week. We are encouraged to surrender our agendas for change and control and to bask for a day in the light of creation, the delight of just being. The Sabbath is a day to abandon contention and dissatisfaction. It is a powerful practice of trust. It is a sublime teaching of interdependence.

The Sabbath is the pause between the out breath and the next in breath. We can grasp our way past it. We can dread falling into its absence. We can fill it with the stuff of the week. Or we can find a way to bathe in the bottomless pool; we can allow our souls to be restored.

6. In this last example I would like to bring a text from the Torah portion for this week, Toldot. Isaac relives many of the events of his father's life. In Genesis 26:18 we find him redigging the wells that Abraham had dug that had been stopped up by the Philistines. Then Isaac's herdsmen find a well of spring water and quarrel over it with the herdsmen of Gerar. He names that well "Esek," which means contention. They then dig another well, dispute over that one too and call it "Sitna," which means hostility or harassment. Then Isaac moves on and digs yet another well. But there is no quarrel this time and he calls the well "Rehoboth," which means spaciousness.

What is all this digging and quarrelling about? When we sit down and are quiet we too are digging into the emptiness of the earth. We are excavating our ancestors' legacies. We often discover shadows from our past. We may meet them with aversion, fear, and anger. And we may simply name what is, name the contention and the hostility, the esek and sitna.

As we name these shadows lurking in the darkness, we may see how insubstantial they really are. As we gently touch the resistance and as we soothe the inner tantrum, we notice how these shadows are empty of power and content. Clouds change shape and dissolve in the spaciousness. We are released into the open awareness of rehoboth—"Ki ata hirchiv adonai lanu . . . Now at last the Eternal has granted us ample space . . ."

The teachings of Judaism and the practice of mindfulness urge us to explore emptiness as the birthplace of patience, generosity, kindness, creativity, wisdom, and love. They urge us to be suspicious of symbols and solutions that fail to honor the mystery, the uncertain, the empty. While I understand the emergence of the American flag as a symbol of solidarity and comfort, I am concerned about its use as a symbol of allegiance. I am wary of being too certain, too impatient, too set on the sound of one voice above all others.

Some of us have changed the words of Jewish prayer over the years to be more aligned with what we really believe. It has become essential to pray with all our ancestors, men and women, and it has become crucial to pray explicitly for the peace of all who dwell on earth, not just peace for Israel.

We cannot live a life without allegiances to identities but we need our identities to be transparent enough to affirm interdependence. Your peace is a condition of my peace and vice versa. In mindfulness practice when we touch our own suffering, we look through a window to the greed, hatred, and ignorance that lurk in the human heart. When we touch our own fear, we know every mortal, ever dying, ever entering the unknown. When we yearn for peace, this yearning, too, transcends all boundaries and frontiers.

Just as we added to the Hebrew prayer—May God grant peace to Israel and all who dwell on earth—I wish we could change "God Bless America." I do not believe that our love of country, as dear as our own mountains and prairies are to us, should restrict the geography of our prayer for God's blessing. God's blessing should be over all the inhabitants of this fragile, violence-ridden, struggling, magnificent, purple mountained, white foaming oceaned majestic planet.

Perhaps this expanded notion of "God Bless America" could translate into upholding the ABM treaty and the Kyoto accords, and engaging in a form of globalization governed by an ethic of care for workers and the earth.

When I reflect on Judaism and mindfulness practice, I am reminded of the words of Gandhi, "You have to be the change you want to see in the world."

Or the words Vaclav Havel (playwright, dissident, prisoner, and president of the Czech Republic) spoke when he addressed the U.S. Congress: ". . . consciousness precedes being, and not the other way around. . . . For this reason, the salvation of this human world lies nowhere else than in the human heart, in human responsibility. Without a global revolution in the sphere of human consciousness, nothing will change for the better in the sphere of our being as humans, and the catastrophe toward which this world is headed—be it ecological, social, demographic or a general breakdown of civilization—will be unavoidable."

I would like to share a few very humble stories about the transformation of the human heart. They are beginning stories because that is where we are in this endeavor. The species, which has caused so much trouble already, is hardly beyond infancy in the aeons of life on this globe. We are young and oh so rowdy and willful despite the wise and sacred teachings that have already threaded their way through human history. These are stories of waking up in the moment, stories of peering over the hilltop; of our isolation and hurt to glimpse a more spacious view of life.

A young rabbi (we'll call him David) was on a mindfulness retreat that I was leading. David was having a very difficult time. He didn't get the chair that he wanted in the hall. He had a sore knee when we sat. He was getting a cold. He was annoyed that we had moved the meditation space to another room that was not to his liking. He was disappointed that one of the teachers arrived two days late. He was finding the food had too much garlic which disagreed with him and there was not enough fruit for breakfast and on and on. In the silence, nearly each breath brought a fresh complaint.

The teachers kept encouraging David to attend to his judgment and dissatisfaction—to note how he was feeling rather than to engage the content of the stories that were eager to proliferate in his mind.

One afternoon at an interview, David burst into the room where I was sitting—on his face a look of triumph and delight. "I get it," he told me. "I really get it!"

"Would you like to talk about it?" I queried. "Definitely!" his grin broadened. "In my congregation there is a faction that I have been calling the malcontents. These are the people that are always complaining about something. They may not like the tunes I use or the topics of my talks or the fact that the board raised tuition for the Hebrew school. Whatever it is, these people cannot tolerate any change. They are making my life miserable and I have been annoyed at best and furious at worst with them. I keep worrying that I am just going to blow up at them one day. They are trying my patience.

"Well, I saw them inside of me. I have been acting like a malcontent. I felt how they feel. I experienced my own discontented mind as a body of suffering and grief and I got it. They are suffering too. They are people in pain. Rather than hate them I actually felt compassion for their suffering. I am not sure yet how this is going to play out when I get home. But I know that something cracked. I am less isolated. They are less 'other.' It is so funny, so sweet."

David had been willing to dig in the wells of contention and hostility and lo and behold, "hirchiv adonai lanu"—"the Eternal granted ample space"—the straits of separation had broadened into the wide plains of connection and understanding.

Another time I was teaching mindfulness to rabbis in a one-day retreat. One of the young women named Lois had been very anxious for this opportunity to spend a day in silence. She enjoyed the instructions for sitting and resting the attention in the beginning of each in breath, then sustaining the attention as the breath moved through the body. Then I gave instructions for walking as mindfulness practice and invited the participants to spend the next period of forty-five minutes using the sensation of each step as a way to develop concentration.

When the participants returned after the walk, I invited questions and comments. Lois was eager to share her experience:

"I was so happy to have this silent time. I found a lovely side street and began to focus on each step. In a few minutes a car passed by and someone leaned his head out. He wanted information, directions, indeed to strike up a whole major conversation.

"I felt really annoyed. I felt invaded. My precious, long-sought-after silence had been intruded upon. I felt my face flush. I heard the irritated tone beginning to form in the back of my throat.

"But I waited for a second. Before I reacted, another thought arose. If I treated him kindly, perhaps he will go away sooner than if I start to react with anger and meanness. There was enough space in my heart and mind to engage the man in a friendly way. It just took a few minutes and he was gone. I made a wise and compassionate choice. No disturbance lingered in the air or in my mind."

"Wow," I responded. "That is a beautiful example of freedom. You had the spaciousness, the awareness to hold your aversion, to see it, not to start to fight with it but to realize a wiser response would come from a place of patience and good will. You acted with power—rather than as a victim."

Another rabbi story. All over the country rabbis were struggling these High Holy Days with their sermons. Rosh Hashanah came a mere week after September 11 and most rabbis were intensely rewriting their talks to speak to the catastrophic events. Even in places far away from New York and D.C., it couldn't possibly be business as usual. There were many special services and interfaith gatherings—literally all over the world. We all did our best in making the necessary adjustments.

Then came Yom Kippur. I struggled with what to say or not say; how to respect this moment in history and not obscure other aspects of the sacred day. Like all the other rabbis, I did my best and hoped for the best.

Two days after Yom Kippur a letter arrived in my office from a man who is not particularly active in the synagogue. He was irate. He came to shul only on Kol Nidre but was severely disappointed that I didn't offer him the solace and comfort he had expected by sufficiently addressing the events of September 11. He blasted my general insensitivity and poor leadership.

I was still pretty drained after Yom Kippur and my first response to the letter was hurt and anger. "Who was this guy to be criticizing me after all my hard work at trying to balance the needs of the congregants, after all my this and all my that." My initial response was very self-centered.

Then I practiced mindfulness. I stopped telling the story and just felt what I was feeling. I made room for the ache in the chest and the tightness in the shoulders. Then that changed and something new entered my mind. This man was hurting. This man was crying out to me for solace.

Suddenly my wounded pride and ego moved aside, and I actually saw another person's grief and fear arrayed before me. It was a relief. I was able to write to him and express my concern for him and invite him to come and see me to talk in my office. I didn't need to get defensive or self-righteous.

He wrote back to me.

But he didn't make an appointment because his reserve unit was being mobilized and he was shortly going to be shipped out with his company. Oh.

These are all small moments when the heart opens to something new— a moment of freedom and nonviolence, a moment of being the change we want to bring to the world. They are tiny moments, but they create the possibility for the next moment of freedom, the next opening to love and trust. It is true that amidst the radical and profound emptiness of September 11, many such moments have arisen like the flowered altars that are woven through the ruins and the thoroughfares of this great city.

The first week in September, I was asked to speak at the dedication of the kosher-hallal dining room at Mt. Holyoke College near where I live in Western Massachusetts. I agreed. The event took place on September 13.

It was amazing to gather with Jewish and Muslim students and faculty for the opening of something that had taken years to conceive and execute—a way for observant students to eat according to their own traditions and get to know one another across the divide of their communities.

The Imam spoke and then I spoke. I would like to share what I said that day while the world was still reeling.

> Today's dedication of the Kosher-Hallal Dining Room at Mt. Holyoke College is a moment of grace.
>
> We have been shattered by the violence in New York and Washington.

This dedication is a moment of wholeness—shalom—salaam.

We have been terrified and confused.

This is a moment of calm and clarity.

We have been filled with anger and helplessness.

This is a moment of friendship and meaning.

It is a small act compared with the enormity of the violence, rage, and suffering in the world. But in terms of spirit, we know that every act flowing from a true desire to honor the Creator and show deep respect to one another is of infinite worth.

I am often asked, "Is it possible to preserve and celebrate my unique heritage and practice and still remain connected to the whole earth and all of humanity? Is it possible to be true to my unique path and not be isolated from others?"

We say emphatically, "YES!"

We can uphold the sacred inspired teachings and guidance of our traditions and create bridges to one another.

And the bridges to one another ultimately lead us to the ONE.

We nourish the bodies that house our spirits.

We receive the bounty of the earth so that we have the strength to serve our true purpose.

And we bless the Source of All who nurtures us and sustains us daily.

We all eat.

We are all part of this miraculous creation.

In Hebrew, the word for bread is lechem.

And the word for war is related—milchama.

Wars can be fought over bread.

But sharing bread can lead us to peace.

This is my prayer for this bold and visionary community.

The story of the kosher-hallal dining room was picked up by news media all around the world, so eager were we for hopeful news. It became a little star on the horizon beckoning us in the darkness that abounds.

We cannot pretend the darkness isn't real. Sometimes we can move through it to the emptiness and beyond. Sometimes we just need to linger and pour out our hearts like water. Sometimes we remember that when we say L'Chayyim, we don't say L'Chaim Tovim—to a good life or a long life or a life of wealth and contentment—but we just say L'Chaim.

As Rachel Naomi Remen teaches in *My Grandfather's Blessings*, "L'Chaim . . . [means] that no matter what difficulty life brings, no matter how hard or painful or unfair life is, life is holy and worthy of celebration.

'Even the wine itself is sweet to remind us that life itself is a blessing. . . .' It has always seemed remarkable to me that such a toast could be offered for generations by a people for whom life has not been easy. But perhaps it can only be said by such people, and only those who have lost and suffered can truly understand its power" (p. 78).

L'Chaim strikes me as an apt byword for practicing mindfulness as Jews, for our willingness to open to all of life, the mystery, the terror, the emptiness, the fullness, the love, and the hope.

Along with the authors of Eicha—Lamentations—another ancient Jew lived through the dark days of the Ninth of Av and went off to exile with his weeping people to the River Babylon. We don't know his name, but his poetry constitutes the second third of the Biblical Book of Isaiah.

I would like to close with his words as a prayer for us all: the citizens of this city and this country, the grieving friends and families of all the innocent victims of hatred and revenge, the leaders of our nation and all leaders everywhere, and the hurting, hungry, and homeless all over the world.

The poet writes: "Fear not, for I am with you, be not frightened for I am your God; I strengthen you and I help you, I uphold you with my victorious right hand" (Isaiah 40:10).

May we be victorious in finding ourselves in each other.

May we be victorious in our trust of Spirit and our willingness to dig new wells that are ample and deep.

May we be victorious in our capacity to be present L'Chaim—the great miracle and blessing that is life.

May we celebrate the victory together—the victory of compassion and generosity, the victory of justice and the rule of law, the victory of kindness and love.

JEWISH SPIRITUAL THOUGHT

THE TREE OF KNOWLEDGE
AND THE TREE OF LIFE

Adin Even-Israel Steinsaltz

WITHIN THE OCEAN OF BLOOD and fire that now surrounds us, there are seemingly isolated islands. Here we are, sitting and talking about Torah, *Mitzvot* and good deeds. On the one hand, it may be comforting to know that there are such islands of serenity. But is it right, at a time like this, to be in a kind of bubble of goodness?

Maimonides (in his Laws of *Teshuvah,* Chapter Three, halachah 6) gives a list of people who do not have a share in the world to come. This list includes "apostates, skeptics, those who deny the Torah," etc. However, it also includes "he who separates himself from the congregation." This person, says Maimonides, may be flawless in faith and deeds, yet he doesn't want to be part of the Congregation of Israel. He wants no share either in its troubles or in its joys. It is as if he says: "Let me live alone!"

For that reason, such a person has no share in the world to come. He is rejected forever. If we do not wish to be included in that category, we must remember that even the islands of quiet exist within and struggle against the noise of the world around us. Therefore we must not seclude ourselves. Rather, we must always remember that we are living within the current reality, with all its confusion, flames, danger, and blood.

I do not want to speak about politics—not because politics is inherently loathsome; on the contrary, it is part and parcel of our cultural environment. In a place like ours, whoever wants to keep away from politics is to be considered "one who separates himself from the congregation." Yet with all that, I choose to speak about a completely different issue, though one that is profoundly related to what is happening now.

I believe that the foundations of things around us are not always visible. Often they are to be found much deeper, and sometimes they seem totally abstract. So too, the topic about which I am going to speak may seem abstract, but I believe it is deeply connected with our current reality. This connection is not a mystical one; it is the direct link between the blemishes of the mind, heart, and consciousness, and what is happening to us now.

The topic is "sophistication."[1]

The only place in the Torah in which one may, perhaps, find a similar term is in Genesis 3:1, which says: "The serpent was more subtle than any beast of the field." In contemporary terms I would translate it as, "the serpent was more sophisticated." Indeed, this is what he was. He was neither wise nor clever, but he was sophisticated, the very first sophisticated being.

Defining sophistication is not easy (because any simple definition cannot possibly be fully satisfactory, and any sophisticated definition will necessarily lead—as has happened—to a vicious circle of defining sophistication by means of increasingly sophisticated concepts). I shall therefore not speak about the term itself, nor about the many ways—from storming in to creeping in—whereby it enters our lives. I would like to focus on the fact that sophistication forces the most basic things not only out of our discourse, but even out of the very process of thought. Sophistication demolishes the possibility of conducting a simple conversation, making a simple statement, or touching the fundamentals of existence. The abundance of explanations and points of view that is the hallmark of sophistication blinds us to the simple knowledge of what is right and what is wrong, what is truth and what is falsehood. We forget the meaning of simple words such as "I hate," and "I love." Instead, we get dragged into a heap of complex, convoluted talk that is completely detached from reality, from genuine experiences and emotions. After sophistication has done its work, there is no longer a need to deny or ignore the basics; sophisticated people no longer believe in, or understand, anything.

Consequently, what is most fundamental not only ceases to be self-evident; it becomes totally incomprehensible. I am speaking about basic words such as: "I believe," "I am afraid," "I am a Jew." One can explain these things at great length, with or without footnotes, in complicated sentences that no one understands—for deliberate obfuscation is part of what sophistication is about. Unlike sophistry, sophistication is not an attempt to mislead. Rather, it may be likened to cutting down flowering, fruit-bearing trees, grinding them, turning them into paper, and then replacing them with paper trees and flowers. The sophisticated person converts living things into much more complex, complicated, "wiser" surrogates—and in the process loses touch with the basics.

The curse of sophistication today affects mainly educated people, or those who want to be considered educated. Before becoming sophisticated, a person could go to an exhibition, see a painting, and say, "This is beautiful!" Today, one can no longer say such a thing, just as one can no longer say that something is horrid. Rather, one needs to demonstrate knowledge of the precise era to which this painting belongs; the genre used; and whether it is outdated, modern, or postmodern; how this painting relates to the works of other painters; and whether the brush strokes go from right to left or from left to right. After all that, who knows anymore if the thing itself is beautiful or ugly?

This applies also to religion, as well as to an increasing number of religious people. Today, religious people are becoming sophisticated. They speak a highbrow language and write highbrow poetry and literature. They explain Judaism in a metaphysical way and in a kabbalistic way and in a poetic way and in a literary way. All these explanations brush aside the simple reality of speaking and thinking about basic concepts, and of experiencing the most fundamental things.

Sophistication is a deadly poison to Judaism because it eradicates all those things that—even if somewhat "primitive"—are *real*. The sophisticated person no longer has children; he has state-of-the-art dolls (sometimes living ones). He has no life; he has super-modern machinery. All this sophistication creates a complete and self-sustaining structure, which I often encounter in religious life. All the explanations, all the attempts to be bigger and brighter, make us lose our most basic understandings.

This process also occurs with emotions and reactions. We can no longer say about anything, "how good it is!" just as we can no longer exclaim, "phooey!" Man has become a captive of this style, this jargon. He has become so elaborate, ornate, and refined that nothing true remains.

These matters are now part of the political discourse in Israel. Without referring to the Right or the Left, I can say only this: before we were sophisticated, we knew there was something called "The Land of Israel," whatever it may be. Now that we have become sophisticated, we are no longer aware of its existence. There was a time when we knew there was something called "enemy." Now there is no longer an "enemy." Instead, there is such a profusion of complex, refined terms that we no longer know what an "enemy" is, or who is a "friend."

If we go back to the serpent, we can see that sophistication contains an element that is fundamentally irrelevant. Let us examine the dialogue between the serpent and Eve. Even though the serpent is difficult to describe, he obviously was not a small, simple creature of the reptile family. He was extremely elegant, charming, and educated; in short, he was sophisticated. And there was Eve who, as the Talmud attests, was a beauty, but apparently totally uncultured.

Now, these two have a dialogue. The serpent suggests that Eve eat the fruit, and she replies, in the simplest of terms: "It's forbidden!" But a word such as "forbidden" is so passé! Sophisticated people are no longer familiar with terms such as "forbidden," or "no." So instead of speaking about the issue itself, the serpent starts discussing the motivation of He who forbade: "Yea, has God said you shall not eat"—what was it that made Him say such a thing?

Poor Eve! Prior to that encounter, she knew that some things were permitted and others were forbidden. Now she no longer knows. True, the serpent does not tell her that everything is permitted; but he says: "Look, here is a world that is much more complicated, more sophisticated." And he tempts her to enter this world: "Eat it!"

Indeed, if one looks at how a serpent moves, one can understand what sophistication is. The serpent does not move in a straight line; it is incapable of that. The serpentine way of moving is one of the most beautiful things there is, something between a wave and a dance. But the serpent is a serpent, and it kills. For the fruit—not the fruit of the Tree of Knowledge, but the fruit of the serpent—is death, the total annihilation of human relations, of basic understanding and feeling.

Once upon a time, everyone—simple and intelligent alike—knew that one should awaken and *daven Shacharit*. People may not have known why. Nobody provided subtle explanations about the vibrations and metaphysics of the thing, but they knew they had to get up and get moving. Now, people are no longer aware of that, because they are sophisticated. And sophistication kills. On the face of things, sophistication only seems to add more refined structures of thought. If so, why not build these Rococo towers even higher? Why not add filigree of thought, the more the better? It turns out, however, that these thought-towers destroy the foundations from which they sprout. They destroy the most basic concepts: "no," "yes," "I am for," "I am against"—all those things that are simple, rudimentary, elementary, perhaps even somewhat foolish—but they are *life*.

Ecclesiastes puts this very succinctly: "A little folly is dearer than wisdom and honor" (Ecclesiastes 10:1). There is grandeur in honor and splendor in wisdom, but both of these may freeze and die due to a lack of inner vitality. "A little folly"—a little simple, naïve, innocent emotion: love, fatherliness, compassion—is what endows wisdom and honor with the minute, yet so absolutely necessary seed of life.

Indeed, what prevented Adam from eating from the Tree of Life? I imagine that the Tree of Life was not more difficult to reach than the Tree of Knowledge. In fact, the two trees may have been adjacent to each other, in the middle of the Garden. But after having eaten the fruit of the Tree of Knowledge, Adam was no longer capable of recognizing the Tree of Life. The Tree of Life may have been right in front of him, but it just didn't occur to him to consider the possibility. He probably thought to himself, "The Tree of Life cannot possibly be this wretched little shrub; it must be something a lot more splendid and sophisticated." He did not reach for the Tree of Life at that moment because he was sure that he had to meditate and read a lot of professional literature first. This is why man is still so far from the Tree of Life.

As I have said before, I do not want to speak about politics, nor about the present. I want to speak about one thing only: the need to reconnect with the basic things, the points of truth that we can grasp, and which are the roots of existence. I mean the simplest things: "good," "bad," "beautiful," "ugly," "I love," "I hate," "this is my homeland," "this is my religion," "this is what should be done." I know that these concepts are not in fashion these days. Nevertheless, if we want to live, let us come—before the curse of the serpent befalls us—and hold on to the Tree of Life.

NOTE

1. The Hebrew equivalent, *tihkum,* which I dislike at least as much as I abhor the English original, is a relatively new word. Its very existence in Hebrew is surprising, given that Hebrew contains quite a number of synonyms for "wisdom." Obviously, the word was imported into the language to serve as a translation for the English term.

A HUNDRED BLASTS SHATTER
THE SOMBER SILENCE

Mordechai Gafni

A HUNDRED BLASTS SHATTER the somber silence of the biblical New Year ritual. The shofar, Rosh Hashanah's major prop, is a ram's horn blown in a strange and evocative combination of notes. In mysticism, the words *Rosh Hashanah*—literally "New Year"—are understood to have deeper shades of meaning. *Rosh* means "the beginning," while the word *Shanah* derives etymologically from *Shinnui*—meaning "change" or "transformation." *Rosh Hashanah*, in the mystic's pen, then becomes "the beginning of transformation." Beginning here is in the sense of entry point, a portal or pivoting point on our journey towards fulfillment, or what Tzadok the Priest from Lublin calls "He'arah"—enlightenment.

This Satori transformation, according to spiritual master Schneur Zalman of Liadi, is essentially connected to shofar. The shofar blasts "break through," leaving imprints of their plaintive and yet audacious sounds in the realm of "Atik"—the innermost folds of the divine face.

What is the secret of the shofar's sound, the pleading, broken, and yet triumphant notes?

The word for shofar in biblical myth is *Teruah*. *Teruah* is understood by Targum[1] to mean *Yevava*—crying. Shofar is a crying instrument; a crying which resounds beyond words, beyond the narrow confines of language. These are tears sourced in the limbic brain—in that fantastic seat of intuition and raw emotional—the amygdala. These are transformative tears.

"But whose tears?" asks the Talmud.[1] "Whose tears are we trying to access in the ecstatic and painful ritual of shofar blowing?" While the ultimate answer is of course "our own" the nature of biblical myth ritual is to access self through the image of an archetype. In effect the Talmud is asking—who is the archetype for the tears of the shofar?

And here our discussion truly begins. For the Talmud responds—the tears of "Em Sisera." Em Sisera, literally translated, means the Mother of Sisera. Sisera, a figure from the early chapters of the Book of Judges, is depicted in the biblical midrashic literature as a heinous villain—a Saddam Hussein/Hitler type of character, guilty of every atrocity imaginable against the Israelite people.

One day Sisera is late, very late, in returning home from battle. The reader of the Book of Judges knows that his intended massacre has been averted. Sisera's forces have been routed and Sisera killed. His mother cries as she peers out the window. Her handmaidens comfort her, assuring that her victorious son will soon cross the threshold of the house once again. Yet Sisera's mother continues to cry—understanding, as only a mother can, that she will see her son no more.

Empathy for Sisera's mother notwithstanding—the Talmudic masters are virtually inexplicable. Why is shofar blowing—the one ritual described by the sources as Sanctum Sanctorum[2]—patterned on the tears of Hitler's mother? Not only do we trace the crying of shofar back to the tear ducts of Sisera's mother—we go out of our way to pattern the notes of our shofar blasts precisely after the patterns of her tears. Indeed the reason for the variation of different kinds of blasts in the shofar ritual is because we are not quite sure how she cried, and we want to make sure to get it right! Adds a medieval writer seven hundred years after the Talmudic period, "We blow a total of a hundred shofar blasts on Rosh Hashanah because Sisera's mother cried a hundred times."

Why "Em Sisera"? What in the nature of this woman's tears did the wisdom masters find so compelling?

One approach to our quandary, which I have already alluded to above, is to understand the choice of Sisera's mother as a way of driving home, in the most powerful way possible, the full humanity of our enemies. As studies of propaganda materials have shown, the enemy is never depicted with a face. Certainly not with a face that has a tear rolling down the cheek of the enemy's mother. The loss of face is the part of the process of dehumanization which allows us to kill. And sometimes we must kill. Sometimes pacifism is deeply immoral. Yet we can never erase the enemy's face. And the path towards the refacing of the enemy is to image his mother's tear-stained eyes.

And yet poignant and powerful as such a reading may be, it still feels insufficient. One intuits another layer of meaning pining to be unfolded;

an additional nuance which understands Sisera's mother as expressing a moment in our own souls; a stage of our journey in which only she can be our guide.

I want to share with you a different understanding of the shofar's music—an understanding that found its way into my soul one night—many years ago—in a moment of connection and clarity.

I begin with a mystical passage from the writings of Abraham Kook—the philosopher, mystic, and Chief Rabbi of Palestine.

> I am in the midst of exile.
> The inner essential I of the individual
> only reveals itself . . .
> to the extent of the higher courage
> which is drenched with the pure light of higher radiance
> which burns within.

The first line of the quote comes from the Prophet Ezekiel who, before receiving the Vision of the Chariot, the lodestone of the Kabbalah, cries out "אני בתוך הגולה-‏"—I am in the midst of exile!" Kook understands Ezekiel's statement to refer not only to physical exile, to the fact that Ezekiel was standing on foreign shores, but as expressing a far more profound sense of inner fragmentation, an inner exile. The inner exile stems from the inner essential "I" being lost. I've lost my self some place, I'm looking for myself, I'm playing all sorts of roles and many assorted games but I haven't found my self. This search for the I is taken by Kook to be the subtext of the Garden of Eden story. Original sin, writes Kook, is the inability to find essential I.

> The first man sinned.
> He became alienated from his own person-hood.
> For he turns to the opinion of the snake and lost himself.
> He did not give a clear answer to God's question where are you,
> for he did not know his own soul
> because his I-ness had perished
> in the sin of bowing to a foreign god.

Original sin is listening to the snake. The snake here is not the fiendish villain. Rather, snake represents any external voice or source of authority which is not my own. The snake however is paradoxically almost always a positive value, idea, or group that we have coopted in our process of identity formation.

Clearly the questions at stake for Kook are questions of identity. How do we locate our essential I? In the modern western context, books like Riesman's *Lonely Crowd* or Whyte's *Organization Man* come to mind.

Growing up, we were familiar with people who defined themselves by their corporation or workplace. A Westinghouse man, a military man, or a General Electric man. In other societies—Israel for example—political parties played a similar role. One was either left or right—whether from a kibbutz or a development town—and that was part of one's essential self-definition. While these old identities have broken down somewhat, the vacuum they left has been quickly filled by other no less insidious false voices of personhood. You walk into a party and say "Hi, I'm Mark, I'm a doctor," or "Pamela, a corporate lawyer," or . . .

We wait for the earliest opening in the conversation which will allow us to establish our place by almost casually introducing our "profession." We feel like we have little else to profess. We have used competence and training to replace or at least drown out the call of soul and spirit.

If we manage to free ourselves of the professional identity trap, relationships lurk in the wings to seduce us. Our relationships become more than places of commitment, growth, and loving. Our relationships become us. Notwithstanding feminism, the image of "the wife of" remains prevalent in our culture with the image of "the husband of" beginning to emerge as well. If "of" dies, then the "wife of" becomes the "widow of" (or widower). What is important is that "of" still provides a matrix of identity.

And the most beautiful, and therefore insidious, identity trap is children. The Jewish mother is but one archetypal representation of how we use children to form our identity. My children are me and I am my children—is the mantra of this particularly common modern idolatry. When I first began teaching as a too-young Rabbi in Palm Beach, an originally Israeli couple approached me to talk about their marriage, which was apparently on the verge of dissolution. I sat there trying to look appropriately wise but was utterly baffled by the complexity of their issues and surely did not have an inkling of what I could do to be helpful. That is, until they got up to leave.

He turned to her—in a familiar voice—and said "Ema . . ." (Hebrew for Mom) and she responded to his rote referral with, "Okay Abba" (Hebrew for Dad). In our next conversation it emerged that their first child was born just a few short months after their wedding. Their youngest son had left about a year ago for school. And it was about a year ago when their marital issues began to take on a new intensity.

They called each other Ema and Abba—indeed their whole relationship was based on being parents. Neither of them had done any of the work and reflection necessary to form an identity independent of their children. Consequently, when the children were no longer an active part of their lives, their relationship began to naturally dissolve.

There is a story about the Chassidic master Levi of Berdichev. He used to walk home from Synagogue through the marketplace to see firsthand the lives of his disciples. One morning a man rushing to fulfill some apparently urgent task barreled headlong into the master, sending him sprawling. The master however was not offended, indeed he noticed the man's alacrity and apparent perspicacity in pursuit of his goal. So he asked him, "Where, my friend are you running?" "Why I'm running to make a living!" The Master, not yet satisfied, queried further, "Why is it so important to you to make a living?" The man was somewhat taken aback—no one had ever challenged that assumption or asked that question. He thinks and he thinks and—light bulb! "For the children, for the children. I am working for the children." The master nods with a strange smile on his lips, and they each continue on their respective ways. Some twenty-five years pass and the master is walking—a little slower perhaps—as he always does, through the marketplace to Synagogue. And again, a man running in the opposite direction bowls into him. Again the master gets up, a little slower perhaps, and says "Young man, where are you running?" The young man amazingly gives the same response, "I'm running to make a living." And the master asks—you know masters try and be consistent—"Why is it so important to make a living?" And no one of course has asked the young man such a question before, so he stops and thinks—light bulb! "For the children, for the children, of course." The master lifts his eyes heavenward and says, "Master of the Universe, when will I meet that one child . . . for whom all the generations labored so mightily?"

We use our children to define ourselves. That is wrong. We need to love our children; one of the most gorgeous, beautiful, demarcating characteristics of the biblical culture is the love and commitment of parents to children through the generations. Nonetheless, even this love can become idolatrous.

Returning to shofar: it therefore strikes us as particularly significant that in biblical literature, where name is such an essential interpretive key, our heroine has none. The name of the biblical archetype for shofar tears is "the mother of Sisera." Sisera's mother is totally defined by being Sisera's mother. She is the paradigm of using our children to form our identity—so much so that Sisera even overshadows her name.

We need but one more link to reveal the secret of shofar.

I ask the reader to return to an earlier scene in your life. Did you ever babysit? If you have, you will recall that there are two distinct kinds of crying that a babysitter might hear. The first is a sort of gentle, sometimes incessant, quiet crying. These are spilt tears which we sometimes respond to and sometimes ignore. There is however a second kind of crying. This form of crying, a heart-rending, earsplitting kind of cry, rivets our attention and brings us instantly to the bedside of the baby. More often than not we find that the baby's security blanket or teddy bear or some other object of that nature has fallen from the crib or been otherwise lost.

When we lose one of what psychologist Donald W. Winnicott called one of our "transitional objects"—those objects we use to give us a sense of place and security in the world—we cry, a uniquely poignant and piercing cry. Ideal healthy development—which is indeed only an ideal—requires that we let go of our security blanket and claim our true identity. What we so often do instead is trade up. We exchange our teddy bear or security blanket for the Organization Man, for the title of professional competence, for a relationship—wife or husband of—or even for the title of mum or dad. Anything to avoid the terror of having to claim our own identity. For perhaps—we think in our most private subconscious moments—perhaps I don't have a self.

Now although they are not our highest selves, our masks are important. The masks we choose are also part of our identity. The biblical imperative "You shall not make for yourselves molten Gods" is better translated as you shall not make for yourselves Gods of masks. The Hebrew for *molten* is Masecha—literally mask. The implicit notion: masks have their place but "do not make Gods of your masks." If you do not take off your mask then it becomes a God—the sum total of your identity. Masks, however, are hard to take off—it is enormously painful to stand naked in the mirror and say, "who am I for real?" Yet that is the essence of Rosh Hashanah—the beginning of transformation.

This is precisely the moment of shofar crying captured by the biblical archetype of Sisera's mother. She has no other name. Sisera is her life, her self, her identity. She realizes that he is not coming home . . . ever again. In one instant her mask has been torn from her face. She is left, in the words of Rilke, "with her face in her hands." She cries—the cry of a baby who has lost his teddy bear or security blanket. A heart-rending, painful, and potentially liberating cry. The cry of shofar. This is the experience we are called to on Rosh Hashanah. We are invited to the liberation of tears which wash away our pseudoselves, revealing underneath—if we dare but look—a lustrous, shining, and beautiful me just waiting to be noticed and loved.

NOTES

1. The authoritative translation/interpretation.
2. Babylonian Talmud, Tractate Rosh Hashanah 26a.

POWER AND THE OPEN HEART

Shefa Gold

OUR PARENTS, WORRIED for our safety, instilled in us the notion that fear would keep us alive. Being careful meant being afraid of the hazards that the world laid in our path. The world indeed seems a dangerous place. Each day new calamities shock us. Dangers that we hadn't even imagined a few years ago lurk around each corner. Our conditioning says that if we are afraid, then we will be careful, and if we are careful, then we are more likely to survive.

Unfortunately, we pay a price in following this strategy. Fear sends us to our "survival brain" and cuts us off from our deepest wisdom. The survival brain's flight-or-fight mechanisms are fine when it comes to reacting to black and white, but in a world of rainbow complexities we need access to the full range of possible responses.

When I teach a meditation retreat, everyone ends up so very open-hearted. Fear that once armored the heart dissolves, laying bare the tender core of compassion for all . . . loving themselves, each other, and the world . . . feeling God's love with each breath. It feels alive and wonderful, but then the question usually arises—How can I possibly go out in the world like this? Without my fear, which is the source of my caution, I'll be clobbered! With so much trust in my heart, someone will surely take advantage of me.

One answer, of course, is to help everyone close down. Closing the heart is a means of protection. If I am going to teach my students how to open their hearts, I also have the responsibility to teach them how to protect themselves. The problem with closing down at the end of a retreat is that this creates a dichotomy between the spiritual life and the mundane. If I am to teach open-heartedness, it must be open-heartedness in the face of both the wonder and the agony of this unpredictable world.

The answer that I'm coming to in my own life is that teachings that open the heart must be balanced by practices that cultivate personal power. The power that I'm talking about comes from deep within the heart. Its source is in God, and it radiates out through the body charging up the energy field. As I build the strength of that field, my heart can open wider. Within that field of power I can be vulnerable, honest, exposed, loving, and open-hearted.

I also ask, "Is there another source, besides fear, for my care and vigilance and warriorhood in the world?" The alternate source that I cultivate is Love. I am a lover of Life and the passion of this love moves me to nourish, preserve and exalt Life. All my heart and soul and might stands behind this love. My fear of death is not ultimately what keeps me alive. At the center of my open heart is a power, a light that radiates outward into my life. It is the best protection. It is a shield that lets the world in (but doesn't let its destructiveness distract or confuse me).

Within the strength of this field of power (not my power, but God's power) I am confident that I will meet the world with the light of my soul, with a presence and a radiance that is not diminished by suffering. Practices that cultivate personal power without paying attention to sustaining the openness and vulnerability of the heart run the risk of self-corruption. Without the open heart, power stands behind the ego and is filtered through its distortions.

My choice of cultivating trust doesn't mean that I am being naïve. To trust is to search out the goodness in the world and call it forth without attention. Trust transforms the world. When I cultivate trust, I also cultivate discernment. When I work to open the heart, I also learn the power of radiance, a radiance whose source is in God. I speak to that power that is shining through me and say, "Use me." And then I work to become a clear and powerful instrument. This work is expressed by a commitment to a daily practice which maintains the strength and openness of my energy body.

On September 11, when disaster struck, I looked inside and found myself disconnected from that center of radiant power. All I found there was a shakiness. The fear was in my body as it was in the corporate body. A few days later was Rosh Hashanah, and it felt as though I had nothing to say, nothing to give to my congregation. I only knew that I would somehow be with them. Since it wasn't clear that the airlines would be flying, my husband and I rented a car and drove from our home in New Mexico to the congregation in California.

The moment we hit the open road, something in me shifted. Because I had surrendered in service, my access to that radiant power returned. The shakiness was gone and a calm spaciousness took its place. A rainbow appeared in the sky over Route 40 in western New Mexico, surprising us, sending us. About a dozen other cars pulled off the side of the road to watch this miracle. I stopped long enough to notice that when I am on my way to do God's work, the work of serving, the work of presence, then I am freed from my enslavement to fear.

Freedom in our tradition is not merely a "freedom from". . . from oppression, suffering, or servitude. It is a "freedom to". . . to be in direct relationship with God our liberator. Being in that relationship means serving the One, the Whole, the Holy. It means serving the Truth that emerges from the widest perspective even as we pay attention to the smallest detail. Our freedom depends on this servitude.

RELIGION IS NOT THE ANSWER

Arthur Hertzberg

MANY YEARS AGO, I was invited by the Harvard Divinity School to take part in a discussion of what the role of religion should be in solving the Jewish-Arab conflict. I shocked my hosts with a very short speech in which I asserted that the greatest contribution that religions—all the biblical religions—could make to peace in the Middle East would be to disappear from the debate.

This assertion ran counter, and still runs counter, to the cliché that if only the combatants "got religion," the wars would disappear and those who have been shooting at each other would mend their ways.

This image of the religions as peacemakers is patently false. On the contrary, it is quite true, today, before our eyes, that many passionate believers in their own traditions have no compunction about encouraging and even fomenting murderous attacks against those who belong to a different faith. In the present warfare between Palestinians and Israelis, the Palestinian rioters did not hesitate to destroy a Jewish shrine, the Tomb of Joseph in Nablus, moments after the Israeli guards left and entrusted the safety of this holy place to the Palestinian police. Several days later, the representatives of the Palestinian Authority detained four Israeli soldiers in the police station in Nablus, but did not or could not protect them from the mob that stormed the station and lynched two of them. On the Israeli side, the angry counterdemonstrations and the military response to the lynching of the two Israeli soldiers in Ramallah expressed more religious than even nationalist anger.

One of the sources of the present rage is Ehud Barak's offer of most of the Holy City of Jerusalem—the center that contains the great religious shrines of Judaism, Christianity, and Islam—to the Palestinians, and that nonetheless his offer was rejected by Yasser Arafat. That he made the offer outraged many Israeli fundamentalists; that the offer was rejected persuaded many more Israelis that the Palestinians do not want peace on any terms that represent a pragmatic compromise.

Therefore, I am emphasizing again that it is simply not true that the religions have a major, self-evident role in bringing peace. On the contrary, they need to reform themselves so that they become more peaceful. In each of the biblical traditions, there are elements enjoining kindness to the stranger, understanding for his needs and his traditions, and an awareness that the one God is the God of all humanity and that He wants all His children to make peace with each other. It is clear that those teachings are not the ones being emphasized by today's combatants.

Religion will make a contribution to peace only when the major traditions, whether in the Middle East or Yugoslavia or Africa, learn to emphasize that side of their teachings that points to love rather than hatred, or, at the very least, reminds all men and women that they should tolerate each other. Until that day, it would be best if the religions got out of this conflict.

So long as people believe they are killing other people in the name of God, to carry out His will, there can be no compromise. Such believers can foment atrocities of the most heinous kind while feeling good because they are "carrying out the will of God." Compromise is possible only among believers who are willing to accept that accommodations that make peace are better than holy wars.

THE TEMPLE OF AMOUNT

Eliezer Shore

IT HAS BEEN YEARS since I've enjoyed the sweetness of a symbolic life, since the time when the world spoke to me like a metaphor. In those early days of spiritual awakening, the world was strangely transparent, and every chance encounter, every passing sight seemed to hold the promise of deeper meaning. All of life pointed to the existence of a higher reality. It was a time of openness and wonder, and of deep contemplation.

And so I became religious, for religious life is symbolic life, devoted to uncovering the truths that lie beneath the surface of this world. Every symbol carries some inner meaning, whether simple or complex. In all cases, a symbol is an object whose content is greater than its form, for with just a few lines or gestures, it conveys a message that would otherwise require many words. But precisely because of this meager form, because their meaning is not overt, symbols demand that the viewer reconstruct the original message *within himself*. As such, they are vehicles for inner transformation, and are among the primary tools of the religious life, which seeks to convey truths that are altogether beyond words. Symbols are points of contemplation, for only by dwelling upon them, do they reveal their contents. And the more one contemplates them, the more meaningful they become. Furthermore, religious symbols, whose subject is the Infinite, have the potential to convey an infinity of meaning.

In Judaism, symbols give expression to every facet and stage of life: symbols of covenant, of renewal, of redemption—from the bitter herb eaten Passover night, symbolizing the harshness of exile, to the blast of the shofar on the New Year, symbolizing the great horn of Messiah. The Torah puts such emphasis on symbols because it understands that, ultimately, all of life is symbolic, and that the entire creation is only a vehicle through which we relate to G-d. Torah study is above all an exercise in interpretation. Texts are endlessly examined for their inner meaning, and new interpretations are put forth constantly. For by learning to uncover the inner meaning of a text, one can eventually learn to uncover the inner meaning of the world. And when the world is understood as a symbol in the Divine-human relationship, then its every detail is also seen to contain the potential for infinite meaning.

Yet, while all things can be meditated upon to discover G-d's presence, ultimately, the most important symbol is the human form itself, which reflects the Divine Image. "From my very flesh, I will behold G-d," says the prophet (Job 19:26). According to Kabbalah, contemplation upon the different aspects of the human dimension—one's thoughts, feelings and actions—can bring a person to an understanding of the Divine attributes. For the human arm is only a symbol of G-d's "arm"—His power and influence in the world. The human heart is only a reflection of the Divine heart; yet through it, we can learn about His infinite love for creation.

Within the human dimension, the richest symbol of all is the self, and contemplating the self is the primary means of apprehending something of the Divine Being. The beauty of contemplative life is that it allows a person time to engage in a pure act of self-reflection, until the self yields up its secret as the very expression of G-d's Being—His *malkut*—in the world. Through contemplation upon the "I" of the self, one can achieve knowledge of the true "I" of creation. On the verse "I am Pharaoh" (Genesis 41:44), the midrash comments: "From the 'I am' of flesh and blood, one can deduce the 'I AM' of the Holy One."[1] Even the "I am" of Pharaoh—the biblical model of selfishness and egotism—can eventually bring a person to the realization of the true I AM of creation.

However, all that was years ago. Today I am lost in a world of numbers. The great challenge of a life devoted to symbols is the constant necessity to penetrate ever deeper into their hidden meaning. No symbol remains relevant forever. After a time, the personal meaning found in the symbol begins to lessen: words of prayer become empty, religious images become hollow. What is called for now is a new act of contemplation, a further opening of the mind and heart to G-d. But at this important juncture, there lies the possibility of a mistake, that a person will look elsewhere for fulfillment. To do so is to leave the world of symbols and enter the realm of numbers, where quantity, rather than depth, serves as the criteria for meaning. It is not a question of how many symbols a person has at the center of his life, but in which direction he turns when the meaningful elements of life fall silent. This can be thought of in terms of a relationship. What do you do when the relationship with a loved one fails? Do you look elsewhere for love, or do you look deeper? Eventually, the new symbol will also lose its meaning, as will all those that follow. But once this horizontal movement has been established—this constant pursuit of the novel—one soon forgets the intrinsic value of things and judges them solely in relative, external terms. Worth becomes a product of amount: i.e., how much, and how many.

I do not remember when I fell away from the symbolic life—it must have happened gradually—but I am aware of the consequences. It is the difference between feeling fulfilled in life and feeling empty, between a sense of closeness to G-d, and the fear that one is never doing enough. On the lowest level, it manifests itself in the pursuit of meaning through material acquisition. On the highest level, it means a spirituality based upon accomplishment and attainment, and the constant desire for spiritual experiences. This is the story of our society. We have long ago lost the symbolic approach to life, as we have lost a truly religious perspective. Today, we are looking desperately for symbolic meaning in a world based on quantity.

Yet there is a solution. Not a way back, but a way through the numerical to something higher. When one looks at the Torah as a spiritual document deeply concerned with the oneness of G-d, one is immediately struck by its fascination with numbers. Everything is listed: people, places, dates, chattel. This is especially evident in the biblical passages describing the building of the *Mishkan,* the portable desert Sanctuary. Six chapters are devoted to its design and construction—entailing two years of work, three tons of silver and two tons of gold, six hundred yards of curtain, forty-eight standing boards, ninety-six sockets, incense, oil, skins, and dyes. Then the moment of assemblage arrives:

> And the L-rd spoke to Moses, saying: On the first day of the first month shall you set up the tabernacle of the Tent of Meeting. And you shall put in it the Ark of the Testimony, and hang the veil before the Ark. And you shall bring in the table, and set in order the things upon it; and you shall bring in the candlestick, and light its lamps. And you shall set the altar of gold for incense before the Ark of the Testimony, and put the screen of the door to the tabernacle. And you shall set the altar of the burnt offering before the door of the tabernacles of the Tent of Meeting . . .

Thus did Moses, according to all that the L-rd commanded him, so he did . . . Then a cloud covered the Tent of Meeting, and the Glory of the L-rd filled the tabernacle. And Moses was not able to enter the Tent of Meeting, because the cloud rested on it, and the Glory of the L-rd filled the tabernacle [Exodus 40:1–7, 16, 33–38].

An almost identical scenario is recorded in the Books of the Kings, occurring five centuries later with the building of the Holy Temple in Jerusalem. Again, after four chapters of detailed descriptions, the verses conclude:

And Solomon made all the vessels that belonged to the house of the L-rd: the altar of gold, and the table of gold, upon which the show-bread was, and the candlesticks of pure gold, five on the right side, and five on the left, before the inner sanctuary, with the flowers, and the lamps, and the tongs of gold, and the bowls and the snuffers, and the basins, and the spoons, and the firepans of pure gold; and the hinges of gold, both for the doors of the inner house, and the most holy place, and for the doors of the outer house, namely, the Temple.

So was ended all the work that King Solomon made for the house of the L-rd. And Solomon brought in the things that David his father had dedicated; the silver, and the gold, and the vessels, he put in the treasuries of the house of the L-rd. . . . And the priests brought in the Ark of the Covenant of the L-rd to its place, into the sanctuary of the house, to the most holy place, under the wings of the Cherubim.

And it came to pass, when the priest came out of the holy place, that the cloud filled the house of the L-rd, so that the priests could not stand to minister because of the cloud: for the Glory of the L-rd had filled the house . . ." [I Kings 7:48–51, 8:6, 10–11].

This is number transformed! These verses tell us that when the elements of creation are incorporated into a structure with the single goal of serving G-d, then a shift can occur that transforms number into something higher—a vessel for revelation. Kabbalah teaches that the Temple was a microcosm of creation, in which all the components worked together to reveal the will of G-d. It also compares the Temple to the human body, with the Divine Presence filling it like a soul. What is implied here is a harmony so great that it can only be defined by the word "organism." For the nature of an organism is that it exists only through the unity of its parts—with each part deriving life only to the degree that it is connected to the whole, and through the whole, something greater than all the parts—soul—becomes revealed.

Rabbi Adin Steinsaltz sees this as an integral aspect of entire Torah:

> The system of the mitzvot [commandments] constitutes the design for a coherent harmony, its separate components being like the instruments of an orchestra. So vast is the harmony to be created by this orchestra that it includes the whole world and promises the perfecting of the world. Seeing the mitzvot in this light, one may understand on the one hand, the need for so great a number of details and, on the other, the denial of any exclusive emphasis on any one detail or aspect of life. The mitzvot as a system include all of life, from the time one opens one's eyes in the morning until one goes to sleep, from the day of birth to the last breath.[2]

This is the great mystery at the heart of all true religious traditions: the fallen state of number is redeemed precisely in terms of its flaw, and out of diversity, the greatest unity can emerge. Likewise, on the individual level, when a person devotes all of his talents and resources in the service of the spirit, he can be lifted above his own divided nature and produce in himself something much more whole. Even when his practice is based upon selfish motivations, the very act of moving in a G-dward direction can deliver him from his flaws. "Let a person study Torah even for self-centered reasons, for eventually this will lead him to study it selflessly," says the Talmud.[3]

This brings us to our present time. Never in human history has there been a generation more obsessed with achievement and acquisition, with number and detail. Never have people had to deal with so much information and specificity of knowledge. Logically, this should result in a fragmentation of society, and a decreased ability for human beings to interact. Yet, we see that the opposite is true; there has never been a greater potential for communication between people and ideas, never have distant territories become more interdependent.

These two contrasting forces are propelling our civilization forward. Certainly, in all our hearts, we dream that their interaction will produce a larger whole—an era of world peace and harmony. All of creation is G-d's house, and every individual can be a holy vessel. When all the parts have been put into place, G-d's glory can once more fill His house. However, without a clear statement of this goal, without the basic religious perspective that leads to transcendence, it is almost unthinkable that this should occur. For the self is only valid as a framework of meaning when it operates in the symbolic mode. When it finds meaning in the realm of number, in its own strength and autonomy, there is no limit to its potential for avarice and destructiveness. Only within the context of a religious system, where self-interests are harnessed as motivation for personal growth and transformation, can the fallen world of number be redeemed. If our society is to reach its goal, we must reenvision human life and social organization in terms of cooperation and community—as an organism moving toward G-d—rather than in terms of quantification, with the egoism and competition that result.

Day by day, I am driven by forces that I do not understand—striving to be better, longing for G-d, moving toward a goal that I cannot foresee. Sometimes, a person can be so obsessed with the parts that he does not see the whole he is slowly building. Perhaps it is precisely the search for the symbolic in the world of numbers that transforms number into something higher. My deepest hope is that before the last day, G-d will assemble the disparate pieces of my life into a structure that reveals His will. "And the L-rd, whom you seek, will come suddenly into His Temple" (Malachi 3:1). For in the end, only G-d can create this whole, shining His light from above to bring unity out of diversity. "Who can bring the pure out of the impure?" asks the prophet. "Only the One" (Job 14:4).

NOTES

1. Genesis Rabbah 90:2.
2. Rabbi Adin Steinsaltz, *The Thirteen-Petaled Rose,* Jason Aronson Inc., Northvale, N.J., 1992.
3. Pesachim 50b.

KABBALAH

THE HERETIC

THE MYTHIC PASSIONS OF GERSHOM SCHOLEM

Cynthia Ozick

ONE MORNING EARLY IN February 1917, Gerhard Scholem, a tall, jug-eared, acutely bookish young man of nineteen, sat at breakfast with his parents in their comfortable Berlin apartment. It was an hour of family crisis. Gerhard, the youngest of four sons, was the only one still living at home. The three others had all been conscripted for the Kaiser's war. Reinhold and Erich were solid German patriots like their father; Reinhold went so far as to call himself, in right-wing lingo, a *Deutschnationaler*—a German nationalist. Werner, Gerhard's senior by two years, was a hot-head and a leftist—he later became a committed Communist. He had been wounded in the foot in the Serbian campaign and was recuperating in an Army hospital. Limping, wearing his uniform, he abandoned his bed and made his way to an antiwar demonstration. He was arrested and charged with treason.

Over the uneaten pastries, yet another brand of treason was brewing. Gerhard had declared himself to be a Zionist, and was openly preparing for emigration to Palestine. Two years earlier, exposed as the author of an antiwar flyer circulated by a Zionist youth group, he had been expelled from high school. Arthur Scholem, the paterfamilias of this opinionated crew (half of them mutinous), could do nothing about Werner, who was in the hands of the military. But Gerhard was near enough to feel his father's rage, and Arthur Scholem had devised a punishment of Prussian thoroughness. A businessman, he was demanding, authoritarian, uncompromising, practical above all; he presided over a successful printing enterprise and a household that could keep both a cook and a maid. At Christmas, there was an elaborately decorated tree, surrounded by heaps of presents. When Gerhard was fourteen, he found under the tree a framed portrait of Theodor Herzl, the founder of modern Zionism. "We selected this picture for you because you are so interested in Zionism," his mother explained. ("From then on," Scholem commented decades later, "I left the house at Christmastime.")

This interest, in Arthur Scholem's view, had increasingly turned excessive and unreasonable. Gerhard had not only hurled himself into the study of Hebrew; he was entering, with the identical zeal he gave to Latin and German literature, the capacious universe of the Talmud, an oceanic compilation of interpretive Biblical commentaries. Every element of these ancient canonical texts attracted him: their ethical and jurisprudential preoccupations; the vitality, in equal measure, of their rational and imaginative insights; their famous dialogic and often dissenting discourse across the generations. Martin Buber's romanticized work and Heinrich Graetz's panoramic "History of the Jews" (both of which Scholem eventually took issue with) were the initial stimuli, but he went on to search out the Zionist theoreticians of the time, and anything in Judaica that a bibliomaniacal teen-age boy haunting secondhand bookshops could afford.

All this was too much for the elder Scholem, who paid dues, after all, to the vehemently anti-Zionist Central Association of German Citizens of the Jewish Faith. The faith might be tepidly Jewish; the primary allegiance— the unquestioned identity, both social and personal—was German. Arthur Scholem believed himself to be an established and accepted member of a stable society. No wonder "the discussions at our family table became heated," as Scholem wryly points out in *From Berlin to Jerusalem,* his concise little memoir of 1977. But by then Gerhard had long since been transmuted into Gershom.

On that February morning in 1917, the family table was less heated than quietly tense. Arthur Scholem had made his preparations; he waited. The doorbell rang, heralding the arrival of a registered letter. It had been composed two nights earlier and was addressed to Gerhard:

> I have decided to cut off all support to you. Bear in mind the following: you have until the first of March to leave my house, and you will be forbidden to enter it again without my permission. On March first, I will transfer 100 marks to your account so that you will not be left without means. Anything more than this you cannot expect from me.

... Whether I will agree to finance your further studies after the war depends upon your future behavior.

Your father, Arthur Scholem

The father could not fathom a young man opposed to a patriotic war. Having a prodigy on his hands bewildered him—a rebellious prodigy given to devouring Plato and Kant, uncommonly gifted in higher mathematics, and determined to add to this conceptual stew an unfashionable, unpredictable, altogether obstinate dedication to Jewish history and thought. And, beyond these perplexities, Arthur Scholem scarcely recognized what Gerhard, in choosing to become Gershom (the name of a son of the biblical Moses), was crucially repudiating—and would continue to repudiate for the rest of his life. Despite the younger Scholem's ardent mastery of European culture, it was Europe, and Germany in particular, that he meant to renounce. His father's loyalties—the passionate love of the *Vaterland* that the majority of German Jews plainly felt—he could see only as self-deception. The Jews might be in love with Germany, but Germany was not in love with the Jews. To a Jewish friend who had professed "boundless adoration for German art, Goethe, and our contemporary Rudolf Borchardt," and who provocatively added, "I hate Martin Buber with all my heart," the nineteen-year-old Scholem responded with what he called "a tremendous intuition" for Judaism:

> I confess that I've never had such a central relationship with any other thing; it has commanded my full attention from the time I began to work and think for myself (to wit, from the age of fourteen). The confrontation with German culture which presents so many Jews with such painful dilemmas has never been a problem for me. Nor has the absolutely un-Jewish atmosphere in my home been able to change this. I have never found or sought out values whose legitimacy was rooted in the German essence. Even the German language, which I speak, disappears for me completely when compared to Hebrew.

To another correspondent, a few days before, he had announced, "We [Jews] have had a relationship with Europe only to the degree that Europe has acted upon us as a destructive stimulation." Both these assertions were made from a bed in a military hospital, where, he reported, "the heavy footsteps of anti-Semitism are always thumping behind my back." Like his older brothers before him, he had been inducted into the military; unlike Werner, he had not been wounded in battle. He was, instead, in a mental ward, suffering from a kind of nervous disorder—and then again it was an invention, "a colossal fabrication," as he put it, to get himself out of the Army. In fact, it was partly one and partly the other, and it succeeded in freeing him. "I'll be able to *work* once again," he crowed. "I won't be squandering my youth in these odious circumstances, and I can celebrate my twentieth birthday wearing civilian clothes."

The three-month interval between his father's throwing him out of the house and his enforced Army stint had turned out to be remarkably fruitful. He went to live at the Pension Struck, a boarding house in an unfashionable neighborhood of Berlin catering to a group of Russian Jewish intellectuals who held perfervid, if conflicting, Zionist views. Among the polyglot and fiercely literary boarders was a future president of Israel, and it was here that Scholem undertook a translation from the Yiddish (a language new to him) of a volume of memorial essays devoted to Jewish victims of Arab rioters in Palestine: his first full-length publication. During this same period, he began his enduring friendship with the Hebrew novelist S. J. Agnon, who would one day be awarded the Nobel Prize in Literature, and whose stories Scholem rendered into pellucid German. Scholem had already encountered Walter Benjamin at a Jewish discussion club for young people—"an utterly original mind," he marvelled. He was then seventeen; Benjamin was five years older. Not long afterward, they met again, as university students. (Despite Scholem's expulsion from high school, he was permitted to take his graduation exams and managed to gain university entrance through an academic loophole intended for Junkers.) The two talked of phenomenology and philology; they talked of socialism and historiography; they talked of Chinese philosophy and of Baudelaire, Pindar, and Hölderlin; they argued over Brecht and Zola and Zionism; they were mutually immersed in Kafka. These astonishing exchanges—the bulk of them through a decades-long correspondence indefatigably pledged to ideas, experimental, often playful, and on Benjamin's part somewhat elusive—continued until Benjamin's suicide, in 1940, in flight from the Germans. Scholem was frequently the first reader of Benjamin's newest work, and Benjamin was briefly inspired by Scholem's example to study Hebrew, though he never progressed much beyond the alphabet. Both these extraordinary young men were beguiled by the transcendent nature of language. Both were out to re-create intellectual history—Benjamin with the uncertainty of his genius, wavering from subject to subject, Scholem with the certainty of his, leaping with scholarly ferocity into the hitherto untouchable cauldron of Jewish mysticism.

It was untouchable because it was far out of the mainstream of Judaism, excluded by rabbinic consensus. Normative Judaism saw itself as given over to moral rationalism: to codes of ethics, including the primacy of charity, and a coherent set of personal and societal practices; to the illuminations of midrash, the charms of ethical lore—but mythologies and esoteric mysteries were cast out. The *Zohar*, a mystical treatise, was grudgingly admitted for study, but only in maturity, lest it dazzle the student into irrationality. For normative Judaism, ripe sobriety was all; or, if not all, then a significant social ideal.

Scholem saw something else, and he saw it from an early age. Unlike Freud, who dismissed religion as illusion, Scholem more ambitiously believed it to be crucial for the structure of the human mind as language itself. At twenty, he wrote to Escha Burchhardt (whom he later married and divorced), "Philology is truly a secret science and the only legitimate form of historical science that has existed until now. It is the greatest confirmation of my view of the central importance of Tradition, though of course in a new sense of the word." He named his idea "the philosophy of the Hebrew language" and exclaimed, prophetically, "Oh, if only someday these things could be the focus of my worthy labors!"

Two years on, he was a doctoral student who described his dissertation as "a vast foundational philological-philosophical monograph on an early kabbalistic text from around the year 1230. . . . Nothing worthwhile that's any longer than four pages has been written about it." His work on the text, "Sefer ha-Bahir," was pioneering scholarship, but it was far more than that. In the framework of conventional Jewish historiography, it signalled a revolution. Scholem was divulging a tradition hidden underneath, and parallel to, normative Jewish religious expression. Below the ocean of interpretive commentary lay another ocean, also of interpretive commentary, but in imagistic and esoteric guise. Scholem's encyclopedic research took him through the centuries; no one before him had ever systematically ordered and investigated the manifold varieties of Jewish mysticism. The position of classical Judaism was that the essence of God is unknowable: "Thou canst not see My Face." The Kabbalists sought not only to define and characterize the Godhead—through a kind of spiritualized cosmogonic physics—but to experience it. Kabbalah had been shunned for its claims of ecstatic ascent to the hidden sublime; it had been scored for its connection to folk religion and magic.

Scholem was determined to uncover the more exalted strata of a suppressed tradition, partly to complete and clarify the historical record, and partly to disclose arcane and majestic imaginative constructs, themselves marvels of the human intellect. It was a kind of literary archeology. His chief excavating tool was philology—the study of texts and their origins. Scholem has been compared to one of the greatest of the grand exegetes and codifiers of Jewish tradition: Maimonides, the twelfth-century physician and polymath, who read Torah with an Aristotelian eye. But Maimonides was a proponent of rationalism. Scholem was in pursuit of the opposite. He looked to theosophy, as manifested in Kabbalah: "those religious streams within Judaism," he explained, "which strive to arrive at a religious consciousness beyond intellectual apprehension, and which may be attained by man's delving into himself by means of contemplation, and the inner illumination which results from this contemplation."

This is almost too general a definition, given the complexities of the many generations and branches of Kabbalah (a word that means tradition, literally "what is received") in its luxuriant fecundity from the first millennium to its latest expression in the eighteenth century. The most influential of all these movements came to fruition in the town of Safed, in Galilee, in the sixteenth century, when a community of initiates gathered around Rabbi Isaac Luria and began to compose the astonishing works that make up what is called the Lurianic Kabbalah. Not all the Lurianic ideas were new, but they expanded in an original direction under the pressure of one of the most catastrophic upheavals in Jewish history: the Inquisitorial persecutions of the Jews of Spain, and their expulsion after a golden age of high creativity. Here was yet another historic exile (the destruction of the Second Temple, in the year 70, inaugurating the dispersion, was primal), and its thunderous effects had their echo in a cataclysmic symbolism.

In the beginning—indeed, before the beginning—God's luminous essence filled the pleroma, the stuff of nothingness that was everywhere. Then God performed an act of *tsimtsum,* self-limitation, contracting in order to make room for Creation. "Without contraction there is no creation, as everything is Godhead," Scholem writes. "Therefore, already in its earliest origins, the creation is a kind of exile, in that it involves God removing Himself from the center of His essence to His secret places." But certain lights, or sparks, or brilliant emanations of God trickled out nevertheless. These were the *sefiroth,* God's qualities or potentialities— the vital ten arteries, so to speak, of His Being. They can be listed as Primeval Will; Wisdom; Intuition; Grace; Judgment; Compassion; Eternity; Splendor; All Fructifying Forces; and, last, the *Shekhinah,* "the hidden radiance of the totality of the hidden divine life which dwells in every created and existing being." These powerful divine lights flowed into the vessels that are the material of the created world; too fragile to contain such magnitudes, they broke apart, scattering the godly sparks. Some fell among the shards of the sundered vessels and were held captive, themselves damaged and given over to darkness. Because of this rupture, called *shevirah,* the ideal processes of Creation have been thwarted, and, ever since, nothing has been in its right place; all is exile. In Safed there arose, finally, the concept of *tikkun,* the reintegration of what has been fragmented, the correction of confusion, the return of harmony. In this way, the Kabbalists of Galilee, through a cosmological myth of exile and redemption, were able to map a people's shattered experience and adumbrate a vision of restoration.

It may have been in the early 1940s (there are no living witnesses, and no one of the current generation is certain just when) that Scholem was invited to New York to deliver a lecture on Kabbalah at the Jewish Theological Seminary. He was introduced by Saul Lieberman, a leading Talmudic eminence, and thereby an adherent of Jewish rationalism. "Nonsense is nonsense," Professor Lieberman pronounced, "but the history of nonsense is scholarship." Whether Scholem responded to this now legendary maxim is not known. But the immensity, and the passion, of his scholarship intimates that he did not include visionary symbolism among the artifacts of nonsense.

In 1923, at twenty-five, Scholem set off for Palestine, as he had promised ten years before. He had completed his dissertation summa cum laude, and might easily have attained a post in a German university. Instead, he arrived in Jerusalem with six hundred volumes of Kabbalistic literature and no academic prospects. But there were plenty of secondhand bookshops: Jerusalem, he noted, "was saturated with old Hebrew books the way a sponge is saturated with water." By 1925, the Hebrew University of Jerusalem was established (it had been in the planning stage since 1913), and before long Scholem became its first professor of Jewish mysticism. And now began that torrent of innovative historical and literary inquiry which quickly marked him as a twentieth-century luminary. He was not a man penetrating a field of learning; he was a field of learning penetrating the world. He wrote in a Hebrew that rivalled his native German in literary quality. He read Greek, Latin, Arabic, and Aramaic. His English was fluent and polished. *Major Trends in Jewish Mysticism,* lectures composed chiefly in English and first published in 1941, has become the standard introductory work: the dedication is "to the memory of Walter Benjamin, a friend of a lifetime." Scholem's magnum opus, *Sabbatai Sevi: The Mystical Messiah,* which appeared in English translation in 1973, is a consummate history of a seventeenth-century messiah figure who aroused, among the diasporic Jewish masses, the hope of a return to Jerusalem; it is a book enormously suggestive of the origins of Christianity.

All this and more—lectures, teaching, travel abroad, a second marriage to Fanya Freud—Scholem accomplished during times of tumult and violence. In Germany, the crisis of postwar currency inflation was followed by the rise of Nazism. Scholem's brother Werner, against whom the earlier charge of treason had been ameliorated, was again arrested, both as a former Communist and as a Jew; he was finally murdered in Buchenwald in 1940. In the late nineteen-thirties, Scholem's widowed mother and his brothers Reinhold and Erich escaped to Australia. During these same years, Palestine was troubled by periodic Arab rioting, notably in 1920, 1921, 1929, 1936, and 1939. "For the past three months, we in Jerusalem have been living under a state of siege." Scholem wrote to Benjamin in August, 1936. "There's a considerable amount of terrorism. . . . A few days ago a colleague of mine who teaches Arabic literature was murdered in his study while reading the Bible. . . . No one knows whether someone will toss a bomb his way or around the next corner." In June, 1939, he again told Benjamin, "We live in terror," and spoke of the "capitulation of the English"—the Mandate power—"in the face of violence." And in 1948 there was outright war when the surrounding Arab nations, rejecting the United Nations plan for the partition of Palestine, sent five invading armies to converge on the newborn Jewish state. Whole sections of Jerusalem were destroyed or overrun. Before Scholem's death, in 1982, he had lived through the terror incursions of 1956, the Six-Day War of 1967, and the Yom Kippur attacks of 1973.

Scholem defined his Zionism as metaphysically and historically rooted rather than political. "I don't give a rap about the problem of the state," he said, and styled himself an anarchist. Nevertheless, he joined colleagues at the Hebrew University in the formation, in 1925, of Brit Shalom (Peace Covenant), a political group favoring a binational state, which was to include both Arabs and Jews on equal terms—but, since few Arabs were attracted to the idea, and, of these, some were assassinated by other Arabs, it failed. He had once affirmed that by leaving Europe behind he was stepping out of world history in order to reenter Jewish history; yet world history, it seemed, had an uncanny habit of following the Jews wherever they were. Scholem was compelled to endure intermittent chaos even as he probed into Kabbalistic theories of exile and redemption.

He also wrote letters. His father, toward whom he was never cordial, had died some months after Scholem's emigration. But he wrote often to his mother, who replied copiously, and now and then shipped him the familiar delicacies he requested—marzipan and sausage. He wrote to old friends still in Germany; to new friends in America; to his students; to Walter Benjamin, Theodor Adorno, Martin Buber, Hannah Arendt, George Lichtheim, George Steiner, Jürgen Habermas, Friedrich Dürrenmatt, Elias Canetti, Daniel Bell, Emil Fackenheim, Leo Strauss, Franz Rosenzweig, and scores of others. The German edition of the letters occupies two thousand pages. The recently published *Gershom Scholem: A Life in Letters, 1914–1982,* edited and translated by Anthony David Skinner, is a lively and considerably shorter collection, which followed Scholem from his fevered adolescence to the sovereign authority of his final years. The editor's illuminating biographical summaries set out useful links from decade to decade, but it is Scholem's uncompromising voice that gives this volume its unified force and striking crescendos. In their unstinting energy, the letters show a man exactly where he wanted to be, and conscious of exactly why.

His correspondents who were fleeing Germany were not so sure. Scholem repeatedly offered refuge to Benjamin, holding out the hope of a post at the Hebrew University; Benjamin repeatedly vacillated, finally admitting to a procrastination "which is second nature to me when it comes to the most important situations in my life." To Scholem's exasperation, Benjamin was contemplating the feasibility of an island off Spain. "You could, of course, do your literary work here," Scholem countered. "Jerusalem offers more than Ibiza: first of all, there are people like us here; second, there are books. . . . But it seems to us doubtful that you'd feel comfortable in a land in which you took no direct part. . . . The only people who can survive all of the difficulties here are those who are fully devoted to this land and to Judaism." Benjamin, Scholem had come to recognize long before, had refused any such devotion. It was Hannah Arendt (then Hannah Stern), writing as a refugee in the South of France, who informed Scholem of Benjamin's suicide.

But for Scholem the most commanding chronicler of the growing Nazi harassment of Jews was Betty Scholem, his despairing mother. In a flood of anguished letters from Berlin (reminiscent of Victor Klemperer's diaries of gradual engulfment), she was recording a week-by-week tightening of the German noose. "I cannot digest what is happening," she wailed. "I'm completely speechless. I simply can't imagine that there are not 10,000 or 1,000 upright Christians who refuse to go along by raising their voice in protest." Her accounts of her futile trips to the offices of the Nazi police to appeal for information about the imprisoned Werner have the resonance of an atrocity foretold. In March, 1933, commenting on the Jewish lawyers, teachers, and physicians who were being barred from their professions, she wrote:

> It's a real stroke of luck that you're out of harm's way! Now, suddenly, I want to see everyone in Palestine!! When I only think of the outcry heard among German Jews when Zionism began! Your father and grandfather Hermann L. and the entire Central Verein beat themselves

on the breast and said with absolute conviction, "We are Germans!"
And now we're being told that we are *not* Germans after all!

Despite intervals of relative quiet, the Jewish population of Palestine
was never entirely out of harm's way; but his mother's terrified response
to the danger in Germany, years after his own prescient repudiations, left
a bitter imprint on many of his later exchanges. Scholem declined to meet
with Heidegger (as Buber had done), because Heidegger had been an unabashed Nazi. He was impatient with tendentious distortions of Jewish
history. When an editor of *The New York Review of Books* asked him to
review Arthur Koestler's *The Thirteenth Tribe: The Khazar Empire and
Its Heritage,* Scholem's reply—"sensationalist humbug"—was scathing:

> Sigmund Freud told the Jews their religion was foisted upon them by
> an Egyptian, so that there was nothing for the Jews to be proud of.
> The Jews found it baseless but rather amusing. Some Gentiles loved
> it because it would [teach] those supercilious Jews a lesson. Arthur
> Koestler wants to give them the rest by telling them that they were not
> even Jews and that those damned Ashkenazim from Russia, Romania,
> and Hungary who had invented Zionism had not even the right to ask
> for Israel as their homeland—which their Khazaric forefathers had
> never seen. . . . There is nothing more to be said by me about Koestler's
> scholarship.

In 1962, as part of a postwar, post-Holocaust effort toward official public remorse in Germany, Scholem was invited to contribute to a volume
intended as homage to "the indestructible German-Jewish dialogue." He
answered with a trenchant polemic:

> There is no question that Jews tried to enter into a dialogue with Ger-
> mans, and from all possible perspectives and standpoints: now de-
> manding, now pleading and imploring; now crawling on their hands
> and knees, now defiant; now with all possible compelling tones of dig-
> nity, now with a godforsaken lack of self-respect. . . . No one re-
> sponded to this cry. . . . The boundless ecstasy of Jewish enthusiasm
> never earned a reply in any tone that could count as a productive re-
> sponse to Jews as Jews—that is, a tone that would have addressed
> what the Jews had to give and not only what they had to give up. To
> whom, then, did the Jews speak in this famous German-Jewish dia-
> logue? They spoke only to themselves. . . . In the final analysis, it's true
> that Germans now acknowledge there was an enormous amount of

Jewish creativity. This does not change the fact that you can't have a dialogue with the dead."

This was not Scholem's most acerbic riposte, though it touched on one of the central passions of his historical thinking. A year later, in 1963, Hannah Arendt published *Eichmann in Jerusalem: A Report on the Banality of Evil,* an account of the trial of Adolf Eichmann, the high-ranking S.S. officer who had ordered the deportation of Jews to the death camps, and whom Israeli agents had captured in his Argentine hideout. Scholem's rebuttal ignited an intellectual conflagration that tore beyond the boundaries of their private exchange into a ferocious public quarrel. Arendt and Scholem had been warm correspondents for two decades. But as early as 1946 a faultline—not yet a crevasse—opened in their friendship. Arendt had sent Scholem "Zionism Reconsidered," an essay he dismissed as a "patently anti-Zionist, warmed-over version of Communist criticism" and "an act of political balderdash." He accused her of attacking the Jews of Palestine "for maintaining an otherworldly separation from the rest of mankind, but," he contended, "when these same Jews make efforts to fend for themselves, in a world whose evil you yourself never cease to emphasize, you react with a derision that itself stems from some other otherworldly source." He set out his credo, both personal and political:

I am a nationalist and am wholly unmoved by ostensibly "progressive" denunciations of a viewpoint that people repeatedly, even in my earliest youth, deemed obsolete. . . . I am a "sectarian" and have never been ashamed of expressing in print my conviction that sectarianism can offer us something decisive and positive. . . . I cannot blame the Jews if they ignore so-called progressive theories which no one else in the world has ever practiced. . . . The Arabs have not agreed to a single solution that includes Jewish immigration, whether it be federal, national, or binational. . . . [They] are primarily interested not in the morality of our political convictions but in whether or not we are here in Palestine at all. . . . I consider it abundantly obvious (and I hardly need emphasize this to you) that the political career of Zionism . . . has created a situation full of despair, doubt, and compromise— precisely because it takes place on earth, not on the moon. . . . The Zionist movement shares this dialectical experience of the Real (and all its catastrophic possibilities) with all other movements that have taken it upon themselves to change something in the real world.

He concluded by charging Arendt with cynical rhetoric aimed "against something that is for the Jewish people of life-or-death importance." Her view, he believed, was motivated by a fear of being classed as a reactionary, "one of the most depressing phenomena to be seen among clever Jews." He knew this, he said, from reading *Partisan Review.*

Vitriol ebbed and affection resumed. In the long run, it was a friendship that could not be sustained, and with the appearance of *Eichmann in Jerusalem,* Scholem's regard for Arendt dissolved; in old age he felt their dispute to have been "one of the most bitter controversies of my life." He disposed of "the banality of evil" as no better than a slogan: it contradicted and undermined the "radical evil" Arendt had testified to in *The Origins of Totalitarianism,* her earlier study. He argued against her merciless condemnation of the Jewish Councils whom the Germans had forced to run the ghettos: "I don't presume to judge. I wasn't there." He disagreed that the prosecution had failed to prove its case, even while he asserted his opposition to hanging Eichmann: "We should not make it easier for the Germans to confront their past. . . . He now stands as a representative for everyone." He did not altogether quarrel with Arendt's criticism of the weaker elements of a people in extremis, but, "to the degree that there really was weakness," he protested, "your emphasis is, so far as I can tell, completely one-sided and leaves the reader with a feeling of rage and fury." Rage and fury boiled up from a still deeper source:

> It is the heartless, the downright *malicious* tone you employ in dealing with a topic that so profoundly concerns the center of our life. There is something in the Jewish language that is completely indefinable, yet fully concrete—what the Jews call *ahavath Israel,* or love for the Jewish people. With you, my dear Hannah, as with so many intellectuals coming from the German left, there is no trace of it. . . . In treating such a theme, isn't there a place for the humble German expression "tact of the heart"?

Arendt's response was unrelievedly hostile. She denied coming from the German left; she had come from German philosophy. She had no love for any nation or collective. As for her opinion of Zionism, the Jews no longer believed in God; they believed only in themselves. "In this sense," she told him, "I don't love the Jews."

Scholem's term for what is now commonly known as the Holocaust was "the Catastrophe." In his scholarship the word hardly appears. But it is clear from the letters that the Catastrophe was one of the overriding preoccupations of his life, and a clandestine presence in his books. A number of his correspondents were refugees; a few, among them his most treasured friend, were suicides. At the close of the war, he roamed Europe, rescuing the surviving remnants of Judaica libraries and transporting them to Palestine. Together with Theodor Adorno he succeeded in preserving another endangered archive: Walter Benjamin's papers, which he edited and guided into print. (Along the way, he was delighted to learn that Benjamin was a direct descendant of Heinrich Heine.)

In the public arena—exemplified by the obsessions evident in his private letters—he pursued two salient themes: the historical imperatives of modern Zionism; and German culpability and its subset, the delusions of German Jews in their unrequited love affair. As for the Germans themselves, "I can and would speak to individuals," but he withdrew from addressing the nation collectively. "We should allow time to do its work," he advised in 1952. World upheaval had buffeted his generation and cut down its most productive minds. "It's pointless to entertain any illusions," he wrote. "We have suffered a loss of blood, whose effects on the spirit and on scholarly achievement are simply unimaginable." Doubtless he had Benjamin in mind—but also the loss to intellectual history, especially in the form of advanced Jewish historiography. So it was left to Scholem to accomplish, single-handedly, the new historiography he envisioned, until the time when his students might take up his work and his legacy. In order to understand Kabbalah, he slyly told them, they must first read Kafka.

He formulated Kabbalah as myth—he was, after all, a modern. And, as a modern transfixed by the unorthodox and the symbolic, he cast a seductive influence over realms far from his own demanding skills. Over the years, the tincture of his mind colored the work of Harold Bloom, Jacques Derrida, Umberto Eco, Jorge Luis Borges, Patrick White. These vagrant literary spores bemused him—"It's a free country," he once remarked—but he knew them to be distant from his powers and his mission. The uses of Kabbalah were not the enchantments of art or the ingenuities of criticism. For Scholem, Kabbalah was a fierce necessity, "the vengeance of myth against its conquerors." To the elitism of classical Judaism, and its judgment of Kabbalah as heresy, he retorted:

> From the start this resurgence of mythical conceptions in the thinking of the Jewish mystics provided a bond with certain impulses in the popular faith, fundamental impulses springing from the simple man's fear of life and death, to which Jewish philosophy had no satisfactory response. Jewish philosophy paid a heavy price for its disdain of the primitive levels of human life. It ignored the terrors of which myths are made. . . . Nothing so sharply distinguishes philosophers and Kabbalists as their attitude toward the problem of evil and the demonic.

For centuries, through persecutions and expulsions, forced conversions and torchings, to the abyss of the Catastrophe, Jews had suffered terror. Responding to these recurring crises, the mystical imagination had devised a cosmogony that incorporated Jewish historical experience. In Kabbalistic symbolism, with its tragic intuition that the world is broken, that all things are not in their proper places, that God, too, is in exile, Scholem saw both a confirmation of the long travail of Jewish dispersion and its consolation: the hope of redemption. In short, he saw Zionism.

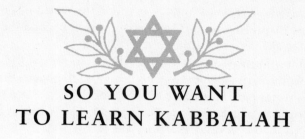

SO YOU WANT
TO LEARN KABBALAH

Zalman Schachter-Shalomi

KABBALAH, THE WORD ITSELF comes from Kabel, ka bel—to receive—to be in a state other than the usually active state, so that that which comes from G-d, which the Bible characterizes as the small still voice or more precisely translated, the sound of subtle stillness, can be received.

It is in that receptivity that some things become revealed. So it is different than reaching out, as one usually does, for concepts and ideas. Although we must use concepts and ideas, they are meant to be used in such a way in which I allow myself and my imagination to be engaged to receive the images that arise. Because that will lead me to be attuned to the worlds that are being referred to.

In Kabbalah, we begin by saying this is not the only universe, the one of sensation, of technology, of our social world. Underneath this world, there is an entire other universe which deals with energy. And if we could see the flow of that energy, feel it, we would, when attuned to that, become attuned to a world that is called the world of function. The spiritual aspect of the world of function is the world of Assiyah. The world that we usually occupy is called the world of Asslyah, the physical world. So already we see two worlds parallel. One in which our phenomena occur, and a world above that which is how our phenomena express themselves, because in them is invested energy. Still, deeper than that, deeper in the sense of we have to reach farther to be in touch with that, is the world where our feelings are. And, there are ebbs and tides of feelings. So there is day feeling and there is night feeling, and there is feeling of compassion and mercy and grace and there is feeling of rigor and severity. And in those worlds where these feelings operate is called the world of Formation, the world of Yitsirah. And, it is seen as one world beyond the spiritual world of Assiyah.

Beyond these feelings, and that world, there's another world still. And that is the world where all ideas are, all theory is, all understandings are, all the reality maps are located there. The world where Plato's ideas reside. The world in which all the myths are told. That world is called the world of B'riyah, the world of creation. The world of Assiyah, the world of Yitzirah, the world of B'riyah are spiritual worlds beyond which there is yet a Divine universe, which is the universe called Atzilut, the universe of emanation. A place where the attributes of G-d are at home. A place where the great archetypes are located. And so, when we feel, somehow in the parenthood of G-d, the father aspect of that, or the mother aspect of that, these are the deep archetypes, in which, the Divine dresses itself to face us from the world of Atzilut.

These four worlds are also connected to the four letters of the Divine name. Sometimes spelled Jehovah, sometimes spelled Yahweh. This time think of it as spelled YHVH or with the Hebrew letters Yod, Hey, Vav, Hey. The highest world, that place where the Divine attributes are at home, is the world of Atzilut, the world of the Yod. Where the ideas are, is the world of the Hey. And the world where the feelings are resident is the world of the Vav. And the world of energy is the world of the other Hey. And this physical world is governed by the other Divine name and the one which we express and use in language when we talk of Yod, Hey, Vav, Hey and call that Adonai.

That has to do with this totality in which G-d's dimension of governance of all that there is, is understood. And that is the first strong principle of the Kabbalah. That we simultaneously inhabit four universes. And in each one of these universes there exists that which we call "in the image of G-d." When we speak of human beings as made in the image of G-d, the word in Hebrew, Tselem, means "like silhouettes." And if you take the Yod and place that over the Hey and place that over the Vav, and place all three over the other Hey, you get an image as if a person: where the head is, is the Yod, and where the arms and shoulders are is the Hey, and where the spine is, is the Vav. And where the legs and pelvis are is the other Hey. And so, in each one of these regions of the being, we see attributes, so that we now speak of the ten sephirot. As if to say ten dimensions in each world. There is a dimension which is called Keter, the crown. There, the will for it to exist is at home. There is a dimension that is called Chochmah, wisdom (Sophie is another name it has). Where the first notion of wisdom arises there from the deep will. And when that first notion of wisdom arises there and lightens up the mind like a lightning, like a spark, we still cannot speak of understanding something until that spark of insight lands in the womb of Binah, of understanding, where it assumes shape and form, and difference and detail. And so we have Keter, where the will is, Chochmah and Binah, which is wisdom and understanding coming to that place where cognition and consciousness arise in us.

Then there is below that, the realm of the arm that gives, that bestows, that is generous, where grace is located. And that is called Chesed. And that sephira corresponds to the first day of creation. Let there be lights! Give all blessing and all light to the universe! And then comes the second sephira after Chesed of the seven days of creation, which is now the fourth sephira in the system after Keter, there where the second day of the week is. "Let there be a firmament dividing the Heaven from below." Distinction making and severity enters, with judgment on the second day of creation and that is called Din or Gevurah.

And the working of these two together, where grace intersects with severity, there is begotten the place of compassion. That is the sephira of Tiferet. It represents the feeling most heard in the universe. Where the seat of compassion for all creation is. From there compassion moves, Tiferet, moves to Netzach, which is called victory, represents the fourth day of creation, and it is there where all things effective, efficient happen. Representing the fourth day of creation, and that is the clockwork of the Heaven. To balance that comes the fifth day of creation when all the egg layers are formed, when the fishes and the fowl are created. And where effectiveness is balanced with beauty and elegance and that is called Hod. And the collaboration of effectiveness and beauty, there is begotten the next sephira, called Yesod, Foundation. And it is this sephira that is also connected to our feeling of our own libido, genitality, where children and begetting are. And then proceeding from that sephira of Yesod, we move to the last sephira, called Malchut, and it represents majesty and kingdom. And it is also that place to which, in our relationship with G-d, we are caused to surrender ourselves to. And so Malchut is our connection to the other sephirot of the ten sephirot of the Divine. And they are replicated in each of the four worlds.

By such a reality map, we can then proceed to look into what is in the interior of a human being, where we find the body and it is animated by the Nefesh (Nefesh translates into our breath and animation), and more interior to that is the aspect of soul called Ruach, spirit. And it is the seat of our feelings, of our emotions. And beyond that is the seat of the soul, that is, the intellective soul, called Neshamah, in which reside all consciousness and awareness with which we want to reach out. Deep seated in Neshamah and beyond it is an aspect called Chiyah. That is the place where our deepest longing is to become united with the One. And deeper than that still, is that aspect of the soul called Yichidah, which is as if a part of a hologram. So are we part of the living infinite G-d. These are the words that accompany the Kabbalah. And I hope that as you hear them from time to time, and you allow yourself to be receptive to the images that it creates in you, that the words of the Kabbalah will not remain opaque to you and that you understand depths that you did not manage to feel or know or encounter before. All blessing in your study of Kabbalah.

So now we perceive in ourselves that pattern through which there flows will and intellect and the emotions and the functions in us, the light that comes from above and becomes reality for us. So the Kabbalist moved to understand that as below, so above as we know it in ourselves as human beings. So that this pattern must also obtain beyond in the larger cosmos. And so the Kabbalist saw that there was this process that saw itself going through the ten sephirot as the large patterns in which the cosmic person, that kind of Incarnation coming from the infinite, invests itself in the world. And this is then done through the sephirot in which Keter is the will that there should be a universe of all these dimensions. And Chochmah is where the plan begins. And Binah is where the plan gets detailed. And then comes the aspect where G-d so loves creation that it can be and sets limit to it so that it might be firm and fills it with compassion so that all life can live. And creates the paths so that there could be a flow of energy from world to world and an interaction of life. And creates the beauty that makes it so that it is what we now perceive as ecological. And gives it that intense energy that leads all creation to want to procreate. And then builds in it also that which causes it to be transformed and recycled and that is Malchut. So let us now review how this shows itself in the Sephirot.

Hasidim and Rebbes: The teachers are the Rebbes, and the Hasidim are the followers, who turn to the Rebbes for guidance, and for teaching, and for blessing, and for intercession in prayer. Sometimes Hasidim tell stories about their masters. And sometimes they report the sayings of their masters. And I would like to share with you some of the sayings of Hasidic Masters. One was Reb Pinchas of Koretz. Someone asked him, "How can we pray for someone else to repent, when this prayer, if granted, would curtail another person's freedom of choice? Is it not said by the Rabbis that everything is in Heaven's Hands, except the fear of Heaven?" And he answered, "What is G-d? G-d is a totality of souls. Whatever there exists in the whole, can also be found in the part. So in any one soul, all souls are contained. If I turn in t'shuvah, in repentance, I contain in me the friend I wish to help, and he contains me in him. And my turning makes the him in me better and the me in him better. And in this way it becomes so much easier for the him in him to become better."

One who studies the Kabbalah has to face a certain dilemma. *If I want to read more traditional, more source originating Kabbalah coming from the past,* I must not expect that its wording and its rhetoric will be at home in our current understanding and the maps of reality. So as we read these texts and become acquainted with them, we hear cosmologies that are hierarchic, divisions between good and evil, between us and them, between above and below, between permitted and forbidden, and between male and female. And in all these one is seen as higher or better than the other. And this is basic to these texts. When, however, the humanistic Kabbalist reformats these deep teachings for the present, it is now understood deeper and more differently, how everything is organically connected and how each needs the other in order to balance. And male needs the female and physical needs the spiritual and how everything is integrated. And if we hear it in this way, it is no less authentic to our day and age, than an earlier version was authentic to that time.

A person can live in the same house with a Tzadik and still be stupid. What can you expect me to say. If you hear one word, you think you know it all already. The Bracha, the blessing, is not found in what is manifest to everyone's eyes. What is a Bracha? A Bracha is the very mystery of the Shekhinah the Divine Presence. And that is what the *Zohar* calls a true blessing. Do you want to know when you have a Bracha? When all the chambers of the body vibrate with it, then you have the Bracha.

To disperse the clouds you need wind, and there are clouds that hover over the mind. And the wind to disperse those clouds that hover over the mind comes from the movement and prayer, the in and out from the lungs. This is what the *Zohar* calls Ruach, the spirit, the breath. If I had told of this some years ago people would have served G-d by breathing and all the clouds would have dispersed.

Sometimes a person needs to be told, and needs to be reproved. And when I must reprove a person, I tell them something gentle and wise. This helps them get in touch with the soul and the soul gives life to its owner so he begins to live the soul life. If I helped him get in touch with his soul. This is what Rabbi Moshe Cordevero says in his Pardes. Sometimes I help him get in touch with his soul by telling him a joke. Ha! Still there are those in this generation of ours who preach morals at people, urging them to repent, but the poor one to whom they preach to has no way to help themselves get to repentance if they can't get in touch with their living soul. So this is why I tell something gentle, something wise and sometimes a joke.

In the *Tikkuney Zohar,* the holy book connected to the *Zohar* literature, it is stated: Hidden worlds that can be revealed and hidden worlds that cannot be revealed. There are deep insights one ought not to reveal at all because in talking about them one causes the G-d within the insight to die away. Now if a person talking about them could say them with the feelings of love and awe alive in them, G-d would not die away from the insight. But this is extremely difficult for those who haven't learned to offer their feelings along with their speech.

But if a person serves G-d with his insight at least for half a year, he has thereby moved himself and the whole world toward the scale of blessing and merit. Then he has accumulated so much power to that insight, that even if he talks about it the G-d within the insight will not die away. Try and understand this very deeply.

Our sages tell us that all of scripture is holy. But the Song of Songs, in which the love between the lover and the beloved is celebrated, in the Song of Songs, the Shir Ha Shirim, that our sages have said, is the most holy. All scripture is holy and it is the connecting link between this world and the higher ones. So according to one's inner connection, one can understand the scripture. However, the Song of Songs is so holy, that it connects this world to the Ayn Sof infinities, and these are way beyond mind.

WHAT I KNOW FROM KABBALAH

Rodger Kamenetz

I CANNOT EXPLAIN KABBALAH in this brief space in a way that would leave a reader knowing what it is. I would not want the reader to think that I could do so. But I can explain what I know because of kabbalah.

Because of kabbalah, I know that whatever is born—whether it is the birth of a child, the birth of the next moment, or the birth of the cosmos—emerges from a shattering and is damaged in some way. We can read the story of this imperfection in the Torah, in human history, and in our lives. It is the same pattern on different scales: a withdrawal of meaning into the mystery of itself, followed by a terrible shattering of whatever inadequate vessels we have gathered to hold meaning, followed by the effort of repair. This is the pattern in our lives over and over again—it is the thumbprint of creation pressed into every moment.

I know that the first phase of creation, the initial withdrawal of meaning, gives us the freedom to make our own meaning, along with our own errors. This freedom also enables us to go back to the beginning and make a repair. In many ways, our duty as human beings is to see what needs fixing, to adjust what is imperfect, and to seek to make it better. This is called *tikkun*—repairing—and it happens on many levels. On the physical level, *tikkun* is healing. On the political level, *tikkun* is a fight for justice, freedom, and dignity for all human beings. *Tikkun* on the spiritual level is focusing our intention with every prayer and every good deed. These levels of *tikkun* are all part of one effort.

I know from kabbalah that God is hidden. I know that this is for a reason and is part of the mystery of creation, and of creativity. I know that the language kabbalah uses to talk about God is necessarily obscure, not just accidentally obscure. And that understanding why it is necessarily so obscure also explains why there is evil in the world, and imperfection all around. I know that our search for God involves names that are wrong, and that the process of lifting the veils is the same as the process of learning how the names are wrong, and learning the right names. We ourselves shatter and ruin the names of God by the way we use them. Only through a shattering of ourselves and the names we use for ourselves can we get a glimpse of the actuality behind the names of God.

I know from kabbalah that all the names of God, especially the name "God," are masks and personae, are inadequate but also all we have. Our common language for talking about spiritual matters is inadequate. Language is both our gift and tragedy, and the nature of what we talk about when we talk about God is the impossibility of its being talked about. Our very efforts to talk about it obscure the subject. Yet hidden within the apparent language is a secret language which is the only proper language to suggest a being whose nature precedes time, space, and language.

I know from kabbalah that we who live in time and space dwell in the world of doubleness and duplicity. This is encoded in the first letter of the Torah, the letter Beth, which stands for the number two. And I know indeed that every letter of the Torah, if read properly, has a secret. The Torah itself is not just a book of stories or of laws—though it is also that—but it may be read with such a deep reverence for its particulars that a whole new revelation of wonder is exposed. In "The Gates of Light" by Joseph Gikatilla, for example, we see that every word in Torah is connected to a particular name of God.

I know that the reading of Torah and Bible that we have inherited from the nineteenth century "higher criticism" is less interesting and perceptive and whole than the reading of Torah as we get from a kabbalist like Gikatilla of the thirteenth century—and I feel humbled. The kabbalists saw the same seams in the text, and the same doubling and "errors" as the logical analysts who split the text into strands of J, E, P, and D—according to the God names they found used there (YHVH for J, Elohim for E, and so on). But the kabbalists gave the Torah a reading that healed the splits and gave the work a unity and power no analyst could imagine. And I know then from Kabbalah that the soul of Torah is deeper than analytics, and that a text is not only a plaything of the mind but can be a guardian of soul and an opener of the heart. I know that the scholarly intellectual way of reading Torah so common today only breaks the text down into bits, and that there's a deeper way of reading: a way that performs a *tikkun* on the text and finds the light hidden in the text. I know this from kabbalah.

I know that the texts of kabbalah contain the results of countless spiritual journeys, in which meditators traveled to realms and depths and came back with a new profound reading of the Torah. It contains meditations and elaborations on the book of Genesis—the secrets of creation—and on the book of Ezekiel, the secret of making those visionary journeys.

People today are also meditating on creation. Some are doing it in prayers and synagogues, others in the laboratories doing stem cell research or accelerating particles in a cyclotron. And certainly we are making spiritual journeys and hoping to find an adequate language to describe what we have experienced, as the kabbalists found.

Now if people still were to ask the historical question, "All right, that's fine but, where does kabbalah come from?" meaning what are its historical antecedents and influences, let them look in the books of the great scholars, such as Gershom Scholem, Moshe Idel, and Joseph Dan. From the scholars they will know that kabbalah has its roots in Torah commentary and is a textual mysticism, a hyper-midrash or super-commentary, that uses a set of symbolic relations known as the *sefirot*. They will learn the similarities between kabbalah and the teachings of the gnostics and the neo-Platonists. They can trace the historical roots of kabbalah in Jewish thought from the time of the chariot riders through the medieval period to today.

But really, the best answer to the question, "Where does kabbalah come from?" I heard from Rabbi Zalman Schachter-Shalomi, the most creative kabbalist I've personally encountered. He told me simply and stunningly, and with a bit of mystery, "Where does kabbalah come from? It comes from the future."

SAFED, ISRAEL

MYSTIC ECHOES FROM THE MIDDLE AGES

Todd Pitock

THE FIRST MYSTIC I EVER MET was in Jerusalem in the mid-eighties. She was a melange of seemingly conflicting identities: an English subject living in France, a Jew who bathed in the light of Sufism, Islamic mysticism. Her spiritual master, as she called him, had pointed her to Israel to study Cabbalah, her own religion's mystical tradition, and she was en route to Safed, where it had flourished in the sixteenth century.

My own family was somewhat disengaged from matters of the soul, and at first, when she told me about her master, and how, when she visited the Pyramids in Giza it had taken eight hours to draw vibrations from the stones, I was inclined to dismiss her out-of-hand. But she was so matter of fact, as if she were only telling me about the weather, and she wasn't proselytizing. Nor was she asking for money, and as we walked around Jerusalem, an appropriate place for this sort of encounter, her descriptions of transcendental bliss—I pictured a Chagallesque nimbus rising out of her—were alluring and not a little disorienting. When it gets right down to it, faith is an either/or proposition. If you don't believe, religion is deluded or fraudulent, and devotion is a waste of time. If you do believe, the waste is devotion to anything but.

The next day she caught the bus to Safed, one of Judaism's four holy cities, and I didn't see her again. Then, this spring, fourteen years later, I went to that part of the Galilee myself. I wasn't looking for an out-of-body experience. My own attempts at meditation only succeeded in putting me to sleep, and my body, if not my soul, has not responded enthusiastically to the sort of self-abnegation mystics typically relish. (My wife's cousin, who spends part of the year at an ashram in southern India, has often commented on her elevated soul, and in the midst of such evaluations, I sense he is looking at me as a sort of Untouchable.)

Rather, I was intrigued by Safed's medieval history, a period of cruel power struggles and mystifying plagues that left people from Asia to Europe brooding and anxious and certain the world was about to end. A period, in short, not unlike our own, when, whether it's a form of Y2K bug or the Age of Aquarius, spiritualism is once more all the rage, and people who have not otherwise observed a particular religious tradition are trying to satisfy inchoate spiritual longings.

We actually started our trip to Safed in Meron, a hilltop village in the Galilee in northern Israel, where on a warm early summer afternoon, the sun dangles like a big white bulb. A fanning breeze from the valley pulls up dust, and between that and the bright light, you squint like you're trying to see something in the distance. Meron's main attraction is the legendary grave of Shimon Bar Yochai, the second-century rabbi revered for purportedly having plumbed life's deepest mysteries during thirteen years he spent in a cave hiding from the Romans. His teachings, say believers, were passed on orally for centuries until they were set down in a thirteenth-century volume, the *Zohar*, the Cabbalah's main text.

The crypt is covered by a stone building with a modest white dome, and as you step through the blue gates at the entrance, you enter a world of perfect belief. Men and women daven on two sides of the *mechitzah*, their eyes sometimes focused on an open book, sometimes closed, their prayers either personal or committed to memory. Their lips move; words come out in a firm murmur. Candles flicker, and there's an abundance of well-used religious books and signs with Cabbalistic charts and large Hebrew letters. Velvet curtains and coverings veil the gravesite itself.

Not everyone is praying. A few ascetically thin young men make conversation, and one man, with cavernous eyes and a figure as exaggeratedly elongated as in an El Greco painting, surveys the room. In an open space, some women carry trays with pretzels, cookies, and dates, while a corpulent beggar insists loudly on adequate donations. He is not, after all, a lowly street beggar but a beggar in a holy place. Despite the fact that almost no two people are doing quite the same thing—even the ones praying are on different pages—the place has a discernible rhythm, a hum.

A copy of the *Zohar* lay open on a lectern.

"People devote their entire lives just to understand a piece of this," a religious man tells me. "They study a single page for five years. You can never master it. Either you will go insane or die."

This perilous view of Cabbalah is something of an anachronism, even among traditionalists who now guide the perplexed, and the merely curious, to study.

"You don't have to be a huge scholar to get the gist of it," says David Friedman, a Denver-born artist and mystic who has lived in Safed for almost two decades. Friedman's roots are traditional Orthodox. Ten years ago, though, a battle with cancer caused him to reconsider his own spiritual journey. At a studio on the upper fringe of Safed's Old Jewish Quarter, he fuses primary colors, geometric shapes, and Hebrew letters to create Escher-like images that take on depth as you focus on them. "It depends on what you put into it," he says. "If you are shallow, you will have a shallow experience."

The route from Meron to Safed wends through hills, past more *tzaddik* graves marked by tiny structures shaped almost like igloos, until a long switchback road climbs the steep face of Mount Canaan. Here, set like a stone mold, is Safed. Now a sleepy town of twelve thousand people, for the mystics who settled here in its medieval heyday, it was the City of Air. Little wonder. On a typically clear day, the view is so expansive that distant hills on the horizon seem to ripple like waves, and the sky is a brilliant shade of blue. The Cabbalists saw in it the lapis lazuli of heaven itself. By midday in summer, the sun heats the smooth stone walls and streets and draws out a blinding glare. In winter, I'm told, misty clouds wrap like shawls around the hills, a phenomenon that must surely have encouraged the mystics, though they famously preferred the night, when they would study and gaze at the profusion of stars and ponder eternity.

The city has been destroyed by earthquakes, rebuilt, and grown well beyond its medieval boundaries. The use of similar materials on newer structures helps them suggest or acquire an old look almost as soon as they're finished. A late Mamluk postal station, one of a number of five-hundred-year-old buildings still in use, is the Rimon Inn. Street lamps, ensconced on smooth stone walls, cast a pale light at sundown like medieval torches.

In the center of the Old Jewish Quarter the dense cluster of synagogues have their own characteristics, from the lively contemporary ones that hold well-attended services thrice daily to historical ones that, despite their stacks of religious books and arks housing ancient Torah scrolls, feel more like dysfunctional museums than houses of worship. With its modest dome and Cabbalistic motifs incorporated into a design brought from medieval Spain, the Abuhav Synagogue has an unkempt air, with stacked folding as though an event is about to happen though none is planned. Caretakers watch small batches of tourists parade through, their disinterested expressions hardly changing as they tap or hold out donations boxes when visitors leave. Someone asked one caretaker to explain the numerology motifs. He shrugged as if to say he didn't know, but the tinkle of coins inspired his memory. Three arks, he said, stood for the patriarchs (Abraham, Isaac, and Jacob); four marble columns for the four elements (fire, water, earth, and air) or four worlds (physical, emotional, intellectual, and spiritual); nine arches represent the nine months of pregnancy.

The most accessible walking route through Safed, the standard tourist track, isn't necessarily what's most worth seeing, and the town's inner life exists just slightly off its most visible paths. Chaya Bracha Leiter, a tour guide whose husband, Shaul, runs the Ascent Institute, which gives seminars on Cabbalah, takes me first to the Cave of Shem and Ever, where Noah's son and great grandson, respectively, are said to have learned Cabbalah, and where, according to Muslims, Jacob was given Joseph's colorful jacket and told his favorite son had been devoured by a lion. Dank and cool, two subterranean rooms are lit by candles placed in what were obviously burial crypts. Without lights, signs, or anything artificial to brighten the cave, the atmosphere is heavy, cloistered. "I don't like it here," says Leiter. "It just doesn't have a good feeling to me. I don't know why."

So we drive across Safed's narrow streets to the Ari Sephardic Synagogue, the only extant house of prayer where Isaac Luria, the sixteenth-century mystic who claimed to be an incarnation of Bar Yochai, is known to have prayed. Leiter, who came here twenty years ago from Denver to study Torah for a summer and never left, tells stories about famous mystics with love and humor, so that someone just joining the conversation might think she's recounting episodes involving close family members.

Constructed on an enormous stone foundation, with a long stone staircase, the synagogue has the appearance of a fortress. Leiter directs me to a blossoming citron tree in the courtyard of the synagogue's entrance and pulls off leaves for me to smell. The fragrance is clean and sweet—and to Leiter quite literally divine. She has me say a prayer; the truly spiritual find transcendence through natural splendor and do not miss opportunities to sanctify anything that signifies a spark of creation itself.

As we leave, an old woman, her back curled like a question mark, is making her assault up the stairs one step at a time, pausing at intervals to recuperate. She is determined to pray and the laborious ascent will be rewarded, I sense, by the scent of the citron tree.

The town has grown over the border of forests that once ringed it. The Ari Ashkenazic Synagogue now stands on a meadow where Isaac Luria, the Ari, would gather his followers to contemplate reincarnation and the transmigration of souls, God's hidden aspect, and techniques for attaining higher realms of consciousness. He taught that the messiah's arrival depended on the purity of their faith and penitence.

In the aftermath of a calamitous century of pogroms and deteriorating circumstances that culminated in the Spanish Expulsion, the Jews were convinced that the world was coming to an end. Many of them went to the Holy Land to prepare for the messiah's arrival. Jerusalem was then a backwater of less than four thousand people, so they came to Safed, a thriving textile center twenty miles north of the Sea of Galilee. Prosperous and free, the city also held the graves of the great rabbinic figures of the second century, a period of suffering under Roman rule that the medieval Cabbalists saw as their own distant mirror. Not many Jews lived in the area between that period and the Middle Ages, but as they gathered from Spain, North Africa, and other parts of the Middle East in the 1500s, Safed became home to the greatest concentration of scholars and rabbis since that earlier time.

They dedicated themselves to revelation and self-purification through fasting, prayer, study, and ritual observance, and wrote volumes of liturgy, theosophical treatises, and codes of ethics. The complex body of work revealed, they said, the Bible's hidden, inner dimension.

Notwithstanding the ethereal metaphors—their work is strewn with imagery of crowns, lights, vessels, and chariots—that they used to help apprehend supernally ineffable ideas, the Cabbalists provided a spiritual rationale for down-to-earth ethical behavior. Once, they said, there was a cosmic shattering, and divine light was scattered. The work of humanity, the Cabbalists taught, was to retrieve the sparks through devotion to God and love of fellow man. Done with the right intention, God would reveal Himself and the universe would be repaired. Humankind was made not just in God's image but was, in a vital way, His partner in creation. Every human action had a spiritual repercussion somewhere else in the universe.

David Friedman, the artist, likes the image of a cosmic shattering. It suggests the Big Bang Theory. "Evolution is Cabbalistic," he says. "It says what all religious traditions have always said: all life springs from one source." His rationalistic approach, though, puts him outside the circle of Safed traditionalists who insist the world is six thousand years old. "How much greater is God, how much more can we appreciate His greatness, if we try to comprehend more time, billions of years, and unending space."

For Friedman, science affirms faith. Others reject it without consideration. I ask one of them if dinosaur fossils prove the world has to be older than six millennia. "Ah, yes, dinosaurs," he says, waving the whole notion away with his hand. "They're very fashionable these days." He is not threatened; the topic is merely irrelevant.

Yuval Ashorov probably spends little time debating subjects like dinosaur fossils. He has more immediate concerns. An acupuncturist and former member of an elite military combat unit, Ashorov became religious several years ago. His spiritual mentor instructed him to come to the Galilee. If just ten people can dissolve their egos, his rabbi told him, the messiah will come. We are sitting in his home in Or Ha-Ginuz, a community built on the gentle rocky slopes just outside Safed. "The real way to live," Ashorov tells me, "is to work in a community. To be spiritual, you must give, not just receive. The secret is to be close to others, to cancel your egoism."

He speaks of mysticism as a sort of apprenticeship. "The study of Cabbalah pulls down the light and purifies the soul, which becomes stronger than the body. You must work and work, and all the time it grows inside you. It's like a baby in a woman. When she first gets pregnant, the life is growing within but she can't feel it, and it takes time before there are outward signs.

"God is hiding from us. We have to earn the light to be worthy. If you give a child a hammer, he only knows to destroy. You must develop skills to use the tool. That is what [religious law and rituals] do. They prepare you for the Cabbalah, which is the real thing."

In the sixteenth century, the intense Safed community began to dissipate as appointed dates for the messiah's arrival passed and its luminaries began to die. But its influence only grew. Of all the schisms in Judaism—Christianity is but one example—Cabbalah is one of a few that gained full acceptance in the Jewish mainstream, from Chasidim, who are the next link in the mystical chain, to the proudly rational Reform, who use rituals and liturgy developed by the Safed mystics.

And though the messiah hasn't come, today's Cabbalists have not given up just yet.

"We are living in the End of Days," Yuval Ashorov says. That prospect does not disturb him; on the contrary, he is looking forward to it. I ask what will happen. He shrugs and puts out his lower lip. "We know the messiah must come, and the world must go through a period of correction called *tikkun*, and then will come the Judgment. What will happen then, no one knows."

By definition, eternal questions have no answers; every generation grapples with them. To the extent that I am looking for an answer, I finally get one to mull over these matters at Rabbi Akiva's grave on a high slope overlooking Tiberias, about forty minutes from Safed. In the distance, the glassy pane of the Sea of Galilee sends back a harsh glare, and here, a group of young men pray while friends smoke cigarettes in a parking lot as they wait for them to finish up.

An elderly man steps down the path, his black hat tilted back, his belly protruding, and he holds out a hand for me to take. Without any introduction or greeting, he says, "*Im atah ma'amin, zeh nachon.*" If you believe, then it's true.

He laughs and pats my back and repeats himself, pleased and certain with a remark that balances on a thread between everything and nothing—revelation or nonsense. Then he walks down the path to Akiva's purported grave and I walk in the other direction, squinting into the bright light.

THE HOLOCAUST

A FORCE FOR LIFE,
NOT FOR ANGER

Irving Greenberg

HOLOCAUST REMEMBRANCE HAS struck a resonant chord with the American people. More than 15 million people, 80 percent of them non-Jews, have visited the United States Holocaust Memorial Museum since its opening. Surveys show that, exposed to the enormity of death unleashed by the Shoah (the Hebrew word for the Holocaust), visitors are emotionally moved to take greater responsibility for society and for potential victims of persecution. Paradoxically, Holocaust remembrance pulls people to the side of increased life, a kind of unexpected testimony to the decency of the human spirit.

Logically, Holocaust memory should be a force for anger and revenge, for it is the result of a uniquely absolute, government-sponsored plan to kill all Jews. The murder of six million Jews; the systematic degradation, stripping of human rights, deprivation of elemental living needs before the actual genocide began; the gypsies, Poles, and gay people who also were swept into persecution and death in the Nazi mechanisms of the Shoah; the fact that all this was made possible by the relative apathy of the civilized world: these truths should enrage us and lead us to moral despair.

Jews should fault Christianity for creating a ring of hatred and stereotyping around Jewry, which the Nazis perversely exploited. And Christians might well be tempted into blaming secular, pagan Nazis, or even into faulting Jews for their own victimization. Similarly, Americans might avoid the museum as being too painful, too foreign in its evil world.

In fact, the opposite has occurred. Survivors, marked by memory, reaffirmed life and raised a generation of children disproportionately involved in human service professions. Goaded by Shoah remembrance, Jews have embarked on the greatest outburst of Jewish life ever, including the creation of the State of Israel. Diaspora and Israeli Jews worked together to rescue communities in danger and to recreate Jewish life. Rabbinic and Talmudic study has been reestablished on an unprecedented scale after being 80 percent decimated in the Holocaust. These are the signs of life, not of death.

Lashed by the horrors of the Holocaust and spurred by a sense of self-critical accountability, the leading Christian churches have purified classic teachings, removing demeaning stereotypes of Judaism and confronting hostile elements in their own sacred texts. They now affirm the dignity of Jews and the ongoing validity of Judaism.

Who can forget Pope John Paul II, frail yet immensely strong on a visit of repentance and prayer at the Western Wall? Moved by the Shoah, he restored Christianity as a Gospel of Love. In parallel response, last year, a major group of Jewish teachers and rabbis issued the most comprehensive Jewish affirmation of Christianity's dignity and contribution as a religion in two millennia.

Visitors to the museum come out with an intensified urge to take more responsibility to ensure a society of law and equality. Polish Americans and Jewish Americans are meeting to create a new era of friendship that goes beyond the cycle of rejection and anger of the past. Today controversy is unfolding in the aftermath of documentation of a mass murder of Jews in 1941 by their Polish neighbors in the town of Jedwabne. There are enormous pressures and emotional conflicts within Poland over surrendering the image of Poles as solely victims of Nazism, rather than perpetuators of atrocities. Extremists urge scapegoating the murdered Jews. Yet, the Polish government's top leadership, sensitized by the Holocaust memory, acknowledges the failures of the past, freeing Poland to build a more humane future.

In 1979, the American government acknowledged its failure to fight for Jewish refugees in the Evian Conference of 1937. The United States then pledged to take in 20,500 boat people fleeing Cambodia and Vietnam and arranged to absorb a total of 250,000 refugees. During the 1990s, U.S. interventions in Bosnia and Kosovo, however belated and limited, reflected the greater sensitivity of the American public to the past failure to stop genocide. We need more searing memory to empower further interventions by the Americans and the world's other powers. This past year, the museum's Committee on Conscience found Sudan to be a potentially genocidal situation. The force of remembrance operates to raise the norms of international accountability for murder and genocide.

Holocaust remembrance is not a feel-good experience; it is shattering. It summons up devastating historical failures and the need for unvarnished self-criticism. If we do not flinch from the pain, then remembering the Holocaust—evil and tragedy without relief—is turned by the alchemy of human spirit into a powerful force for life.

SHOAH BUSINESS

Andrew Wallenstein

AS PRESIDENT OF THE entertainment division at NBC, Jeff Zucker usually worries more about sitcoms than he does about sports. But this past spring he had a question about football for Lawrence Tisch, CEO of the Loews Hotels chain and a member of the family that co-owns the New York Giants franchise. In a private e-mail to Tisch, he posed a rather unusual question: Which team has more Jewish fans, the Giants or the New York Jets?

Strange as the query might seem, there was cause for Zucker's curiosity. *Uprising,* a two-part NBC miniseries about the Warsaw ghetto uprising, was slated to air during the last of the three all-important sweeps months when networks schedule their most ratings-grabbing programs. If Zucker scheduled *Uprising* on Oct. 28, 2001, the miniseries would compete for viewers with ESPN's evening broadcast of the Giants-Redskins game. But if he postponed the premiere to the following Sunday, he would go head-to-head with a Jets-Saints game. If he could help it, Zucker did not want Jews to have to choose between the Holocaust miniseries and a football game.

In his response to Zucker, Tisch sided with the Jets; Jews and Jets fans both happen to populate Long Island, Westchester, and New Jersey in high concentrations, according to his rationale. But before Zucker even settled on the date that would attract the most Jewish viewers, word of the e-mail leaked out, exposing how a Holocaust drama found itself at the center of a network strategy to maximize its audience.

Uprising is hardly an isolated case. During the 2001 TV season, all three sweeps months—February, May, and November—featured heavily promoted Holocaust miniseries in primetime. In February, CBS broadcast *Haven,* an account of how one woman saved hundreds of Holocaust survivors. ABC followed with *Anne Frank* and in May, HBO and Showtime featured two more original films with Holocaust themes on cable TV.

Nine years after Steven Spielberg's groundbreaking *Schindler's List* there has been an unmistakable boom in what Israeli diplomat Abba Eban once dabbed the "Shoah business." With at least a dozen dramatizations in various stages of production or development set to hit TV and movie theaters—featuring top actors like Jodie Foster, Haley Joel Osment, and Harvey Keitel—the obvious question is, why now?

In the wake of *Schindler* and the Oscar-winning Italian film *Life is Beautiful,* some skeptical observers suspect Hollywood producers and directors now perceive the Holocaust as Academy Award bait. "I'm sure there have always been serious people who wanted to make films on the subject and couldn't," said Raye Farr, director of the Department of Film and Video at the U.S. Holocaust Museum in Washington, D.C. "Now seeing that . . . [a Holocaust film can] be a runaway commercial success, all kinds of people want to get in on the act."

But a more generous view sees a new generation of producers and executives expressing their ethnic pride with unprecedented boldness. "The old Hollywood represented studio heads who were ashamed of being Jewish," said Rabbi Marvin Hier, dean and founder of the Simon Wiesenthal Center, an organization devoted to fighting bigotry and anti-Semitism. "That has changed."

Today, the list of upcoming Holocaust films is seemingly endless. On the big screen, Miramax Pictures is developing the movie version of the Leon Uris novel *Mila 18,* a fictionalized account of the Warsaw rebellion. Fox 2000 is preparing another movie version of *The Diary of Anne Frank,* which will mark its tenth Hollywood reincarnation. Acclaimed directors Sidney Lumet and Roman Polanski are each adapting best-selling survivor memoirs from writers who experienced the ghetto. Jodie Foster plans to star in a biographical film she is also producing about Leni Riefenstahl, the propagandist filmmaker who glorified the Third Reich in her work. Even Charlton Heston is part of the trend, switching from Moses to Mengele; the legendary *Ten Commandments* star will depict the Nazi doctor for an upcoming independent film. Adolf Hitler will also be reexamined. CBS is planning a four-hour miniseries about the life of the führer, and a big-screen biography about Hitler's early days as an artist, titled *Max,* will be released this fall. Cable television is also part of the action. HBO is preparing a sequel to *Conspiracy,* its November 2000 film about the Wannsee Conference, where the Nazis plotted the Final Solution. And *Broken Silence,* five Holocaust documentaries presented by Steven Spielberg and the Shoah Foundation, airs April 15 through 19, timed to run just after Holocaust Remembrance Day (April 9).

The irony of this profusion of films is that Hollywood once paid the Holocaust scant attention. Though the highest ranks in Hollywood have always been filled with Jews, the Jews who built the film industry—moguls like Adolph Zukor of Paramount and Louis B. Mayer of MGM—stayed far away from everything overtly Jewish. As books like Neal Gabler's *An Empire of Their Own: How the Jews Created Hollywood* (Anchor, 1989) documents, these moguls rarely produced movies that depicted Jewish people or issues, let alone the Holocaust. They severed their own religious roots to gain access to the WASP establishment, and their movies were free of any ethnic signifiers that would have betrayed their humble beginnings in the shtetls of eastern Europe.

The trend continued in the decades following World War II: American television and cinema producers mostly ignored the Holocaust. The earliest successful movies on the subject, like 1959's *The Diary of a Young Girl* and 1961's *Judgment at Nuremberg,* played down the Jewish element of their stories. This disregard in part reflected that the systematic murder of six million Jews wasn't always understood by the American public as the "Holocaust"—a tragedy distinct from the overall toll taken by World War II. Not until the 1978 TV miniseries *Holocaust* did pop culture identify the Shoah as a uniquely Jewish tragedy. "In contrast to previous media representations like *Judgment at Nuremberg,* the television series forthrightly present[ed] the Holocaust as a Jewish event rather than a universalized catastrophe in which the Jews were incidentally numbered among the victims," writes Jewish Theological Seminary Professor Alan Mintz in his new book, *Popular Culture and the Shaping of Holocaust Memory in America* (University of Washington Press, 2001). Though critics, including Nobel Peace Prize laureate and Holocaust survivor Elie Wiesel, blasted *Holocaust* for turning tragic history into a "soap opera," the tragedy had entered into people's homes like never before. Close to one hundred million viewers saw some portion of that NBC miniseries, according to Peter Novick's *The Holocaust in American Life.*

But it wasn't until *Schindler's List* in 1993 that the Holocaust genre regained mainstream success. *Schindler* grossed $321.2 million worldwide, and its 1997 NBC broadcast was seen by sixty-five million viewers, twice the number of people who had seen it in theaters. The next big hit, in 1999, was *Life is Beautiful,* which depicted a father's madcap efforts to shield his son from the Holocaust. It grossed $229 million worldwide, making it the most successful foreign language film ever in the American market until the Asian martial-arts showcase *Crouching Tiger, Hidden Dragon* came along.

No single factor can explain the boom. But experts speculate that the escalation of Holocaust commemoration over the past two decades, as well as the media spotlight on Holocaust reparations, have paved the way for a more Holocaust-sensitive culture. Holocaust commemoration has also emerged as something of a primary ritual for American Jews. In the 2000 Annual Survey of American Jewish Opinion conducted by the American Jewish Committee, 81 percent of the respondents rated "remembering the Holocaust" as either "extremely important" or "very important" in terms of defining their Jewish identity. Nothing else ranked higher, not even "celebration of Jewish holidays" (68 percent) or "participating in synagogue services" (37 percent). And the dwindling number of Holocaust survivors increases the urgency to focus on that horrific event, according to Jeffrey Shandler, author of *While America Watches: Televising the Holocaust* (Oxford University Press, 1999). "There's a crisis of memory," he said, "because people who are eyewitnesses to the war are an aging population that is passing away."

In light of this new climate, it seems that a new generation of producers and executives is expressing its ethnic pride with unprecedented boldness. While the impresarios of Hollywood's golden age reinvented themselves through cinema, contemporary producers are using film to reconnect with the heritage of their forebears. Much of that is because of the success of *Schindler.* "Spielberg did his best work on the Holocaust, which gives permission to other filmmakers, particularly Jewish filmmakers who may have been a little bit afraid of appearing parochial, to touch this area," said Michael Berenbaum, a former director of the Shoah Visual History Foundation, now a consultant to makers of historical films, including *Uprising.*

According to this next wave of would-be Spielbergs, the decision to depict the Holocaust was purely personal and devoid of financial motives. For instance, Polanski was inspired to direct an adaptation of Wladyslaw Szpilman's memoir *The Pianist* because of his own childhood experience in the Krakow ghetto. Of his decision to finance the upcoming film *The Grey Zone*, Avi Lerner, the Israeli-born head of Millennium/Nu Image Films, told the *New York Times,* "This is the first—and only—time I am making a movie that has nothing to do with financial considerations." Millennium is also releasing *Edges of the Lord*, a film starring Osment of *The Sixth Sense* as a Jewish boy hiding from the Nazis. And Miramax's own CEO Harvey Weinstein said he is considering directing the upcoming movie

Mila, which would mark his directorial debut. In a *Times* interview, Weinstein explained why. "Guys like me, we grew up with two kinds of Jews you know, the Jews who marched into the concentration camp and the Jews who fought. Uris's books were about the Jews who fought." Miramax also won a high-six-figure bidding war for the film rights to another book about Jewish resistance fighters, *The Brothers Bielski.*

Still, not everyone is convinced that Hollywood's motives are completely pure. Since *Schindler,* Holocaust movies have been surefire formulas for Academy Awards. In fact, there have only been two years (1995 and 2000) since 1994 when the genre didn't claim at least one Oscar win: *Schindler's List* earned seven statuettes in 1994; *Anne Frank Remembered* and *One Survivor Remembers* each earned Oscars in 1996; *Shine* won in 1997; *The Long Way Home* and *Visas and Virtue* took Oscar honors in 1998; *The Last Days* and *Life is Beautiful* (three awards) won in 1999. In 2001, *Into the Arms of Strangers: Stories of the Kindertransport,* won for best feature-length documentary, one of three Holocaust productions nominated last year. With such a track record it's not surprising that Holocaust movies are considered a ticket to success.

Consider a comment made by Lance Bass, a member of the chart-topping "boy band" 'N Sync, in an October interview with *Reuters.* Discussing his unlikely bid for respectability as a film actor, the non-Jewish Bass elaborated on the reason his production company chose to adapt *Children of Willesden Lane,* a book about a Jewish piano prodigy fleeing the Nazis. "It's very Oscar material," he said, "and I would love to have that little Oscar on my shelf someday!"

While not all Holocaust movies are successful—many have flopped, including the 1999 movie *Jakob the Liar,* starring Robin Williams—many studios are more comfortable taking a risk on a Holocaust project because they are typically cheaper to make than other films. (For example, they don't require a lot of special effects.) And since the Holocaust is essentially an international story, the genre has the advantage of translating to foreign audiences.

But what may be most enticing for filmmakers is the way a significant Holocaust movie can catapult them from mere entertainer to venerated artist and humanitarian. Spielberg, once known for movies like *Jaws* and *Jurassic Park,* is a case in point. *Schindler* not only made an impact on American culture and education, inspiring endless newspaper editorials, TV news programs, scholarly tomes, and high school curricula, it turned Spielberg into an activist. The Shoah Visual History Foundation, which he helped create, videotapes and preserves testimonies of Holocaust survivors. "Certainly if you look at the career of Steven Spielberg, *Schindler* transformed the level of respect accorded to him as a filmmaker, as a figure in Hollywood, and as a figure in the Jewish community, too," said Shandler, a professor at New York University. "I think that can make the prospect of creating another *Schindler's List* very appealing to filmmakers."

The genre's surge comes as many historians are casting a skeptical eye on the value of extensive Holocaust commemoration through contemporary movies, museums, books, plays, college courses, and memorials. The ideology of these critics differs markedly, ranging from the University of Chicago's highly respected Peter Novick, author of *The Holocaust in American Life* (Houghton Mifflin, 1999), to leftist fringe figures like Norman Finkelstein, whose *The Holocaust Industry: Reflections on the Exploitation of Jewish Suffering* (Verso Books, 2000) was widely criticized last year for insinuating that Jewish institutions exacting reparations from foreign countries are engaged in a "shakedown." (In fact, Finkelstein claims his position recently cost him his college teaching job, according to a report in the January 18 *Forward*.) Critics of the Holocaust-centric approach to Jewishness argue that repeated portrayal of the Shoah in film, on TV, and in memorials has a long-term detrimental impact. Novick, who has studied Holocaust consciousness in America extensively, calls the United States Holocaust Memorial Museum in Washington, D.C., "the principal 'address' of American Jewry," and laments that the Holocaust has become "the emblematic Jewish experience" for many American Jews, according to an article in the 2001 *American Jewish Yearbook*.

That imitation is the sincerest form of creativity in show biz is self-evident. Producers send in clones until the public tires of them. And Holocaust films won't be the exception, according to Paul Dergarabedian, a film industry analyst with Exhibitor Relations Co. Inc. "After so many of these films," he said, "the audience is going to get burnt out."

The consequences of this trend may extend beyond box-office burnout, since these films have a tremendous impact on how Americans view the Holocaust. Of the movie-going public, said Farr, the director of film and video at the Holocaust museum, "I think that they assume that the artistic representation *is* the reality." The sum result of the overexposure could jade Americans to the Holocaust, some experts say. "As the Holocaust is used more for the form of melodrama, for a cheap effect," said Thomas Doherty, a Brandeis University film-studies professor who presided over a seminar on Holocaust films in July 2000, "you lose your confrontation with the reality of the horror of the event."

When faced with too much Holocaust coverage versus too little, Rabbi Irving Greenberg, former chairman of the U.S. Holocaust Memorial Council, would settle for overexposure. After all, it's easier for educators to correct "overcommercialization or cheapening" than it is to counter simple omission. "What really breaks your heart," Greenberg says, "is when they don't care or don't pay attention."

HIDING PLACES

Daniel Asa Rose

ONE WAS SAID TO HAVE ESCAPED with her jewelry by wearing it all at once so the Nazis thought she was a whore displaying her baubles. Another hid in the circus, stashing grenades under his cot and using oil from sardine tins to oil his guns. There was even supposed to be a widower over in Europe somewhere who'd changed his name from Jacov Pesach Morganstern to J. P. Morgan and smuggled diamonds inside chocolate bonbons and in the hollow stems of bread knives.

These were great aunts and second cousins, and there seemed to be dozens of them. The New York branch was a patriarchy headed by Yudl and Velvl, who in appearance and habits would strike you as not unrelated to computer nerds except that they were in diamonds. Diamond dorks, if you must, but in the best sense possible: they were elegant eccentrics, politely resting their teacups half off their saucers, stubbornly closing one eye when crossing the street against traffic instead of troubling to get a new eyeglass prescription, ceremoniously leaning into the light from the window to read the Sunday *Times* rather than wasting electricity flicking on the light. Eternally bemused and with bottomless tact, they were at the same time cosmopolitan and deeply insular, with equal amounts of delicacy and certainty in their movements. You imagined they pressed their PJs and went to sleep with their watches on; and none of your digital watches but choice old Swiss timepieces on leather bands, genuine calfskin bought at discount. For all their wartime exploits (though they didn't see them as exploits—they saw them as *mishaps*), they weren't physical folks. If there had been a Morganstern family crest the legend would say: Be Timid In All You Do . . . and yet by escaping the Nazis they pulled off one of the most audacious feats of the twentieth century.

There's a line in Isaac Babel that jumped out at me in college: "The Philosophers Who Cut Diamonds." This they were: courtly, mild-mannered burghers who saw in diamonds not only an order and a geometry but also an aesthetic to live by and even a moral code. With due modesty they saw themselves as philosophers entering into a dialectic with each stone, bringing out the argument inside; as scholars, studying each stone's individual makeup; as artists, like Michelangelo sculpting forth the soul of each diamond from where it was hidden in the rough. In discussions with my father the shrink they even allowed as how they functioned as diamond psychiatrists, bringing to the surface and grinding away those imperfections that have been dogging it all the centuries. Gentlemen diamond dealers, in a word, who were gratefully out of sync with the late twentieth century, so old-school that with Victorian disdain they regarded the stock market and movies and even soft drinks as vulgar, who reluctantly owned maybe one television in the kitchen and that only for select educational programs. Did people who speak six languages watch *Cheers* with the rest of America after dinner? They did not. Did they read fiction? "Not lately," they'd say, meaning not for the past thirty years. Instead they studied: history, religion, philosophy, mysticism. They learned ancient Greek so they could read Plato in the original. They read Maimonides in bed, or Baudelaire if they were feeling frisky—the only people in New York to consider *Les Fleurs du Mal* foreplay.

Still, their smiles were a wonder to me. Their faces were informed with a subtlety and tact; their humor was dapper and restrained; their wit was dry. (*Why don't Jews drink? It dulls the pain.*) So long as a joke was low-key, preferably of a jewel-like clarity, their mouths would pucker to smile, then when you were least expecting it erupt in a silent laugh with a shocking display of long, horse-like yellow molars. But even when not smiling their faces contained a mysterious flicker of self-mockery; what was *that* about?

It made you want to hug them. But so breakable did they seem, it'd be like hugging Audrey Hepburn. The uncles as well as the aunts were so frail as to be Audrey-like: thin and brittle as though their bones were made of Limoges porcelain. And just as you can see a glow through a piece of Limoges if you hold it up to the light, so could you make out a faint glow behind their faces, an ambient kindness, an aura of goodness that permeated their features and raised the temperature in your heart half a degree.

The bottom line was they seemed more like ancestors to me than elders. That's how I thought of them, as my Venerable Jewish Ancestors.

They were of that peculiarly dated upper middle class school that still re-cites telephone numbers using the prefix word (as in ENdicott Three in-stead of 363), that still navigates the curbs of the Upper West Side with varnished canes and a quarter inch of starched hankie running across their breast pockets, taking tiny steps in their rubber galoshes as their diminu-tive wives clutch to their wrists. When these old souls are gone, what will the modern world know of finish? Of manners? Of the sort of refinement that, if they stumble into a parking meter, will say excuse me?

Tall and stately and hunched, these ENdicott Jews were civilized to a fault. It was the noisy Americans who lost out in the manners game. Con-versations with my New York relatives didn't proceed at a normal Amer-ican clip; they loped along, stopped mid-sentence, and were attended by something almost unheard of in American parlance: thinking. You'd ask a question, they'd pause before responding. The pause could last twenty seconds. They were polling their intellect, prior to fashioning their replies. Such reflection was not meant to but could often be disconcerting, mis-taken for reticence. If you were a typically impatient American, your in-stinct would be to forge ahead and fill in the embarrassing blanks. In this manner you could conduct an entire conversation without ever actually hearing from them; an unfortunate outcome because their responses, when finally phrased, would always be salient and frequently droll.

My father, the American, a Harvard Jew who'd met his share of bul-lies growing up brainy in Boston and who cultivated charm to cope but who nevertheless always struck my great uncles as suspiciously Jamesian (Jesse *and* Henry), once asked my great uncles how business was going. The two brothers looked back and forth to each other for some time.

"Not bad," they finally said.

My father bided his time. "That good?" he asked at last.

Mirth was occasioned. My great uncles arched their eyebrows. They liked this snappy rejoinder so much that they raised the corners of their lips and smiled, showing the barest tip of tongue.

"Now he's catching on," they congratulated each other.

○

Inside, the apartment was like a mini Versailles, a hallette of beveled mir-rors and abbreviated chandeliers. It was opulent but not stiflingly so: the function of the opulence was to give. We were aggressed by generosity: crystal bowls of raisins awaited us, silver platters of walnuts, pale tea in gleaming glass tankards. And always, at the center of every apartment was a dining room table with an embroidered tablecloth upon which sat a bowl of waxed fruit—apples with a perpetual dull sheen or grapes that never got gnats. These were the waxed version of my relatives with their squeezably pale skin, their soft-hard flesh, their manner that was both re-silient and resistant at the same time so you felt that if you seized their elbow to keep them from falling you'd leave a full set of fingerprints. Even their blemishes seemed wax-perfect, etched in for show. Their warts, their wens, their kempt or remarkably unkempt eyebrows, were almost too super-realistic to be real. The only jarring note were those six watery blue numbers etched on their arms. Why would the manufacturer leave the lot number on their arms?

Waxed Jews. . . .

The gentleman diamond dealers had their smocks off now to reveal their French linen shirts, they were relaxed as the smell of cooked cabbage clung faintly to their V-neck cashmere sweaters. Here Yudl and Velvl were at home, the wife needle-pointing Vasarely, the husband using a diamond loupe to read the fine print on a matchbook instructing him to keep the cover closed when striking. They chipped their butter from the top, in-stead of oafishly taking a slice from the end; just a little chip, and then an-other little chip, why waste a speck? They were diamond cutters at the table, wielding their words as they wielded their butter knives, managing both their badinage and their bread sticks with an economy that was dainty, good-natured, cautious, occasionally even ribald, but ribald in the most virginal way, so that any dirty words that happened to pass their lips sounded squeaky clean, like an experiment in phonetics only. Here Velvl was at ease, and his dignity was never so overbearing that some adoles-cent grandson couldn't stand behind him as he presided over the table, twaddling his earlobe . . . for minutes on end! And Velvl would just sit there taking it, doodling to himself and smiling mysteriously with that twinkle of self-mockery on his lips.

I couldn't suss them out. All the ENdicott Jews—the women as well as the men—were both more formal and, paradoxically, more gay than we were. It occurred to me that our Americanism came too cheap. We hadn't quite earned it. They were at once more skeptical and more aware than we were, more furrowed but somehow more cheerful than us. We were spontaneous but they were tolerant. Their laughter bubbled forth from a deeper place in their chests. Their sorrow was sorrier, their joy more joy-ous. Yet they maintained such a scrim of fineness that they were forever blushing for us, forever lowering their eyes, and giving off such a sense of sweetness that I felt wicked in their world.

One still held his nose when he sneezed, a holdover from hiding days when his life depended on not being heard. Another who built apartment complexes couldn't bring himself to go into an underground parking garage. Yudl himself was unable to straighten up completely, the result of spending four months hunched over in a chimney. Yet another whose eyes were shadowed with kindness and fatigue was for a medical experiment given the option of having his neck vertebrae fused up or down and chose to have it fused upwards, the better, as he said, to spit in God's eye; and if you thought that sacrilegious, if you thought perhaps he should have spit instead in the eye of a Nazi, he would reply with precise gentle diction that he wanted to go to the head Nazi and that was God. No false piety for these survivors.

You could spot the women who'd spent time in concentration camps: Their eyes watched you while their faces were affectless. Their effervescence was removed, like the 7-Up I hadn't quite finished and was going flat on the floor of the station wagon in the street below. One who was so wispy she looked as if she was going to vaporize on the spot, had been pregnant when she arrived in Auschwitz and Mengele let her have her baby, only to learn that she was part of an experiment to see how long it would take to starve the baby to death. Another was lugging a suitcase full of ammo with a few leaves of basil on top to disguise the smell when she was stopped by a German who asked her what she was carrying. "It's full of ammo!" she said, and thinking of course that she was joking, he helped carry her suitcase. Yet another was said to be quite beautiful, in her day. She used to lure Germans soldiers to ride bikes with her through the park. Where they'd be ambushed. *Kilt! Kaput!* Old ladies in Adidas running shoes who harbored terrible secrets, these were the wary ones, and like birds too wounded to fly south for the winter, they watched and waited, not trusting the world that had changed around them too many times.

Seeing such people at home in their element, you realized that a more docile and less presumptuous group of individuals it would be hard to find. And you realized something more. Sitting in their drawing rooms, watching them stutter gracefully and tinkle their glasses of sparkling cider and with great spunk maintain their veneer of stateliness against all the depredations of the twentieth century, you knew that Hitler's targeting of them to exterminate was not some higher social ideology, no advanced philosophy based on questions of genes and race. He had merely picked on the meekest people he could find. He wasn't a political scientist, a social architect with a comprehensive *Weltanschauung*. He was a schoolyard bully, picking on those least able to defend themselves.

---
o

Nevertheless I snickered. I cackled. I persevered in my ridicule. During the seder, when it came time to go around the long table reading, I made my siblings laugh by putting my finger over the lines they were supposed to read. I planted whispered images in their ears of Velvl on a Harley-Davidson or Yudl going over a mogul at Stowe. I tittered beneath my breath about a Low Salt Holocaust Diet and muttered jokes about a Holocaust aerobics class. But the best part came when the room fell silent to allow a small second cousin to stand on a chair and sing the Four Questions. He was named "Little Henry," in distinction to an older devout Henry nicknamed "God's Henry," and I couldn't help but snortle. On and on went his sing-song voice as the bright-eyed boy gazed about the room eager to please, and I got my brother and sisters to snortle, too. Giggle, sputter, trying to avoid each others' eyes, staring hard at a piece of chipped plaster on the ceiling to take our minds off the syrupy-sweet singing, till we would catch each other's eyes and the snortling would erupt out of control and we'd shoot our hands in front of our mouths and double over, ashamed at last of our glee.

But here was the thing that truly shamed us. Little Henry's parents would keep smiling, their eyes shining with pride, as their son kept singing. Little Henry's parents had been married before the war, to other people. They had each lost their spouses and children at Birkenau, at Dachau. Penniless, dazed, wandering Europe after the war, they'd met in a refugee camp, gotten married, had a son. A miracle. Out of the ashes, a baby boy. That boy developed leukemia and died at age five. Though they were aged before their time, they mustered the courage to try again. They had a second miracle: another boy. This boy was standing on the chair now, singing the Four Questions.

Unlike most of the other grown-up men in the room, Little Henry's father was not well-off. He dealt not in diamonds but in diamond dust. Diamond dust is necessary, of course, because only diamonds can polish other diamonds, and diamond dust is the thing to do it. But it's not the most glorious part of the business. It's the most humble, and Little Henry's father would come to the basement of my great uncle Velvl's apartment building to grind some of Velvl's leftover stones into dust to make his living, an act of charity that was never spoken of. Little Henry's father would lose his wife in a few years but he would remain close to his son. Little Henry would grow up to be a renowned neurologist, always on call, rushing off to do important operations. As an old man, Little Henry's father's eyes would fill with dusty tears, his eyelashes glittering with diamond dust, when he would report that no matter how busy he was, Little Henry would still call him once a day at five, every day, like clockwork. Later still, six months after Little Henry's father died, Little Henry would die of prostate cancer at age forty-one, never having married, never having furthered his race, a sweetly bitter man, eager to please till the end.

But for now, Little Henry was on the chair, singing the Four Questions. His parents' eyes shone, the candle glow reflecting on their smooth cheeks as they mouthed the words in time with his singing. They took no notice of our giggling. All their attention was focused on their pride and joy, standing on the chair and singing. It didn't matter to them that we laughed. They forgave us. God had been generous with them by giving them this boy, and they could afford to be generous with the privileged children from the countryside, the sons and daughters of Connecticut.

Afterwards they smiled warmly at us, pretending to share in our laughter, as though the whole time we'd been laughing at how nice it was. This was their most generous gift of all.

Why didn't Little Henry's parents slap me across the face? Why didn't they rip the shirt from my body, pull my pants down right there in front of everyone and spank the smugness out of me?

They did better. They tolerated me. They let me live with it for decades until I came to understand.

At Passover, the Haggadah tells the story of four sons. It is a very simple and profound story. The first son, the wise son, asks what Passover means. The second son, the wicked son, asks what it all means to you—to you and not to him, for he removes himself from the group. The third son is dim and just says, What is this? The fourth son does not know how to ask.

What it took me half a lifetime to understand was that I was not that wicked son. Though I thought the Holocaust happened to them and not to me, though I mimicked my stuttering relatives who survived their exodus from Hitler's Europe and parodied the ones with Parkinson's so bad the numbers on their saggy arms shook, still I was not that wicked son. I was a different son, a fifth son who had been damaged.

It took me half a lifetime to understand that for this damaged son, making fun was his way of metabolizing the Holocaust, of filtering the horrors through at his own speed; that he had to have sons of his own and take them to see the tragedy of his people in the land where it happened, before he could pay for his blasphemy, and redeem himself.

The trip I took in my late thirties, with two sons to find the hiding places where our ancestors survived the Holocaust, was not only a trip to bond ourselves into a family after our divorce, not only a chance to heal and to get in touch with our deepest selves, in a land where our people died for being Jews.

It was, above all, a trip of atonement.

9/11

FORGIVE THE TERRORISTS?

Benjamin Blech

G-d, I need your guidance. I grieve for all the victims of September 11th. My heart is filled with pain, and with anger at the terrorists responsible for the horrible crimes committed on that day. But I know that you teach us to forgive those who sin. In the Bible you often tell us that you are a G-d who is slow to anger, merciful and forgiving. We are supposed to imitate you and adopt Your behavior as guidelines for our own personal conduct. Does that really mean that no matter how difficult it is, I have to tell myself to forgive all those who turned the twin towers into a mass graveyard? Am I guilty of failing my spiritual obligations if I'm not willing to respond to terrorism with love and forgiveness? G-d, how far does clemency go? In the name of religion, must I be prepared to pardon even those who committed murder?

Forgiveness is a divine trait. It defines the goodness of G-d. Without it human beings probably couldn't survive. Because G-d forgives, there's still hope for sinners. When we do wrong, G-d reassures us that he won't abandon us as a result of our transgressions. Divine forgiveness is the quality that most clearly proves G-d's love for us.

That's why the many passages in the Bible that affirm G-d's willingness to forgive our sins are so important. They comfort us and they fill us with confidence. We know none of us are perfect. If we would be judged solely on our actions, we would surely all fall short. Thank G-d the heavenly court isn't that strict. We can rest assured, as the prophet Isaiah told us in the name of the Lord, "Though your sins be as scarlet, they shall be as white as snow."

It makes perfect sense, then, for us to understand that if we expect G-d to forgive us for our failings we have to be prepared to forgive others as well. What we need when we're being judged from above certainly deserves to be granted to those we are judging. So we obviously have to be guided by the profound words of Alexander Pope: "To err is human, to forgive, divine."

That all makes it seem like we have no choice in the matter. Forgiveness appears to be our only moral option. But the more we study the Bible, the more we recognize a peculiar paradox. The same G-d who preaches forgiveness very often doesn't forgive. Instead, he punishes sinners. He holds people responsible. He criticizes, he condemns, and afflicts those who committed crimes. Adam and Eve sinned, and they were kicked out of the Garden of Eden. Cain sinned, and he was condemned to become a wanderer over the face of the earth. The generation of Noah sinned, and a flood destroyed them. The builders of the Tower of Babel sinned, and their speech was turned into babble. In one story after another, from the five Books of Moses through the works of the prophets, we read of retribution, of accountability, of divine punishment.

Isn't this an innate contradiction in the Bible? The same book in which G-d identifies himself as merciful and forgiving repeatedly shows us a G-d of justice who withholds undeserved pardons. It almost sounds hypocritical to hear G-d glorify forgiveness as an ideal way to act and then most of the time not put it into practice in his dealings with human beings.

There must be something we're missing. There can't be such an obvious contradiction in the Bible. And sure enough, just a little reflection makes clear why there are times when G-d forgives people for their sins and why at other times he refuses.

The Price for Forgiveness

G-d's great gift to us is a heavenly pardon. But His present is predicated on a condition. What He asks us to do before He grants us forgiveness is to acknowledge that we were wrong and that we renounce our sinful behavior.

"Let the wicked forsake his way, and the unrighteous man his thoughts; and let him return unto the Lord, and He will have mercy upon him; and to our G-d, and He will abundantly pardon" (Isaiah 55:7).

Forgiveness is willing to overlook the sins of the past for the sake of an altered future. It is ready to pardon the most terrible wrongs for the price of remorse, regret, and the desire for a new beginning. But the one thing G-d's forgiveness is unwilling to do is to condone vicious crimes by simply accepting them. An unrepentant sinner mistakes G-d's mercy for permission to continue in his ways. To forgive such a person isn't kindness; it's cruelty to all those who'll be hurt by the evil that wasn't stopped before it could do more harm.

Yes, it was the same G-d who drowned the wicked generation of Noah and who saved the evil people of Nineveh. Those who were destroyed by the flood were given plenty of warning. They watched Noah build his ark for many years. Noah told them what G-d planned to do if they didn't repent. But they didn't believe him—even when it started to rain and to pour like never before. So of course people who didn't see the need to ask for forgiveness weren't forgiven.

But when Jonah told the residents of the city of Nineveh that they were doomed because of their evil behavior, they took the message to heart and committed themselves to a new way of life. And the people who changed were immediately forgiven. G-d wasn't going to hold their past against them—because it was really a thing of the past.

To speak of forgiveness as if it were the automatic entitlement of every criminal is to pervert a noble sentiment into a carte blanche for mayhem and chaos. We might as well open the doors of every jail and release all the thieves, rapists, and murderers. Our wonderful act of compassion wouldn't take too long to be followed by the cries of the victims of our folly!

As a Jew, I recognize this idea as a basic principle of our faith. In our tradition we are taught that, "He who forgives the wicked hurts the good." But you don't have to be Jewish to acknowledge the validity of this concept. The Christian Bible unambiguously affirms it as well: "And if your brother sins against you, rebuke him; and if he repents, forgive him. And if seven times of the day he sins against you, and seven times of the day turns to you saying, I repent, you shall forgive him" (Luke 17:3–4). Forgiveness isn't an orphan. Its parent has to be repentance.

Don't Forgive Them Unless . . .

Forgiving people who aren't sorry for what they did makes a statement: Repentance isn't really necessary. No matter what you did, you don't have to change. Can anything be more immoral than encouraging evil by refraining from any condemnation of those who commit it?

The day after the Columbine High School massacre, a group of students announced that they forgave the killers. A short while after the Oklahoma bombing, some people put out a call to forgive Timothy McVeigh.

And, on September 12th, on several American campuses, college groups pleaded for forgiveness for the terrorists responsible for the horrific events of the previous day.

These weren't just misguided gestures of compassion. They were serious sins with potentially tragic consequences. Evil unchallenged is evil condoned. To forgive and forget, as Arthur Schopenhauer so well put it, "means to throw valuable experience out the window." And without the benefit of experience's lessons we are almost certain to be doomed to repeat them.

The terrorists who piloted the planes into the twin towers never asked us to be forgiven. They expressed not the slightest remorse as they went to their deaths together with their victims. Those who sent them, those who financed them, and those who applauded their mission never for a moment regretted what happened. Forgiving them is no less than giving them license to murder four thousand more innocent people. That's why to forgive in a case like this is to become an accomplice to future crimes.

What If a Nazi Asked for Forgiveness?

But what if a brutal murderer realizes the enormity of his crimes and honestly regrets his past deeds? What if the plea for forgiveness is accompanied by sincere remorse? Can the crimes of the past be forgotten? Is a troubled conscience sufficient to secure automatic forgiveness?

That's not just a theoretical question. Something exactly like that happened towards the end of the Holocaust. And the man who had to decide what to do in such a situation, a concentration camp victim who had suffered indescribable mistreatment and torture, wrote a remarkable book about his experience.

Simon Wiesenthal was a prisoner of the Nazis confined to slave labor in a German hospital. One day he was suddenly pulled away from his work and brought into a room where an SS soldier lay dying. The German officer, Karl, confessed to Wiesenthal that he had committed atrocious crimes. Although raised as a good Catholic and in his youth G-d-fearing, Karl had allowed himself to become a sadistic accomplice to Nazi ideology. Now that he knew his end was near and he would soon be facing his Maker, Karl was overcome by what he now realized was the enormity of his sins.

More than anything else, Karl knew that he needed atonement. He wanted to die with a clear conscience. So he asked that a Jew be brought to him. And from this Jew, Simon Wiesenthal, the killer asked for absolution.

Wiesenthal has been haunted by this scene his entire life. When it happened, he was in such shock that he didn't know how to respond. His emotions pulled him in different directions. Anger mixed with pity, hatred with compassion, and revulsion with mercy. His conclusion was to leave in utter silence. He didn't grant Karl the forgiveness the German desperately sought.

Years later, Wiesenthal shared the story with a number of prominent intellectuals, theologians, and religious leaders. How would they have reacted? he asked them. In the light of religious teachings and ethical ideals, what should have been the proper response? Was there a more suitable reply than silence?

Wiesenthal collected the answers and had them published as a book called *The Sunflower.* The ranges of responses offer a fascinating insight into different views on forgiveness. Some, like the British journalist Christopher Hollis, believe that the law of G-d is the law of love, no matter what the situation. We have an obligation to forgive our fellow human beings even when they have caused us the greatest harm. A remorseful murderer deserved compassion.

On the other hand, Cardinal Franz Konig believes that Wiesenthal did Karl a favor just by listening to him. Wiesenthal did pass up the chance to offer his forgiveness to Karl, although in those circumstances doing so would have been "superhuman."

Rabbi Abraham Joshua Heschel, a prominent American theologian and author, offered a different perspective. No one can forgive crimes not committed against him or her personally. What Karl sought could only come from his victims. It's preposterous to think that one solitary Jew can presume to speak for six million.

And Who Are *You* to Forgive?

Some years ago, Rabbi Heschel had occasion to elaborate on this idea. He had been invited to address a group of prominent business executives. Among them were some of the most important CEOs in the country. His lecture dealt with the Holocaust and its lessons for us. He stressed the importance of memory and the need to continue to bear witness to the crime of genocide.

When he finished, one of the very famous names in American corporate life angrily rebutted the essence of Heschel's talk. "I'm tired," he said, "of hearing about the Holocaust. You claim that you're speaking in the name of morality. Why can't you demonstrate true morality by learning to forgive and forget?"

To a stunned audience, Heschel replied by asking them for permission to tell a story. Before beginning, he introduced his listeners to the man he would be speaking about. In the history of the Jewish people, he explained, there has hardly ever been someone considered as saintly as Rabbi Israel Kagan, commonly known as the Chafetz Chaim ("the one who desires true life"). A Polish rabbi and scholar of the late nineteenth and early twentieth century, he was universally revered not just for his piety but more importantly for his extreme concern for the feelings of his fellow man. It is an incident in the life of this holy figure that Heschel said he wanted to share before he would respond to the question put to him.

Rabbi Kagan was traveling on a train, immersed in a religious book he was studying. Alongside him sat three Jews anxious to while away the time by playing cards. The game required a fourth hand so they asked the unrecognized stranger to join them. Rabbi Kagan politely refused, explaining that he preferred to continue his reading. The frustrated card players refused to take no for an answer. They began to beat the poor Rabbi until they left him bleeding.

Hours later, the train pulled into the station. Hundreds of people swarmed the platform waiting to greet the great sage. Posters bore signs of Welcome to the Chafetz Chaim. As the Rabbi, embarrassed by all the adulation, walked off the train with his bruises, the crowd lifted him up and carried him off on their shoulders. Watching with horror were the three Jews who had not long before accosted the simple Jew sitting in their cabin, now revealed as one of the spiritual giants of their generation. Profoundly ashamed and plagued by their guilt, they managed to make their way through the crowd and reached their unwilling card player partner.

With tears, they poured out their feelings of shame and remorse. How could they possibly have assaulted this great Rabbi? They begged for forgiveness. And incredibly enough, the Rabbi said no. The man who spent his life preaching love now refused to extend it to people who harmed him and regretted their actions. It seemed incomprehensible. So the three Jews attributed it to a momentary lapse. Perhaps, they thought, it was just too soon for the Rabbi to forgive them. He probably needed some time to get over the hurt. They would wait a while and ask again at a more propitious moment.

Several weeks passed and it was now close to Yom Kippur, the Day of Atonement. Even the simplest Jews knew that they had to gain forgiveness from their friends if they wanted to be pardoned by G-d. With trepidation, the wicked three wrangled an appointment and once again were able to speak to the Rabbi. They pleaded their case. Still the Rabbi said no. He would not forgive them.

The Rabbi's son was present as this strange scene played itself out. Puzzled by his father's peculiar behavior, he couldn't contain himself. It was so unlike anything he had ever witnessed before. Why did his father suddenly act so cruelly? Why would he persist in tormenting people who only asked for a simple expression of forgiveness?

The son dared to ask. His father explained. "Do you really think I don't want to forgive these poor Jews before the High Holy days? If it were only in my power to do so, don't you know that I would have forgiven them when they stood before me at the railroad station? Of course I, Rabbi Kagan, forgive them for what they did to me. When they learned who I was, they were mortified and filled with shame for what they had done. But the man they beat up was the one they presumed to be a simple, unassuming poor person with no crowd of well-wishers waiting to greet him. He was the victim and only he is the one capable of granting them forgiveness. Let them go find that person. I am incapable of releasing them from their guilt."

Rabbi Heschel completed the story. He then turned to the executive who suggested that it was time for us to move on after the Holocaust and to forgive and forget. "I would be more than happy to do so if I only could. But I was not the one who was sealed in the gas chambers to die a horrible death. I didn't have my child pulled from my breast and shot in front of my eyes. I was not among the tortured, the beaten, the whipped, and the murdered. It is they and they alone who can offer forgiveness. Go and find those six million and ask them if they are prepared to forgive and forget."

Should we forgive the murderers of the thousands of victims of terrorism on 9/11? Perhaps the most appropriate response is simply this: We are not the ones who have the right to make that decision.

FROM A KABBALIST'S DIARY

PENSÉES ON A POST-9/11 UNIVERSE

Bezalel Naor

THE EVENTS OF SEPTEMBER 11, 2001, have created a new configuration in man's spiritual universe. The attack by Islamists on the symbols of America's power, financial and military, is cause for radical reevaluation not only by political analysts but also by theologians of every creed. There were those so smug in their vision of a "new world order" and the doctrine of a "global economy" that they were ill-equipped to portray the rise of Islamism as other than the final pocket of resistance of a few "obscurantists." For such pundits, the shock of 9/11 came as that of the Mahdi to the inhabitants of the Imperium in Frank Herbert's *Dune* (1965), a science fiction classic which in retrospect appears an example of modern prophecy.[1] Needless to say, these observers underestimated both the determination and resources, physical and spiritual, of this twenty-first century *jihad*.

The most profound of all the portions of the *Zohar,* the *Sifra di-Zeni'uta* (Book of Concealment), introduces the concept of the *mitkala* (balance).[2] There is a divine balance at work in the universe. No political system in the history of mankind is so perfect that it is undeserving of criticism. Capitalism was first critiqued by communism, a system that has fallen into such disrepute that it is hard to remember that there was ever a "spark of holiness" contained in the socialist ideal. But there were many salient features to the socialist critique: The value of community over and against the "rugged individualism" that ends in loneliness and "anomie" (to use Durkheim's term); the fact that workers had become alienated from the fruits of their labor; the concept that work could be "holy" and spiritually rewarding. With the fall of the greatest bloc of communism in Eastern Europe, the disintegration of the Union of Soviet Socialist Republics, and its coopting by capitalism (though perhaps "mafiacracy" rather than "democracy" is the more apt term to describe Russia's present-day form of government), the cosmic balance was upset. This vacuum was quickly filled by Islamism.

It is no coincidence that in the very region (Afghanistan) and the very time (end twentieth century) that Russian-style "socialism" fell, militant Islamism rose. Once again, the antipode to capitalism is so distasteful to us that it is hard to imagine where in the Taliban or al-Qaeda version of reality there might possibly lie a "spark of holiness." The truth is that the Islamist critique of the West, loathsome though it may be to us, is not devoid of value. Islamists home in on many sore spots in contemporary Western civilization: unabashed greed and materialism, the pursuit of hedonistic pleasures, outright pornography, the widening gap between rich and poor, spiritual hypocrisy and vacuity, to name a few examples. The sickness of our society that has gone unnoticed or unprotested by our own clergy comes in for close scrutiny by the Islamists.

○

Entering a new millennium, it is appropriate that we reflect on the previous millennium and how the three "Abrahamitic" faiths comported themselves throughout. I refer specifically to their performance in the sciences.

Someone living a thousand years ago, say in Spain, could hardly have predicted what our world would look like today. Based on trends at that time, one certainly would have prognosticated that Islam would be the world leader in the exact sciences. Judaism would be a close runner-up, with Christianity lagging far behind. There would be many factors militating for this projection. Europe was enveloped in the "Dark Ages." The Church was a repressive body, highly suspicious of scientific revolution, and would continue to be so half a millennium later when it confined Galileo to house arrest. Islam at the other extreme, was at the forefront of scientific endeavor, whether it be in the field of astronomy, mathematics, or medicine. And the Jews? As so often in their history, they were "middlemen," translators of scientific treatises from Arabic to Latin.

We now know that this forecast would have been all wrong. The "dark horse" of Christendom has emerged at the forefront of scientific advancement. Able to free itself of the stifling influence of the Church (though even most recently, President George W. Bush thought it judicious to confer with Pope John Paul II concerning the morality of pursuing stem cell research), the West eventually arrived at a secular society conducive to science.

For Islam however, the millennium was "downhill all the way," if one is speaking of the exact sciences. As time went on, Islam was eclipsed by the West. Even the formidable Ottoman Empire, once capable of striking fear in Christian Europe, took its last gasp of air in the 1920s, unable to cope with modernity and the march of progress. Whereas the West was able to free itself from the oppressive clutches of the Church, the religion of Islam, though having no central governing body even vaguely resembling the Vatican, became increasingly hostile to the sciences. Where once they had provided a comfortable climate for scientific research, the lands of Islam were now most inhospitable in that respect. This transformation is not lost on the brightest minds within the Islamic community. One cannot have but the greatest respect and admiration for Iranian-born, Washington-based Seyyed Hossein Nasr, who in his books attempts to recapture the lost glory of Islam, or Egyptian producer Yusuf Chahine, who in his film *Destiny,* a portrayal of the life of the twelfth-century philosopher Ibn Rushd (Averroes), all too transparently pleads the cause of academic and artistic freedom.

And the Jews? Where do we figure in all of this? Candidly, our religion was not tremendously supportive of scientific pursuit, but neither was it overly repressive. (It has been suggested by some historians that Christian-influenced Ashkenaz was hostile to secular knowledge, while Islamic-influenced Sefarad was positively disposed.) If the Nobel Prize is a barometer of scientific distinction, it is a well-known fact that Jews are disproportionately represented in Stockholm. One might counter that the *yeshivot,* the traditional bastions of Talmudic learning, have grown increasingly rigidified and disapproving of secular studies. Though Maimonides' Code of Law might be studied day and night in the *yeshivah* of Brisk let us say, Brisk is not likely to turn out a Maimonides at the forefront of medicine, philosophy, and astronomy. But the *yeshivot* are only one sector within the Jewish People. Viewed as a whole, Judaism has held constant vis-à-vis science and technology. As a people, we have certainly not lagged behind in terms of scientific advancement. We need not gloat, but neither should we be ashamed if there seems to manifest in Judaism a healthy attitude to the by-products of human intellect.

A Parisian student of Kabbalah, the late Rabbi Eli Munk, wrote a generation ago:

> Judaism has much to offer, for it has long been aware of the fact that the grasp of things requires a balancing; it has long exhibited an un-

derstanding that the full life required reason and faith operating in their respective domains but continuing to produce a harmonious life. Nor will Judaism today join the chorus of the anti-scientific ones, of the anti-intellectualists, of the escapists into the untrammelled emotional deification of unreason. It will cherish its nurtured past as a vital exhibition for present use, illustrating the correlation of the manifold aspects of human effort. If Judaism today can maintain and advance its balanced view of life, applying its reason and faith to the daily problems confronting us, it will thus not only restore to its own followers, but also to a sadly disturbed world, a measure of sanity.[3]

○

While on the topic of the three "Abrahamitic" faiths, in kabbalistic typology, Abraham symbolizes *hesed* (love); Isaac, *gevurah* (rigor), while Jacob (or Israel) is the synthesis of these two, *tif'eret* (beauty). Where do Ishmael and Esau figure in this scheme? It was taught that Ishmael is the "overabundance of love" (*motarot ha-hesed*), and Esau the "overabundance of rigors" (*motarot ha-gevurot*). Which is to say, Ishmael represents an exaggeration of his father Abraham's quality of love of God. Likewise, Esau is overendowed with his father Isaac's quality of fear of God.[4] Without sounding jingoistic or disrespectful of other faith communities, perhaps this kabbalistic critique can place our world today in some perspective.

Love is the desire for proximity and intimacy. Fear seeks distance and space.[5] Too much closeness is suffocating. Too much distance is absence. Today Islam (Ishmael) is in a position of *motarot ha-hesed*, disproportionate love of God. It is being consumed by its closeness to Allah.

Once upon a time, the rabbis would refer to Imperial Rome as Esau.[6] Today, Esau is the heir to Rome, Western civilization in general, and specifically America. Our society suffers from *motarot ha-gevurot,* excessive fears. Esau is overly fearful of God to the point that God, if not altogether absent, is reasonably remote from our everyday lives.

Perhaps once again, Judaism can assume the role of a middleman teaching the proper space to insert between Creator and created.

NOTES

1. By the way, Herbert's term for accelerated human evolution, *Kwisatz Haderach,* was lifted from Jewish mysticism, where as *kefizat ha-derekh,* it refers to the ability to travel great distances in relatively no time. "Kwisatz Haderach: 'Shortening of the Way'" (Frank Herbert, *Dune* [New York: G.P. Putnam's Sons, 1984], p. 506). With the exception of this one incursion of Hebrew, the linguistic landscape of *Dune* is bedrock Arabic.

2. *Zohar* II, 1976b.

3. Eli Munk, "Reason and Mysticism," in Leo Jung, ed., *Judaism in a Changing World* (London: Soncino Press, 1971), p. 157.

4. Rabbi Shneur Zalman of Liady, *Siddur* (Brooklyn: Kehot, 5731/1971), *Sha'ar ha-Lulav*, 265c.

5. See Maimonides, *Mishneh Torah, Hil. Yesodei ha-Torah* 2:2.

6. Babylonian Talmud, 'Avodah Zarah 10b–11b.

A CONGREGATION
OF HOLY SOULS

REFLECTIONS ON 9/11 ONE YEAR LATER

Avi Weiss

ON TUESDAY MORNING, SEPTEMBER 11, immediately following the attack on the World Trade Center, I set out from 53rd Street making my way south to the site of the devastation. It was as if something—someone, a congregation of holy souls—was calling me.

As I drew nearer it became difficult to breathe. I waded through a white, otherworldly dust, which, at times, reached up to my ankles. The scene was apocalyptic, horrifying; the extent of the evil inflicted upon it made it seem almost polluted, impure. But soon I was overwhelmed by the very opposite realization—my sense of the sanctity of the place. This was where innocence had been violated by evil. It had become a holy place—a *makom kadosh*. I had entered the precincts of holiness.

This holiness encompassed not only those who had been lost to terror, but those (unlike myself) endowed with essential life-saving skills—firefighters, police personnel, doctors and nurses—who had converged on the site. Among these men and women, I discovered quite by accident and with great emotion my own son-in-law, Dr. Mark Levie, who led a group of volunteers with the call "We can't just stand here—let's go." The heartbreaking image of the makeshift triage center on the evening of 9/11 will never leave me. Set up in Stuyvesant High School with beds and a full array of emergency equipment, doctors and nurses stood awaiting the casualties.

The wounded never arrived. As the stark realization of the finality of the catastrophe set in, medical personnel sat down with heads in hands, overcome. I understood, to my great sorrow, that what remained now was to comfort and minister—and this, at least, with my pastoral experience, was a service I could offer. An image that will remain with me from those early days is of standing as one member of the clergy among many others of all faiths as police and firefighters snapped to attention when the remains of a comrade were taken out—remains not necessarily whole or intact, a limb, perhaps, a finger, a toe—all holy. And those rescue workers who stood there, giving them honor—all holy.

This black hole in the world, which has become known as Ground Zero, was beyond anything I had ever before witnessed. I have been to devastated zones—in Israel, in Argentina—but nothing could compare to this. Those devastations could be placed in a corner of this hole. This hole will remain forever in my consciousness as a dark foreboding of what is possible—an emptiness, an absence, a silence.

And it is with a ritual of silence—of reflection and meditation that transcend the limitations of words—that we shall remember this tragedy in our synagogues when its first anniversary falls during the Days of Awe. First, we will ask for silent meditation. We will recall where we were at that moment. We will reflect on how our brush with death can help renew our appreciation of those closest to us. We will close our eyes and imagine those dearest to us, and say prayers for each of them.

Firefighters and police officers will be invited to join us in the sanctuary, and, right there on the High Holy Days, we shall rise to express our gratitude. I'll remind my congregants that—as I first heard from a colleague, Rabbi Jonathan Rosenblatt—those who died in the service of the people did not fall as buildings collapsed upon them; rather, they ascended toward God as they worked selflessly to save others. We'll listen closely as portraits of the lives of some of the victims are read by congregants from throughout the sanctuary. In this way, the victims, although no longer on this earth, are brought briefly to life. We'll raise our hands in prayer, and then reach out to embrace those closest to us in an expression of love and song—of how good it is, brothers and sisters together.

This has been an enormously difficult year. The fate of being targeted, which had once seemed to mark and isolate Israel, has now expanded outward to include America. But common victimization by terror will lead only to common resolve to combat the evil. At the Twin Towers during those terrible days, I felt a profound sense of Universalism. Jewish Particularism had expanded outward, encompassing all innocents. Suddenly, all humanity had become Jews.

When faced with evil, the goal cannot be to dispel the darkness; that is often impossible. It's much like walking into a dark room crowded with furniture. The first time we enter, we grope blindly, we bump into everything, we stumble everywhere. But after a time, when we enter, although the room is still dark we know where the obstacles lie; we no longer fall, we have found our way. Meditating on Rosh Hashana and Yom Kippur to commemorate this first anniversary of September 11, we will hold fast to hope as we struggle in the midst of the darkness to find our way.

ANTI-SEMITISM

THE NEW ANTI-SEMITISM

Phyllis Chesler

ON SEPTEMBER 11, 2001, at about 11 A.M., I walked over to my computer and typed the sentence: "Now, we are all Israelis." Later that week, Osama bin Laden announced that the twin towers of the World Trade Center had fallen in retribution for U.S. policy supporting Israel and the Jews. The new anti-Semitism had been formally declared, and I began writing this book.

I was not a direct victim on 9/11. I did not personally know anyone who was killed that day in the World Trade Center or in the Pentagon. I was at home in Brooklyn, transfixed before the TV set, watching it live, as it continued to happen, and did not move from my spot. I knew that when I got up nothing would ever be the same again, I would no longer feel safe in my native city or country or world, I would no longer be able to assume that life as I'd known it—with all its illusions—would continue.

The twin towers had burst into flames and were tumbling down; firemen and policemen rushed in, people with horrified eyes and covered with white soot burst out of the building, a tornado of debris whooshed after them as they kept on running; incredibly tiny people were holding hands as they jumped to their deaths from high floors, and still the towers continued to burn and melt and fall; in my mind, they are falling still, out of heaven, into hell. Falling into memory for all eternity.

By late afternoon the wind had begun to carry bits and pieces of charred stuff into my neighborhood in Park Slope less than two miles as the crow flies from Ground Zero, and the air smelled of scorched souls, acrid and agonized. It was a sickening combination of industrial fuels, hate, and human cries; it burned my throat and my eyes and my mind. I will never forget it. Nor will I forget the small impromptu shrine that instantly, instinctively, arose spontaneously at the corner of my block: flowers, candles, an American flag, a small umbrella to shield this makeshift memorial from the elements—I paid my respects there almost every day for more than a year.

I survive them, we all do. In their place and for their sakes we must find the courage to stand up to evil as best we can; there are many ways to do so. We owe it to them to speak softly, to act wisely, and to listen respectfully to those with whom we disagree. From now on, we will be pleading their case—and the case of all civilians everywhere who are now hostage to terror.

———————— o ————————

I find it incredible that I am writing a book about a new plague of anti-Semitism, which is so closely connected to those events on September 11, 2001. Who would ever have thought that such a work would be necessary in the twenty-first century?

But I must speak out. Something awful is happening to the world's Jews. If the daily violence and demented propaganda against them is not countered effectively, I fear that the Jews may again be sacrificed to a world gone mad and in need of a sacred scapegoat.

The new anti-Semitism, a virulent epidemic of violence, hatred, and lies has become, how ironically, politically correct. In Islam, in Europe, on the old right, and on the new left, Israel has become the scapegoat, the cause of evil, the beast of the world. And simmering beneath that smoke screen of anti-Israeli fervor is, as we shall see, the terrible but familiar hatred of the Jew, the "other," the separate people, the powerful, secret international conspiracy, the pariahs of the earth.

Fifty-five years ago, Israel was created in order to solve the problem of the old anti-Semitism. Now Israel is the Jew of the world; its citizens are being ghettoized and isolated, just as Jews once were in Europe and under Islam. The Jews of Israel are facing the gravest danger, but Jews elsewhere, especially in Europe but also in South America, Africa, and Asia, are increasingly at risk.

Today, the new anti-Semitism speaks a hundred languages. The mob's infernal, heart-stopping chants, flag-burnings, bombings, and executions are shown on television over and over again. The demonization of the Jews and of Israel has created an atmosphere in which the unthinkable and the horrific are becoming possible. There is a thrilling permissibility in the air, the kind of electrically charged and altered reality that acid-trippers or epileptics may experience just prior to a seizure; purple haze, unreality, a disassociation from normalcy, responsibility.

Jews and Zionists are being blamed for 9/11 in Chinese as well as in Arabic. Nobel Prize winners, European and American academics, anti-globalization activists and Jews on the Left have all condemned Israel for daring to defend itself while remaining silent about the suicide-bombings of Israeli civilians. Doctored footage of fake Israeli massacres have now entered the imagination of billions of people; like pornography, these ideas can never be forgotten.

'Tis a season of blood that's upon us. I knew it from the moment the two Israeli reservists were lynched in Ramallah in the fall of 2000. The Palestinian crowds cheered when the smiling murderers proudly displayed their hands smeared with Jewish blood. I saw them dancing in the blood of my people, *partying*, like ghouls. No one on the airwaves drew back in horror, they showed these scenes but did not condemn them. International human rights activists and intellectuals remained silent, as did the United Nations. I wept because I understood that Jewish history was, once more, repeating itself. How foolish I'd been to think that we had finally escaped it.

But, will six million more have to die before the blood-letting stops?

o

These days, "Israel" is far too dangerous a word to pronounce in a western intellectual or social setting. Say it—and you risk uncivil argument.

For example, it's ten months after 9/11, and I am having dinner with a friend and colleague of thirty-five years. We are talking up the usual storm, laughing a lot, enjoying each other's company, when one of us uses the word: "Israel." My friend, an independent and sophisticated thinker, stops talking. Suddenly, the air becomes thin. She takes a deep breath. Her tone is no longer light, it has become dark, coarse, mocking.

"Israel?! It deserves exactly what it's getting. And more. And don't think America doesn't deserve what it's getting too."

We are sitting a mile away from Ground Zero in NYC.

"Have you no compassion for the innocent?" I say, shocked by her cold, driven vehemence.

"Innocent? No one is innocent. We are all guilty. Don't tell me that you would dare to defend the Zionist apartheid state or the multinationals."

Her dear face has been utterly transformed into the face of a one-woman lynch mob. I do not want to fight, I can't bear the ridicule and intimidation, I know that I must say something, I am tired of having to do so. I do not want this friendship to shatter over the Jewish Question, that perpetual elephant in the living room of the world.

My friend is a Jew, a feminist, a leftist, and she prides herself on being an independent thinker.

"According to you," I say, "only Americans and Israelis deserve to die for the sins of their leaders? I don't hear you wishing a hellish death upon Chinese or Iraqi civilians because you disagree with their government's policies." But my heart is not into "making points." My heart is beating too fast. I am afraid of her anger.

o

I have been talking to a number of Arabs and Muslims from around the world. They are all educated and worldly people. One man, let me call him Mohammed, came for dinner last week. He is fluent in five languages, tells charming stories, knows "everyone" in the Islamic world. He enjoys unmasking the hypocrisy of tyrants and mullahs. He shocked even me as he described the foibles of major Islamic figures who are cocaine and opium addicts, alcoholics, liars, thieves, incredibly stupid, vain, insane, etc.; they shall remain nameless since I have no way of knowing whether this information is true or not.

He joyfully zeroed in on hypocrisy. For example, according to my friend, "The Saudi princes *use* religion, they themselves are not particularly religious. For example, they drink. [Muslims are not supposed to drink alcohol.] Once, when I was in Pakistan, my host and I went to five black-market liquor stores. They were all sold out. And why? Because a world Islamic conference was taking place in town!"

This man—so charming, so well-informed, earnestly pressed upon me three Internet articles that "proved that the Zionists really do run America." The fact that he himself understands that America is the world's only and supreme superpower does not stop him from believing that the Zionists—who run a country about the size of New Jersey—also control both America and the world. Nothing I said could change his mind. Eventually, he politely, wisely, changed the subject.

If I cannot persuade him that the Zionists really do not run America, how can I hope to persuade other educated Muslims?

Another friend, an elegant woman from an Islamic non-Arab country who has lived in exile in Paris for a long time, unsettled me with a long and eloquent diatribe against America. She reminded me of Europe's colonial past, the untold grief it caused, the arrogant carving up of the Ottoman Empire by Britain and France, and of America's long and ugly history of funding corrupt and sadistic tyrants in every Islamic country. She is, by and large, correct. (Strangely, she is not angry at the French who, I have been told, "went native" in a way that the British did not.)

She tells me: "Please understand, what is going on is that the frustration of the people has finally boiled over. It has come time to pay the price for America's having backed the Shah of Iran, a man who was not even royal, just the son of an army colonel, bought and paid for by the Americans. The Shah stole thirty-six billion dollars from his people when he fled Iran, and who protected him and his money? The Americans. The American oil companies—that's who runs the American government! They wanted to create a pipeline running through Afghanistan and they wanted to stop the Soviets. That's why they approached and funded the Pakistanis, who are hardcore religious zealots, who turned around and created the Taliban out of the illiterate and Islamically brainwashed Afghan refugees. The Taliban were originally supposed to ride shotgun and protect the new gas and oil pipeline that would run through Afghanistan. Well, that did not work out. So now, America has put a new puppet, Hamid Karzai, in place. Everyone knows that Saddam Hussein is a bloodthirsty animal. But who put him there? The Americans. Again, the reason was oil and gas. If the Americans get rid of him, they'll only put another puppet in his place. *That's* why 9/11 happened."

She pauses, briefly. Then says: "And that's why America has got to stop backing Israel. When and if it does, that will signal to the Islamic world that America is interested in brokering some justice in the world."

I am somewhat speechless but quickly say: "Assuming America abandons Israel to its enemies, assuming that another sacrificial bloodbath of Jews takes place, how will that change the historical record or improve matters in the rest of the Islamic world now?"

She answers me by coolly saying that "fifteen percent of the United States Senate is Jewish. The American Jewish Israel lobby is very powerful. They will never allow America to broker a just peace in the Middle East." Actually, the 108th Congress (which includes both the Senate and the House) has 535 members of whom 37, or 7 percent, are Jews. But no matter.

Actually, most Arabs and Muslims sound angrier and far more hateful than this. In a 2001 sermon televised by the Palestinian Authority, Sheikh Ibrahim Madhi said that the Almighty had described Jews as "apes and pigs, (and as) calf-worshipers and idol-worshipers." He also said: "We blow them up in Hadera. We blow them up in Tel Aviv and Netanya. And in this way Allah establishes us as rulers over these gangs of vagabonds."

This would be comic if it were not so tragic.

○

Israel, like America, is a country of immigrants and a democracy. Like America, Israel has high ideals which it does not and cannot always achieve. Because both America and Israel symbolize and promise so much—equality, democracy, justice, modernity, the right to pursue individual happiness—people are disappointed and embittered when the promise does not include *them*.

I also know that Israel does not have a perfect government; no country does. But Israel is not a colonial, apartheid state. The Jews came to Israel in the late nineteenth and early twentieth century, not as conquering Europeans backed by a royal treasury but as the wretched of the earth in search of respite from ceaseless persecution. They were impoverished, young, and idealistic. They were not mercenaries or colonialists. They had no "mother country" behind them, only hatred hard on their heels. They were not in search of natural resources to plunder (Israel was arid, rocky, swampy), nor did they intend to create a permanent subordinate class of workers based on racial difference. Jews and Arabs are both Semites. Jews come in all colors: black, brown, olive, yellow, white.

When Zionist idealists first returned to Israel/Palestine, what ensued was not merely a clash between white-skinned Europeans and dark-skinned Arabs. The clash that ensued—and that continues still—was also one between modernity and a hide-bound traditionalism that had not changed for twelve or thirteen centuries; between active-doers and passive survivors; between secularists and religionists as well as between extreme followers of different religions; between those who wanted to bring modern medicine, agriculture, industry, government, and jurisprudence to the region and those who rejected such possibilities.

I am no longer willing to say that colonialism and global capitalism are solely responsible for all human suffering, that America and the West are *essentially* evil, beyond redemption, and must therefore be destroyed in order to purify the world. Things are more complex than that.

European colonialism also imported "foreign" concepts such as nationalism and individual rights, which ultimately led to the overthrow of the colonialists; in addition, colonialism also sponsored "foreign" practices such as education (for girls, and the children of peasants too), hygiene, health care, governmental infrastructures, technology. So too: global capitalism both exploits and educates, impoverishes and enriches. If America and the West are reduced to apocalyptic rubble, that will not improve the material or cultural future of the rest of the world.

o

First, let us be clear: the absence of anti-Semitism is what's unusual, not its presence. As we have seen, for more than two thousand years, classical anti-Semitism denied individual Jews the right to live safely or with dignity as equal citizens anywhere in the world. Today, this historical strain of anti-Semitism continues but, in the last fifty years, has also metamorphosed into the most virulent anti-Zionism which, in turn, has increasingly held Jewish people everywhere, not only in Israel, accountable for the military policies of the Israeli government.

In the last three years, the most soul-shaking incidents of anti-Semitism have increased enormously in the Western world, in both Europe and North America, as well as in the Islamic world. On campuses, at demonstrations, and at international conferences—ugly words, sneers, threats, beatings, riots, broken bones, broken windows, torched synagogues, vandalized synagogues—the works. It's as if Hitler's Brownshirts have returned from the dead in greater numbers and are doing their dirty kristallnacht-work every day, everywhere.

The Jews are experiencing four simultaneous *intifadas:* one in the Islamic world, a second in Europe, a third on North American campuses, and a fourth one too—the one that is directed at America and the West by al-Qaeda.

Jews are facing the full force of two thousand years of racism (anti-Judaism, anti-Semitism) recycled. Lies, propaganda, myths, and half-truths are being advanced through modern technology and presented as if they were factual. Right-wing politicians in Europe, left-wing politicians in North America, print and broadcast media pundits of all stripes, feminists, filmmakers, journalists, students, esteemed professors—all proclaim Big Lies to be the truth. As advertising companies well know—most people eventually come to believe whatever they continually hear and see. We are the species who hum the jingles from commercials.

Indeed, this is one of the things that is new about the new anti-Semitism: that it is worldwide, and carried around the world instantly via mass communications. And, as this epidemic of violent deeds and propaganda rages, the world media, prominent left-wing Western intellectuals, and activists either deny that this plague is happening or merely note it in passing, without context or mercy; or, they simply blame Israel for causing the anti-Jewish violence. By definition, Israel is a rogue state because it is a *Jewish* state that insists upon defending itself.

———————— o ————————

The world—including many in the Jewish world—still seems to have one standard for Jews and for the Jewish state (and it's a high standard), and another, much lower standard for everyone else. Most barbarism goes completely unnoticed, no one is ever held accountable, the crimes are denied or covered up, the whistle-blowers killed or imprisoned. In contrast,

Israel's most minor imperfection is continually criticized; serious mistakes are demonized.

What's *new* about the new anti-Semitism is that, for the first time, it is being perpetrated in the name of politically correct ideology. Because the charges of "apartheid Zionism" and "American capitalist imperialism" are being leveled by those who champion the uprising of the oppressed, what they say, by definition, cannot be racist. Therefore, when such champions of freedom chant "Death to the Jews" or "Divest in apartheid colonialist Israel"—by definition, these are not racist remarks. The new anti-Semites are not anti-Semites because they *say* they're not. Even George Orwell would be astounded.

What's *new* is that acts of violence against Jews and anti-Semitic words and deeds are being uttered and performed by politically correct people in the name of anti-colonialism, anti-imperialism, anti-racism, and pacifism. Old-fashioned anti-Semitism was expressed in the name of ethnicity, Aryan idealism, white purity, superiority, and nationalism. Nazi-era Germans and Americans viewed Jews as inferior racially and biologically. The new anti-Semite cannot, by definition, be an anti-Semite racist because she speaks out on behalf of oppressed people.

LETTER FROM FORMER NEW YORK MAYOR ED KOCH TO WOODY ALLEN

Edward I. Koch

May 17, 2002

Dear Woody:

I take the liberty of using your first name because, as I hope you will recall, I made a cameo appearance in *New York Stories* when I was mayor, and I really enjoyed it. And, of course, we often visit the same restaurants at the same time.

You were quoted in yesterday's *New York Times* on the subject of anti-Semitism in France as saying, "I never felt that the French people in any way were anti-Semitic . . . I think one can be very proud of France for the way they've acquitted themselves in the last election and I don't think a boycott is in order. I just don't feel that it's right . . . I think any boycott is wrong. Boycotts were exactly what the Germans were doing against the Jews."

Some who disagree with you, not only now, but in the past as well, have referred to you as a "self-hating Jew." I think that is unfair. Your humor, movies, and scripts all convey in an intelligent and humorous manner your positive Jewish identity.

I also believe you were wrong in your comments about the French.

While you defended the outcome of the last election and Le Pen's defeat as a "clear-cut response to the extreme right," Le Pen received 18 percent of the total vote. If a party whose leader is widely recognized even in France as a defender of the Nazi regimes were to receive 18 percent of the vote for president here in the United States, would you feel proud of America or would you sit up and take notice?

Were you not offended when the French ambassador to Great Britain, Daniel Bernard, recently attending a dinner party, called Israel "a shitty little country," adding, "Why should the world be in danger of World War III because of those people?" The implication to many was that Ambassador Bernard thinks Jewish lives lost in terrorist suicide bombings are not as precious as others requiring our concern. It is a fact that during World War II, French cops in unoccupied Vichy France rounded up and delivered sixty-one thousand Jews to the Nazis at Drancy without a request by the Nazis that they do so. Those Jews ended up in Nazi death camps where they were gassed. It is generally accepted that the French in large numbers were collaborators with the Nazis. And a relatively small number continued to fight underground before France was liberated as a result of the D-Day invasion. In January of this year, Israel's Deputy Foreign Minister, Michael Melchior, singled out France as the European country where the greatest number of anti-Semitic attacks have occurred.

Historically, one of the most outrageous acts of French anti-Semitism is the infamous Dreyfus trial followed by his imprisonment on Devil's Island before his exoneration. Dreyfus was lucky that Emile Zola was on the scene and not intimidated by or infatuated with the French government of his time.

Many knowledgeable observers believe anti-Semitism in France and elsewhere in Europe is equal to what it was in 1939. I do too.

Abraham Foxman, national director of the Anti-Defamation League, has denounced French anti-Semitism and the lack of governmental response, saying, "Time and again, we have called on President Chirac to come forward with strong denunciations of the violence and incendiary anti-Semitic and anti-Israel rhetoric, and take responsibility for Jewish citizens by better protecting them."

Apparently, the French government (Chirac having been reelected after Jospin, the socialist prime minister, was defeated in the first election by Le Pen) is now acknowledging and taking appropriate, albeit belated action to protect its Jewish citizens and their synagogues from assault and arson. Apparently, most of the incidents are perpetrated by the French Muslim population.

Last year, Roger Cukierman, president of CRIF, the Representative Council of the Jewish Organizations of France, asked his French countrymen and the French government to recognize the seriousness of the anti-Semitic acts targeting Jews in France. He wrote in *Le Monde* in February 2001, "The leaders of the country like to play down the anti-Jewish acts. They prefer to see these as ordinary violence. We are deluged with statistics designed to show that an attack against a synagogue is an act of violence and not anti-Semitism. Some Jews who have lost touch with reality like to buttress their personal status by turning a deaf ear and a blind eye to danger, in order to curry favor with the public consensus. The media like to give the widest exposure to voices critical of Israel and Jews, all the more so when these voices are Jewish. This way, media can't be charged with anti-Semitism or anti-Zionism. Judicial authorities don't like to mete out strong punishment for acts of anti-Jewish violence, even when the perpetrators are caught red-handed: a three-month suspended sentence or nothing for an attack on a Jewish place of worship, compared to a year in jail for burning a straw cottage in Corsica."

It is true that Mr. Cukierman, with whom I have had a correspondence, is currently opposed to a boycott, writing to me on April 8, 2002, "Things have changed in two ways. First, we have more and more anti-Semitic acts, clearly connected with the Middle East situation. We are fortunate that we have no death casualty. Secondly, the Prime Minister and the President have changed, at last, their attitude. They stopped minimizing and are now taking the situation seriously." I responded on April 15, "Silence never works. I understand your needs living in France, and I can appreciate your frustration and inability to respond the way people like me, living in a free, democratic country where anti-Semitism is at an all-time low, will respond."

There are those equally concerned with the protection of French Jews who join Mr. Cukierman in opposing a boycott at this time. So, in opposing a boycott, you are not alone. But your explanation and reasoning are badly flawed. What do you mean when you compare a call by Jews for a boycott against the French with the Nazi boycott against the Jews? Do you really believe all boycotts are the same? Did you oppose the boycott of South Africa in order to end apartheid? Did you oppose Martin Luther King's support of a boycott of segregated buses in Birmingham, Alabama, as well as a boycott of the white commercial establishments in that city?

I believe a boycott directed at the French government, until it apologizes for its ambassador's scurrilous comments, is in order. Those comments, still not repudiated by the government, when viewed in the context of the physical assaults on French Jews, convey gross hostility and indifference on the part of the French toward Jews in general.

I am convinced that your comments have given the French people and their government undeserved cover for their tolerance of anti-Semitic behavior and shamefully inadequate response to it.

I do hope that you will reconsider your defense of France, and if you do, convey it to the American and French public, as only you can.

All the best.

Sincerely,

Edward I. Koch

FEELING ALONE, AGAIN

THE GROWING UNEASE AMONG GERMANY'S JEWS

Alvin H. Rosenfeld

DURING A TWO-WEEK PERIOD in May 2002, I visited Germany to give a series of lectures on the Holocaust in Berlin, Leipzig, and Munich. In addition, I had intense conversations with an array of German academics, journalists, political figures, and others. I also met with Jews living in Germany to get an understanding of the country from their perspective. The situation of these Jews—their social and material well-being, the nature and vitality of their community lives, their sense of belonging or estrangement—is of particular interest, and I devoted a lot of time in all three of the cities I visited talking with Jews about these matters.

The very first thing one notices about Germany's Jews is their numbers, which have been steadily growing and may now be as high as one hundred thousand, or more than double what they had been a decade ago. This increase is owing in large part to Germany's willingness to absorb significant numbers of Jews from the former Soviet Union and other eastern-bloc countries. Government officials and others want their "Jewish fellow citizens," as they are commonly called, to feel at home in their new country, and they offer a range of benefits to ease their adjustment. In many respects, the process seems to be working. While still only a tiny fraction of the country's total population, the Jews and all things Jewish are highly visible. Indeed, it is not an exaggeration to say that the successful "return" of Jews to Germany and the "normalization" of German-Jewish ties have been high priorities for German political leaders for many years now.

The aim is clear: if Germany truly can attract sizable numbers of Jews to once again inhabit the country and sustain living Jewish communities within its borders, it will prove, to itself as well as to others, that the worst chapters of the country's past really are behind it. There are few things that Germans want more than to put the final seal on this shameful past and also few that they work at harder. Without denying German responsibility for the Nazi crimes, the country's leaders are determined to place the accent decidedly on the future, to integrate Germany within a larger European context, and to be recognized, at last, as a "normal" country.

The very striving to achieve such "normality," of course, is a sure sign that all is still far from actually *being* normal. Nor can Germany hope to become "normal" by a sheer act of national will or by extending even the most attractive package of material and social benefits to its new Jewish citizens. What is required to achieve such a goal is for these Jews to feel genuinely welcome and, if not yet fully "at home," then at least relatively at ease in a country that is free of overt anti-Semitic tendencies. Or, barring that—for anti-Semitism remains stubbornly alive among segments of the German population, as it does among Europeans at large—at least for Jews to feel confident that Germany's leaders will actively oppose those who try to promote anti-Semitic hatred. In short, German "normalization" is only achievable with the consent of the Jews.

My visit to Germany occurred at a time when assaults on Jews and Jewish institutions throughout Europe had reached a level of intensity that surpassed anything that had been seen on the continent since the end of World War II. France, in particular, has been the site of hundreds of such attacks, which have ranged from the burnings of synagogues to the stoning of Jewish school buses to assaults on individual Jews in their shops and on the streets. Anti-Semitic graffiti have become commonplace, and the vandalization and desecration of Jewish cemeteries are likewise all-too-familiar occurrences. And not only in France but in Belgium, Holland, Italy, Greece, Ukraine, Russia, and elsewhere. Accompanying these outrageous acts, and to some degree perhaps also inciting them, have been verbal attacks on Jews, and especially on the Jewish State. In general, European news coverage of the Israeli-Palestinian conflict has been more negative in its reporting on Israel than on the Palestinians. In addition, the media have been less than scrupulous in drawing distinctions between Israelis, whose military actions are often deplored in strong terms, and Jews in general. In certain European countries, movements are under way to boycott Israeli products and also Israeli scientists and scholars. And as the capstone of this new, harsh mood, which has been developing even as Israelis are being blown up by Palestinian suicide bombers, the right to "criticize" Israel is one to which European intellectuals, journalists, and political commentators have been laying eager claim.

Within this Europeanwide context of anti-Semitic and anti-Israel aggression, Germany has seemed to present a milder face than most. But shortly before my departure, I read a short article, released by the Jewish Telegraphic Agency, that was disturbing. Titled "German Jews Warn against Racism, Say Taboo on Anti-Semitism Is Gone," the article began as follows:

> BERLIN, May 13—Jewish leaders and politicians are condemning what they perceive as a growing anti-Semitic atmosphere in Germany.
>
> As the alarm was sounded, there was an attack on a Jewish site in the German capital that Jewish leaders said was motivated by anti-Semitism.
>
> "The mood here clearly has changed," said Paul Spiegel, head of the Central Council of Jews in Germany.
>
> "Anti-Semitism in Europe is worse than at any time since the Nazi era," Spiegel said in a recent interview. Nor is he alone in issuing such warnings.
>
> "Something seems to have changed in Germany," Foreign Minister Joshka Fischer told the *Frankfurter Allgemeine Zeitung* newspaper.
>
> "No one feels this more directly and more urgently than the German Jews," Fischer said. "They feel alone again, and that cannot be permitted to happen. Not in Germany."

Joseph ("Joshka") Fischer is a respected figure, as is Paul Spiegel, and their views are to be taken seriously. In traveling to Germany, therefore, I felt obliged to investigate the nature of the change that was worrying both of these men and to try to gauge how it was impacting on Germany's Jews. I also wanted to see if the German Foreign Minister would be joined by others who would speak out as openly as he on behalf of the Jews and against those whose words and deeds evidently were making them feel less than fully welcome.

My first stop was Berlin, Germany's new capital. Ever since the wall came down in 1989 and the western and eastern sectors of Berlin were reunited, the city has been rebuilding its urban face in bold and ambitious ways and now boasts a wealth of modernist and postmodernist architecture that is truly impressive. Prominent among the buildings in the former East Berlin is the New Synagogue on Oranienburgerstrasse. A large, strikingly ornate structure originally built in 1866 and almost totally destroyed during World War II, the building has been restored in more recent years, and its handsome domes and towers have been returned to their former elegance. Like much else in Germany that touches on Jewish life, though, there is an element of illusion in the New Synagogue's appearance, for while its facade is one of grandeur, the interior is largely a shell. A small group of Jews attempts to gather once a week to pray in a side room, but apart from this activity and programs sponsored on occasion by the Berlin Jewish community in other rooms, the Oranienburger Street synagogue is today mostly a museum, and, as such, a sad reminder of its former self.

Not far away is the newly opened Jewish Museum of Berlin. The creation of Daniel Libeskind, the building is singular in its conception and architecturally stunning. Justly praised as a work of genius, it exhibits absence as much as it does the history of German Jewry. After only a few minutes in its halls, one has the feel of being in a space that is simultaneously rich and empty, welcoming and disorienting. It was during my visit to Libeskind's museum that I began to glimpse some of the unease that Jews in Germany are experiencing these days. My guide, a well-established member of Berlin's Jewish community, expressed more than just her own apprehensions when she described the unanticipated introduction of anti-Semitic rhetoric into German political discourse. This kind of verbal aggression was new and unsettling, she explained, and to date it was not being forcefully opposed by the country's political leadership. Given what was happening to Jews and Jewish institutions in France and elsewhere in Europe, she went on, the Jews in Germany were beginning to grow anxious about their own situation, which suddenly seemed less secure than they had supposed.

To hear these words in Berlin's new Jewish Museum was troubling, for one aim of this place is to show how Jews have been rooted in German history and, until the catastrophe of the war years, had been feeling increasingly integrated into the country's life. Was this sense of wished-for security now, once again, coming undone?

An important article by Salomon Korn in the *Frankfurter Allgemeine Zeitung* of May 6, 2002, offered evidence that Jews were, in fact, beginning to feel a kind of isolation and insecurity that they had not known for years. Korn, the head of the Jewish community of Frankfurt, is also a prominent member of the Central Council of Jews in Germany. His article carries a disturbing title—*Ende der Schonzeit: Es gibt keinen neuen Antisemitismus—der vorhandene wird entlarvt*—which does not translate easily into English. One can render it as "The End of the No-Hunting Season: There Is No New Antisemitism—The One That Has Been with Us All

Along Is Now Out in the Open," or, perhaps, "Open Season for Anti-semites: There Is No New Antisemitism: The Existing One Is Now Dis-closed." However one takes Korn's title, it is unnerving and points to a troubled situation—among other things, reports within the German media that have been critical of Israel in ways that go beyond the norms of ob-jective news coverage. Many German Jews see such reporting as skewed by still-lingering biases, which have begun to make an appearance in Ger-man political and cultural life as well. Among other expressions, they have taken the odd form of declaring repeatedly and sometimes passionately that Germans have the right to "criticize" Israel. I refer to this phenome-non as "odd" because, like all other countries, Israel is hardly perfect and clearly is not above legitimate criticism. Moreover, Germans have not been shy to voice negative judgments of Israeli policies and actions and have been doing so for many years. Why, then, a public debate about a Ger-man "right" to engage Israel in a critical way?

Korn offers a brief but acute analysis of some of the things that may explain the current German preoccupation with Israel, and I will present his views shortly. First, though, consideration needs to be given to one of the figures at the center of this contentious debate—Jürgen Möllemann—whose high-profile political maneuverings in recent months have con-tributed much of the venom that accompanies public discussion about Israel within Germany.

As German politicians go, Mr. Möllemann, a deputy chairman of the small but politically strategic Free Democratic Party (FDP), is an unusual figure. The chairman of his party in the important state of North Rhine-Westphalia, he is also the long-serving head of the German-Arab Society and, in this capacity, a vocal lobbyist for Arab interests. For years a stri-dent critic of Israel—as far back as 1981, for instance, he accused Israel of employing "state terrorism" against the Palestinians—Möllemann has leveled especially bitter attacks on Ariel Sharon, whom he has denounced for, among other things, "trampling on international law." As if that were not enough, he recently has escalated his rhetoric against the Israelis to new levels of vituperation.

In a much-quoted comment on attacks within Israel by Palestinian sui-cide bombers, for example, Möllemann seemed to endorse the murder of Israeli civilians when he stated, "I, too, would resist, forcefully so, and not just in my own country but in the aggressor's." The comment drew no public censure from his party leadership, but it was denounced in strong terms by Michel Friedman, a vice chairman of the Central Coun-cil of Jews in Germany. In light of Möllemann's remarks, the FDP should distance itself from their deputy chairman, Friedman advised, if not drop him altogether. Möllemann, not one to shirk a public fight, responded by acknowledging that anti-Semites unfortunately do exist in Germany and that "hardly anyone makes them more popular than Mr. Sharon and, in Germany, Friedman, with his intolerant and malicious manner." Jews immediately recognized that in putting the blame for anti-Semitism on the Jews themselves and then complaining that he was being unfairly victimized by these same Jews, Möllemann was employing a tactic from the familiar repertoire of anti-Semitic clichés. Möllemann then proceeded to make a bad situation worse still by bringing into his parliamentary group a former Green Party politician, Jamal Karsli, who had accused the Israeli army of using "Nazi tactics" against the Palestinians. A Syrian-born citizen of Germany for the last twenty years or so, Karsli also pointed to a "Zionist lobby" that was exerting too much media control in Germany and, beyond that, to the nefarious workings of a worldwide Jewish conspiracy, which was powerful enough to cut down anyone it disliked.

Jews within Germany saw these developments as alarming and began to say as much in print. Paul Spiegel, the chairman of the Central Council of Jews in Germany, labeled Möllemann's perverse charge against impertinent Jews such as Friedman "the worst insult a political party has delivered in Germany since the Holocaust." Susanne Thaler, a Jewish member of the FDP and the head of the party's chapter in Berlin-Dahlem, announced that she was leaving the FDP and that others would soon follow. Michel Friedman stated that in all of his years in Germany, no experience had hurt him so much as this mean-spirited attack by Möllemann.

The earliest reactions to Möllemann and Karsli by Guido Westerwelle, the FDP chairman, however, were mild, almost to the point of being inaudible. Moreover, Westerwelle's reply to some of Möllemann's critics was that it was "shabby" of them to label those who criticized Israel as anti-Semites. "Surely it must be possible for friends to express criticism," Westwerwelle added. The FDP chief seemed to endorse Möllemann's populist appeal and even went on record as stating that he would personally welcome into the party those who, in the past, had voted for the far-right Republikaner Party (this would be roughly analogous to an American politician declaring that he welcomed the support of Ku Klux Klan members).

To some degree, these were obvious political maneuverings by both Möllemann and Westerwelle to heighten their party's appeal in the run-up to Germany's next national elections, scheduled for September 22, 2002. The FDP had not done well in the last election campaign, and something was needed to give the party a lift. Former kingmakers, they were edged out of power in 1998 by their rivals, the Greens, and now were looking for support among newly enfranchised Muslim voters, who might respond positively to Karsli's presence in the FDP and the openly aggressive stance towards Israel and the Jews that Möllemann represented. To reach a higher standing in the polls by appealing to some of the basest instincts of the German electorate, however, was to engage in a kind of dirty politics that Germany's mainstream parties had largely shied away from in the postwar period.

As proven by the examples of Jörg Haider in Austria, Jean-Marie Le Pen in France, and others elsewhere in Europe, anti-immigrant and anti-Semitic populism has its attractions, but its successes are purchased at a dangerously high price. Before long, German politicians denounced Möllemann's rough tactics and warned of the dangers to German democracy if anti-Semitism were to become instrumentalized as an acceptable political practice.

Pressure mounted on both Möllemann and Westerwelle to distance themselves from Jamal Karsli and do what was necessary to repair their party's now badly strained relations with the Central Council of Jews in Germany. After a short time, Karsli announced that he was stepping back from the FDP, and Möllemann offered public regrets for his words if, as he put it, they inadvertently offended the sensibilities of Germany's Jews.

But the damage had been done. This episode contributed to the anxieties of Germany's Jews. A poll released in June 2002 showed that 28 percent of the population at large and 40 percent of FDP members agreed with Möllemann's charge that Jews like Friedman were responsible for provoking German anti-Semitism. Other studies indicate that 15 to 20 percent of Germans hold anti-Semitic views and that a still larger number may harbor latent anti-Semitic feelings. While these figures may be comparable to those one can find elsewhere in Europe, they are nevertheless unsettling and, when exploited by German politicians for electoral gains, they point to the possibility of trouble ahead.

Salomon Korn signals the nature of such trouble in referring to the end of the "Schonzeit," or "no-hunting season," on Jews. This term became popularized in Germany in the mid-1980s at the time of another public debate about the German desire to "normalize" relations with Jews, this one triggered by a controversial play, *Garbage, the City, and Death,* by Rainer Werner Fassbinder. The play uses overtly anti-Semitic language in referring to the "Rich Jew," a character who is charged with shady financial manipulations in making lucrative real estate deals. While this character otherwise goes nameless in the play, it was widely recognized that Fassbinder was focusing his ire on Ignatz Bubis, a Frankfurt real estate developer and a powerful figure among Jews in Germany. Among the many questions debated at the time was this one: are Germans not free to "criticize" Jews if they see them as capitalist predators or otherwise as financially corrupt? Or are Jews to remain beyond the reach of moral judgment, as if special restrictions (a "Schonzeit") were in place to permanently protect them from such criticism?

Looking back, the debate in the mid-1980s now seems to be only a variant of a debate that is under way in Germany today. Both seem to spring from a German need or desire to "normalize" relations with Jews by focusing on perceived Jewish flaws or shortcomings—a "normalization" that is not attainable if the "special considerations" that Germans have afforded Jews ever since the Holocaust remain forever in place. Some of those involved in the debates that swirled around *Garbage, the City, and Death* saw such "special considerations" as tantamount to an unfair and unwanted taboo. And while they may have acknowledged that Fassbinder's play was bound to be offensive to Jews, it had the salutary effect of breaking this taboo, enabling people to freely speak their minds, thereby putting German-Jewish relations on a more "normal," or acceptable, plane.

In the latest effort to achieve such "normalization," the focus has shifted from "criticizing" questionable "Jewish" money dealing to "criticizing" questionable "Jewish" politics. The issue is now commonly posed in terms that are blunt and often have an edge to them: why should Germans not be permitted to criticize Israel without in turn being labeled anti-Semites?

As Korn tunes in to this debate, what he finds has much more to do with the inner struggles that many Germans continue to have with their complex identities than with the external realities of the Middle East conflict. The latter, he believes, is only a convenient site for Germans to deal with the "Jew," who represents for many "the darker sides of German history and of their own family history." Calling such a problematic figure an "Israeli" is a lot easier for most Germans than calling him a "Jew," a term that still causes "heart palpitations and anxieties," especially among the older generation. Yet the two—"Jew" and "Israeli"—have become blended within the German psyche, Korn believes, and by aggressively "criticizing" the latter, one can finally (and more safely) deal with the former. As Korn pursues the psychodynamics of this equation by looking at media coverage of the Israeli-Palestinian conflict, what he discovers is more than a little troubling.

The Israelis are ultimately transformed into "Nazis," the Palestinians into persecuted and murdered "Jews." In the repeatedly cited picture of the "beer-bellied Sharon" (was Helmut Kohl ever described in this way?), the stereotype of the ugly "Stürmer-Jew" finds its current Israeli-Jewish rebirth.

At this point, the German-Jewish and German-Israeli relation intersect to the point of total overlap. All Jews are assigned collective liability for any action of Israel against the Palestinians. On the basis of this circular "interior logic," anti-Semitism can now, under the appearance of legitimacy, unburden itself, sometimes more subtly, at other times more openly. The Israeli military actions remain a temptation for Germans to relieve themselves of their historical burden of guilt, and also the unease toward Jews that they continue to feel, by the oblique means of engaging in "legitimate" criticism of Israel.

What all of this gets down to is something like the following: until recently, Jews within Germany were largely perceived in the role of victim, which meant that non-Jewish Germans were cast in the unenviable role of being victimizers. Jews typically have been seen as admonitory figures, reminding Germans about what had gone horribly wrong in their country in the past and warning them about what might still go wrong in the future. By contrast, non-Jewish Germans have felt compelled to see themselves as being, if not eternally burdened with guilt, then at least on long-term moral probation. This internal drama, devised chiefly by Germans themselves although often attributed to Jews, is full of unwanted tensions and, not surprisingly, has proven to be increasingly intolerable for many. The numerous "debates" that periodically take place in Germany about the Nazi Holocaust, anti-Semitism, and related matters testify to the unease that many Germans continue to feel about their own identities vis-à-vis those of Jews. Within this context, the most recent of these debates, focusing on the German right to "criticize" Israel, might be understood as an effort to break free of these roles by changing the terms of this story. According to the new script, if the Israelis/Jews can be regarded as the "new Nazis" and the Palestinians as the "new Jews," then the Holocaust, for all of its horrors, is not such a singular event and, as the writer Martin Walser famously put it a few years ago, should not be eternally held over the heads of Germans as a kind of "moral cudgel." For as bad as Nazi treatment of the Jews was during the Second World War—and responsible people in Germany do not deny that it was bad indeed—Israeli/Jewish treatment of the Palestinians shows that Jews can be victimizers, too.

Korn probably represents the thinking of many Jews in Germany when he views German "criticism" of Israel along these lines as little more than the old hostility expressed in new terms. Far from advancing "normalization," the current situation only serves to further burden German-Jewish relations, so much so that Korn is moved to raise a question that is as inevitable as it is painful: "In the face of an anti-Semitism in Germany and in Europe that becomes more manifest in the course of the conflict in the

Middle East, the old sword-of-Damocles question once again hangs over the heads of Jews residing in this country: did the Jews make the right choice when they chose to remain in Germany?"

Joshka Fischer, Germany's Foreign Minister, found Salomon Korn's troubling question serious enough to respond to it almost immediately. In an important article published in the *Frankfurter Allgemeine Zeitung* of May 11, 2002, Fischer lamented the silence that greeted Möllemann's "unspeakable statements" in support of the Palestinian terrorist bomb attacks against Israel: "There was no national outcry, no resignation, nothing of the kind." What there has been instead, as Germany's Jews perceive it, is the unfolding of a new and unfriendly mood. "Something seems to have changed in Germany," Fischer notes, and German Jews "feel alone, again, . . . That ought not to be so. Not in Germany."

Among his other reasons for writing, Fischer meant to tell his Jewish countrymen that they are not alone. "Can we criticize Israel?" Fischer asks. "Yes," he answers, but not if by doing so one is only devising a new means to address a long-standing and difficult German identity question. Rather, "criticism is possible only on the firm foundation of indelible solidarity" with the Jewish State. Möllemann and those who have supported him, however, are far from exhibiting such solidarity. In fact, they are doing something else, something that has "turned the descendants of the victims into perpetrators, believing this could salve one's conscience. But this is a dangerous misconception that, under the slogan of presumed 'normalization,' can end only in the abyss of antisemitism."

Fischer well understands the growing anxieties of German Jews in the face of such maneuverings. If "such an attentive and sensitive observer of German-Jewish relations as Salomon Korn" no longer "feels secure in our democracy," he remarks, then the "credibility of German democracy" is put into question. That simply must not be permitted to happen. As Fischer argues, "The extent to which we succeed in supporting and promoting the life and well-being of Jewish communities in Germany is also a yardstick of our ability to create an open and tolerant society. For that reason, each and every instance of antisemitism is not only a threat to Jews in Germany, but also to our society and democracy as a whole." Fischer recognizes that the stakes are high in this new German debate about Israel, and he is forthright in affirming German support of Israel and warning against those who would use ill-conceived "criticism" to "release Germany from responsibility for its history. One should not even attempt that, for it will end in disaster."

Others who have issued warnings of an incipient anti-Semitism have tended to speak the language of politics alone and have shown little sympathy or understanding of the position articulated by Salomon Korn and other Jewish voices. Thus, Thomas Schmid, a political commentator for the *Frankfurter Allgemeine Zeitung* and not a supporter of the FDP's vice chairman's tactics, nonetheless saw some good in what Mr. Möllemann was up to. In an article in the *FAZ* called "Breaking an Old Taboo," Schmid wrote that public criticism of Israeli policies had a salutary effect, for it helped to break an artificial and increasingly uncomfortable silence. In breaking this "taboo," Möllemann and others like him were giving voice to the desire of many who would like to put the past behind them and "think, feel, and live solely in terms of Germany's postwar history." And "that is progress."

Not everyone agrees. The journalist and filmmaker Richard Chaim Schneider, for instance, takes strong issue with the notion that any "progress" has been made or taboos broken as a result of Möllemann's attacks on Sharon and Friedman and the new debate on anti-Semitism that has followed. In a revealing article of his own, published in the Berlin newspaper *Der Tagesspiegel* on May 25, 2002, Schneider notes that for at least the last fifteen years, no one in Germany has adhered to any imposed restrictions on criticizing Israel. The language of taboo has been self-produced by Germans themselves against "the background of German culpability" for the Nazi crimes against the Jews. By leveling harsh "criticism" against the Israelis/Jews today, "the FDP seems to have found a mouthpiece for the disposal of its own history."

Schneider is seriously troubled by these developments and even goes so far as to state that they constitute a "paradigm shift . . . that will cause the Jewish community great trouble."

By justifying terror attacks within Israel and employing old anti-Semitic clichés for political purposes, Möllemann, Karsli, and their supporters have broken not so much an old and unwanted taboo but a former consensus within German political culture against the instrumentalization of anti-Semitism. In the face of this new situation, Jews living in Germany are beginning to wonder if they really can find a permanent home in Germany or if instead they should begin to seriously think about "packing their bags."

The metaphor of the "packed bags" is a familiar one in German-Jewish parlance and, as Schneider notes, has undergone significant change over the years. Jews of his father's generation—many of them Holocaust survivors—often thought of themselves as residing in Germany only temporarily or on conditional terms. They would remain as long as conditions were hospitable, but with their bags packed in case things changed for the worse and they had to flee.

The sons and daughters of this older generation have been in the process of shedding this mentality. In fact, some are likely to see themselves not just as "Jews residing in Germany" but, increasingly, as "German Jews," and they could put away the metaphorical suitcases that their parents had packed. One of the crucial sources of this emerging confidence among younger Jews has been memory. And not only Jewish memory but "primarily Germans' remembrance of the Nazi period and the responsibilities that accompanied it." This confidence has now been badly shaken, Schneider concludes. For with the introduction of anti-Semitic language into politics, the premises undergirding the permanence of Jewish life in Germany have been put into question.

It is not possible at this time to know how many German Jews share this dire analysis. The German-Jewish writer Ralph Giordano is quoted in *Der Spiegel* as stating that "many Jews are already at the point of 'packing their suitcases'." He is convinced that a "firm foundation for anti-semitism exists" in Germany and that its exploitation by Möllemann, with support from Westerwelle, is "changing the face of the Republic." Otto Romberg, the founder and editor of *Tribüne*, a journal dedicated to advancing German-Jewish understanding, wonders if his efforts over the years to foster constructive dialogue have not been in vain. The Berlin Rabbi Dr. Chaim Z. Rozwaski sees these tendencies as already out in the open, and he warns that if something is not done soon to check them, Jews in Germany will soon need to ask themselves, "What am I doing here?" Other Jewish voices could be added to those already cited above, all of them displaying similar feelings of outrage and worry.

Since these matters are still unfolding, it is not easy to put them in perspective and know for certain what they might signify for Germany and its Jews in the period ahead. Michael Brenner, a professor at the university in Munich, explains that a certain kind of anti-Semitism can exist even in the absence of anti-Semites. Or at least of old-style anti-Semites, those who would openly declare, without embarrassment or inhibition, "I just don't like Jews." No one in Germany today, apart from those in hard-core neo-Nazi groups, is apt to speak in such terms. However, there are people in public life who may not think of themselves as anti-Semites but who have no reservations about drawing on the traditional storehouse of anti-Semitic accusations or otherwise using code words that refer to Jews negatively, even if sometimes covertly or obliquely.

Unless present conditions get appreciably worse, it is doubtful that very many Jews living in Germany will actually pack their bags and leave the country. The debates discussed in this essay are serious ones, and there is no doubt that they are symptomatic of a mood swing within segments of

German society. And yet, while public discourse about Israel, the Jews, and anti-Semitism is changing, policy is not. There is much discussion about the dropping of "taboos" and the right to "criticize" Israel, but to date Germany remains second only to America in its support of Israel; and, from all one can see, this support is likely to continue, at least in the short term. Germany also has clear laws against the public advocacy of anti-Semitism and the incitement and execution of anti-Semitic deeds. Obviously, these laws are not enforceable against whatever it is that people may privately think and feel about Jews, but they do prevent such feelings from giving rise to organized anti-Jewish hostility. In both of these respects, Germany's record not only compares favorably to that of other European countries but in some notable respects surpasses it.

And yet Jews living in Germany do have cause for concern. In general, politics in Europe have been drifting to the right, and populist, racist, anti-immigrant feelings are becoming more intense. So is anti-Americanism, a complex set of passions that some observers believe may be a cover for anti-Semitism. Seen in these terms, the high visibility given to Jews and things Jewish within Germany in recent years may have less to do with any genuine interest in Jewish culture than with the need to maintain a kind of anti-anti-Semitism. If the latter begins to erode, the place of Jews within Germany may become less secure.

Something similar might be said as well for German support of Israel. The bedrock of such support is the special obligation that German governments have felt toward the Jewish State as a result of the country's historical and moral responsibility for the Nazi crimes against the Jews. Of late, though, there are signs that this sense of responsibility may be weakening at the popular level. German public opinion, like that in other European countries, is undergoing a change that does not favor Israel. According to poll findings released in April 2002 by the Pew Foundation, for instance, only 24 percent of Germans say they feel sympathy for Israel, whereas 26 percent express sympathy for the Palestinians (these figures contrast sharply with sentiments expressed by Americans, where some 41 percent say that they sympathize with Israel and only 13 percent side with the Palestinians). Moreover, among highly educated Germans, 40 percent back the Palestinians, a significant change from the past that, if continued, may challenge Germany's traditional support for Israel in the Middle East conflict. If German "criticism" of Israel grows and intensifies, there may over time be consequences for German foreign policy that will make Germany's Jews even more uneasy.

The most visible sign of this uneasiness was made clear to me towards the end of my visit in Berlin. It was Shabbat, and I went with a German friend to the synagogue on Fraenkeluferstrasse, in the Kreuzberg section of the city. As is the case virtually everywhere in Europe, we first passed through a police line (this one reinforced by plainclothes security agents) before entering, a procedure that is now routine and widely accepted as "normal." What struck me as decidedly abnormal was something else—clear signs of a wall going up around the synagogue. When I turned to my friend and asked him what *that* was about, he told me there have been a couple of attacks against this synagogue, one involving a firebomb, and that a wall was deemed necessary to protect the synagogue and the Jews praying within it.

The irony of this situation was suddenly all too painful. Here I was in Berlin, the capital of the new Germany and a city that had suffered decades of division marked by a wall. With the fall of the wall in 1989 and the unification of Germany shortly thereafter, the Berlin Republic would come into its own as an enlarged, free, and democratic country. But while Germans were now moving towards "normalizing" their condition, the Jews living among them were beginning to feel increasingly uneasy, especially as they became party to the torturous confrontation that Germans were having with their own history, an encounter that cannot fail to implicate the complex dynamics of anti-Semitism.

It would be a fine thing if anti-Semitism could be confined to historical discussions alone, but reality, sadly, dictates otherwise. In 1998, German authorities recognized a rise in anti-Semitism, and in the fall of 2000 attacks against Jews and Jewish institutions grew more violent as racist and anti-immigrant assaults in general escalated. There were attacks against synagogues in several German cities (Düsseldorf, Essen, Halle, and Berlin); a bombing at a Düsseldorf train station that apparently targeted a group of Ukrainian Jews; and the desecration of numerous Jewish cemeteries. Despite these occurrences and a few similar incidents more recently, though, the present condition of Germany's Jews does not appear to be seriously endangered. And yet the more I think about my time in the country and the new mood that is developing there, the more I come back to my Shabbat morning visit in Kreuzberg. One can get used to entering a synagogue by passing through police lines, it is true, and even be grateful for the presence of the police, but whatever else such protection may signify, one should not mistake it as being "normal," for it is anything but that.

A dozen years ago, an infamous wall came down in Berlin, providing the people of Germany with immense opportunities for bettering their situation. Today another wall is going up, and not only in Berlin/Kreuzberg. It separates and restricts and imposes on the people it is meant to protect a special and unenviable status. It is this increasingly uneasy situation that moved Salomon Korn to raise the troubling question: "Was it right for the Jews to remain in Germany?" I close by citing Joshka Fischer's reply to Korn, a reply meant as a challenge to the German public at large: "The ease or difficulty with which our Jewish compatriots are able to answer yes to this question depends crucially on whether they can live perfectly 'normally' as Jews in Germany, and as Germans."

The present state of German-Jewish relations, exacerbated as it has become by the developments recounted in these pages, right now renders any positive answer to this question uncertain.

POETRY

ALLEN GINSBERG FORGIVES EZRA POUND ON BEHALF OF THE JEWS

Rodger Kamenetz

This is something I was too shy to ask you in that interview:
Was it arrogance, your public relations brilliance
some deep desire to heal the split in American poesy . . .
a rascally fuck you to all the rabbis you never loved
the synagogue hens, the shalt nots you burst one by one—
or was it that his Cantos gave you permission
to empty your battered mind into the walls of verse
that you felt a kinship and personal debt?

You called his work a graph of the American mind
so that whatever was in that mind—Dolmetch's lute,
a fine eye gathering fire, Duccio, Rothschild and Jewsevelt,
all poured into a cracked vase bleeding syrup and lye.
Obscurities like dust blowing across the page,
raw jokes, fits of sweetness, Chinese characters, the Doge of Venice
dull history Adams and Jefferson, ledgers and correspondence,
Yeats in his tower, a "peacock in the proide of his oye"—
Irish black Yiddish vaudeville routines,
exact details with small significance:
Vasco da Gama wore striped pants—
and then, rising out of the mutter and ripple of mind:

an upturned nipple, bronze in the light
—the light Pound saw and made us see—
so that you Allen Ginsberg, the biggest Jew in po bizness
would hunt him down in Venice to plant a kiss on his cheek.

He was by then a broken man besieged.
"We get hippies" his Olga said.
One pitched a tent in the garden, she ran him off with a hose.
Journalists rang the bell, "announcing they will tell both sides.
What do they think we are? Ezra Pound is no pancake."

You came in the summer of '67,
chanting Hare Krishna outside his window
back from India, Morocco, Japan
another stop on your wisdom journey:
Martin Buber, Jerusalem's sage,
and your first Tibetan teacher, Dudjom Rinpoche.
Eyeing your hippie entourage, Olga asked,
"Would you like to wash your hands?"
But you said, "Do you people need any money?"
Olga thought you "a big lovable dog
who gives you a great slovenly kiss
and gets lots of hair all over you."

Dog Jew, hairy Jew.—Allen, who sent you?
Did you stop first in Rome for Primo Levi's blessing
whose hands trembled in Birkenau?
Did you sing hare krishna outside Paul Celan's window
before he jumped in the Seine
or say kaddish for his mother, murdered by men
who also had theories about economics and race?
Was there a depth of kindness in your public relations?
Were you able to hold not only forgiveness
but the knowledge of all that needed forgiving?

You met again that fall, at the Cici restaurant in Venice.
You in dark glasses, rich Adamic beard,
Pound's thin aged face, wisps of white hair.
Across the table you asked to say,
"more than a few words."

You did most of the talking, Pound in his silence and regret.
Then pausing in the yakety yak of your eternal sentences,
you asked, "Am I making sense?"
To which Pound said, Yes, and then mumbled
"but my poems don't make sense."

"Any good I've done has been spoiled by bad intentions."

And then very slowly, with emphasis
"But the worst mistake I made was
that *stupid suburban* prejudice
of anti-Semitism."

So Pound half-confessed to a bearded Jew,
for a Jew he saw in you, not a Buddhist
with the Jewish fire and sweetness and the eagerness to explain

From the time you heard Blake's voice in Harlem
you butt your head against the Hebrew God
until Buddha lifted your prophet's mantle—
when Rinpoche told you,
"If you see something horrible, don't cling to it.
If you see something beautiful, don't cling to it."

You told Pound, "I come to you as a Buddhist Jew."
Fair enough. He shouldn't think himself
forgiven by the other kind.

Or was it Martin Buber who sent you
when he told you to forget
the voices of angels and demons.
"Our business is with the human."

Pound learned that in the iron cage,
you in the asylum.
Celan knew it, but couldn't live with it.
Primo Levi knew it but let go of the rope.

Whoever sent you, Jew or Tibetan,
when Ezra confessed you forgave.

"Do you accept my blessing?" you said.
Pound, "I do."

But a year later, outside a McDonald's,
(strange American life)
Pound shuffled off into the woods.
Laughlin found him muttering,
"Why don't you just discard me here?"

Now in the suburbs of Elysium,
Ezra Pound, wander as you will
past Big Mac wrappers and a few extra fries.
Go into the dark woods where Dante roamed
and hear once again the clear sweet voices
that drove you to make a beautiful thing.

Or crack your pot against the stone of time.

And you Allen Ginsberg, in the land of 10,000 Buddhas
or in the simple heaven of your mothers and fathers
or raw bone under the earth,
       tell me, which is it now—

"If you see something beautiful, don't cling to it?"
Or is our business with the human after all?

MIRIAM'S SEDERS

Enid Dame

1

I strolled into history
surrounded by family:
famous brothers, nervous parents, wrangling gangs of cousins,
the old uncle's bones in a box.
Our God stolen out of Egypt
under the slaveowners' noses.
(A few women took goddess statues secretly—
you'll never find this written anywhere.
Some even took cats.)

On the desert
we cemented our relationship
with the God we never saw—
a bit like learning to lean against the air.
If you do it correctly, you'll never fall
spinning, dizzy, into inner space,
while your body collapses like a limp tent around you.
No, you'll learn how to pick up your bags
and keep moving.

I was a gutsy kid,
a bold girl.
I wore my knowledge
not like a face painted on,
but like the movement
shaping itself to my dance.
I strode through the world in large steps
banging my timbrel
never thinking how others saw me.

In those days,
I could do anything.
I wrote my mother back into our story.
I made the second wedding, midwifed
the birth the basket the royal adoption.
I wrote the music
that made the bricks finally crumble
the walls we'd built thick split
letting in a few spurts of sky,
tunnel enough
for our God to slide through.

(Our God who never put on physical clothes:
never a woman never a cat never water, or rock.
Our God who only spoke to brothers.)

On the desert we became a Nation.
Our newly freed men found women's music troubling.
We were told to dim down our batteries,
to let our songs loose only in locked rooms
as if they were bad-smelling birds.

I hurled words like stones
at the brick-closed wall of faces.
I threw back my hair and shouted at God,
who'd never seemed more like a brother.

2.
Today at thousands of feasts,
families assemble.
Doors are cracked open even in dangerous neighborhoods.
The prophet strides in he sips majestically

But I'm already there in the chair in the corner:
the unmarried sister the widow
the strange aunt nobody notices.

I'm not the good son who knows all the answers
I'm not the bad son who storms out of the room
    leaving a curse like a stain on his mother's upholstery
I'm not the simple son who only likes the drama, the dessert
or the baby son who drowsily perceives everything
    through closed eyes.

I'm nowhere at all in this story!

No, that's all wrong.
Let me try that again:

I am the good girl the smart one, the whiz kid
I am the bad girl tromping on feet, screaming to get attention
I am the simple girl who only likes music and the sway of her
body
    the baby girl absorbing the ritual through her pores.

I am like everyone else in the room.
We are all, all the children in the story.
A nation of children sits down at the tables
for the time it takes to revisit the story,
which changes as we move through our lives,
which changes us as we move through it together.
No two tellings are ever alike.

3.
So let me tell the story my own way.
Tonight will be different from all other nights.
Today I will sit down between my brothers.
We will sing loud songs to each other.
I will beat out the rhythm on the tabletop.
Moses will sing the melody sweetly off-key.
Aaron will spill red wine across the tablecloth.
Mother will quickly blanket it with salt.

We will laugh and watch the good salt do its work,
sucking the hurt out of the wound.

THE LATE YEAR

Marge Piercy

I like Rosh Hashona late,
when the leaves are half burnt
umber and scarlet, when sunset
marks the horizon with slow fire
and the black silhouettes
of migrating birds perch
on the wires davening.

I like Rosh Hashona late
when all living are counting
their days toward death
or sleep or the putting by
of what will sustain them—
when the cold whose tendrils
translucent as a jellyfish

and with a hidden sting
just brush our faces
at twilight. The threat
of frost, a premonition
of warning, a whisper
whose words we cannot
yet decipher, but will.

I repent better in the waning
season when the blood
runs swiftly and all creatures
look keenly about them
for quickening danger.
Then I study the rockface
of my life, its granite pitted

and pocked and pickaxed
eroded by the sun and
the wind and the rain—
my rock emerging
from the veil of greenery
to be mapped, to be
examined, to be judged.

VILLANELLE: IS BUTTER CHURNED THESE DAYS, IS LOVE DENIED?

Leo Haber

Is butter churned these days, is love denied?
Is wax removed from ears, is hate possessed?
My soul still yearns for Thee, my God, my guide.

All waves still wash the shore, my child, my pride.
Does ten divide by three, is greed impressed?
Is butter churned these days, is love denied?

The sun is up at dawn, my dear, my bride.
Are sickly bodies cupped, are sins confessed?
My soul still yearns for Thee, my God, my guide.

The moon waxes and wanes, no law defied.
Are swords still made of steel, are hearts distressed?
Is butter churned these days, is love denied?

If God is dead because six million died,
Are heavens numbered seven, angels a jest?
My soul still yearns for Thee, my God, my guide.

The world turns, the smallest quark espied,
The final night approaching, fear repressed,
Is butter churned these days, is love denied?
My soul still yearns for Thee, my God, my guide.

WHAT THE RETURNING RAVEN SAID

Leo Haber

And [Noah] sent forth the raven, and the raven went out
[from the ark] and returned, went out and returned. . . .

Genesis 8:7

Six months in the ark with all creation, nested
in giant rooms fit for elephants, yet little
or no flying space within infested
walls, stinking hovels, yearning for brittle
boughs shuddering with fear in the ceaseless rain,
the blackened sky a magnet of delight,
pregnant clouds a pulsing target, I gain
the other side, the sun, my life, flight.

Noah needs a vineyard, the heady drink
that is his consolation. Shem requires
a yeshiva's claustrophobic walls. The wife

of Japheth longs for dressing rooms, the wink
of love, beauty's nest. My wing desires
a world beyond the ark, beyond the knife.

YIDDISH

I. Century

I was born in the land of Yiddish,
a place where nouns and verbs,
like its soups and breads,
were of mixed origins.
How I left, and when, I do not remember.
I seemed to have leapt from the mother country
into a land full of children speaking
Ringolivio, Skelly, and punch ball.
I became a citizen of English.

Years later I visited the holy land
and found *mishpocheh* from the *shtetl* of Pultusk.
I was smothered with embraces
as warm and comforting as *cholent*.
I could not speak Hebrew;
they could not speak English,
and as though I had never been away,
I returned to the land of Yiddish.

TO DREAM IN HEBREW

Leslie Cohen

I never dreamed I'd learn to dream in Hebrew
A tongue so strange its "hello" means "goodbye!"
Yet my middle-of-the-nighttime conversations
Resound with *bakashah, todah,* and *dai.*
I never dreamed I'd learn to dream in Hebrew
A tongue so turned around it says "night-good!"
Yet *yofi* squirts from out of my unconscious
As El Al touches safely down at **Lod.**
I never dreamed I'd learn to dream in Hebrew
A gendered tongue where breasts are masculine!

VEINED-GARDEN

Valerie Wohlfeld

Before he was pure, Adam was impure.
Birth-bed silt,
he and Lilith a muddy pair,
each given a tail, some said.

Before Eve was impure, she was pure.
Eve with no mother but the cold-boned rib.
Skin of the apple, sweet compote in her teeth,
red as the heart's hibiscus-colored veined-garden.

Lilith came out of dust, Eve out of bone.
Holding the ivory rib, cupping the handful of dirt:
satiated in unspeakable name
as others were on remnants of jewel-red fruit.

FICTION

EMPTY CHAIRS

Talia Carner

I WAS TEN YEARS OLD, and my mother was the class mother on a one-day trip to Jerusalem when Miriam got her first period.

My mom didn't tell me. Miriam did, a couple of days later, assuming that my mom had. In the separate building that housed the school lavatory, Miriam also wanted to show me the special belt her mother had bought her to hold the pads, which she was supposed to wash every day, but the whole thing was just too gross. I fled.

All through the next two years, weird and mysterious things were happening around Miriam. Not awesome, but rather repulsive, like the curious importance she gave the gigantic mounds that filled the front of her dress, and her basking in the boys' attention, which I so dreaded.

The boys' after-school hangout had shifted from the schoolyard to the front of Miriam's four-story apartment building, where the massive branches of an aged sycamore offered a chance to climb up closer to Miriam's perch on the third floor. On my daily trek with Sarah, Bella, and Debbie to the private library off Allenby Street, where, for a monthly fee, we took out three books each day, we would spot Miriam at her window. Her pretty face with warm brown eyes was framed by light brown curls, and she smiled easily, although I didn't always see a reason for the smile. If the boys weren't around, Miriam walked with us to the library, although she rarely even read the one book a week from the school library, while the four of us would often finish a book on our walk back home.

For a long time, Miriam wasn't even the subject of discussion among us four. Whatever was taking place around her dwelled in the periphery of my consciousness, but had I been interested, I wouldn't have known what questions to ask. My three friends had begun to bud, and Debbie's mother badgered her not to stoop and to let her buy her a bra. We had perused the drawings in the midwifing book my grandmother had brought from Russia in 1920 and had been horrified to discover what we really had "down there." Yet none of it had anything to do with the way Miriam walked about pushing out her large breasts, or with the boys, mostly a head shorter than she, sniggering or just acting crazy, punching and hitting one another just to show off, but looking like idiots.

In fifth grade, on the nurse's day off, I tore a ligament in my ankle. I sat in class, whimpering, until the teacher could no longer ignore it and sent Miriam with me to the Red Star of David emergency room. I couldn't hobble the four blocks, so Miriam carried me on her back. After the doctor bandaged my leg and ordered home rest, she carried me uphill on Mazeh Street all the way home. Her sweat was tangy and full-bodied, like an adult's.

A couple of weeks later, when she invited me to come to her home to play, it would have been rotten of me to refuse.

Miriam's mother had blue numbers tattooed on her forearm. She was a handsome woman, older than everyone else's mom, her hair coiffed, her white dress tailored, and she smelled clean in the heat of summer. She was so different from my Israeli-born mom who, like me, wore her dark hair in a waist-long braid, walked around in blue shorts and biblical sandals, and who favored industrial soap for our bedtime shower.

Miriam's mother said something in German to Miriam, and Miriam led me to their dining room. Their furniture—heavy, dark, and smelling of lemon and wax—was the kind salvaged from Europe. The inlaid-wood table was so shiny that I could see my reflection in it. Miriam's mother gave us cloth napkins trimmed in lace and served us tea in a silver set and home-baked butter cookies that were the best I had ever tasted.

After her mother had left the room, Miriam pointed to the corpulent buffet, made of the same shiny, grainy wood as the dining table. Above it hung a framed beveled mirror. On top of the buffet were two framed photographs, one of a woman with a boy and a girl, and one of a man with a younger set of a boy and a girl. Although the boys in both pictures wore knee-long dark pants held up with suspenders and their hair was plastered to their foreheads as if still wet, they weren't the same boy. The older girl was blonde. The younger one was just a toddler, with a huge bow on top of her brown hair. Her pretty eyes looking into the camera reminded me of Miriam's.

"My parents' families before the war," Miriam whispered.

My stomach lurched as it caught the implication. I had seen photographs of Jews being rounded up, of cattle cars, of barbed wire, of gas chambers. Bella's dad from Poland and Debbie's mom from Romania had lived through the Holocaust. But the photos they had in their homes were of young people and grown-ups, not of little kids.

Miriam went on. "Then my parents met and made me. To make up for the kids they'd lost."

I swallowed. I thought it wasn't polite to keep staring at the dead children.

We moved to her corner room, which had large windows and was filled with dolls with real clothes and a cabinet with as many board games as a store. The pink bedspread matched the curtains. As I explored Miriam's treasures, I couldn't take my mind off her four siblings. Dead siblings she had never met. I thought it must be very sad to live in this home. I tried to imagine that my sister had been born before me and had been gassed or hurled against a wall, her scalp smashed. It made me want to cry.

Otherwise, the whole afternoon was a drag. I beat Miriam easily in the board games. We practiced our flute lessons, and she was okay, but got bored. When playing with dolls, she agreed too quickly with my plots, never offering a new idea. Miriam was so unlike Sarah, Bella, and Debbie, with whom I could stage plays and then serialize them for weeks. It was like playing alone, so I finally just ignored her as she sat cross-legged on her bed and watched me dress and undress her dolls while I made up stories.

———— o ————

The boys' interest in Miriam climbed up a notch when she started showing them her bra. One by one, she took them behind the lavatory. I knew about it because she told me and once even asked whether I, too, wanted to see it. I was incredulous at her stupidity. I didn't want to laugh at her because of her dead siblings and how sad it was to have to make up for their loss, but neither did I want to have anything to do with her.

In March, when she turned twelve, her mother sent pretty hand-written invitations to her Bat-Mitzvah the following Tuesday. It was to be a small dinner for Miriam's "best friends."

Tuesday was a school day, but since it was the day when, during Creation, God had said twice that the day had been "good," it was all right to have a party. But I was mortified to be considered among Miriam's best friends. Sarah, Bella, or Debbie surely weren't her friends, and I kept the invitation a secret. They no longer allowed Miriam to walk with us to the library, because the boys would follow and would taunt us. Besides, there was something contaminating about associating with Miriam. People might think that I, too, was the kind of girl who showed the boys my bra, or would when I needed one, that is. I had discovered that the females in my family all wore "falsies," and with the twin almonds I was growing, I wasn't about to break this tradition.

I wondered who were the other girls who had been invited and figured that they must be the ones living behind Miriam's building in the next block, which was zoned for the other neighborhood school. I wished I hadn't been invited. I felt protected in the virtuous company of Sarah, Bella, and Debbie, who thought boys were disgusting. I was embarrassed that these other girls might think I was really Miriam's friend and had anything in common with her. But after the trip on Miriam's back to the emergency room, I couldn't refuse the invitation. I thought about those butter cookies.

My mom gave me money for a set of three pretty handkerchiefs folded in a flat cardboard box under clear plastic. I drew a picture of Miriam carrying me on her back. I rhymed birthday wishes that all her dreams would come true so she wouldn't be blue. I starched and ironed my lemon-colored organza dress with the black velvet bow. Along with my patent leather mary-jane shoes and white socks, no one would think I wore a bra or had dirty pads. No one would think that I took boys behind the lavatory to show them anything.

Miriam was dressed in a red Tyrolean dress, the section below her chest criss-crossed with a thin cord. The cloth of a white blouse underneath was gathered on top but embarrassingly stretched wide over her ample breasts. Below the full, embroidered skirt, the one-inch heels did nothing to make her look taller than wider.

I felt like a fraud as I handed her the present and nodded politely to her mother. I wanted to find the opportunity to explain that this was a mistake because I wasn't Miriam's "best friend," or even "a friend." But I took a glimpse of the dining room and felt as if I had stepped into a fairy tale.

The dining room table was open to its full length and covered with a white tablecloth. It was set with silver candelabra and silver finger bowls and silver napkin holders and multiples of silver forks, knives, and spoons. There was a bouquet of red roses in the center. The first course was already waiting in each of the plates, half a grapefruit sectioned and topped with a cherry. On a teacart, crystal glasses of lemonade with mint leaves were ready. Another flower arrangement sat on the buffet, where silver serving platters awaited the food. The smells coming from the kitchen were foreign and delicious and made saliva gather in my mouth.

The pictures of the dead children remained in their spots, untouched, old-world in their clothes and hair, the sepia-color pinning them to those bad times less than twenty years earlier, when the Nazis exterminated Jews like cockroaches.

Miriam's father, a big man with a broad face and wisps of white hair neatly combed back, and kind brown eyes like Miriam's, came in and carefully placed the needle of a gramophone on the record. Classical notes poured into the room, the kind of late night radio music that old people went to concerts of, but I had never met anyone who actually played it at home.

I tugged at the black velvet bow of my dress and waited. Miriam's mother gave me a glass of lemonade and invited me to sit down on the sofa in the adjacent living room whose two open double doors combined the two rooms into one. I obeyed, and Miriam came to sit next to me. We didn't speak. Her father said something in German, and she replied, her tone polite like to a teacher, so unlike the easy tone I used at home. I remained seated, sipping my lemonade and examining a glass cabinet that contained magnificent porcelain figurines. Their faces were angelic, with tiny, pointed noses, their hands graceful, the tilts of their necks delicate. I was awed by the beautiful, flowing dresses with porcelain lace petticoats. And there were princes wooing the princesses, kneeling or striking princely poses, always with rapture in their eyes. I put down my empty glass on the coaster on the side table, rose up, and stood fixated in front of the display.

"This princess went out to the woods, following the enchanting sound of gurgling water," I said, pointing at two of the figures. "She's sitting by the spring and she doesn't know that the shepherd who walks down the lane is really a cursed prince. When the wizard who hates him will try to also cast a spell on the princess, this dog will bark to alert the prince, and the prince will draw his sword and fight the wizard—"

"Then the dog will pee on her shoes," Miriam added.

I was mortified. I couldn't bear the thought of ruining that delicate stroke of muted red on the tiny feet. "No. She has satin shoes." I tried another story, pointing to other figurines. "This princess with the baby blue dress went to the ball. The prince wants to know which of the many princesses is the kindest so he can take her hand in marriage. With that cape, he dresses up like one of the musicians. As he strolls outside with his mandolin, the princess, so in love with his music, follows him to the palace garden—"

"There's no garden."

"Pretend garden." I pointed at a magnificent porcelain bird on a tree branch. "The princess falls in love with the prince, but when he reveals his identity, she realizes that their fathers are arch enemies." I stopped, waiting for Miriam to take over, and when she didn't, I said, "It's your turn."

"The wizard casts his spell on her."

"That was the first story. You need to make up a new one," I said with exasperation. What was the use? Standing quietly, filled with rapture, I went on weaving new stories in my head, the music filling the room blending them into wonderful pictures.

I forgot about Miriam until she spoke behind me. "Maybe no one will come."

I turned and my first thought was that I was the only one stupid enough to come to her party. Then I felt anger about the way Miriam had brought it all upon herself and how she now involved me. But then I saw the tears in her eyes and felt bad. I felt pity for this big girl who towered over me but who wanted to be my friend. Pity for this girl whose life both at home and at school I couldn't comprehend. I wanted to ask about the girls who went to the other school and were supposed to be here, but I wasn't sure if I should.

"Are Sarah, Bella, and Debbie coming?" Miriam asked me.

I swallowed. "I didn't know you invited them."

Miriam kept looking down at me, her gaze pleading. I felt so small, so uncomfortable with the power she handed me. I shrugged and kept my shoulders high up in a gesture of helplessness. I wished I could just leave.

The record had ended for the third or fourth time. Miriam's father changed it once more. Her mother went to the window again and again. She spoke in German. She gave me another glass of lemonade. Her skin was as translucent as the figurines', and I realized that I had never before met anyone who had escaped the Israeli sun. We waited.

Miriam began to cry, a soft, silent weeping. Her father stroked her hair. Her mother's lips tightened into a line as she stepped into the kitchen and closed the door. With all that lemonade in me, I wanted to pee badly, but dared not move. Miriam went on weeping.

Finally, her mother came out of the kitchen carrying a tray with steaming food. They spoke in German, and Miriam's father lit the candles in the candelabra. I walked back to the dining room and sat down, Miriam's parents at both ends, Miriam and me facing each other at the center. On either side, three chairs separated Miriam's parents and us. Twelve girls who hadn't shown up.

The four dead children looked straight at me. Grave, foreign children. Murdered by the Nazis. I wished I had thought of grabbing Miriam's seat first. She had known to avoid them.

I looked at all those utensils and wondered what I was supposed to do. My friends and I had read a manners book for when we would be invited to dine at a palace, and we practiced with whatever was left from the set my father had inherited from his mother, and which my mom hated because it was stupid to polish silver when we had stainless steel. Now I forgot everything the book had said except that it was very important not to make a mistake, so I watched Miriam lift the outside fork and hold it in her left hand as she ate the grapefruit. I did the same, although it was difficult to eat with my left.

My bladder could hold no more. My face hot, I excused myself and went to the bathroom, certain that it was really impolite and now they were talking about me in German. I wished that at least one other girl had come. But when I returned to the table, Miriam's mother was bringing more food from the kitchen, and she smiled at me kindly.

The other dishes tasted as good as they smelled. I ate everything Miriam's mother put on my plate, making sure to thank her each time, to dab my mouth with the lacy cloth napkin in between bites. I wanted to be good, to make up for the absence of the twelve others, to make up for the sorrow of the four dead children.

The last record Miriam's father had changed ended. This time he didn't get up. The record went on turning, obedient in its soft, rhythmic hum, but the needle whimpered. The scratching gave me goose bumps. No one moved to do anything about it. I hugged myself and rubbed the skin of my arms. The twelve empty chairs and the untouched place settings gaped at me. Suddenly, Miriam's father dropped his face in his hands. Miriam's mother said something, but he only shook his head. There was some strange trembling to his shoulders. Miriam's mother bit her lips, her face contorted. I lowered my gaze into my fingers, not knowing where else to look. Then there was this odd sound in the room, like a choked moan, and I looked up to see Miriam's mother rush back into the kitchen.

I shifted in my seat. The four dead children in the photographs were silent. I wondered how old the oldest had been when they killed him. I was sorry that Miriam was not the kind of child who could make up for the loss. I glanced at her and saw that she was a woman in a Tyrolean girl's dress. At least her parents didn't know what she did with the boys.

Miriam's father still didn't move. His exposed scalp shone. A guttural croak tore out of him. My first introduction to unbearable grief bore down on me, seeping into me through the thick air. I wanted to cry with them, but I had no right since the Nazis hadn't killed anyone in my family.

Miriam just looked down, her fingers twisting and knotting the napkin in her lap.

For a split second I wanted to offer myself to them as their child. It was a stupid idea. I slid off my chair. My throat was constricted. "Thank you very much. The food was delicious," I managed to say, even though I was leaving before dessert, before the birthday cake, possibly losing out on those butter cookies.

Neither one answered. I didn't knock on the kitchen door before I left, although it was impolite not to thank the hostess.

Miriam's family—the dead and the living—walked with me all the way home.

RELIGION: GOY

Herbert Gold

TODAY LET'S TALK ETHNIC and allegiance to history; let's admit a touch of rage and the hint of love—a merest whiff, in this case.

The seventy-one-year-old father of a woman friend thought, since I seemed to be keeping company with his daughter, that we should all three share a few wary jokes and comments. The daughter promised: no obligation; just meet Elliott; you'll like him. I accepted: no obligation; I'd like to meet your dad whom you call by his first name; maybe I'll like him.

"Dinner?" she inquired. "Something casual at Allegro? Lots of laughs and food you don't have to wrestle with?"

"I always enjoy a nice seafood pasta paid for by someone else," I said.

"Stipulated," said the lady, who was coming up for partner in a good law firm.

The father in question turned out to be a lanky, tennis-playing, thrice-married, healthy old boy with a last name as clearly marking his origins as mine, but membership in the Episcopal Church. Serves, does something, at Grace Cathedral; I'm not clear on exactly what devoted Episcopalians with the name (say) Shapiro actually do when they're tight into High Church procedures.

The daughter, my friend, Ms. Connie Shapiro, believed he had converted when he married her mother, his first wife. With her name, Connie sometimes had trouble explaining that she was second-generation Episcopalian—mother's maiden name Maclean—but it wasn't an issue in contemporary San Francisco. Connie always thought she might take her husband's name and get rid of the question entirely, assuming she married something less ethnically resonant, but the package hadn't yet pulled together. When I asked, "What if you married a Lipshitz or Weinberger?" she laughed, tossed her curls, and said, a little startled: "If it happens, it happens."

Odd, since she was a high-I.Q. person with occupational training in contingency planning, that she hadn't anticipated the possibility. But then, this is San Francisco, and she had a good mind, warm eyes, Stanford Law School training, constituting an attractive package all by herself, so that people said, "Connie Shapiro. . . . Well, it won't do for ingenue opposite Robert Redford in *Butch Cassidy 2* but it's fine for attorney in a more contemporary, Deborah Winger-type thing."

Settled at our window table at Allegro on Russian Hill, I brought up this history while we tasted our pre-dinner small-talk drinks. The father, Elliott, straightened out some chronology for his daughter (they had never discussed the matter before). "No, it was during the War, I guess I didn't tell you." He was stationed in England and had to deal with anti-Semitic rednecks and decided these quarrels were a waste of time and energy. Already, back in the States, he'd looked at Unitarianism and Christian Science, but there in London, under bombardment, he took instruction from this terrific Church of England guy in a kind of royal purple tunic. It was really nice and comforting, great hymns, processionals like you wouldn't believe. Some of the Jewish boys wailed away with the local rabbis, and one fighter pilot seemed to have died because he was shot down wearing dogtags with the telltale H on them and the Germans, you know, on the ground, when they cut him out of his parachute. . . .

"H for Hebrew," I explained to Connie.

He sighed. "Definitely had a kinder, gentler war this way," he said.

Now, when he played tennis at the Burlingame Club or went in and out of retirement—taking good care of his investments—it was nice to be a long-time Episcopalian, since World War II in downtown London; *way* back.

He turned to Connie, giving her a shot of some family stuff for the first time. "Your mother, my dear, really had nothing to do with it. It just happened that she was Episcopalian and I was sort of more High Church when we met. So there we were."

"It was Destiny, Elliott," Connie said, "just like all your marriages."

He grinned. "Every wife was great in her own way, dear, even if they didn't always work out."

"Can't beat that Church of England karma, Dad," I said. He could tease, too—punched me on the arm—and a shrimp fell back into the lettuce (light appetizers for California eaters).

I called him Dad, probably a mistake even in jest, because Connie didn't. I was, somewhat driftingly, in a position of semi-courtship toward his one and only daughter, a child of his first wife. I began rambling through a joke of which the climax is the question, "What's your religion?" and the answer: "Goy."

Connie laughed, the folks at the next table laughed, and Elliott said, "I haven't heard that one."

I could have bet people told the story while he was rushing the net at the Burlingame Club courts. Instead, I commented that I preferred racquetball to tennis these days because of the really intense aerobics involved. It slipped out that I have five children. Elliott crinkled up boyishly, making a mouth that said, *Whew.* Then I explained: two by my first wife, Jewish, and then three who are half-Jewish by birth but fully educated about their heritage on both sides.

Uh-huh would have been the two words, or the one hyphenated word, he would have uttered, had he spoken aloud, but he didn't. He sipped his wine, ran it across his tongue, and said, "Nice."

"Not that I'm not *aware*, Herb," Connie, the young lawyer, stipulated.

More food came, Angelo boomed, the room turned lively. The alert father of Connie enjoyed his fresh salmon. Connie was staring at me, seeing a whole new side of this formerly tactful friend of hers. "Strange thing about children," I said, "liking them a whole lot may not be as natural as people think. I sort of stumbled into loving my kids. My first daughter taught me. When she was a baby. She taught me."

"I wouldn't know," Elliott said. "I only had that one."

"*This* one, Elliott," said his daughter.

"You always call your father by his first name?" I asked.

"What else should I call him?"

He crinkled up into Kissinger-like humor. "You could call me Your Excellency."

To get off this uncomfortable subject, I returned to the previous uncomfortable subject. I too met with anti-Jewish feeling when I was growing up, I said, and in the Army. But it made me decide to explore what all this meant. "Maybe there's more freedom in connecting with the past, what do you think?"

He had no trouble with this. "Interesting. You took arms against a sea of troubles—that's a poet said that, right?—and spent a lot of your energy that way. Well, I thought I was an American good as anybody else, so why should I get stuck . . . ?"

Didn't bother finishing the sentence. Yawned.

I kept imagining the lean young airman, handsomely grim or handsomely grinning as the bombs fell on London, surviving his war, even brave enough on his missions—coming through okay and thanking Jesus while his (and my) unknown relatives were being destroyed in atrocious herds. I remembered Henri Bergson, the French philosopher, who in his old age had become Catholic by conviction but refused, on his deathbed in Occupied France, to accept formal conversion. He would not abandon the people of his history.

I also remembered my more banal rolling in the dust of an Army dayroom with another soldier who suggested I was a New York Jew (I was a Lakewood, Ohio, Jew), battering him and being battered by him. I couldn't see myself saying, "Well, actually, I'm not, you know."

Connie's dad and I ordered fruit, no cholesterol for dessert. We were at that age. It was odd in this beneficent San Francisco, where Jews are now just beige WASPS, part of the beleaguered majority, to revive old memories and passions. Connie was watching with interest, trying to learn from this conversation between her father and her friend. I thought maybe I should lighten up. I told Connie and Elliott about the blond, blue-eyed, orthodontically perfect crew at my half-Jewish daughter's temple confirmation class, where there was even a non-Jewish kid, not Jewish by either mother or father, who just wanted to join her friends in this ritual. Folks seemed to think, Hey, why not? We have grown ecumenical in our San Francisco.

"I have an Orthodox friend who calls this place of worship, it's too liberal for him, Notre Dame de la Torah."

Elliott cast his sharp, shrewd old man's glance at me. "You have an Orthodox friend? You got many of those?"

"Elliott," said his daughter, "don't be such a snob."

"So how come," I asked, trying for a certain lilt, "you kept the name Shapiro?"

"Wasn't that big a deal. Hey, it was conviction, you know? Liked the music—those hymns are dynamite—the fellowship, the nice clean churches. That's what I've been trying to tell you."

I was dining with a sincere convert: was what he was trying to say.

He reached for the check. "Mine!" he declared.

His daughter stayed my hand. "Elliott *wants* to pay," she said.

We dropped him at his condo on Sacramento Street. He was jaunty, pleased, very healthy, the kind of father-in-law who would never be a burden. Temporarily he was between wives again, but that could be remedied.

Connie and I agreed to differ, agreed to be "friends," that is, to avoid each other. It was hard for me to explain that it was partly her father that I didn't like about her. Geneticists offer no evidence for the inheritance of smarm, but some do believe in the danger of acquired character. From that evening until now, when I look at Connie's alert, intelligent, ambitious face, what I see is the skull beneath the skin of a man who chose, in 1944, in the dark of that night, to deny whatever depths there might have been in his nature.

MAZAL'S DAY

Gloria Goldreich

MAZAL HUDDLES INTO HER oversized hooded plaid coat as she waits for the light to change. It is only late October, but already she can feel the chill of impending winter. Although she has lived in New York for two years, Mazal still thinks of autumn as an alien season. In Israel, at summer's end, thin sere leaves scatter briefly and cypresses sway mournfully in the sea-scented breeze, a peaceful transition from one season to another.

Mazal knows Israelis who marvel at the fall foliage. Her neighbor, Nechama, who like Mazal is the paid companion of an elderly Jewish woman, gave her a basket of small, misshapen gourds in muted shades of russet and orange, purchased during a weekend trip to Vermont. Mazal thinks the gourds ugly, but she does not want to offend Nechama, who is always welcoming, always ready to share her copy of *Ma'ariv*, always ready to discuss the bad news from Israel.

The light changes, and Mazal crosses the wide avenue and enters the Tiberias Gardens where the walls are pasted with faded posters—a view of the Western Wall, a nightscape of Tel Aviv, anemones on a Galilee meadow. Two men sip small cups of muddy Turkish coffee at a table covered with a white paper cloth. They argue vigorously in Hebrew, their voices drowning out Chava Alberstein's wistful voice singing of starry Negev nights. Mazal hums along as she studies the Hebrew-English menu.

Fat Yoram, the owner, is on the phone. He shouts at the suppliers in Arabic, makes another call and shouts again in Hebrew, hangs up and smiles at Mazal, reminding her of her ex-husband, Chaim, who was always swiftly angered and swiftly smoothed. It is the way of Moroccan men, Chaim's mother had once told her, an explanation which had irritated Mazal.

"So, Mazal, how are you?" Yoram asks. "Too cold today. This country. This weather." Yoram has lived in Brooklyn for seven years, but he is still ambushed by autumn.

Mazal shrugs and orders Turkish salad, stewed okra, and tomatoes. As Yoram fills the white cardboard containers, Mazal inhales the mingled scents of his spices and thinks of the spinach and rice patties her mother had cooked in the iron skillet she had carried with her from Saana and the fragrant lamb stews that had simmered on her stove. Mazal cannot cook such foods on the hot plate in her sliver of a kitchen, and the one time she made a lentil dish in Mrs. Klein's kitchen, the old woman had complained to her daughter, Paula, who had tried to be conciliatory.

"I'm sorry, Mazal. Howard and I both love Middle Eastern cooking, but the odor gives my mother a headache. You understand. Eat anything in the refrigerator."

Mazal had nodded, although she did not believe that Paula and her husband have any fondness for the spicy food she craves. They are both tall and thin, Howard a pathologist and Paula a psychiatrist. Mazal thinks that the acrid scent of death and misery clings to them.

Mazal seldom eats Mrs. Klein's food. She is repelled by the soft bland white cheeses, the gray meat and pale chicken in gelid broths, the pureed vegetables and ominously dark compotes. These foods are prepared by Lucy, the younger daughter, who drives in from Great Neck once a week laden with shopping bags. Lucy also buys her mother soft pastel-colored sweaters and long-sleeve silk blouses that conceal the wrinkled flesh that hangs so loosely from the aged arms.

The gifts are grudgingly accepted, the clothing tried on only after Lucy leaves. The previous week, Lucy had brought a pink angora sweater, and both mother and daughter had pressed Mazal for a reaction. Did she like the color, the cut of the neck?

"Pink is beautiful," Mazal had said. "My favorite color. My daughter's too."

Dark-haired Lucy, who is divorced and teaches anthropology at a community college, favors long, loose dresses of rough weaves and heavy pendants of geometric design. Mrs. Klein speaks bitterly of Lucy's ex-husband, a non-Jewish professor of philosophy who never earned tenure. They had never trusted him, never liked him.

Mazal's family, in contrast, had liked Chaim, who was a skilled welder, a steady earner, a Moroccan who had accepted the customs of the Yemenites with ease. Mazal's decision to divorce had bewildered, her explanations had angered. So he had a temper, all men had tempers. Look at the apartment he had given her, the good life.

"But it's not the life I want. I want to see something of the world, to go to America. I want something different." She had choked on the exculpation of her own yearnings, gagged on her guilt and misery. Her mother wept, her father shouted.

"What will you have in that America? Who will understand you there? You'll lay there like a dog, alone."

There are nights when Mazal sits in her rented room and thinks that her father who had understood so little, had, in fact, understood everything.

Occasionally, Lucy brings her children to visit their grandmother. They are twins, wild and noisy, unlike Paula's gentle dreamy daughter, a student at New England College. Cindy writes to her grandmother on oddly textured notepaper, asking questions about her life. Mazal laboriously reads these notes aloud because the old woman's eyes are so weak, thinks of her own grandmother. A wizened gnome of a woman, her dark leathery skin stretched tight against her avian face, her coal dark eyes bright with mysterious memories, she had sat day after day at the window. The children of Rosh Ha-Ayin had waved to her as they scurried past the house. No one in Flatbush, where the curtains are drawn and the doors are double locked, waved to Mrs. Klein. In this America, Mazal thinks, the old people drown in their loneliness. And not only the old. The memory of her own nocturnal misery sours her mouth.

"You heard the news this morning, Mazal. The suicide bomber in Holon. Three dead. School children." Yoram sighs and Mazal shakes her head sadly.

She and Yoram share the cryptic code of the exile with a single focus. The only news of any interest to them emanates from Israel. The death of a child, the wounding of a soldier, paralyzes them with misery.

"What does your daughter think will happen?"

Yoram is impressed that Yael works for military intelligence. He does not know that she is only a typist and that her infrequent letters are largely requests for compact discs and jeans, always ending with the same plaintive question—"*Ima*, when are you coming home?"

Mazal never answers that question. When she was Yael's age, twenty, she was already a mother. Yael should understand that she must save enough to buy herself a flat, furniture, appliances.

"You know that my daughter cannot write about her work," Mazal says curtly.

"Of course." Yoram is apologetic. He wraps a potato boureka and adds it to her purchases. "No charge." He gives her a tattered copy of last month's *Ha-Ishah*.

Mazal pays him, counting out the bills carefully and with pleasure. Each Friday, when Paula hands her the six fifty dollar bills, she riffles through the currency, enjoying the feel of the money she has earned, that belongs to her alone. It vests her with power and independence. She drops a coin in the Babi Sallah canister, another in the Magen David Adom box.

"*Shalom,* Yoram."

"*Shalom u-vrachah,* Mazal."

The quiet blessing of farewell trails her onto Ocean Avenue. Hurrying now, she turns the corner and lets herself into the house just as the phone begins to ring. Mazal knows that it is Paula calling, to make sure that she arrived on time, and this daily monitoring angers her. There is an edge to her voice as she talks to Paula.

"Your mama is fine," she says. "You'll be here today?"

Paula visits each Tuesday and Friday afternoon, and occasionally Lucy arranges to meet her sister. Always then, they urge Mazal to take a few hours off, and Mazal knows that they want to discuss their mother's finances, to arrange the transfer of funds from one account to another, to check her silver, her jewelry. They are, after all, the conservators of her possessions, but their vigilance offends Mazal. When she returns, they stop talking and then chatter with nervous rapidity, complimenting her on how orderly she keeps the house before they broach their mother's small complaints. The dishes are not always properly dried. The light is too often left on in the kitchen.

Mazal always listens sullenly and reminds them that their mother calls to her from the bedroom when she is in the midst of a kitchen chore.

Paula and Lucy nod sympathetically. They know that Mazal works hard and they wish they could spend more time with their mother but they are so busy. What more could they do? Mazal does not tell them how her grandmother's children came each day to the Rosh Ha-Ayin house carrying dishes of food and freshly laundered clothing and linens. They hovered over the old woman, telling stories, singing the songs of Yemen, a frail sweet chorus, their voices wafting through the windows so that passersby stopped to listen. Who sings like this in America? Who takes care of an old mother?

"Yes. I'll be there this afternoon." Paula's voice is irritable.

"Mazal, I'm waiting for you," Mrs. Klein whines from the bedroom.

Mazal replaces the receiver and hangs her coat up, pausing in the living room to push the royal blue ottoman closer to the armchair. She dusts the low table with her handkerchief because Paula sometimes runs her finger across it.

In the bedroom, the old woman sits forlornly at the edge of her unmade bed running a hair brush through her thinning snow-white hair. She is dressed, but her striped silk blouse is incorrectly buttoned, and her navy skirt is unzipped.

"Here, Mama, let me help you." Mazal thinks of Mrs. Klein as *hazkeynah*, "the old woman," but she calls her "mama" because that pleases Paula and Lucy, helps them to think of Mazal as a relative rather than a servant. That is perhaps why they hired a Jewish woman.

Mazal corrects the buttons, zips up her skirt, and kneels to lace the clumsy black space shoes. She notices that the bureau drawer in which the old woman keeps her favorite possessions is open, its contents in mild disarray.

"You want something from the drawer?" she asks.

"No. Last night I was looking for something, but now I don't want it."

Mazal is not surprised. Her employer often rearranges her small treasures, sometimes showing them to Mazal—scarves and sweaters, a cameo, a gold lapel watch, a gray cashmere sweater with a collar of soft gray fur.

She shrugs. In the kitchen, she prepares the old woman's breakfast, counts out her gem-colored pills, which the old woman swallows one at a time, waiting expectantly after each sip of juice as though anticipating an infusion of energy. Mazal settles her in the blue chair and turns the television set on. She makes the bed, clears the breakfast dishes, and returns to watch a talk show about very fat men married to thin women.

"Stupid," her employer says, and she nods in agreement.

"In Israel we don't have such shows." Her tone is disapproving.

"So you should go back to Israel." The sly malice of the rejoinder wounds Mazal, who returns to the bedroom and reads *Ha-Isha*, emerging only when it is time to prepare lunch. She punishes the old woman with solitude.

After lunch, it is time for a nap. Mazal settles her on the bed, covers her with a duvet, and lingers at the bureau, straightening the comb and the brush, the small blue bottle of toilet water.

"What are you doing, Mazal?"

The question, asked in such a sharp tone, startles Mazal, who had thought Mrs. Klein was asleep.

"Nothing," she replies defensively. "Just making a little order."

In the kitchen she spoons some of the Turkish salad onto a pita. She will take the rest of it home and invite Nechama to eat with her. The anticipation of a shared meal and Hebrew conversation lightens her mood. She is still nibbling at the pita when the front door opens and Lucy calls to her from the doorway.

"It's only me, Mazal. I'm early today."

Lucy hangs up her russet-colored cape and drapes her batik scarf over her white wool sweater. She comes into the kitchen.

"You want I should make you coffee?" Mazal asks.

"No. I'll wait for Paula."

Mazal continues to eat, but all pleasure is gone. Lucy wanders restlessly from room to room as she often does, sometimes plucking up an album of old photos, sometimes rearranging the framed portraits in the living room. Paula and herself as children, their children as toddlers, her parents as newlyweds. Mazal thinks of her parents' home, where there are pictures of herself as a baby, a slender school girl, a bride, photos that anchor her, serving as a ballast. Here, no one knows that she is the daughter of Boaz, the spice vendor, granddaughter of Shalom, the silversmith.

Lucy opens the china closet, studies the silver chest. Mazal hears the cabinet doors open and close as she continues to read her magazine. She barely looks up as Paula enters the house, striding into the kitchen still wearing her tan coat which only emphasizes her pallor. Briefly, Mazal pities her.

"Hi, Mazal, how are you?"

But Paula does not wait for an answer. It is understood that she does not care how Mazal is. Lucy comes into the room, and Paula gives her a peremptory kiss. They turn to Mazal.

"Why don't you go out, Mazal? Have some time for yourself. Lucy and I will be here when Mama wakes up," Paula suggests, but Mazal knows that it is, in fact, an order.

"All right. Why not?" It is, after all, only right that they should be there while their mother sleeps. They, the daughters. Mazal's mother and her aunts always sat beside her grandmother's bed as the old woman napped, loving vigilantes, on guard against the angel of death.

"We're sure. We don't mind," Paula replies impatiently.

Mazal takes the bus to the Kings Plaza Mall where she wanders aimlessly. The shops do not interest her today. She wishes she had a friend who would meet her for coffee, a friend with whom she could share her contempt for the cheap merchandise, the careless, inattentive mothers. She walks slowly, hobbled by her loneliness.

She leaves the mall and goes into a luncheonette owned by a large-bellied and balding Israeli named Moshe where she orders a Turkish coffee.

"You're slow, today." She is alone at the counter and the tables are empty.

"It's always slow after lunch. I can't complain. One year more, maybe two, and I'll have enough money to go to Israel, to start my own business in Holon. War or peace, people need sinks, toilets."

"Better to buy a shop that sells bullet-proof vests," she says bitterly.

She picks up a copy of *Ma'ariv* on the counter and reads an advertisement for a new housing complex in Bat Yam. The street name is unfamiliar and she wonders if she will recognize her own country when she returns, or will she wander the streets of Tel Aviv, uncertain and alone.

She finishes her coffee, and she and Moshe discuss Sharon's most recent speech until Moshe is called away by the entrance of a group of old ladies. Disappointed, she leaves, and because she can think of nothing else to do, she boards the bus and returns to the house. Perhaps they will be pleased that she returned early.

She opens the door with her key and closes it very quietly, fearful of disturbing the old woman's nap. But there is no need for such caution. The three women are in the bedroom, and Mrs. Klein's voice is fearful, insistent.

"I know exactly where I put it. You girls think I can't remember where I put things? The sweater's not in the drawer. You looked yourselves. Did you find it?"

"We're not arguing with you. We know it's not there." Paula speaks to her mother with the professional calm that may reassure her patients. "What do you think, Lucy?"

"I saw Mama put it in that drawer myself, and no one comes into this room except Mazal. But it doesn't make sense that she would take something after all these months, something that isn't even valuable."

"Maybe she thought that if it wasn't valuable we wouldn't notice. And she did like that sweater. She even said that pink was her favorite color." Paula appraises the situation with diagnostic reason.

Mazal's cheeks burn, her heart pounds. She strides into the bedroom. They stare at her, their faces very pale.

"You looked for something and didn't find it?" she shrills.

Paula places her hand protectively on her mother's shoulder.

"We can't find my mother's new pink sweater."

Mazal opens the bottom drawer and takes out the sweater.

"I put it there so it shouldn't get creased. I take care of your mother's things like they were my own."

"Mazal, we're sorry. But Mama was so upset." Lucy stumbles over her words, blushes deeply, but Paula's skin remains waxen.

Mazal glares at them. Calm deserts her. The simmering fury of months boils over into a roiling rage. They do not trust her, Paula with her morning check-up calls, Lucy always looking into closets and cabinets. Chutzpah. She tosses the sweater onto the bed.

"You didn't want her to be upset." She mimics Lucy's voice. "Such good daughters. So good that you pay me to take care of her even though you worry that maybe I steal from her. Such good daughters that you leave your mother maybe with a thief. In my family this would not happen. We took care of our own. My grandmother's children came to her every day and her grandchildren too. They came from the army, from their schools. They kissed her hands. They asked her to bless them. Me, I cut her nails, her fingernails, her toenails. Like I cut your mother's. I take care of your mother like she was my own. Ask her. Ask her."

The old woman shakes her head.

"You do, Mazal. Of course you do." Tears streak her wrinkled cheeks.

"Why would I take such a sweater? My daughter, my Yael, she is young, beautiful. She wants a sweater, I buy it for her. That's why I work here. That's why I take money to do what daughters should be doing."

Paula and Lucy lower their eyes like chastened children.

"It was just a misunderstanding," Paula says.

"No! It was an insult." Mazal spits the word out and leaves the room. She takes her cardigan and her sneakers from the hall closet, shoves them into a plastic bag and adds the white cardboard containers of food from Yoram's restaurant. Lucy and Paula race after her, confront her as she struggles into her plaid coat.

"Mazal, what are you doing?" Paula asks.

"You can see. I'm leaving. I don't work where I'm not trusted. You owe me for two days this week. A hundred dollars."

"Mazal, please don't leave. We want you to stay. We made a mistake. Please come into the living room, we'll talk about it," Paula says coaxingly.

Mazal looks at the sisters and sees the fear and regret in their eyes. Energized by a new sense of power, she sits on the royal blue chair still gripping her plastic shopping bag. The tall sisters, penitent supplicants, stand before her.

"Look, we made a mistake. And you said some unkind things. But now it's over. Mama likes you, and she really wants you to be here. We thought we would raise your pay at Chanukah, but why should we wait for December? We'll give you a raise now," Paula says, and Lucy nods vigorously.

"It's not the money," Mazal insists. "If I stay, it's because of how I feel about your mother. But it's a hard job. And it's hard to get here from where I live. Two different buses. Where my friend Nechama works, the family pays her carfare."

The sisters look knowingly at each other.

"All right. We'll pay your carfare," Lucy agrees.

"Mazal," the old woman calls. "I want my tea."

Mazal goes into the kitchen and makes the tea, draping her coat over a chair.

"All right," she calls as the kettle boils. "I stay because she needs me."

When she carries the tray in, the old woman is sitting up in bed holding the gray sweater with the fur collar. She gives the sweater to Mazal.

"For you," she says and lifts the cup.

Mazal's fingers dance across the soft wool, the silvery fur. "I don't need such a sweater."

"But I want you to have it." She takes a sip of tea. "It's good. This tea."

"I made it with honey." Mazal presses the fur against her cheek and carefully folds the sweater.

"Take it, Mazal," Lucy says softly.

She and Paula prepare to leave. They refresh their lipstick and each in turn kisses her cheek. Dustings of her pale face powder cling to their newly painted lips.

"Goodbye Mazal," they say in unison, but they do not meet her eyes.

The door slams behind them, and Mazal turns on the television set. She and Mrs. Klein watch a talk show on which an estranged mother and daughter are reconciled and hug each other. Mazal remembers her mother's embrace, imagines herself putting her arms about Yael. Tears sear her cheeks, and she hurries to prepare the old woman's dinner, staring from the kitchen window into the neighboring house. A man still in his overcoat kisses his wife. A woman sits at a table and helps her children with their homework. Mazal peels a carrot, a cucumber.

The old woman eats quickly and Mazal clears up with matching swiftness. They are both glad to have this day end.

"You took the sweater, Mazal?"

"I have it," Mazal assures her. "Thank you," she adds hesitantly and hurries out.

The night is cold, and the tense early darkness of autumn depresses her. Arriving home, she is relieved to see a light in Nechama's window. She is not yet ready to face the silence of her own room.

The friends eat together and Mazal shows Nechama the sweater.

"It's beautiful," Nechama says. "A good color for you."

"But where would I wear it?" Mazal asks bitterly. The evenings of her life in this land that is not her own stretch before her, a barren desert of time.

That night she showers, using the Ahava soap that she hoards for time of need. She stands for a long time beneath the hot spray. She would wash away all the sadness of the day, the small and bitter betrayals, the solitude that trailed her like a shadow, the rustling of brittle leaves driven by a vagrant wind. She puts on a fresh nightgown of white cotton and over it the soft gray sweater. Her long black hair, damp from the shower, capes the silvery fur. She sniffs her fingers that smell of Israel.

Still wearing the sweater, she lies very still on her narrow bed. A car alarm shrills on the street below and a child's laughter, high and sweet, sounds in the hallway. At last, her hand upon the fur, Mazal sleeps.

JEWISH HUMOR

THE WIT AND PRACTICALITY OF THE TALMUD

Ralph de Toledano

THE *YESHIVA-BOCHERS* HAVE OVERSOLD the Talmud. So, by reputation, it is a many-volumed treatise of Godly wisdom, Biblical analysis, religious nit-picking, legal disquisitions, deep mysticism, and a reminder that Heaven is open to all, whatever their religion, if they lead a just life—a work where only the *chachamim* can share the insights into Scripture, its meanings, and its consequences. But the Talmud is far more than that. Unlike the *Pirkei Avot,* the Talmud is also a compendium of observations, advice, and oftentimes ironic or whimsical commentary on daily life and behavior.

"Asparagus," the Talmud tells us, "is good for the heart and the eyes" (Berachot). And: "In nature there are no rectangles" (Nedarim). Continuing on the nutritionist line, the Talmud warns us, "It is forbidden to eat raw vegetables before breakfast" (Berachot), a practice that seems to have eluded modern man. Nutritionists agree with the Talmud, which noted before there were fast-food emporia, that "more people die of over-eating than of under-nourishment"(Shabbat). But they would disagree that "Food is better for a man until he is forty; after forty drink is better" (Shabbat). On drink, however, the Talmud is ambivalent. Compare "when wine enters, reason departs" with "where there is no wine, drugs are needed" (Bava Batra). Still, drugs must be shunned and "even if you are sick, avoid taking medicine, if you can" (Pesachim).

Of sickness: "Everything is in the hands of heaven except fever and chills" and "every ache—except headache" (Shabbat). The American

Medical Association, moreover, would applaud this adjuration: "A physician who does not take a fee is not worth a fee" (Bava Kamma). Moderation, however, is the key to health and well-being. "A little is good and much is bad in three things: yeast, salt, and hesitation (Berachot) . . . A little is good and much is bad in eight things: travel, sex, wealth, work, wine, sleep, hot drinks, and medicine" (Gittin).

The Talmud spends much time in discussing the merits of marriage and raising a family. Yet it lists "four things that cause a man to age prematurely: a fright, anger, children, and a bad wife" (Chayye Sarah). And, it ominously adds: "Every man gets the wife he deserves (Sotah). . . . A shrewish wife is like a skin disease. . . . Give me all evils—except a bad wife (Shabbat). . . . A woman's weapons are always with her" (Yevamot). Marriage, moreover, is not all honeymoon. "When love is strong, we can lie together on the edge of a sword; but when love fades, a bed sixty feet wide is not wide enough" (Yevamot). And of children the Talmud warns, "A man who gives his property to his children during his lifetime buys himself a master" (Bava Metzia).

"It is pleasant to ascend the pulpit, but hard to step down" (Yalkut Shemoni), the Talmud says in its disposition on man's vanity. "If one man says you are a donkey, pay him no mind, but if two men say it, buy yourself a saddle" (Bereshit Rabbah). And to make the point even clearer: "Man was created on the sixth day. If he becomes vain, remind him that the flea preceded him in Creation" (Sanhedrin).

The Talmudist must have been thinking of rent control when he wrote: "When prosperity comes to my landlord, I do not share it, but when hard times hit him, I also suffer" (Eichah Rabbah). Of commerce: "Once a tradesman has set a price for his goods, it is wrong for him to raise it if he has a chance" (Kiddushin). Moreover, the Talmud says, "Do not offer to sell pearls to those who deal in onions" (Tanchuma Bechukotai).

Recognizing that "there is no society in which everyone is rich or everyone is poor" (Gittin), and considering that "poverty is worse than fifty plagues" (Bava Batra), the Talmudist considers what one man can do to help another. "Let a man be very charitable, but let him beware of giving everything he has" (Arachin). For giving has its bad point. "It is greater to lend than to give, and greater still to lend and with the loan help the borrower to help himself. . . . Lending without interest is better than giving charity" (Shabbat). But charity must be merited. "If you do not work, you should not eat" (Bereshit Rabbah). Work, moreover, has merit beyond what it produces. "A man will die if he has nothing to do" (Avot).

The Talmud ranges far and wide in its observations. Is it laughing at Israel when it remarks, "Who buys a Jewish slave gets himself a master"

(Kiddushin)? Or: "Silence is restful. It rests the heart, the lungs, the lar-ynx, the tongue, and the mouth" (Zohar). It makes one of its infrequent gibes at women with "hypocrisy is like a woman who in the arms of her lover swears by the life of her husband" (Tanchuma Emor).

It makes its point on that great human occupation, thievery. "Steal from a thief and you will acquire the taste" (Berachot). "Deception is the worst form of theft. . . . The thief becomes law-abiding when he can steal no more" (Sanhedrin). "There is no point in scolding a man who cannot tell good from evil" (Sanhedrin). It also puts a barb into the easy excuse of wrongdoers: "No man sins for someone else" (Bava Metzia).

"A man should not put all his money in one pile" (Bereshit Rabbah). And he should understand the envy of his fellows: "Bad neighbors con-sider a man's income, but not his expenses" (Pesikta Rabati)—something the Internal Revenue service should take to heart.

The Talmud informs us that "The Law of the land is law" (Bava Kamma). . . . "As fish die out of the water, so people die without law and order" (Avodah Zarah).

On a loftier plain: "The spirit became pregnant and gave birth to wis-dom" (Shemot Rabbah), though "he who creates wisdom increases dissat-isfaction" (Kohelet Rabbah). But some things transcend wisdom: "The eye, the ear, and the nose are independent of the will" (Vayyikra Tanchuma).

Groucho Marx, a philosopher of sorts, asked: "If I'm not here, I'm there, but if I'm not there, where am I?" The Talmud answers him flatly: "The center of the world is exactly where you stand" (Berachot). At the center of that world, there is the Talmud, explaining the ways of God to man and setting up the rules whereby the world can arrive at just gov-ernment, though acknowledging that "truth is so heavy, few wear it" (Midrash Shmuel). The great question, posed by the great Hillel, is quoted but remains unanswered: "If I am not for myself, who will be, but if I am only for myself, what am I?" (Avot).

But even in ancient days, the Talmud had one warning still to be taken to heart—and pasted on every commentator's and reporter's word-processor: "How many pens are broken, how many ink bottles are con-sumed, to write about things that never happened" (Tanchuma Shoftim).

IT IS NOT A JOKE . . .

Leo M. Abrami

A JEWISH JOKE IS MORE than just a funny story, for it often has a message for the listener. "First you laugh at a Jewish joke or quip. Then, against your will, you suddenly fall silent and thoughtful. And that is because Jews are so frequently jesting philosophers. A hard life has made them realists, realists without illusions," writes Nathan Ausubel, in the introduction to his *Treasury of Jewish Humor.*

Many Jewish jokes and anecdotes have made a definite impact on the mind and character of the Jewish people, because they are inspired by a profound wisdom. Though not always anticipated at first, it becomes manifest as soon as we reflect upon them.

A classic Yiddish story makes the following observation:

When you tell an *am ho-oretz* (peasant) a joke, he laughs three times: once, when you tell it, once, when you explain it, and once, when he understands it.

When you tell a landowner a joke, he laughs twice: once when you tell it and once when you explain it—he will never understand it.

When you tell a military officer a joke, he laughs only once, when you tell it, because he won't let you explain it, and of course, he doesn't understand it.

But when you tell a Jew a joke, he tells you that he has heard it before, and that you are telling it all wrong, anyway.

Humor is one of the most effective ways of confronting adversity and coping with difficult situations, especially when we have little control over them, or none at all. "By laughing at our fate, it is as if we were stepping out of a situation and looking at it from a distance, as if we were outside observers, so to speak," writes Rabbi Reuven Bulka. By so doing, we gain the ability to transcend the circumstances, which may be the cause of our anguish. Theodor Reik, a disciple of Sigmund Freud who settled in New York in the 1920s, remarked that life is often tragic and sad. By joking about it, we succeed in transcending the tragic character of an event and bringing it under our control. "By using humor, the lament often turns into laughter," remarked Reik (*Jewish Wit*, New York, 1962).

What do you suppose makes Jews joke so much about adversity? "It is the instinct for self-preservation" says Ausubel. "By laughing at the absurdities and cruelties of life, we draw much of the sting from them. The jester's bells make an honest tinkle, and his comic capers conceal his inner gravity. His satire and irony have one virtue: you never for a moment suspect that his barbs are directed at you. And so you laugh boisterously, feeling superior to the poor *shmiggege*, while all the time, it is you who are the target!"

In Jewish humor, comedy and tragedy are intertwined and it is often what you might call "laughter through tears," or as we say in Yiddish, "*a bitterer gelekhter!*"

Jewish humor is unique, not only because it pokes fun at our shortcomings and weaknesses, but because it reflects upon the history of our people. Let us consider, for example, some of the anecdotes and jokes that express our determination to stay alive in spite of everything and our resolution to overcome the threatening situations in which we find ourselves.

A classic story, illustrating this instinct of survival, is an anecdote quoted by Reuven Bulka.

> A Jew in Russia falls into a lake, and, not knowing how to swim, he frantically screams, "Help, save me!" But his calls are totally ignored by all present, including a number of soldiers standing nearby. In desperation, the Jew yells out, "Down with the tsar!" At that moment, the soldiers immediately jump in, yank the Jew out of the water, and haul him off into prison.

To stay alive, in spite of all forms of oppression, has been one of the major concerns of the Jewish people through the centuries, and their jesters found many ways to convey this message in humorous terms. In France, during World War II, a funny anecdote circulated among Jews:

A Jew manages to hide in a psychiatric asylum during the war. He is acting like the other demented patients. One day, the director of the institution informs the residents that the führer, Adolph Hitler, is planning to visit the asylum. When he enters into the main hall, they are told, they are to stand up and greet him with the words "Heil Hitler!"

The day comes, and they all welcome the führer with the words they had so carefully rehearsed, except for the Jewish man, who remains seated in the back of the hall.

"You," says Hitler, "why didn't you greet me like everybody else?"

"My führer," says the Jew, "they are all *meshuge*. I am not!"

Even in the face of impending doom there may still be some hope, as the following story will tell us:

Prominent scientists have just announced that, as a result of the global warming phenomenon, an uncontrollable flood would soon devastate planet earth and bring death to every living being. There were only three days left before doomsday.

The Chief Rabbi of Israel goes on international radio and says: "Fellow Jews, we must all accept the will of God with humility. We must prepare ourselves to meet our Maker and pray that God may receive us with love and compassion."

The leaders of the Chasidim address their communities and say, "*Yidn* (fellow Jews), let us do *teshuvah* and repent from our sins, and let us be prepared for the great Day of Judgment, at which time we will appear in the presence of the Court on High."

The science and biology students of the universities of Jerusalem, Tel Aviv, Haifa, the Negev, together with the leading scientists of the Haifa Technion and the Weizmann Institute, immediately go on the air and say, "Fellow Jews, everywhere, we have heard the terrible news, and we must not waste any time, for we just have three days to learn how to live under water . . ."

The lesson of the story is quite significant: the Jews wish the world to know that they are determined to survive even the worst hell, says Bulka. They will mobilize all their energies and abilities to stay alive, even in the midst of severe persecutions. The victims of discrimination and injustice have no other way than to rely upon their wit and intelligence in order to overcome the hatred of their enemies.

Because they faced discrimination and anti-Semitism so many times in the past, Jews had to find ways of responding with dignity, but often also, with a certain amount of biting wit, to these unwarranted attacks on their personalities. One of these stories brings a Jew and an anti-Semite face to face:

> An altercation takes place at a royal reception at Buckingham Palace, between the Jewish philanthropist, Sir Moses Montefiore, and an unfriendly Russian Grand Duke.
>
> Shocked that a Jew should have been invited to an aristocratic gathering, the Grand Duke slyly remarks to Sir Moses Montefiore that he had just returned from Japan, and he had been intrigued to learn that in Japan, there were neither Jews nor pigs. Sir Moses calmly responds to the Grand Duke, "This is indeed quite interesting. Now, suppose you and I were to go to Japan, it would then have one of each!"

In the battle of wits, unlike other battles, a Jew could win an argument by exposing the absurdity of the prejudice. This approach often became the only way that enabled the Jew to retain his sanity and survive the inhuman conditions that were imposed upon him.

> An anti-Semite declares without shame, "All our troubles come from the Jews!"
>
> The Jew responds: "Absolutely! From the Jews—and the bicycle riders!"
>
> "Bicycle riders? Why the bicycle riders?" asks the anti-Semite.
>
> "Why the Jews?" asks the Jew.

"For the past two thousand years, the Jews have been sharpening their wit as well as their wits, on the logical grindstone of the Talmud. This may explain why so much of Jewish humor," writes Nathan Ausubel, "has an intellectual character." For Jewish humor is not just laughter; it is in fact, wisdom! Consider this lovely anecdote from Eastern Europe, which is all about Talmudic logic.

> After months of negotiation with the authorities, a Talmudist from Odessa is finally granted a visa to visit Moscow. He boards the train and finds an empty seat. At the next stop, a young man gets on the train and sits next to him. The scholar looks at the young man and thinks: this fellow doesn't look like a peasant, and if he isn't a peasant, he probably comes from this city. If he comes from this city, then he must be Jewish, because this is, after all, a predominantly Jewish area. On the other hand, if he is a Jew, where could he be going? I am

the only Jew in our district who received permission to travel to Moscow. Ahh? That's no problem; I know that just outside Moscow, there is a little town called Samvet, and Jews don't need special permission to go there. Yes, but why would he be going to Samvet? He's probably going to visit one of the Jewish families that live there, but let me think; how many Jewish families are there in Samvet? There are only two: the Bernsteins and the Steinbergs. The Bernsteins? No, that cannot be; it is a terrible family. A nice looking fellow like this young man, must be visiting the Steinbergs. But why would he visit that family? The Steinbergs have only two daughters. So, my best guess is that he must be their son-in-law. But if he is, indeed, a son-in-law, which daughter did he marry? I heard that Sarah married a nice lawyer from Budapest, and Esther married a businessman from Zhitomir; so, I got it: he must be Sarah's husband, and his name, people say, is Alexander Cohen. But, if he comes from Budapest, a city where anti-Semitism is rampant, he must have changed his name. What would be the Hungarian equivalent of Cohen? It must be Kovacs. But it is well known that not everyone is allowed to change his name in Hungary, and if he was able to do so, it must be for a good reason: he must have some special status. And what could that be? Obviously, this fellow Alexander Cohen must have earned a doctorate from the University.

At this point, our Talmudic scholar turns to the young man and says, "How do you do, Dr. Kovacs?"

"Very well thank you, sir," answers the startled passenger. "But, please tell me, how is it that you know my name?"

"Oh," replies the Talmudist, "it's so obvious; I knew you had to be Dr. Kovacs."

Jews have excelled not only in the art of telling humorous anecdotes, but also in their ability to make use of wit, in order to answer malevolent questions on occasion. Here is an example of wit that conveys a message of wisdom:

In the course of an interview, Isaac Bashevis Singer is questioned by a reporter about his vegetarianism:

"Are you a vegetarian for health reasons?" he is asked.

"Yes," answers Singer, "the health of the chicken!"

Jews invented many jokes about the canards and false accusations that were leveled against them. Here is an anecdote, told by Bulka, which is meant to undo the effect of hostility and to ridicule unfounded prejudice.

A Jewish businessman is on his way home, carrying with him an important sum of money which he needs in order to provide for his family. He is attacked by an armed *ganef* (thief), who robs him of all his possessions. The Jew starts to sob uncontrollably, moving the thief to actually ask him why he was crying so much. The Jew then says that he could bear that his money might be taken away, but how could he face his family, who would ask him where the money had gone, and who might doubt his story that the money was stolen? Could the thief help him by providing clear evidence that he had been attacked?

"How could I help?" asks the thief. The businessman says, "Perhaps you could shoot a bullet through my coat." The thief complies. Then the Jew asks, "Could you perhaps shoot another bullet on the other side of my coat?" The thief gladly obliges. Then the Jew asks if he could put a bullet through his hat, which the thief does. The Jew then asks for one more bullet through his hat, to which the thief says, "Sorry, I have no more bullets."

As soon as the Jew hears this, he pounces upon the thief, pummels him into submission, and takes back all his money. As he walks away to go home, he hears the thief muttering to himself, "This goes to prove that you can never trust a damn Jew!"

The love of learning and the striving for knowledge has been one of the most preeminent motivations of the Jewish people through the centuries. A lovely Chasidic tale beautifully conveys this notion.

Reb Yehuda Leib was a great *Talmid Khokhem* (scholar), and he was often invited to give lectures on Talmudic topics at the most prestigious yeshivas of Lithuania. After the lecture, the Rosh Yeshiva (head of the academy) would usually introduce to him his finest students so that he might examine them.

Everyone knew that Reb Yehuda Leib had a lovely daughter who had reached the age of marriage, and that the *rebbe* was looking for a suitable husband for his beloved Rachel. Reb Yehuda would always ask potential candidates the same difficult question, in the hope that one of them might pass the test. But so far, none had been able to answer the question.

One day, after having lectured at the great Kovno Yeshiva, the Rosh Yeshiva personally introduced to him his best student. He was particularly brilliant in every subject, and Reb Yehuda took a liking to him right away. But when he asked him the same difficult question he had asked all the other candidates, the student could not find the right answer. So Reb Yehuda took leave of his host and his best student. But as he was about to get on the coach that would take him back home, the yeshiva student came rushing to Reb Yehuda and with almost no breath left, he reached him just as he was about to close the door of his coach.

"I beg of you, *rebbe*," asked the student, "would you be kind enough to tell me what the correct answer to the question is?"

And the *rebbe* smiled as he opened wide the door of his coach and he said, "Young man, you are the one; and now, come with me!"

Indeed the desire to know the truth is the beginning of wisdom. Among the other types of people who have become main characters in Jewish humor is the *shnorrer*, the beggar. Theodor Reik contended that the jokes about *shnorrers* express the hope and conviction that the economic gap between the haves and the have nots will be erased one day. But we might even go one step further, says Reuven Bulka. Indeed, Jews have often been forced to *shnor*, that is to beg, for what was legitimately theirs. The *shnor-rer*, therefore, symbolizes the Jew who begs the indulgence of others, so that he might enjoy the basic right to live with decency.

> Here is the story of a *shnorrer* who used to visit the house of the Baron de Rothschild to receive his weekly alms. On one particular visit, he is told that he cannot be supported that week. Visibly upset, he wants to know the reason. He is told that the Baron's daughter had been married that week and that the wedding had been particularly costly and there were no funds left for charitable purposes. The *shnorrer*, reacting with a combination of understanding and protest, says: "I certainly don't mind the Baron marrying his daughter, but not with *my* money!"

It was not always easy for Jews to earn a living when there were so many discriminatory laws limiting their activities; they were not to own land or to engage in many trades, which were regulated by professional guilds that accepted only Christian members. Jews were able to survive only by putting their ingenuity to work. As they could only engage in professions, which were not regulated by law, they practiced international commerce and banking (which was forbidden by the Church in the Middle Ages), they went into medicine, astrology, and map-making, and quite a few became experts in these professions. Many, however, managed to earn a living by practicing simple trades. They became tailors and shoemakers, grocers and butchers, and many shopkeepers and merchants. The next anecdote will reveal to us how students of the Holy Scriptures learn about the commercial trade.

> There are two young *yeshiva bakhurim* (students at a Talmudic academy) in a train compartment, in Belgium. They are discussing the amazing abilities of Jewish merchants and diamond dealers in their city of Antwerp.
>
> "To what would you attribute their success?" asks one fellow of the other. "You know what, let's ask our *landsman* (compatriot), who is sitting near the window," says the other.
>
> "*Ir zeit a soykher* (you are a businessman), aren't you? Please tell us: to what do you attribute the success of businessmen in this *medine* (country)?"
>
> "Oh," he says, "that's very simple. It is due to the kind of food we eat."
>
> "Oh yes, and what kind of food do you eat?"
>
> "We eat heads of herrings and this gives us brains."
>
> "Interesting," say the two young travelers.
>
> "By any chance, would you have some heads of herrings in your bag, and would you be willing to sell them to us?" asks one *yeshiva bokher.*
>
> "Of course," says the merchant. "It will be just one hundred francs a piece."
>
> The two students are anxious to try the experiment without any delay, and they start eating.
>
> "Do you know," one of the students says to the businessman, "in Antwerp, you can buy a whole herring for ten francs, and here, I paid one hundred francs, just for one head . . ."
>
> "You see, my friend," answers the businessman, "it's already working . . ."

The *shadkhn,* the matchmaker, was a vital element of survival in the old country. He or she was instrumental in bringing together eligible males and females for the purpose of marriage and propagation. In the atmosphere of constant threat to their existence, every marriage was regarded as an investment in the survival of the Jewish people.

We all know the answer of Yente, the Matchmaker:

> "The way she sees and the way he looks, it's a perfect match!" *Or,*
> "She is beautiful, intelligent, and from a good family; what else do you

want?" "But why me, I have none of these." "Oh, I should have told you before: she is just a tiny bit pregnant . . ."

Even religious traditions and practices were not spared from the double-edged sword of Jewish humorists.

A ten year-old boy tells his father what he learned in Sunday School that day.

"You know the exodus from Egypt, Dad? That was quite a feat on the part of the Hebrews. They were able to cross the Red Sea in amphibious vehicles while combat helicopters and rocket launchers were protecting them from the Egyptian cavalry. That must have been an amazing victory."

"Tell me, son," asks the father, "is that what your teacher said?"

"Oh no, Dad; but if I told you what he said, you would never believe it."

Another anecdote pokes gentle fun at some of our most important beliefs. It recounts a conversation between two Jews who are comparing the respective merits of their jobs. One says to the other:

"I have a good job and I am getting a good salary, but I have no security. The *poretz* (the owner of the land) may let me go at any time, and I am constantly worried about the possibility of losing my job."

The other one says, "I have a simple job and it does not pay much, but I would say that it is quite a secure job."

"Ah," says the other, "and what do you do for a living?"

"Oh, I work for the *shul* (synagogue)," answers his interlocutor. "Every morning, at dawn, I have to go up on the roof of the *shul* and look all around, as far as I can, to see if the messiah is coming. The moment I see him, I will have to inform the *rebbe* and the president of the congregation immediately. I'll tell you the truth, my friend, it doesn't pay much, but there is plenty security!"

The following story involves a Chasidic *rebbe* and his young assistant in a little town in Russia. It pokes fun at the *Wunder Rebbes,* the rabbis who were believed to have the power of performing miracles.

The *rebbe,* who was walking swiftly in the street accompanied by his assistant, heard a Russian *muzhik* (peasant) make an offensive anti-Semitic remark: "Those accursed Jews are filling our town with dirt . . ."

Without thinking, the *rebbe* spontaneously exclaimed: "May the wall fall upon you and reduce you to silence." But the assistant rabbi immediately intervened and said to his Master: "*Rebbe,* this man has a wife and children. Would you really want the wall to fall upon him?"

"You are right, my son, I am sorry, I should not have reacted that way."

The *rebbe* prayed, and a miracle happened: the wall did not fall upon the *muzhik!*

In Latin America, as well as in the rest of the world, they have always picked on the rabbis and the other members of the Jewish clergy. The following anecdote tells you about the *tsores* (the painful episodes) in the life of a rabbi.

Everyone knows that there is a shortage of rabbis in Mexico. Two congregations in particular had been unable to find a rabbi, for years. So they decided to insert ads in newspapers, and they soon received letters from two potential candidates, who were immediately invited to Mexico. But unfortunately, one of them died soon after he reached Mexico City from the effects of air pollution. As a result, each of the two congregations claimed the remaining rabbi.

The members of one congregation were willing to follow the advice of King Solomon and cut the rabbi in two; the other agreed to let him live, just as in the biblical story of the two mothers and their child.

What did they do? They consulted the Beit Din of Mexico City. The judges heard the case and decided: "The remaining rabbi must go to the first congregation—whose members wanted to cut him in two—because that is, indeed, the fate awaiting all rabbis . . ."

Women have always played an important role in the Jewish community, even when it was not officially recognized. Of course, the situation is much different today, but many are still not willing to acknowledge it. So, women have been campaigning for equal rights.

The mayor of Ra'anana was inspecting a public building site, accompanied by his wife, when one of the construction workers called to the mayor's wife and said, "How are you, Dinah?" and she answered, "Good to see you, David." And she continued to chat with the worker for a few minutes.

After the mayor had completed his inspection, he asked his wife, "How do you know this man?" "Ah," she said, "he was my sweetheart in high school. He even proposed to me, many years ago."

The husband laughed and said, "You should be grateful to me, then, for if I had not come along, you would be the wife of a construction worker, instead of being married to the mayor of the city."

"Not at all," said the wife. "If I had married him, *he* would now be the mayor of this city!"

Even the conflict between Israelis and Palestinians has not escaped the scope of Jewish jesters. Some facts are better conveyed in the form of a joke than in a serious lecture on history, as in the following anecdote:

> At an emergency meeting of the Security Council of the United Nations, the ambassador of Israel and the chairman of the Palestinian Authority, Yasser Arafat, were scheduled to speak from the podium. The Israeli delegate was called first: "Ladies and gentlemen, I would like to preface my remarks by telling you an old story of our folklore. When Moses was leading the Children of Israel through the wilderness, he felt extremely tired one late afternoon, and he decided to take a stroll. He walked away from the camp of the Israelites, and, lo and behold, he saw a lovely lake, right in front of him. He quickly took off his clothes, set them in a pile on the shore, and he went for a swim. Refreshed and relaxed, he came back to the shore and looked for his clothes, but they were nowhere to be found. 'Surely,' said he, 'some Palestinian must have stolen my clothes.'"
>
> At this point, Yasser Arafat could not stand still anymore and he shouted: "Ladies and gentlemen, this is an abject lie, for everyone knows that there were no Palestinians in those days!"
>
> "Thank you, Mr. Arafat," said the Israeli ambassador. "That is correct, and that is indeed my first point. Now, I can proceed with my remarks."

What can we learn from these anecdotes and expressions of Jewish wit? In his book, *Jokes and Their Relation to the Unconscious,* Sigmund Freud suggested that many Jewish jokes point to the ability of the Jewish people to (a) engage in a thorough self-criticism of themselves, (b) advocate a democratic way of life, (c) emphasize the moral and social principles of the Jewish religion, (d) criticize the excessive requirements of it, and (e) reflect on the misery of many Jewish communities. Freud, who wrote this book some hundred years ago, was actually paying homage to the capacity of the Jewish people to overcome the oppressive social conditions that had been imposed upon them and their ability to transcend them by laughing at them.

Some non-Jewish psychiatrists—even disciples of Freud—seem to have had some difficulty in understanding the gist of Jewish wit and have been particularly critical. Their preconceived ideas about the Jews may have had a certain influence in their judgment. Dr. Edmund Bergler, in a book he published in 1956, *Laughter and the Sense of Humor*, expresses the view that a definite tendency to "psychic masochism" is present in Jewish wit, and that certain external situations (discrimination, poverty, the lack of opportunity, and the bitterness of life in Eastern Europe) have predisposed Jews to a certain degree of masochism. Dr. Martin Grotjahn, a disciple of Theodor Reik, published a book on the subject in 1960, titled *Psychoanalysis and the Jewish Joke*, in which he advances the opinion that the witticisms of Jews often start with an aggressive tendency, a shocking thought, or an offensive statement in a disguised form. The release of aggression is sudden, and the hostility or aggressiveness manifests itself in a masochistic way, that is, turned against the Jew himself.

These notions were corrected, however, by Reik himself, who remarked that the masochistic aspect of the Jewish joke may not be authentic. It is only pseudomasochistic, because the masochism of Jewish wit is only a "mask" that does not show the face behind it. For the ultimate aim of this display is the unconscious wish to win the approval—or even the admiration—of the audience, and to regain one's dignity. It is as if the jester were saying, "See how full of weaknesses and failings I am. Therefore you must recognize my humanity, forgive me, and love me again."

Reik justified his conclusion by stating that, contrary to the clinically diagnosed masochist, the Jew does not derive gratification from this type of behavior, as does the authentic masochist. Indeed, the Jew makes fun of himself, but he does not come out humiliated or dirty. His self-humiliation is perhaps only a measure of self-defense, which may protect him against greater dangers. It is thus a kind of sacrifice made in order to survive. Jewish jokes are therefore only pseudomasochistic and not really masochistic.

Reik went on to suggest the possibility of the coexistence of masochistic humility and provocative insolence. As an example of this attitude, he referred to a letter written by the German Jewish poet and writer Heinrich Heine, who had converted to Christianity in hope of being accepted by Western society, in which Heine a few months before his death says to his brother Max, "*Our forefathers were brave people; they humbled themselves before God and were stubborn and fearless towards the worldly powers. I, on the contrary, challenged Heaven with impudence and was humble and servile towards people, and now, I lie on the ground, like a worm that has been crushed under a foot.*"

That does not mean, of course, that we do not have some true maso-chists or paranoid personalities among us from time to time, as the say-ing goes: "*Just because you are paranoid, does not mean that they are not out to get you.*"

What Grotjahn meant by an aggression turned against itself might be expressed in these words: "*You don't need to attack us. We can do that ourselves and even better. We can take it. We know our weaknesses and in a way, we are proud of them.*" Jewish jokes, he writes, contain a kind of resignation and occasionally a stubborn pride. They seem to say: "*This is the way we are and will be as long as we exist.*"

For Freud and for Reik, the truth seemed at once simpler and more complex. There is often a kind of oscillation between a pseudomasochis-tic self-humiliation and a sense of paranoid superiority in Jewish humor. Thus, there are two sides to every Jewish story.

No one will deny that there is a high degree of resiliency and courage that is displayed in many Jewish stories, and that has served as a kind of defense-mechanism enabling Jews to confront adversity. The fact that Jews are capable of making merciless fun of the shortcomings of their own people is a positive trait, not a negative one, as some anti-Semites have tried to construe it. Self-criticism, and even self-sarcasm, are part of the thought process of the individual who is committed to intellectual and moral integrity.

The world has changed considerably in the last forty years since Reik wrote his book, and we may say, today, that the universal character of Jewish wit has come to be enjoyed by many—Jews and non-Jews alike. Some of the finest humorists on the American scene are Jewish, and many gentiles have learned to enjoy and appreciate a good Jewish joke.

Woody Allen is a case in point. He may be ambivalent about his Jew-ishness, but he has certainly not rejected the Jewish tradition of humor. He has been quoted as saying, "*I have frequently been accused of being a self-hating Jew, and while it's true I hate myself, it's not because I'm Jewish.*"

That's Jewish humor in full flower.

SEINFELD

Lawrence J. Epstein

JERRY SEINFELD was standing in front of a live audience. "I grew up in Massapequa on Long Island," he began. Pausing for a second with the comic timing he had perfected, he then explained, "It's an old Indian word meaning 'by the mall.'" When the laughter died down, he continued, "My folks just moved to Florida this past year. They didn't want to move to Florida, but they're in their sixties and that's the law."

The audience loved his jokes, but it wasn't always so easy for Seinfeld. In his early twenties, on the same day he graduated college, he made his first stand-up comedy appearance at New York's Catch a Rising Star. It was open-mike night, and the young comedian had his chance. He walked up to the microphone and froze. He managed to blurt out the subjects of his would-be jokes but not the jokes themselves. He stood there saying words: "The beach. Driving. Shopping. Parents." Unable to continue, he left the stage.

Seinfeld's story, as all American television viewers know, had a happy ending. That is so, in part, because Seinfeld had enormous talent, incredible determination, and a desire for perfection. His comedic talents simply wouldn't be denied.

But Jerry Seinfeld also had another weapon: the rich wealth of the tradition of Jewish comedy. Seinfeld was his generation's follow-up to Jack Benny, the Marx Brothers, George Burns, and literally hundreds of others. Jerry Seinfeld, then, was not alone on that stage at Catch a Rising

Star. Like the Jews themselves, he wouldn't quit. The world saying "no" became just an incentive to go on.

Seinfeld had been attracted to comedy early. When he was eight, he saw a comedian on Ed Sullivan's show. The act, and the audience's appreciative laughter, provided a shock of recognition for the young boy. He knew he wanted to make people laugh. He began to watch endless hours of television, searching out the comedians, observing their manners and material.

Despite his inauspicious debut at Catch a Rising Star, Seinfeld continued to perform onstage. He did well in New York, but Seinfeld never confused activity with achievement. He was working but not getting ahead. So he moved to Los Angeles, where he landed a brief role on the situation comedy *Benson*.

He began to develop his early trademark lines, like "If I'm the best man, why is she marrying him?" He talked about a detergent commercial in which a woman brags that she could remove bloodstains. Seinfeld noted that "If you get a t-shirt with bloodstains, maybe laundry is not your problem now."

Seinfeld was a skillful writer. He carefully constructed his jokes and refused to use obscene language. "I made rules that I wouldn't use profanity because it was a more interesting game for me to try and do certain material or certain subjects without going over the line." He knew swearing released anger, but he wasn't so much angry as bemused or frustrated, with relief coming through cleverness and close observation.

In November 1988, Seinfeld went to see Larry David, widely admired among comedians for his quick mind and writing abilities but hampered in his career by self-admitted neuroses, shyness, and a willingness to confront what he frequently thought to be an underappreciative audience by yelling at them or walking off the stage.

Seinfeld had been speaking with NBC about starting a television show but didn't know what the series would be about. Sharing a taxi back to the West Side in New York, the two stopped at a grocery store. As they walked the aisles, they joked about the products they saw. David suddenly said, "See, this is what the show would be." Seinfeld immediately grasped the idea of finding humor in everyday activities.

They continued to talk about the show, and during ten electric minutes at the Westway Diner on Ninth Avenue they jointly came up with the initial idea for what, after some evolution, would later become one of the most successful sitcoms in television history: describe the experiences during which comedians gather material for their performances. Jerry would play a stand-up comedian seeking material that would then be seen performed in an act at the end.

Seinfeld and David went to see Warren Littlefield, president of entertainment at NBC. Contrary to legend, though, David did not present their idea as "a show about nothing." Instead, he suggested that the humor would come from conversations more than situations. The standard story line would be much less important. Littlefield didn't like it, and David, outraged at what he saw as corporate comedic myopia, told Littlefield exactly how he felt. But one executive in the room, Rick Ludwin, offered to put up the funding for a pilot. The rest has become part of the legend of television.

Seinfeld's story was part of a long and happy saga of Jewish comedians finding a congenial home on American television. Many of them, however, succeeded only after a long struggle.

On his television show, Seinfeld dealt with several intimate subjects including masturbation; the male winner of a contest to refrain was to be known—in words that became a national catchphrase—as the "master of his domain." Always, though, the subjects in the show were handled with deftness. "It's funny," he said, "to be delicate with something that's explosive." It's hard to find another comedy manifesto more at odds with that of Howard Stern. This choice was crucial. Just as Jewish vaudevillians and later comics had used code words to include Jewish material while appearing to be completely within an American tradition, Seinfeld and David used code words to include very adult material while their language remained completely clean.

Seinfeld's appeal was as someone who was, in Carl Reiner's words, "sweet and funny." Reiner saw the combination as rare. However, Seinfeld's television success depended on more than a cute smile, a well-wrought line, and clean observational humor. That combination had worked well in the clubs, but on 1990s television more was needed. Had Seinfeld simply translated his act onto the screen, the show would not have been as successful.

The success came from the grafting of the sweet and funny real Jerry Seinfeld with the selfish and self-absorbed television Jerry Seinfeld. Jerry and his friends—George, Elaine, and Kramer—cheated, lied, and used each other for their own ends. Despite these traits, however, the characters remained lovable, and the four remained friends. Seinfeld's universe, that is, is cynical and unsentimental. It is filled with small failures.

The depressive George, the emotionally distant Jerry, the self-centered Elaine, and the perpetually failing Kramer may seem to be odd characters. The relationship among characters, though, goes right back to Jack Benny. Benny let his audience laugh at him, and in doing so they laughed at those parts of themselves they recognized and perhaps felt guilty about. The young audiences that watched *Seinfeld* got the same kind of emotional release. Laughing at the self-absorbed characters provided a profound letting go of tensions collected from confronting those same characteristics they found in themselves. In the 1930s, Benny's audiences were forced to be cheap and wanted someone who could simultaneously make them laugh about that cheapness while giving them permission to keep being cheap. In the 1990s, the *Seinfeld* audience wanted to focus on their own self-interests, and they, too, wanted to laugh about it while being given emotional permission to continue.

Comparisons to the Benny show don't stop there. Like that show, *Seinfeld* had much more dialogue than other contemporary shows (its scripts were as long as seventy pages, about twenty pages longer than other scripts). The excess of language betrayed a nervousness, a distinctly urban and distinctly Jewish approach to dealing with anxiety. Seinfeld, like Benny, was the main character, though he often let himself be the straight man while the other characters cracked jokes around him.

The characters in the show were unable to commit to a stable romantic relationship. Jerry, for example, was a perfectionist, always finding flaws in the women he meets. The profound Jewish sensibility of the show provided such a relationship phobia with another dimension. The characters' inability to commit to a partner or to maturity itself was a metaphor for their inability to commit to an identity. The long-standing tension between Jewish and American identities was partially overcome in *Seinfeld* by having the characters not choose at all, by refusing to be grown up enough to have to choose. While Woody Allen struggled to define his identity, the *Seinfeld* characters avoided any such conflict. They didn't see the value in their parents' struggles. They didn't see the intellectual or artistic challenges in constructing an identity. They wanted comfort, not confusion.

Jerry did finally say that he was Jewish—to a priest in a confessional where he's gone to complain about a dentist who became Jewish just for the jokes. The Jewish identity was peripheral, however. It did not define him. And he told the priest, he was not offended by the dentist as a Jew but as a comedian. It is as a comedian that he sees life, though with a Jewish comedian's sensibility: clear-eyed observations about life, a sense of annoyance at having to deal with life's petty travails, and as someone smaller than others. This last point is important. Seinfeld once wrote, "As a kid I was small for my age, and when you're small, you like small things. In fact, that's what a joke is, a crystallized observation, a small precision-crafted nugget of truth." Many Jewish comedians are small or were small as children. This physical characteristic might be considered as the source of a psychological feeling of being without power, of having to rely on humor to protect themselves—very much like the Jews in history. Seinfeld's view renders size unimportant as a psychological impediment; indeed it is valuable as a way to see truth and an unusual explanation of jokes as particularly Jewish constructions.

Still, while Seinfeld named his show after himself, he could have called it *Jerry*. He deliberately used his very Jewish-sounding last name. Jerry Seinfeld was at home in America. He—and the networks—felt no need to hide his Jewishness and felt no embarrassment at displaying it.

Seinfeld's cynicism ran deep. The family comedies of the 1950s and 1960s had given way to the social comedies or comedies in which coworkers substituted for traditional families. In both of these the morality passed on by the family continued to be transmitted through other means. By the late 1980s and early 1990s, the gruesomely dysfunctional family shows that appeared were almost gleeful in their mockery of such values.

Seinfeld found a way to express that same moral anarchy in a different way. The amoral perpetual adolescents of *Seinfeld* not only found comfort in each other's company but also felt their views were justified by the sober realities of a cynical world. They tried to do good deeds. Jerry and George decided to visit a boy who had to live in a bubble. The boy fights with George over a game of Trivial Pursuit and asks George's girlfriend to strip. That, too, is *Seinfeld*'s universe: a world in which good deeds always backfire and, therefore, a world in which it is crucial to forge a separate peace with a few friends. It is all right, maybe even moral, not to want to grow up in such a world. The purported amorality of adolescence is, rather, its own bubble, its protection against having to join the hypocritical adult world. This was a message that Americans found congenial—and, with Seinfeld's comic touches, funny. But *Seinfeld* had a message that was ultimately subtler than just a justification of amorality. There was a recognition of legitimate adult responsibility, though that responsibility was seen as an obligation for the future, an obligation the characters were not yet prepared for. For example, in one famous episode, Jerry's parents visit him and intrude when he and his girlfriend are kissing. Jerry, a loving son, insists they remain even after they offer to leave. Several days later, Jerry and the young woman are watching *Schindler's List*. Their frustrated lust bubbles over during the film, and they start kissing in the theater. The adolescent sexual urges trump the appropriate adult response to others' suffering and the obligation to be concerned about it.

The world of *Seinfeld* was one in which the characters relied on each other to justify their existence but recognized that eventually they would have to become adults. The series finale, with its punishment in jail for their refusal to help an overweight man who is being carjacked, was a clever final chapter, for after that purgation they would presumably have grown up. When they did, the show could not go on because they would be so different.

Larry David surely deserves an enormous amount of credit for the show's success. It was his neurotic slant, his hard-to-believe but real experiences that formed the basis for many plot lines, and his writing abilities that formed the perfect complement to Jerry Seinfeld's extraordinary skills as a writer and performer.

The irony of *Seinfeld* is that it prided itself as being a show about nothing, but it was really a complex guide to the deepest needs of the American mind.

THE EDITOR

ARTHUR KURZWEIL is a leader in the world of Jewish book publishing. During his seventeen years as editor-in-chief at Jason Aronson Inc., he published over 650 Judaica titles. He currently serves as Jewish Interest Editor for Jossey-Bass, a Wiley imprint. He is a past president of the Jewish Book Council and serves as co-coordinator of the Talmud Circle Project under the direction of Rabbi Adin Steinsaltz. He is also the editor of two collections of essays by the renowned Rabbi Steinsaltz, *The Strife of the Spirit* and *On Being Free*. An expert in the field of Jewish genealogical research, Kurzweil is the author of the classic bestseller *From Generation to Generation: How to Trace Your Jewish Genealogy and Family History.* Over the past twenty-five years he has been one of the most popular speakers on the Jewish lecture circuit, where he has offered presentations on a wide range of topics to over seven hundred synagogues and Jewish organizations throughout the United States. He is a member of the Society of American Magicians and the International Brotherhood of Magicians, and performs a unique magic show in which he combines entertaining tricks and illusions with an exploration of some of the profound questions in Jewish thought.

THE CONTRIBUTORS

LEO M. ABRAMI has been practicing and teaching logotherapy in Tucson, Arizona, ever since he retired from the pulpit rabbinate. He is also serving as a Jewish outreach mentor in South Africa and Portugal under the auspices of Kulanu, an outreach organization assisting communities of Crypto-Jews and proselytes around the world.

JOSEPH ALPHER is a consultant on Israel-related strategic issues and is director of the Political Security Domain, an independent NGO. Mr. Alpher served in the Israel Defense Forces as an Intelligence officer, followed by twelve years of service in the Mossad. In autumn 2001 he inaugurated, together with Ghassan Khatib from Ramallah, *bitterlemons.org,* an Internet-based Israeli-Palestinian weekly dialogue that focuses on the Israeli-Arab conflict. In December 2001 he published a book (in Hebrew), *And the Wolf Shall Dwell with the Wolf: The Settlers and the Palestinians.*

NORMAN BERDICHEVSKY, an American living in Spain, is a freelance writer and teacher of English. His articles have appeared in a number of journals, including *Midstream.*

SUSAN BERRIN, editor of *Sh'ma: A Journal of Jewish Responsibility,* is editor of two anthologies, *A Heart of Wisdom: Making the Jewish Journey from Mid-Life Through the Aging Years* and *Celebrating the New Moon: A Rosh Chodesh Anthology.*

BENJAMIN BLECH, a rabbi, is an educator, religious leader, author, and lecturer. He has written seven best-selling books on Judaism, including *Understanding Judaism: The Basics of Deed and Creed* and three volumes in the well-known *Idiot's Guide* series.

LAWRENCE BUSH is editor of *Jewish Currents* magazine and *Reconstructionism Today*. His books include *Bessie,* a novel, and *American Torah Toons: 54 Illustrated Commentaries*. He is the coeditor of *Jews,* a magazine of visual arts and literature.

TALIA CARNER is the author of *Puppet Child,* a novel, published in the summer of 2002. Her essays have appeared in the *New York Times* and *Chocolate for Women* (an anthology published by Simon & Schuster). Visit www.taliacarner.com.

I. CENTURY is the pen name and family name of Irving Centor, an attorney practicing in New York City. He has had poems and short stories published in *Midstream, Chelsea Review,* and other periodicals. Currently he is completing a book of poems about old movies.

PHYLLIS CHESLER is an emerita professor of psychology and women's studies, a psychotherapist, and an expert witness. She is a founder of The Association for Women in Psychology and The National Women's Health Network. She is the author of many articles and books, including *Women and Madness, About Men, Letters to a Young Feminist, Women's Inhumanity to Women, Woman of the Wall,* and, most recently, *The New Anti-Semitism,* from which the selection in this book is taken.

LESLIE COHEN, member of Kibbutz Ein Hashofet in Israel, has published numerous book reviews and a book of poetry called *Facets of the Poet*. Her poetry has also appeared in *Midstream*.

ENID DAME is a poet, writer, and teacher and is a university lecturer at the New Jersey Institute of Technology. Her books of poetry include *Lilith and Her Demons* and *Anything You Don't See*. She is coeditor of *Home Planet News,* a literary tabloid, and is coeditor of *Which Lilith: Feminist Writers Recreate the World's First Woman*.

ALAN M. DERSHOWITZ is a professor at Harvard Law School and is well known as a civil libertarian and legal educator. He is the author of many books, including *Why Terrorism Works, Chutzpah, The Vanishing American Jew,* and, most recently, *The Case for Israel*. He has published hundreds of articles in magazines and journals, and as an attorney he has participated in some of the most well-known cases of our time.

RALPH DE TOLEDANO, a writer and journalist, is the author of *Notes from the Underground: The Whittaker Chambers-Ralph de Toledano Letters, 1949–1960.*

CAROL DIAMENT is director of the National Department of Jewish Education at Hadassah. She is the first woman to have completed a doctorate in Jewish Studies at Yeshiva University. Diament has edited *Moonbeams: A Hadassah Rosh Hodesh Guide, Jewish Women Living the Challenge, Ribcage: Israeli Women's Fiction, Zionism: The Sequel,* and Hadassah's newest study guide, *Pray Tell: A Hadassah Guide to Jewish Prayer.*

AMOS ELON is the author of eight books, including *Founder: A Portrait of the First Rothschild and His Time, Jerusalem: City of Mirrors,* and the best-selling *The Israelis: Founders and Sons.* He is a frequent contributor to the *New York Times Magazine* and the *New York Review of Books.*

LAWRENCE J. EPSTEIN is a professor of English. He is the author of such books as *A Treasury of Jewish Anecdotes* and *A Treasury of Jewish Inspirational Stories* as well as *The Haunted Smile: The Story of Jewish Comedians in America.*

MORDECHAI GAFNI is a rebbe, scholar, and teacher, and is the founder of Bayit Chadash, an Israeli spiritual community/movement. He is the host of a leading Israeli TV show on ethics and spirituality and is the author of several scholarly books as well as the national best-seller *Soul Prints,* with accompanying PBS TV special. His latest book is *The Mystery of Love.*

HERBERT GOLD is the author of many novels, including *Fathers, He/She,* and *A Girl of Forty.* Three of his nonfiction books—*Haiti, The Magic Will,* and *The Age of Happy Problems*—are being reissued with new material by Transactions Publishers. He was a Fulbright Fellow and a Guggenheim Fellow, and has received many awards, including the Sherwood Anderson Prize for Fiction.

SHEFA GOLD is the director of C-DEEP, the Center for Devotional Energy and Ecstatic Practice, in New Mexico. She is a teacher, composer, and performer of spiritual music and has recorded nine albums.

GLORIA GOLDREICH has written several novels, including *Years of Dreams* and *That Year of Our War*. Her fiction has appeared in *Midstream* and other journals.

BLU GREENBERG is an author and lecturer who has published widely on the issues of feminism, Orthodoxy, and the Jewish family, as well as on other subjects of scholarly interest. She is the author of *On Women and Judaism: A View From Tradition* and *How to Run a Traditional Jewish Household*. She chaired the first International Conference on Feminism and Orthodoxy in 1997 and the second in 1998.

IRVING GREENBERG is the president of Jewish Life Network. An ordained Orthodox rabbi and a Harvard Ph.D., Rabbi Greenberg is a former chairman of the United States Holocaust Memorial Museum and was appointed a head of the President's Commission on the Holocaust by President Jimmy Carter.

DAVID GROSSMAN is the author of many novels as well as groundbreaking works of journalism, including *The Yellow Wind* and *Sleeping on a Wire*. He has also written several books for children.

LEO HABER is the author of *The Red Heifer,* a novel. His poetry and fiction have appeared in a wide variety of publications. Two of his poems appeared in an anthology of Holocaust poetry called *Beyond Lament*. Mr. Haber is the editor-in-chief of *Midstream*.

DAVID A. HARRIS has been the executive director of the American Jewish Committee since 1990. For the last three years he has been a visiting scholar at the Johns Hopkins University School of Advanced International Studies in Bologna, Italy. His books include *The Jewish World* and *The Jokes of Oppression* (as coauthor).

ARTHUR HERTZBERG received rabbinic ordination from the Jewish Theological Seminary and a Ph.D. degree in history from Columbia University. Since 1991, he has been the Bronfman Visiting Professor of the Humanities at New York University. He is the author of many books, including *Being Jewish in America, The Jews in America,* and *The Zionist Idea*. His most recent book is a memoir, *A Jew in America*.

YITZHAK HUSBANDS-HANKIN is rabbi of Temple Beth Israel in Eugene, Oregon. He is the chair of the Aleph: Alliance for Jewish Renewal project on Ethical Kashrut.

PAULA E. HYMAN is Lucy Moses Professor of Modern Jewish History at Yale University. Her most recent book is *Gender and Assimilation in Modern Jewish History: The Roles and Representations of Women*.

YOEL JAKOBOVITS is an assistant professor of medicine at Johns Hopkins University School of Medicine and the resident physician on the campus of Ner Israel Rabbinical College in Baltimore, Maryland. He maintains a private practice in medicine and gastroenterology. He lectures widely and has often published in specialty medical and rabbinic journals.

RODGER KAMENETZ wrote *The Jew in the Lotus* and won the National Jewish Book Award for *Stalking Elijah*. Northwestern University Press will publish his collection of poems, *The Lower Case Jew*, in the fall of 2003.

EDWARD I. KOCH served as the 105th mayor of New York City for three terms from 1978 to 1989. He is the author of numerous books and articles, including *Mayor* and *Ed Koch on Everything*. He is currently a partner in the law firm of Bryan Cave LLP and a member of the board of directors of the American Heart Association.

JANE LEAVY is an award-winning former sportswriter and feature writer for the *Washington Post*, and is the author of the comic novel *Squeeze Play*.

AMY-JILL LEVINE received a Ph.D. degree from Duke University. She is the E. Rhodes and Leona B. Carpenter Professor of New Testament studies at Vanderbilt University Divinity School as well as a member of the faculty of Vanderbilt's Graduate Department of Religion. She is a self-described "Yankee Jewish feminist who teaches the New Testament to Christians in a predominantly Protestant divinity school in the buckle of the Bible Belt."

ANDREI S. MARKOVITS is visiting professor of social studies at Harvard University. His regular appointment is at the University of Michigan in Ann Arbor, where he teaches courses in European politics with a special emphasis on Germany and Austria. He is currently working on a book on anti-Americanism and anti-Semitism in postwar Europe.

BEZALEL NAOR is an interpreter of Kabbalistic and Hasidic thought. He is the author of several books, including *Lights of Prophecy, Of Societies Perfect and Imperfect, God's Middlemen: A Habad Retrospective* (together with Reuven Alpert), *Post-Sabbatian Sabbatianism, Kabbalah and the Holocaust, Bringing Down Dreams*, and *When God Becomes History: Historical Essays of Rabbi Abraham Isaac Hakohen Kook*.

CYNTHIA OZICK is one of the most gifted and important writers of our time. She is the author of several books of fiction, including *The Pagan Rabbi and Other Stories, Bloodshed and Three Novellas, Levitation: Five Fictions, The Cannibal Galaxy, The Messiah of Stockholm, The Puttermesser Papers,* and *The Shawl,* as well as a few collections of essays, including *Art and Ardour.* She has received many awards, including the National Book Critics Circle Award.

MARGE PIERCY is the author of sixteen books of poetry, including *Colors Passing Through Us* and *The Art of Blessing the Day: Poems with a Jewish Theme.* She has published fifteen novels, including *He, She and It, Gone to Soldiers,* and *The Third Child.* She has also published a memoir, *Sleeping.*

TODD PITOCK is a writer whose essays, journalism, and reportage have appeared in numerous publications, among them the *Washington Post,* the *New York Times,* and *Salon.*

DANIEL POLISH is rabbi of Congregation Shir Chadash in Poughkeepsie, New York. He has served, most recently, as director of the Commission on Social Action of Reform Judaism. He is the author of a number of books and his articles have appeared in a range of magazines both scholarly and popular. His most recent book is *Bringing the Psalms to Life.*

DANIEL ASA ROSE is the author of *Flipping for It,* a novel cited as a *New York Times* New and Noteworthy paperback, and *Small Family with Rooster,* a collection of prize-winning short stories. His essays, stories, reviews, and travel pieces have appeared in *The New Yorker,* the *New York Times Magazine, Esquire, Playboy, Partisan Review,* and elsewhere. The winner of an O. Henry prize and two PEN awards, he is currently the arts and culture editor of the *Forward.*

ALVIN H. ROSENFELD is professor of English and director of the Borns Jewish Studies Program at Indiana University. President George W. Bush appointed him to the United States Holocaust Memorial Council in May 2002.

GILBERT S. ROSENTHAL, a rabbi, is executive director of the National Council of Synagogues. His latest book is *Contemporary Judaism.*

DAVID SAKS is a senior researcher at the South African Jewish Board of Deputies and editor of the journal *Jewish Affairs.*

ZALMAN SCHACHTER-SHALOMI is the founder and Rabbinic Chair of Aleph: Alliance for Jewish Renewal and founder of the Spiritual Eldering Institute. He is professor emeritus of religion at Temple University and professor of religious studies and former World Wisdom Chair at Naropa University. He is the author of many books, including *Paradigm Shift* and *Wrapped in a Holy Flame: Teachings and Tales of the Hasidic Masters.*

PENINNAH SCHRAM, storyteller, author, and recording artist, is associate professor of speech and drama at Stern College of Yeshiva University. She has written seven books of Jewish folktales, including *Jewish Stories One Generation Tells Another* and *Stories Within Stories: From the Jewish Oral Tradition,* and recorded a CD, *The Minstrel and the Storyteller,* with singer-guitarist Gerard Edery. As a storyteller, she is a recipient of the prestigious Covenant Award for Outstanding Jewish Educators from the Covenant Foundation and the Circle of Excellence Award from the National Storytelling Network.

ELIEZER SHORE teaches classes in Jewish thought at Yeshivat Bat Ayin in Jerusalem. He is the publisher of *Bas Ayin,* a journal of Jewish spirituality. His essays have frequently appeared in the journal *Parabola.* He is also a storyteller of both original and classic tales.

LEWIS D. SOLOMON, Theodore Rinehart Professor of Business Law at The George Washington University Law School, Washington, D.C., received rabbinic ordination from the Rabbinical Studies Department of The New Seminary (now, Rabbinical Seminary International). His latest book is *The Jewish Tradition and Choices at the End of Life: A New Judaic Approach to Illness and Dying.*

WILLIAM C. SPEED is a research associate in the laboratory of Drs. Kenneth and Judy Kidd, Department of Genetics, Yale University School of Medicine. The laboratory's research has two foci: the genetics of complex human psychiatric disorders and human population genetics. The Kidd lab has one of the largest and most diverse collections of human DNA from various ethnic groups with which to study human evolutionary history.

ADIN EVEN-ISRAEL STEINSALTZ is a teacher, mystic, scientist, and social critic and is internationally regarded as one of the greatest rabbis of our time. The author of many books, including the contemporary classic, *The Thirteen-Petaled Rose,* he is perhaps best known for his monumental translation and commentary on the Talmud.

ANDREW WALLENSTEIN writes about the entertainment industry for the *Hollywood Reporter.* His work has appeared in the *Boston Globe, Business Week, TimeOut New York,* and numerous Jewish publications. He has taught journalism at the City University of New York.

ARTHUR WASKOW is director of The Shalom Center, author of *Seasons of Our Joy, Down-to-Earth Judaism,* and *Godwrestling—Round 2,* and coauthor with Phyllis Berman of *A Time for Every Purpose Under Heaven: The Jewish Life-Spiral as a Spiritual Path.* He was named by the UN one of forty wisdom-keepers from around the world, in connection with the Habitat II conference in Istanbul, and was presented with the Abraham Joshua Heschel Award by the Jewish Peace Fellowship.

SHEILA WEINBERG has been a congregational rabbi for seventeen years and is a graduate of the Reconstructionist Rabbinical College. She is currently on the faculty of the Spirituality Institute and is engaged primarily in teaching mindfulness and meditation to rabbis, cantors, and lay Jewish leaders. She has been published widely in the Jewish community on topics ranging from feminism to spirituality and politics and is a major commentator in the Reconstructionist prayerbook series.

AVRAHAM (AVI) WEISS is senior rabbi of the Hebrew Institute of Riverdale, president of the Coalition for Jewish Concerns/Amcha, and dean of Yeshivat Chovevei Torah, the open Orthodox rabbinical school. His most recent book is *Principles of Spiritual Activism.*

MARGARET MOERS WENIG is rabbi emerita of Beth Am, The People's Temple, and instructor in liturgy and homiletics at Hebrew Union College-Jewish Institute of Religion.

ELIE WIESEL is the author of more than forty books of fiction and nonfiction, and two volumes of his memoirs. His internationally acclaimed *Night* has been translated into over thirty languages. He is the recipient of many awards, including the U.S. Congressional Gold Medal, and over one hundred honorary degrees from institutions of higher learning. In 1986, he won the Nobel Prize for Peace. He is the Andrew W. Mellon Professor in the Humanities at Boston University.

VALERIE WOHLFELD is the author of *Thinking the World Visible,* which won the Yale Younger Poets Prize. She has published her work in *The New Yorker, The Antioch Review, Partisan Review,* and elsewhere. She received an M.F.A. degree from Vermont College.

CREDITS

Israel

ELIE WIESEL   "Letter to President George W. Bush, May 7, 2002." Appeared full page in all editions of the *New York Times,* May 7, 2002. Reprinted by permission of the author.

JOSEPH ALPHER   "What Everyone Should Know About the Conflict." Reprinted from *Reform Judaism,* Fall 2002, vol. 31, number 1.

ALAN M. DERSHOWITZ   "If a Visitor from a Far-Away Galaxy." Reprinted from the *National Post,* Nov. 4, 2002.

AMOS ELON   "Israelis and Palestinians: What Went Wrong?" Reprinted with permission from *The New York Review of Books.* Copyright © 2002 NYREV, Inc.

DAVID GROSSMAN   "Fictions Embraced by an Israel at War." Copyright © 2002 The New York Times. Distributed by The New York Times Special Features/Syndication Sales.

DAVID A. HARRIS   "Letter from an Anguished Soul." Reprinted from number 20 in a series of occasional letters on topics of current interest. American Jewish Committee, August 5, 2002.

ARTHUR WASKOW   "Torah, War, and the 'Gentle Heart' Today: Israeli Soldiers' Refusal to Serve in the Occupation Army." Reprinted from Shalomctr.org.

ANDREI S. MARKOVITS   "Europe's Unified Voice and Passion." Reprinted with permission from *Sh'ma: A Journal of Jewish Responsibility,* Nov. 2002, vol. 33, number 595. For more information about Sh'ma, see: www.shma.com.

Current Issues

BLU GREENBERG   "Orthodox, Feminist, and Proud of It." Copyrighted by and reprinted with permission of Beliefnet.com. Visit www.beliefnet. com.

YOEL JAKOBOVITS   "Stem Cell Research: What Does Halachah Say?" Reprinted from *Jewish Action,* Summer 5762/2002, vol. 62, number 4.

AMY-JILL LEVINE   "Jesus Who?" Reprinted from *Moment,* August 2002/ AV 5762, vol. 27, number 4.

DANIEL POLISH   "Judaism and the Ultimate Punishment." Reprinted from *Reform Judaism,* Summer 2002, vol. 30, number 4.

DAVID SAKS   "Why Only the Orthodox Can Avoid Intermarriage." First appeared in *Midstream,* Feb./Mar. 2002, and is reprinted here by permission of the Theodor Herzl Foundation, Inc.

WILLIAM C. SPEED   "Y Marks the Spot." Reprinted from *Moment,* June 2002/Sivan 5762, vol. 27, number 3.

LAWRENCE BUSH   "Drugs and Jewish Spirituality: That Was Then, This Is Now." Reprinted from *Hallucinogens: A Reader,* edited by Charles S. Grob, M.D., published by Jeremy P. Tarcher/Putnum.

JANE LEAVY   "King of the Jews." Pages 169–195 from SANDY KOU-FAX: A LEFTY'S LEGACY by Jane Leavy. Copyright © 2002 Jane Leavy. Reprinted by permission of HarperCollins Publishers Inc.

Religious Education and Practice

PAULA E. HYMAN   "Who Is an Educated Jew?" Reprinted with permission from *Sh'ma: A Journal of Jewish Responsibility,* Feb. 2002, vol. 32, number 588. For more information about Sh'ma, see: www.shma.com.

LEWIS D. SOLOMON "Rabbinical Education for the Twenty-First Century." First appeared in *Midstream*, Feb./Mar. 2002, and is reprinted here by permission of the Theodor Herzl Foundation, Inc.

MARGARET MOERS WENIG "Oops! I Shouldn't Say This . . . Or Should I?" Reprinted from *Reform Judaism*, Summer 2002, vol. 30, number 5.

SUSAN BERRIN "Creating a Moral Legacy for Our Children." Reprinted from *The Jewish Woman*, Winter 2000, Revised 2002.

NORMAN BERDICHEVSKY "Hebrew vs. Yiddish—The Worldwide Rivalry." First appeared in *Midstream*, July/Aug. 2002, and is reprinted here by permission of the Theodor Herzl Foundation, Inc.

CAROL DIAMENT "The Parent Is the Child's First Teacher." Reprinted from *The Hadassah Magazine Jewish Parenting Book*, edited by Roselyn Bell.

YITZHAK HUSBANDS-HANKIN "Ethical Kashrut." Reprinted from *New Menorah*, spring 2002.

GILBERT S. ROSENTHAL "Halacha: Divine or Human?" First appeared in *Midstream*, Feb./Mar. 2002, and is reprinted here by permission of the Theodor Herzl Foundation, Inc.

PENINNAH SCHRAM "Rabbi Abraham Joshua Heschel of Apt on Listening." Previously unpublished.

SHEILA WEINBERG "Facing an Uncertain Future: What Jewish Meditation Teaches." Reprinted from *New Menorah*, Winter 2002.

Jewish Spiritual Thought

ADIN EVEN-ISRAEL STEINSALTZ "The Tree of Knowledge and the Tree of Life." Reprinted from *A Dear Son to Me: A Collection of Speeches and Articles* by Adin Even-Israel Steinsaltz, Israel Institute for Talmudic Publications.

MORDECHAI GAFNI "A Hundred Blasts Shatter the Somber Silence." Reprinted with permission from *Sh'ma: A Journal of Jewish Responsibility,*

September 2002, vol. 33, number 593. For more information about Sh'ma, see: www.shma.com.

SHEFA GOLD   "Power and the Open Heart." Reprinted from *New Menorah,* Summer 2002, number 68.

ARTHUR HERTZBERG   "Religion Is Not the Answer." Copyrighted by and reprinted with permission of Beliefnet.com. Visit www.beliefnet.com.

ELIEZER SHORE   "The Temple of Amount." Reprinted from *Parabola,* vol. 24, number 3.

Kabbalah

CYNTHIA OZICK   "The Heretic: The Mythic Passions of Gershom Scholem." the *New Yorker,* September 2, 2002. Reprinted by permission of Raines & Raines, agents for Cynthia Ozick. Copyright © 2002 by Cynthia Ozick.

ZALMAN SCHACHTER-SHALOMI   "So You Want to Learn Kabbalah." Previously unpublished.

RODGER KAMENETZ   "What I Know From Kabbalah." Copyrighted by and reprinted with permission of Beliefnet.com. Visit www.beliefnet.com.

TODD PITOCK   "Safed, Israel: Mystic Echoes from the Middle Ages." First appeared in *Midstream,* Sept./Oct. 2002, and is reprinted here by permission of the Theodor Herzl Foundation, Inc.

The Holocaust

IRVING GREENBERG   "A Force for Life, Not for Anger." Copyrighted by and reprinted with permission of Beliefnet.com. Visit www.beliefnet.com.

ANDREW WALLENSTEIN   "Shoah Business." Reprinted from *Moment,* April 2002/Nisan 5762, vol. 27, number 2.

DANIEL ASA ROSE   "Hiding Places." Reprinted with the permission of Simon & Schuster Adult Publishing Group from HIDING PLACES: A Father and His Sons Retrace their Family's Escape from the Holocaust by Daniel Asa Rose. Copyright © 2000 by Daniel Asa Rose.

9/11

BENJAMIN BLECH   "Forgive the Terrorists?" Reprinted from *Jewish World Review,* Sept. 11, 2002/5 Tishrei, 5762.

BEZALEL NAOR   "From a Kabbalist's Diary: Pensées on a Post-9/11 Universe." Previously unpublished.

AVI WEISS   "A Congregation of Holy Souls: Reflections on 9/11 One Year Later." Reprinted with permission from *Sh'ma: A Journal of Jewish Responsibility,* Sept. 2002, vol. 33, number 593. For more information about Sh'ma, see: www.shma.com.

Anti-Semitism

PHYLLIS CHESLER   "The New Anti-Semitism." Reprinted from *The New Anti-Semitism: The Current Crisis and What We Must Do About It* by Phyllis Chesler. Copyright © 2003 by Phyllis Chesler. This material is used by permission of John Wiley & Sons, Inc.

EDWARD I. KOCH   "Letter from Former New York Mayor Ed Koch to Woody Allen." Reprinted from the American Jewish Congress.org. Used by permission of the author.

ALVIN H. ROSENFELD   "Feeling Alone, Again: The Growing Unease Among Germany's Jews." Reprinted from International Perspectives 49, August 2002.

Poetry

RODGER KAMENETZ   "Allen Ginsberg Forgives Ezra Pound on Behalf of the Jews." Previously unpublished.

ENID DAME   "Miriam's Seders." Previously unpublished.

MARGE PIERCY   "The Late Year." First appeared in *Midstream,* Sept./Oct. 2002, and is reprinted here by permission of the Theodor Herzl Foundation, Inc.

LEO HABER   "Villanelle: Is Butter Churned These Days, Is Love Denied?" First appeared in *Midstream,* Apr. 2002, and is reprinted here by permission of the Theodor Herzl Foundation, Inc.

LEO HABER   "What the Returning Raven Said." First appeared in *Mid-stream*, Apr. 2002, and is reprinted here by permission of the Theodor Herzl Foundation, Inc.

I. CENTURY   "Yiddish." First appeared in *Midstream*, July/Aug. 2002, and is reprinted here by permission of the Theodor Herzl Foundation, Inc.

LESLIE COHEN   "To Dream in Hebrew." First appeared in *Midstream*, Feb./Mar. 2002, and is reprinted here by permission of the Theodor Herzl Foundation, Inc.

VALERIE WOHLFELD   "Veined-Garden." First appeared in *Midstream*, Sept./Oct. 2002, and is reprinted here by permission of the Theodor Herzl Foundation, Inc.

Fiction

TALIA CARNER   "Empty Chairs." First appeared in *Midstream*, Apr. 2002, and is reprinted here by permission of the Theodor Herzl Foundation, Inc.

HERBERT GOLD   "Religion: Goy." Reprinted from *Michigan Quarterly Review*, Fall 2002, vol. XLI, number 4.

GLORIA GOLDREICH   "Mazal's Day." First appeared in *Midstream*, Sept./Oct. 2002, and is reprinted here by permission of the Theodor Herzl Foundation, Inc.

Jewish Humor

RALPH DE TOLEDANO   "The Wit and Practicality of the Talmud." First appeared in *Midstream*, July/Aug. 2002, and is reprinted here by permission of the Theodor Herzl Foundation, Inc.

LEO M. ABRAMI   "It Is Not a Joke . . . " First appeared in *Midstream*, July/Aug. 2002, and is reprinted here by permission of the Theodor Herzl Foundation, Inc.

LAWRENCE J. EPSTEIN   "Seinfeld." From THE HAUNTED SMILE by LAWRENCE EPSTEIN. Copyright © by Lawrence Epstein. Reprinted by permission of PublicAffairs, a member of Perseus Books, L.L.C.